North Korea in Transition

North Korea in Transition

Politics, Economy, and Society

Edited by
Kyung-Ae Park
and
Scott Snyder

ROWMAN & LITTLEFIELD PUBLISHERS, INC.
Lanham • Boulder • New York • Toronto • Plymouth, UK

Published by Rowman & Littlefield Publishers, Inc.
A wholly owned subsidiary of The Rowman & Littlefield Publishing Group, Inc.
4501 Forbes Boulevard, Suite 200, Lanham, Maryland 20706
www.rowman.com

10 Thornbury Road, Plymouth PL6 7PP, United Kingdom

British Library Cataloguing in Publication Information Available

Library of Congress Cataloging-in-Publication Data

North Korea in transition : politics, economy, and society / edited by Kyung-Ae Park
and Scott Snyder.
    p. cm.
  Includes bibliographical references and index.
  ISBN 978-1-4422-1811-6 (cloth : alk. paper) — ISBN 978-1-4422-1812-3 (pbk. :
alk. paper) — ISBN 978-1-4422-1813-0 (electronic) 1. Political culture—Korea (North)
2. Korea (North)—Politics and government. 3. Korea (North)—Economic policy.
4. Korea (North)—Social conditions. 5. Korea (North)—Social life and customs.
I. Park, Kyung-Ae, 1955– II. Snyder, Scott, 1964–
  JQ1729.5.A58N66 2013
  320.95193—dc23

                                                               2012024453

Printed in the United States of America

Contents

PART III: NORTH KOREAN SOCIETY AND CULTURE IN TRANSITION

PART IV: FOREIGN RELATIONS IN THE TRANSITION ERA

PART V: CONCLUSION

Introduction

Scott Snyder and Kyung-Ae Park

As a closed system that has historically distanced itself even from its closest geographical and ideological neighbors, North Korea has proven to be a particularly challenging subject of study for both academic researchers and policymakers alike. Former intelligence official and U.S. Ambassador to South Korea Donald Gregg has famously referred to North Korea as "America's longest-running intelligence failure in the history of American espionage."[1] Even in its reporting to international agencies that have programs in the country, the Democratic People's Republic of Korea (DPRK) provides only sketchy official statistics. This lack of information has had a direct impact on the ability of researchers to study the North, resulting in a relatively thin database of informed, comprehensive studies about the country. The near-complete hermetic seal that the regime places around the country means that outsider accounts are sparse and are largely restricted to highly controlled areas such as the capital, Pyongyang. The extreme secrecy of the country gives truth to the quip that a "North Korea expert" is an oxymoron.[2] Although some might argue that this circumstance reveals more about the limits of the efforts of outsiders to understand the country than about North Korea itself, it is hard to argue with the fact that North Korea has pursued a unique development path that resists easy categorization or study.

Despite North Korea's apparent craving for isolation, the end of the Cold War, the famine in the mid-1990s, and the resulting flows of refugees out of and aid workers into the north have resulted both in greater exposure of North Korea to the outside world and in external changes that have forced it to undergo wrenching internal adjustments. As a side effect, these developments have widened the flow of information about North Korea to the outside world, providing new opportunities to observe its system and evolution. The collapse of North Korea's primary patron, the Soviet Union, in 1991, was a precipitating factor that led to the Great Famine of the mid-1990s, and this human catastrophe in turn resulted in unprecedented flows of refugees from North Korea as well as increased opportunities for international aid workers to gain access to the country. The famine also precipitated dramatic structural changes in the North Korean economy, and specifically in reliance on the market rather than the state as the primary provider of food, the reverberations of which are still being felt today. These forces have no doubt required the adaptation of North Korea's political leadership structures, although it has not resulted in fundamental change to its political system. The end of the Cold War also catalyzed adaptations in North Korea's international strategies and circumstances. The regime's long history of adeptly exploiting great power rivalries on its periphery means that the international context and the survival of the Kim dynasty are inextricably linked.

The year 2012 has long been signaled by North Korea as a potential turning point in its modern history by claiming that the centennial of the birth of the DPRK's founder would mark the emergence of North Korea as a "strong and prosperous nation." The sudden death of Kim Jong Il on December 17, 2011, heightened expectations that 2012 would be a year of transition, either through an unprecedented third-generation family leadership succession or perhaps toward North Korea's systemic transformation. Elections and political transitions among all of North Korea's neighbors are influencing the regional context for Kim Jong Un's—the third-born son and successor to the recently deceased Kim Jong Il—efforts to consolidate his power and political control over the North Korean system. Thus, North Korea must adapt to both internal and external developments that will influence its future direction and prospects.

TOWARD A BETTER UNDERSTANDING OF NORTH KOREA IN TRANSITION

This volume builds on prior scholarship on North Korea by analyzing the forces motivating its transition in three dimensions: the political adaptation of North Korean institutions as the main sources of support for the leadership's power and political control, the impact of dramatic economic changes inside and outside North Korea and their effects on both its institutions and society, and the impact of larger, global developments on North Korea's foreign policy. In each of these three areas, this volume builds on prior efforts to understand the North Korean system, its durability, its vulnerabilities, and prospects for the future.

Leadership and Institutions

The landmark study of North Korean communism by Robert A. Scalapino and Chong-sik Lee provided a baseline for understanding the North Korean ideology and institutions in comparison with the Soviet and Chinese Communist systems, assessed the effects of nation-building and modernization efforts on the North Korean system, and evaluated the intertwining of Communist ideology and Korean tradition as a source of the system's durability.[3] The study, published in 1972, provides a comprehensive introduction to the evolution of North Korea's institutions and methods for maintaining power and political control. The study holds up well, illustrating the lasting, foundational institutional structure and enduring characteristics of the North Korean system as it was established by Kim Il Sung. The book provides an important point of departure both for understanding the extent of institutional adaptations under Kim Jong Il and for the emergence of contemporary debates over the relative influence of North Korean institutions, ideology, and the Kim family to the institutions over which they have presided.

The system Scalapino and Lee describe borrows its primary structural features from the Soviet and Chinese systems and was monolithic, under the complete control of Kim Il Sung. But there has been a gradual evolution of North Korean institutions both under Kim Il Sung's leadership until his death in 1994 and under his son and successor Kim Jong Il. With the transition from Kim Il Sung to Kim Jong Il, the relevance of bureaucratic institutions within North Korea as influences on policy formation under Kim Jong Il's rule is easier to see. One straightforward example is that while Kim Il Sung himself always delivered a New Year's address providing guidance and defining priorities for the North Korean people, that guidance was provided under Kim Jong Il in the form of a Joint Editorial from outlets representing the military, the party, and the communist youth league. A 1998 constitutional revision consolidated Kim Jong Il's rule by enhancing the role of the military at the expense of the party. Kim Jong Il's *songun* (military-first) politics, an institutional prioritization that served as his guiding ideology, was established.

The emerging role and function of North Korean institutions has been the subject of periodic studies over the years. Patrick McEachern, in his 2010 book, *Inside the Red Box: North Korea's Post-Totalitarian Politics*, makes a compelling argument that bureaucratic competition has emerged among the government, the party, and the military as a result of North Korea's evolution from totalitarianism into a posttotalitarian state.[4] His study illustrates how differing positions among these institutions are debated publicly in the absence of opportunities for private interaction in the stove-pipe system over which Kim Jong Il presided—and intervened—as the final decision-maker.

This volume accepts the premise that ideology and institutions have provided the primary foundations for wielding power in modern North Korea and assumes that the main focus of the North Korean leadership in the context of its current leadership transition will be to ensure that various institutions—the party, the military, and the government—are working in concert to support the third generation leadership succession. Kim Jong Il's effort in September 2010 to revamp the party leadership suggests that efforts to align military and party support for the transition to Kim Jong Un are indeed critical for its success or failure.

In part I on the political system, Charles Armstrong provides a historical analysis of the crucial guiding role that ideology has played as an instrument for demanding loyalty from the people and as a way of controlling elites. Ken Gause then examines the institutional underpinnings of the leadership transition in detail, with a focus on the North Korean efforts to align and intertwine institutional branches with each other in support of a new leader. Terence Roehrig further explores the multiple roles of the Korean People's Army in North Korean society, especially as a result of the special place that the military has occupied as a main component of North Korea's guiding ideology. Bruce Cumings argues in support of the durability of the North Korean system and the likelihood of a successful North Korean leadership transition to Kim Jong Un by reviewing the assumptions of many policy analysts who have mistakenly anticipated North Korea's collapse following the end of the Cold War. Analysis of North Korea through the lens of institutions and ideology provides a picture that emphasizes continuity and endurance, or at the very least, evolution, over the prospects for dramatic change. Yet the international context for analyzing regime durability and cohesion in 2011 and 2012 has been the dramatic change brought about by the Arab Spring, which includes a wide range of institutional outcomes resulting from the public challenge to authoritarian rule in the Middle East. If there are clear signs that China is on guard against unanticipated influence from these developments, North Korea is doubly so. Victor Cha and Nicholas Anderson examine the various socioeconomic and demographic factors that have influenced change in the Middle East, drawing the conclusion that although North Korea is at a different stage in its development, it cannot be confident of its immunity from the contagion of popular protest. This backdrop, in which father-to-son successions in Egypt and Libya have been derailed and the son of a dictator is fighting to maintain power in Syria, may be a particularly unsettling moment for North Korea to pursue its own political consolidation under Kim Jong Un.

Despite the increasing availability of information and an improved understanding of North Korea's bureaucratic and institutional structures, the longstanding nature of current academic and policy debates continues to underscore the limits of our understanding of North Korean institutions, leadership, and decision-making procedures. The precise nature of the relationship between the Kim family and other leading elite families within North Korean society to the party, military, and government is still unknown. Debates continue over whether Kim Jong Un is simply a figurehead for a military-led state or whether the military is simply an instrument of his absolute power. It is also anyone's guess whether there is such a thing as a collective leadership in Pyongyang or whether this fundamentally conflicts with an institutional structure in which the *Suryong* is the paramount leader.

Economic Transformation: Marketization, Information Inflows, and the North Korean System

Understanding of the impact of economic crisis on the North Korean system has been greatly aided by the fact that the famine of the 1990s cracked the hermetic seal by which North Korean institutions exercised absolute control over the society. The famine triggered significant population flows by North Korean refugees to China and then onward to South Korea and other destinations including the United States, Canada, and the United Kingdom. In addition, North Korea's dependency on external sources for its economic needs shifted from the Soviet Union, which supported it in the shadows without enhancing transparency, to the broader international aid community, which insisted on the monitoring of humanitarian assistance by aid workers, giving them unprecedented direct access to the North. The famine also had profound impacts on North Korea's Public Distribution System as the markets replaced the state as the primary means by which people gained food. One result was that the energy of the people turned away from the state and toward the markets, as compulsory attendance at state-owned factories gave way to an obsession with private enterprise as the means by which families had to survive. This shift has created an ongoing conflict between the state and the market, with the state simultaneously attempting to emasculate, regulate, coopt, and profit by market mechanisms and the market's potential emergence as a sphere of activity not fully under the state's control.

The emergence of markets and the institutional ramifications for state efforts to impose absolute political control over the people has been well documented by a range of excellent sources. The most comprehensive is Marcus Noland and Stephan Haggard's *Famine in North Korea: Markets, Aid, and Reform*, which exploits the available, albeit still limited, data sets that emerged from North Korea in the context of the famine to assemble a picture of the growing role of the markets and their impact on North Korean institutions.[5] Another valuable book that describes the effects of marketization and monetization on North Korean social organization based on her direct observations as a UN staffer based in Pyongyang is Hazel Smith's *Hungry for Peace*.[6]

With these changing aspects of North Korean society, a valuable strand of literature has resulted from the flow of North Korean refugees and their eyewitness testimonies. This literature is compelling because it provides rare firsthand accounts of the human effects of the North Korean system. For years, there was an almost complete absence of eyewitness accounts. For instance, almost no literature regarding North Korean human rights existed in the early 1990s as a result of the absence of credible eyewitness testimony. A rare attempt from the late 1980s is the result of a standard guided tour of Pyongyang, but in retrospect, based on what we have learned from eyewitness accounts, this barely scratched the surface. However, the stream of literature now available provides chilling evidence of the dire consequences of the failures of the North Korean system, along with a picture of the gradual erosion of political control within the country.[7] But these dramatic accounts have not yet had a direct effect on the North Korean system itself, as evidenced by the fact that such stories have only become available as a result of exit from the country. There is still no evidence of institutionalized mechanisms or collective actions through which internal dissent is possible. While these firsthand accounts are compelling, this volume has confined itself to the question of whether transformations within the North Korean system may emerge as potential accelerants or sources of challenge to the transition of the North Korean system. Refugee testimonies provide the international community with new information regarding human rights conditions in North Korea, but these suppressed populations are utterly marginalized in ways that minimize their influence on the system.[8]

In parts II and III, the volume evaluates the mixed impact of marketization on North Korea. On the one hand, it examines how the state has attempted to meet its needs for outside capital to exploit marketization as a source of hard currency that may perpetuate regime survival. On the other hand, it evaluates the impact of the penetration of markets and outside information on Korean society in spite of state efforts to limit such influences. Nicholas Eberstadt analyzes North Korea's external economic interactions primarily as an effort to extract resources from the outside world in order to sustain its own system and strategies, while pointedly rejecting strategies that might effectively address domestic economic problems or lead to greater integration of the North Korean system with the outside world. Bradley Babson then describes North Korea's recent institutional efforts to interact with its capitalist neighbors through mechanisms such as the establishment of a state development bank and other efforts to attract foreign capital necessary to sustain the regime. Andrei Lankov follows, relying on interviews with North Korean refugees to paint a picture of an emerging grassroots entrepreneurship in North Korea's system of jungle capitalism. With this, he illustrates how the differing levels of economic risks grow in proportion to the relative closeness or distance of economic activity to cooperation with the state. Woo Young Lee and Jungmin Seo study the penetration of South Korean cultural influences into North Korea through the illicit distribution of DVDs, CDs, and USBs that are formally outlawed in North Korea but that have become high-demand forbidden fruit, especially among North Korea's younger generation.

The aggregate picture painted by these four chapters is one that illustrates both how the North Korean system has adapted to manipulate marketization to its own ends, exploiting commercial activity at all levels as sources of hard currency, while fighting off the expanding influence of capitalism on the people's minds through rearguard actions and more intensive indoctrination. But the verdict is still out on whether the penetration of grassroots capitalism in North Korea will ultimately fuel bottom-up reform and opening-by-default. There are still considerable gaps in understanding how North Korea's failed economy may serve its political objectives or the ways in which a rapidly increasing demand for higher-end goods among elites and the masses alike will ultimately be resolved.

The International Context: North Korea's Dynastic Succession and the Regional Environment

The literature regarding North Korea's interactions with the outside world is voluminous in comparison to research devoted to the North Korean system itself. The former reveals both the frustration and difficulty that the international community has faced in its attempts to find the right combination of incentives and coercive measures that might more deeply institutionalize North Korea's cooperation with the outside world. This literature includes periodic assessments of developments in inter-Korean relations and in North Korea's relations with the four great powers that have historically interacted over the Korean Peninsula: the United States, China, Japan, and Russia. Since 2003, the need for greater institutionalization of a regional mechanism designed to facilitate stable management of inter-Korean tensions has been filled by the establishment of the Six-Party Talks, comprising these four powers and North and South Korea. Despite the fact that they have not convened since December 2008, the existence of the Six-Party Talks has yielded a framework and process of enhanced consultation among these actors as the parties most directly concerned with tensions on the Korean Peninsula.

Samuel S. Kim has led the most ambitious efforts to place North Korean foreign policy in the context of international relations theory. His conclusion is that none of the traditional schools of international relations theory are fully adequate to explain North Korean behavior, and his instinct is to frame North Korean behavior as primarily a product of division by which "incomplete nation-states" pursue the "politics of national identity mobilization in order to maximize their exclusive security and legitimacy."[9] The founding of the North Korean system under Kim Il Sung, through its ideology, its personality cult, and its totalitarian subordination of all other interests to the task of pursuing legitimation through the pursuit of reunification, certainly provides ample evidence to support Kim's view. He carries his argument further by attempting to evaluate Korean identity through its relations with major powers in northeast Asia,[10] but ultimately his effort is limited by the fact that two now starkly divergent Korean national images stand against each other, with South Korea resoundingly winning legitimacy from the international community in a verdict that North Korea ultimately will not accept.

In part IV, the book provides updated current assessment of North Korea's foreign policy by examining its relations with South Korea, China, and the United States and the greater international community. Will North Korea find a path toward peaceful integration with its neighbors and with the other economies in the region? Or will it take advantage of strategic mistrust between the United States and China, between China and Japan, and between South Korea and China? Liu Ming conducts the difficult task of analyzing North Korean attitudes and actions toward China in an attempt to tease out North Korea's strategy for maintaining autonomy and freedom of action in the face of overwhelming dependence on China, both politically and economically. Haksoon Paik examines North Korea's consistent efforts to pursue "survival and development" over the course of the past two decades, analyzing the motives and ideational influences that have affected the North's response both to the Sunshine Policy of engagement under the progressive Kim Dae Jung and Roh Moo Hyun governments, and the "Denuclearization, Opening, $3000 Policy" of Lee Myung Bak, which offered massive economic assistance to North Korea on the condition that Pyongyang abandon its nuclear weapons. David Kang considers the history of U.S.-DPRK relations and the dilemmas posed by North Korea for the United States as an extraordinarily "hard target" for American efforts to effectively and positively influence North Korea's provocative behavior. Finally, the concluding chapter broadly surveys the persisting dilemmas and assumptions that will inform the choices of the United States and others as the parties collectively attempt to influence North Korea's future path.

Although North Korea's transition had been planned for several years, there was no way to anticipate that its leadership succession would in fact come prior to 2012, when we initially identified the need for a book on the topic. The political transition unfolding in the next year or two will set the stage for a new round of efforts to address the seemingly intractable tensions surrounding the Korean Peninsula. It is not yet clear if the consequence of these tectonic shifts will be a greater convergence of mutual interest and common purpose to cooperatively address Korean issues, or if they will reveal gaps and mutual mistrust that North Korea might once again exploit as it continues to pursue its own regime survival. As North Korea's post–Kim Jong Il leadership charts its course, both its domestic circumstances and its external interactions will unfold dynamically in ways that will either accelerate transition or perpetuate longstanding patterns of crisis and provocation. The pages that follow provide a systematic analysis of the challenges and prospects for North Korea in transition, based on the available information, recognizing that the study of North Korea from its origins has consistently been an enterprise that generates more questions than answers.

NOTES

1. John Diamond, "U.S. Intelligence Keeps America Guessing," *USA Today* (March 10, 2003), http://www.usatoday.com/news/world/2003-03-10-korea-usat_x .htm (accessed April 28, 2012).

2. Peter Ford, "Did North Korea's Kim Jong-il Take a Secret Train to China?" *Christian Science Monitor*, May 3, 2010.

3. Robert A. Scalapino and Chong-sik Lee, *Communism in Korea*, Vols. I and II (Berkeley, University of California Press, 1972).

4. Patrick McEachern, *Inside the Red Box: North Korea's Post-Totalitarian Politics* (New York: Columbia University Press, 2010).

5. Marcus Noland and Stephan Haggard, *Famine in North Korea: Markets, Aid, and Reform* (New York: Columbia University Press, 2009).

6. Hazel Smith, *Hungry for Peace: International Security, Humanitarian Assistance, and Social Change in North Korea* (Washington, DC: U.S. Institute of Peace Press, 2005).

7. See, for example, Chul-hwan Kang and Pierre Rigoulot, *The Aquariums of Pyongyang: Ten Years in the North Korean Gulag* (New York, NY: Basic Books, 2001); Kongdan Oh and Ralph Hassig, *Hidden Lives of the North Korean People: Everyday Life in the Hermit Kingdom* (Lanham, MD: Rowman & Littlefield Publishers, 2009); Barbara Demick, *Nothing to Envy: Ordinary Lives in North Korea* (New York, NY: Spiegel and Grau, 2010); Marcus Noland and Stephan Haggard, *Witness to Transformation: Refugee Insights into North Korea* (Washington, DC: Peterson Institute for International Economics, 2010); Blaine Harden, *Escape from Camp 14: One Man's Remarkable Odyssey from North Korea to Freedom in the West* (New York, NY: Viking Penguin, 2012).

8. Here, see Kyung-Ae Park, "People's Exit, Regime Stability, and North Korean Diplomacy," in Kyung-Ae Park, ed., *New Challenges of North Korean Foreign Policy* (New York, NY: Palgrave, 2009), pp. 43–68.

9. Samuel S. Kim, "In Search of a Theory of North Korean Foreign Policy," in Samuel S. Kim, ed., *North Korean Foreign Relations in the Post–Cold War Era* (London, UK: Oxford University Press, 1998), p. 19.

10. Samuel S. Kim, *The Two Koreas and the Great Powers* (Cambridge, UK: Cambridge University Press, 2006), pp. 1–41.

Part I

NORTH KOREA'S POLITICAL SYSTEM IN THE TRANSITION ERA

Chapter One

The Role and Influence of Ideology

Charles Armstrong

> To maintain socialism and lead it to victory, we must intensify ideological work. Only when we have solidly armed the popular masses with socialist ideology and strengthened the ideological bulwark of socialism can we consolidate and develop socialism and firmly defend it from any storm. This has been clearly proved by our revolutionary experience.
>
> —Kim Jong Il, 1995[1]

In no country in the world is political ideology more visible than in North Korea. Billboards, banners, and signs in cities, towns, and villages throughout the country proclaim officially correct "thought" (*sasang*—usually translated as "ideology") rooted in the words and ideas of Kim Il Sung and Kim Jong Il. Arts and mass media are always supposed to contain a core ideological message. Loudspeakers broadcast state propaganda to farmers in the countryside as much as eight hours a day. North Korean citizens attend regular, often daily, study sessions on Kim Il Sung and Kim Jong Il thought. The ideological apparatus has continued unrelenting after the death of Kim Jong Il, building up his son and successor Kim Jong Un as a "military genius," although his writings are not yet apparently part of the ideological curriculum. A large portion of written publications, both those intended for internal consumption and those intended for foreign audiences, focus on ideology. Since the 1970s, North Korea has declared that a "monolithic ideology" (*yuil sasang*) unites its people.

Yet for all the pervasiveness of ideology in the Democratic People's Republic of Korea (DPRK), it is difficult to determine the extent to which such ideas influence the behavior of individuals or of the state. This is true of ideology in every society, of course, but it is particularly problematic in North Korea, where there is such a large gap between the abundance of ideological

3

messages and the inaccessibility of public (let alone private) opinion. Among observers outside of North Korea, opinions about the "ruling ideology" of *juche* range from the view that *juche* is a complete sham, merely disguising the Kim family despotism, to those who see it as a quasi-religion more or less believed by a majority of the population.[2] Despite these limitations, however, there are a number of ways in which the evolution and role of ideology in North Korea can be evaluated, two of which will form the core concerns of this chapter. First, behavior—both at the individual and the collective level—refers back to ideology and is justified by it. Therefore there is a connection, if not necessarily causal, between action and ideology. Second, North Korean ideology has evolved over time. This ideological evolution has been more a process of accretion than the substitution of one ideological form for another. Marxism-Leninism, the foundational ideology of the DPRK in the 1940s, has not been entirely discarded, although its content has been radically transformed. North Korean official media still refer to "socialism" and to Marx, although not frequently. *Juche*, as it was developed into a full-blown native ideology in the 1960s and 1970s, was referred to as the "creative application" of Marxism. *Juche* in turn has been the foundation of *songun* ("military-first") politics—sometimes referred to as *songun* ideology (*songun sasang*), a term which began to appear in North Korean media in the 1990s, although North Korean sources claim it started in the late 1960s.[3] By tracing the evolution of North Korean ideology over time, we may get some idea of how the regime has adapted to changing circumstances and where it might be going next in the new, post–Kim Jong Il era.

THE RISE, REVISION, AND RENEWAL OF *"JUCHE* IDEOLOGY"

From the late 1960s onward, North Korean media had emphasized the concept of *juche*, often translated as "self-reliance," in all areas of political, economic, and social activity. *Juche* was in turn closely linked to the leadership and ideas of founding leader Kim Il Sung. The DPRK Constitution of 1972, the first version of the constitution to institutionalize *"juche* thought," declared North Korea to be "the socialist motherland of *juche* which has applied the idea and leadership of the great leader Comrade Kim Il Sung." No mention of Marxism appeared in this or subsequent constitutional revisions in 1992 and 1998.

In the 1990s, following the collapse of socialism in Eastern Europe, North Korea frequently evoked the slogan *urisik sahoejuui*, "our-style socialism" or "socialism of our style." On the surface, "our-style socialism" might be reminiscent of Deng Xiaoping's "socialism with Chinese characteristics," a slogan that gave Communist Party legitimacy to market reform in the 1980s. But the content of "our-style socialism" was unclear. On the one hand, the slogan clearly suggested that North Korea's political system was not of the same family as Eastern Europe's and would not suffer the same fate. On the other hand, the term neither promoted nor precluded the possibility that North Korea might engage to some degree with the global capitalist economy. Largely interchangeable with *juche*, "our-style socialism" was a potentially flexible concept, and North Korea in the 1990s and early 2000s greatly expanded its political and economic ties with the capitalist West, and embarked on limited economic reform, while insisting on unwavering adherence to *juche*. The DPRK maintained that fidelity to *juche sasang* (*juche* ideology or thought) was the sine qua non of the regime. In practice, however, the core principle of *juche* was not economic autarky, but political self-determination and freedom from outside control. In this sense, "our-style socialism" was not so much Marxist-Leninist, perhaps not even socialist, as it was nationalist. "Our-style socialism" was a defensive attempt at national identity mobilization, the legitimation of an incomplete nation-state that found itself besieged by stronger external powers as well as a powerful competitor for national legitimacy in the form of the Republic of Korea in the south. The dilemma North Korea faced in the post–Cold War era was that its legitimacy was based on the guiding principle of *juche* and "socialism," however they were defined, yet at the same time the DPRK had little choice but to seek assistance from the capitalist West and even from South Korea in order to salvage its economy—a move that could undermine the Northern regime's very raison d'etre.

By the beginning of the new millennium, North Korea had weathered the storm of communist collapse and economic disaster under the leadership of Kim Jong Il and the new slogan of "Military-First Politics." But by the end of the first decade of the 2000s, even relatively minor attempts at reform and opening had been scaled back, and the regime based its security less on engagement with the West and South Korea than on Chinese economic support and the development of nuclear weapons. In the meantime, *juche* and "our-style socialism" had been supplemented, and to some extent superseded, by the slogan "Military-First Politics" (*songun chongch'i*). "*Songun*" was closely associated with Kim Jong Il—by now regularly referred to as "the General" (*Changgunnim*)—just as *juche* had been identified with his father Kim Il Sung and with the Korean Workers' Party (KWP). Although sometimes seen as a new "ruling ideology," *songun* did not simply replace *juche* in North Korean propaganda. Rather, *songun* appeared to be a more military-oriented version of *juche*. In the early 2010s, as North Korea moved toward third-generation succession with the rise of Kim Jong Il's son Kim Jong Un in the military and party leadership, *juche* seemed to make something of a comeback, an ideology refined for a new era, one in which the Korean Workers' Party appeared to be returning to a more central role in the society. Yet at the same time, Kim Jong Un's close association with the military and frequent visits to military sites in the early stage of his leadership suggest that "*songun*" and "*juche*" remain inextricably tied in the post–Kim Jong Il order. North Korea's attempt to balance party and army as leading forces in society may be reflected in one of the most common sobriquets given to Kim Jong Un in the immediate aftermath of his father's death: Supreme Leader of the Party, the State and the Military.

NORTH KOREAN IDEOLOGICAL DIVERGENCE

Ideology has always played a key role in communist systems, and North Korea is no exception. Marxist-Leninist regimes all depended on ideology and information control when neither coercion nor material incentives were sufficient. As Katherine Verdery argues in her work on socialist Romania, such regimes appear to be strong but in certain respects are actually quite weak: in terms of efficiency, in terms of dependence on unreliable local actors to implement central policies, and in terms of the internalization of official ideology among ordinary citizens. Such weaknesses, Verdery suggests, require these states to rely extensively on normative or "symbolic-ideological" strategies of control,[4] what in North Korea is called *sasang* or "thought." But from very early in the regime, North Korea diverged from Marxist-Leninist socialism as dictated by the Soviet Union. As early as the beginning of the 1960s, observers from Soviet-aligned states in Eastern Europe complained of North Korea's "deviation" from Marxist-Leninist orthodoxy. This deviation was most troublingly expressed in the cult of personality surrounding Supreme Leader Kim Il Sung, and the strident Korean nationalism that went with it. For example, the East German embassy in Pyongyang reported in March 1961 that in the DPRK,

> Party propaganda is not oriented toward studying the works of Marxism-Leninism, but rather is solely and completely oriented toward the "wise teachings of our glorious leader, Comrade Kim Il Sung." . . . Dogmatism in the Korean Workers' Party is closely linked to mystical ideas of Confucianism, which extend to certain nationalist tendencies.[5]

Although "mystical ideas of Confucianism" may not have been quite accurate, the East German analysis pointed correctly to the East Asian basis of the familial cult, strongly linked to nationalism, a trait North Korea shared with China—another "deviant" in the communist world—as well as with (North) Vietnam. The three East Asian communist regimes also shared a similar emphasis on ideological indoctrination and "correct" thought leading to proper economic and social relations, rather than the other way around, as one might expect in a Marxist, materialist framework.

Thus, North Korea's emphasis on ideology derived from Soviet-style socialism, but it was reinforced by the deep-rooted values of education and moral guidance inherent in Korea's neo-Confucian tradition. Soviet Marxist-Leninist ideas were overlaid upon, and in some ways reinforced by, the legacy of aggressive wartime nationalism from the Japanese colonial period. The content of North Korea's official ideology has always mixed socialist ideas with homegrown Korean nationalism, with a noticeable shift in emphasis to the latter after the Korean War in the 1950s. Like its counterparts in China and Vietnam, the ideology of North Korean state socialism has much greater grounding in popular nationalism than was the case for Soviet-dominated states in Eastern Europe. Although both Marxism-Leninism and nationalism coexisted in North Korean ideology from the beginning of the regime, as the regime evolved, the language of socialism became increasingly sidelined (or absorbed) by the language of nationalism.

Kim Il Sung's first known reference to *juche* was in a speech in December 1955, although later North Korean texts claimed that the idea originated in Kim's anti-Japanese guerilla days of the 1930s. While in foreign analyses this term is most often associated with economic matters, it is significant that Kim's original *juche* speech was concerned with ideological work.[6] Much more than a slogan for economic self-reliance, *juche* has been the preeminent expression of North Korea's emphasis on the ideological over the material, thought over matter, superstructure over base. Portrayed as a supplement to and an improvement on Marxism-Leninism, *juche* in effect reversed the historical materialism of Marx. Rather than superstructural transformation resulting from changes in relations of production, in North Korean official ideology, "thought revolution" is the first step in transforming individuals and society, out of which "correct" political organization, and finally increased economic production, will emerge.[7] *Juche* became official orthodoxy when it entered the DPRK Constitution in 1972. In 1997, three years after the death of Kim Il Sung, North Korea established a new "*juche* calendar" based on the birth year of Kim Il Sung, 1912. In this way the elder Kim, who was declared the "Eternal President" in 1998, became fully identified with *juche*, while his son was becoming associated with the new principle of *songun*, which will be discussed below.

THE POST–COLD WAR PERIOD: "OUR-STYLE SOCIALISM"

The collapse of communist regimes in Eastern Europe, the People's Republic of Mongolia, and the Soviet Union contributed to economic catastrophe and famine in North Korea in the mid- to late 1990s. North Korea's crisis was also an ideological one, and Pyongyang's response was to turn inward and disassociate itself from the failed socialist experiments of the Soviet Bloc. This ideological introversion was encapsulated in the slogan "our-style socialism" (*urisik sahoejuui*). The precise content of "our-style socialism" was left vague, except to insist that it was unique, inseparable from the leadership of Kim Il Sung and Kim Jong Il, and "people-centered"—exactly what the DPRK had been saying about *juche* for decades.[8] Indeed, our-style socialism was presented as a further application of *juche*. A typical editorial statement of the 1990s declared, "The socialism of our style centered upon the masses is developing fully under the refined leadership of Comrade Kim Jong Il by imbuing the whole society with the Juche idea."[9] This "socialism" had little to do with class struggle, economic redistribution, or social equality. It had everything to do with national independence and autonomy, and the primacy of ideas over material circumstances. The article makes this quite explicit: "The ideal of socialism, *the people's idea of independence*, can never be suppressed or destroyed."[10]

Within such ideological parameters, North Korea could even engage in limited experiments in economic reform. During the first post–Cold War decade, DPRK media gave extensive coverage to foreign investment and noted approvingly the moves toward improved relations with Japan and the United States. In the mid-1990s, the DPRK media covered with some enthusiasm the new Free Economic and Trade Zone (FEZ) in the Rajin-Sonbong area of northeastern North Korea, where the DPRK held its first-ever international investment conference in September 1996.[11] This was especially the case in publications intended for foreigners, such as the English-language, Japan-based *People's Korea*.[12] This contradictory stress on economic flexibility on the one hand, and unswerving ideological uniformity on the other, may have reflected differences within the leadership on the desirability, extent, and nature of economic reform, as well as differences between pronouncements intended for domestic consumption and those aimed at foreigners. No doubt, the regime would have wanted the best of both worlds: the economic benefits of Western investment and assistance, without any compromise of the existing political system or weakening of the ruling elite. As material circumstances deteriorated, the DPRK increasingly stressed the supremacy of thought over "objective conditions," turning Marx on his head. North Korea's neo-Hegelian Weltanschauung was expressed ever more openly; an article in the 1990s stated, "The decisive factor in the victory of the revolution is not objective and economic conditions. . . . The decisive guarantee for the victory of socialism is *giving precedence to the enhancement of the independent ideological consciousness of the popular masses*."[13] Following this logic, a sufficiently indoctrinated population need not fear the introductions of capitalist means of production so long as those means are kept subordinate to larger collectivist concerns, including the maintenance in power of the current leadership. "Our-style socialism" could, in theory, be compatible with market reform. For a time, North Korea seemed to be preparing for that path.

For example, at a DPRK-sponsored "*Juche* Seminar" held in Moscow in February 1996, the director general of the Institute for the *Juche* Idea, a Japanese by the name of Inoue Shuhachi, quoted Kim Jong Il as saying,

> The Juche idea explains that the motive force of social movement is not the objective conditions, but man himself, not as an isolated individual, but as a socio-political collective united with the common idea of independence.[14]

The complete identification of North Korean ideology with nationalism reflected simultaneously the abandonment of Marxism and a rejection of liberal democracy. In Russia's first post-Soviet decade, Boris Yeltsin treated the DPRK with undisguised contempt, as if it were a relic of the past about to disappear. On the other hand, North Korea's *juche* was praised both by die-hard Russian communists and ultranationalists such as Vladimir Zhirinovsky.[15] Upon coming to power, President Vladimir Putin mended fences with North Korea, and in 2000 he became the first top Russian or Soviet leader to visit the DPRK. In 2001, Kim Jong Il paid a reciprocal visit to Russia.

The accelerated shift from Marxist orthodoxy to nativist themes was also linked to the death of Kim Il Sung in 1994. One longtime North Korea watcher called this a "shift from the politics of patriarchy to the politics of filial piety."[16] At one level, this meant that Kim Jong Il had to show loyalty to his deceased father's policies and ideas and undergo a long and respectful period of mourning before assuming his official political positions in 1997–1998. The three-year gap between the elder Kim's death and the younger Kim's assumption of power did not reflect a power struggle among the elite. Kim Jong Il's succession had been prepared since the 1970s. Rather, this gap resonated with the traditional three-year mourning period of Korean subjects for their deceased kings, or sons for their fathers.

At a deeper level, after Kim Il Sung's death, North Korea sought to situate regime legitimacy more solidly in Korean history, bypassing the historical dead end of Soviet socialism. The media placed greater emphasis on traditional Korean history, virtuous and benevolent leadership, and the central importance of the family to society—including the symbolic and literal lines of paternal descent of the Kim family. Thus, North Korean propaganda focused not just on the actual ancestry of Kim Jong Il, but also on tracing a kind of symbolic ancestry that linked Kim Jong Il and Kim Il Sung to great leaders of the past—not the communist pantheon of Marx, Engels, Lenin, Stalin, and Mao, but Korean historical figures, especially dynastic founders such as Wang Kon of Koryo and Yi Song Gye of Choson. This process was already under way before Kim Il Sung's death, with the North Korean "discovery" in 1993 of the alleged remains of Tangun, the mythical progenitor of the Korean race some 5,000 years ago.[17]

The family unit became more than ever the metaphor and explicit foundation for regime legitimacy. The family itself had never come under attack in North Korea, as it had in the early years of the Soviet Union or in China during the Cultural Revolution. Rather, from the beginning of the North Korean regime, the family was extolled as the basic "cell" of Korean society.[18] In the post–Cold War years, North Korean publications and media turned toward traditional themes of popular Korean neo-Confucianism: filial piety, respect for elders, and moral education. Needless to say, the DPRK did not refer to neo-Confucianism as its guiding principle in the 1990s and made appropriate references to "revolution" and "socialism" in its pronouncements. But the sentiments behind this modern language were deeply traditional. For example, an article by Kim Jong Il appeared in the *Rodong Sinmun* on Christmas Day, 1995, which made much use of the phrase "respect for revolutionary elders."[19] The article is suffused with the language of love, benevolence, duty, family, and history. Society is represented as harmonious, indivisible, and centered around the Great Leader (that is, the deceased Kim Il Sung). The key social value is collectivism, and the recurrent metaphor is the family, in particular the parent–child relationship: the leader is the father, the party is the mother, and the people are the children. The highest duty of the revolutionary is reverence for the leader, and the relationship between "elders" (*hubei*) and "juniors" (*sonbae*) should also be like that between parents and children. "Our-style socialism" is said to mean that the people "love and help one another as one family," and the goal of revolutionaries is to "create a sublime and beautiful model of moral duty arising out of the tradition of anti-Japanese revolution." One could hardly find a language farther removed from Marxist materialism or Leninist internationalism.

As in his other writings of the time, such as his 1994 treatise "Socialism Is a Science,"[20] Kim Jong Il in his *Rodong Sinmun* article argued that Korea followed a unique path very different from that of the failed socialisms of Eastern Europe. Without naming any countries specifically, the article attacks "opportunists, traitors to socialism, and modern revisionists" who have distorted Marxism-Leninism, become tainted by the ideology of bourgeois individualism, and (temporarily) set back the cause of socialism worldwide. The key to maintaining ideological correctness, the loss of which led to the disasters in Eastern Europe and the USSR, is the education of the young. This had long been a prominent theme in North Korean propaganda, going back at least to Kim Il Sung's speeches in the 1960s. If Eastern Europe was a negative example of youth education, North Korea presented itself—and Kim Jong Il personally—as a model of proper transgenerational indoctrination. "History teaches us," Kim Jong Il writes, "that if the youth of a socialist society are not properly educated, they cannot grow up believing in revolution, and cannot maintain socialism." In proper Confucian fashion, youth must learn from the experiences of previous generations; school education, social education, and family education must be harmonized; education must have a strong moral element; and young people must behave as "filial sons" (*hyoja*). North Korea's emphasis on morality, respect for leadership and tradition, and "family values" was more than a conservative defense of the communist status quo. The ideology of "our-style socialism" reflected a reformulation of Marxism-Leninism as cultural nationalism and resonated with a long history of Korean defense of a neo-Confucian order against the Western incursions of the late nineteenth century. Echoing the neo-Confucian traditionalists of one hundred years before, the North Korean leadership of the 1990s argued that only a moral revitalization of the people could save Korea, the last holdout of civilization (Confucian in the 1880s, socialist in the 1990s) against barbarism.[21]

MILITARY-FIRST POLITICS

North Korean ideological discourse shifted again in the new millennium, and the dominant slogan of the 2000s was "Military-First Politics" (*songun chongch'i*) or sometimes "Military-First Ideology" (*songun sasang*). North Korea had been a militarized society from the beginning of the regime, but after the collapse of European communism, the newly isolated and defensive DPRK became militarized as never before. This military emphasis was evident immediately after the fall of the USSR, reflected in—among other things— new titles for North Korea's top two leaders. In December 1991, Kim Jong Il assumed North Korea's top military position as head of the Korean People's Army, and on April 20th, 1992, he was named "Marshal" (*Wonsu*).[22] Kim Il Sung had been named "Generalissimo" (*Taewonsu*) one week earlier, on April 13th. The leadership succession to Kim Jong Il was fully consolidated by April 1992, and the younger Kim—despite his lack of any real military experience— would henceforth be known primarily by his military titles: as commander-in-chief (*ch'oego saryonggwan*) in North Korean state media, in popular parlance simply as "the General" (*Changgunnim*). Kim Jong Il became chairman of the National Defense Committee in 1993, and his position was reconfirmed in 1998, four years after his father's death. The younger Kim, thus, ruled North Korea primarily as a military leader.

The term *songun*, relatively rarely used before, grew in frequency and importance in DPRK media in the years after Kim Il Sung's death. In 1999, *songun* appeared in the joint New Year's editorial among the three leading newspapers in the DPRK, representing the party, the military, and the youth organization; in 2003, the New Year's editorial referred for the first time to *songun sasang*, or military-first ideology, implicitly putting *songun* on the level of *juche*. In one sense, *songun* was the logical next step in the evolution of *juche* as an ideology of militant nationalism. But more specifically, *songun* placed the institutional military as the vanguard of the revolution, replacing the working class. Indeed, the army was now placed above the party; the *Rodong Sinmun* announced that North Korea "puts the People's Army, not the working class, to the fore as the main force of the revolution" and "the army is precisely the party, the state and the people."[23] If *juche* represented North Korean independence and autonomy, embodied in the Great Leader Kim Il Sung, *songun* placed the defense of that independence in the vanguard institution of the military, closely identified with General Kim Jong Il. As Kim Jong Il explained in a 2003 essay, "The underlying aspects of Songun politics are that military affairs are of paramount importance, that the army is the hard core and main force of the revolution, and that the army must be strengthened in every way."[24] Kim acknowledged that "precedence of the army over the working class" was unprecedented in Marxist revolutionary theory. But times had changed, and the working class of the Information Technology age was not the same as that of the industrial revolution. In the present age, the military is the vanguard necessary to "awaken and rally the broad sections of the masses who oppose the domination of monopoly capital and the aggression and war policy of imperialism."[25] For North Korea, that meant "giving prominence to the People's Army as the core unit and main force of the revolution."[26]

For most of its existence the DPRK has been a highly mobilized, militarized society that served as a living example of what Marx once called "barracks communism." *Songun* seemed merely to remove any remaining pretense of North Korea's adherence to Marxian class struggle and to be an acknowledgement of the preeminent role of the military in the leadership and in society. The rise of *songun* also coincided with North Korea's retreat from economic reform in the mid-2000s. Having lost confidence in its modest experiments with reform and opening, the DPRK instead put its stock into military defense, successfully exploding a nuclear device in 2006 (and again in 2009) in an attempt to guarantee regime survival through nuclear deterrence. North Korea's clashes with South Korea in the West Sea in 2010, including the shelling of Yeonpyeong Island by Northern artillery in November, seem to reflect this heightened militarism of North Korea as well. Once again, however, *songun* did not replace *juche* but was proposed as an improvement upon it. And with the emergence of third-generation Kim leadership at the beginning of the 2010s, *juche* appeared to be regaining prominence, and *songun* somewhat to be declining as a dominant slogan.

"NEO-*JUCHE*" FOR THE NEXT GENERATION

On September 28, 2010, North Korea hosted a "Conference of Party Delegates" (*tang taep'yoja hoe*), the third in its history and the first since 1966. This was ostensibly not a "Party Congress" (*tang taehoe*), the sixth and most recent of which took place in October 1980. It was at the Sixth Party Congress in 1980 that Kim Jong Il officially emerged as the successor to Kim Il Sung. At the September 2010 Party Conference, Kim Jong Il was reaffirmed as party secretary and chairman of the Military Defense Commission, but much of the world's attention was focused on the question of his own successor. There was no obvious choice of successor to Kim Jong Il when he disappeared from view in 2008, apparently the victim of a stroke. Given the consolidation of the regime as a "family business" over the last four decades, it was almost certain that Kim would pass power to one of his sons. Kim's eldest son Kim Jong Nam appears to have fallen out of favor after his arrest at Narita Airport in 2001, when he tried to sneak into Japan with a false passport. Little is known about Kim Jong Chul, the second son, but he seems not to have been a contender. Rumors that the third son, Kim Jong Un, was the Chosen One began to emerge in early 2009. By midyear he had gained the official sobriquet "*Yongmyong-han Tongji*" or "Brilliant Comrade." He joined the National Defense Commission and traveled to China with his father in August 2010. On September 27 he was named a "*taejang*" or "four-star general" (along with, among others, Kim Jong Il's younger sister Kim Kyong Hui), and the following day he was designated a vice chairman of the Central Military Commission of the KWP and appointed to the Party Central Committee.

On October 3, a few days after the party conference, the *Rodong Sinmun* dedicated a signed article to the twentieth anniversary of Kim Jong Il's essay "The Workers' Party of Korea Organizes and Guides All the Victories of Our People." The article emphasized the centrality of ideology in the North Korean system, and in the leadership of Kim Jong Il. *Juche* was reaffirmed as the central ideological slogan, while *songun* was reduced to a supporting role:

> What is important among the undying exploits of Kim Jong Il is that he has developed the WPK [Workers' Party of Korea] into an ideologically pure party equipped with the revolutionary idea of President Kim Il Sung, the Juche idea, invincible militant ranks united as firm as a rock around the headquarters of the

revolution and an experienced and tested guiding force advancing the Songun revolution to victory. Only Juche type blood is running in the veins of all its members and they are advancing along the road indicated by the Juche idea no matter which way the wind may blow. This is the real picture of the WPK.[27]

The Party Delegates' Conference marked the beginning of the transition to the third-generation Kim's leadership, and possibly a Seventh Party Congress in the not-too-distant future will make the succession official. All of this has been couched in the Leninist-cum-nationalist-cum-militarist language that has characterized North Korean ideological discourse for the last twenty years. While the elements of nationalism, militarism, and Kim-centrism have long been at the core of this ideological discourse, there has been a shift away from *songun* and back toward *juche* in the last few years. It might be going too far to call this a "Neo*juche* revival," as *juche* in fact never went away.[28] But the shift in discourse may suggest a return to a more conservative ideology (evoking the "good old days" before the abortive experiments in post–Cold War reform), greater emphasis on the party and less on the military as the vanguard of the North Korean revolution, and the association of Kim Jong Un with the heroic period of his grandfather. There is some evidence that this is indeed the case and that the regime is trying to evoke the relatively more prosperous Kim Il Sung period through propaganda, not least in the image of Kim Jong Un, who seems quite consciously cultivated in dress, deportment, and even his haircut to look like the young Kim Il Sung.

This image making coincides with the one hundredth anniversary of Kim Il Sung's birth in April 2012. In that sense, Kim Jong Il's death was well timed. Kim Jong Un's image seems deliberately linked to that of his grandfather in order to focus the North Korean population's attention away from the difficult years of Kim Jong Il's rule—a time of famine, uncertainty, and confrontation with the outside world—and to bring back memories of a relatively better-off past as a model for the future. In the buildup to 2012, North Korea declared its goal of building a "powerful and prosperous nation" (*kangsong taeguk*). This phrase was first promoted in January 1999, as North Korea was emerging from the disaster of the late-1990s' famine.[29] But the phrase became prominent in the late 2000s and associated with the 2012 anniversary of Kim Il Sung's birth. To that end, North Korea began large-scale construction projects in Pyongyang in 2008, under the direction of Kim Jong Il and his brother-in-law Jang Song Taek, with the goal of 100,000 new apartments by April 15, 2012.[30] Arguably the "powerful" part of the phrase is linked to North Korea's military-first policy and in particular to its nuclear deterrent. If Kim Jong Un can be associated with a revived economy and strong defense, his legitimacy will be strongly grounded. Or so the regime appears to hope. Whether North

Korea will achieve these goals, and even if does, what this will mean for the future leadership of Kim Jong Un, remains to be seen.

CONCLUSION

It is difficult if not impossible to ascertain how much ordinary North Koreans believe in the ruling ideology. Defectors' testimonies in recent years suggest that economic decline has led to a weakening of ideological controls and a decline in general belief in the system.[31] Partly this is due to growing awareness of the world beyond North Korea's borders and recognition of a gap between that external reality and what North Koreans are told by their leaders and official media. Despite the best efforts of the regime to keep its population isolated, ordinary North Koreans are much more aware of realities beyond their country's boundaries than they were a decade or two ago. Even if overt criticism of the regime is forbidden, North Korean people have increasingly been evading the official system in various ways, whether it be through local entrepreneurship, fleeing the country altogether, or tuning in to officially forbidden but increasingly tolerated news media and entertainment from outside the DPRK, including South Korea.[32] The control of the state is not what it once was, and North Koreans are dealing with the state not (yet) through resistance, but through evasion and cynicism, similar to Eastern Europe in the 1970s.

While leadership transition proceeds in the DPRK, and despite a turn toward a more conservative form of *juche*, North Korea may now be moving away from revolutionary mobilization toward a "mature" communist state.[33] All other communist states moved from that stage to either substantial economic reform or collapse. In some cases, such as Hungary, reform was followed by collapse. North Korea's dilemma for over two decades has been that reform is necessary for survival, yet reform could cause the whole system to fall apart. In this situation North Korea's leaders have taken the conservative path, more fearful of the political threat of a genuine opening than of the economic consequences of maintaining the status quo. So far North Korea has avoided either reform or collapse, largely through falling back on ideological exhortation and enforcement of social controls. Both of these methods, however, seem to be showing diminishing returns. As North Korea declares its emergence as a "strong and prosperous nation" under the leadership of Kim Jong Un, the regime seems to be promising improvement in the material quality of life for its citizens. Without such improvement, it will take a great deal of ideological work indeed to maintain a docile and satisfied citizenry.

NOTES

1. Kim Jong Il, *Giving Priority to Ideological Work Is Essential for Accomplishing Socialism* (Pyongyang: Foreign Languages Publishing House, 1995).
2. See Han S. Park, *North Korea: The Politics of Unconventional Wisdom* (Boulder, CO: Lynne Rienner, 2002). On the concept of political religion, which may be a particularly useful lens through which to understand North Korean ideology, see Hans Mair, ed., *Totalitarianism and Political Religions: Concepts for the Comparison of Dictatorships*, trans. Jodi Bruhn (London: Routledge, 2004).
3. Kim Chol U, *Songun Politics of Kim Jong Il* (Pyongyang: Foreign Languages Publishing House, 2008), 3.
4. Katherine Verdery, "Theorizing Socialism: A Prologue to the 'Transition,'" *American Ethnologist* 18, no. 3 (August 1991): 419–39.
5. Embassy of the German Democratic Republic in the DPRK, Report, March 14, 1961, Federal Republic of Germany, Federal Archives, Archives of Party and Mass Organizations of the German Democratic Republic (SAPMO-BA), DY 30, IV 2/20/137.
6. Kim Il Sung, "On Eliminating Dogmatism and Formalism and Establishing Juche in Ideological Work," in Kim Il Sung, *Works*, vol. 9 (Pyongyang: Foreign Languages Publishing House, 1981), 395–417.
7. See Bruce Cumings, "Corporatism in North Korea," *Journal of Korean Studies*, no. 4 (1983): 1–32.
8. The September 2010 Workers' Party Conference referred to the DPRK with the neologism "People's Regime" (*Inmin Chongkwon*) and made no reference to Marxism or the ultimate goal of communism. See Korean Central News Agency, "Resolution of WPK Conference on Revision of Rules," http://www.kcna.co.jp/index-e.htm.
9. Ch'oe Chol Nam, "Socialism Unites People with One Mind and Will," *Korea Today*, January 1993, 5.
10. Ch'oe Chol Nam, "Socialism Unites People," 5; emphasis added.
11. Jonathan Pollack, "Behind North Korea's Barbed Wire: Capitalism," *New York Times*, September 15, 1996.
12. See for example "Rajin-Sonbong Zone Being Developed as International Economic Center," *People's Korea*, January 20, 1996, 5. This full-page article included names of foreign companies that had sent representatives to visit the zone, and boasted that the region would become "an international economic center like Singapore," with "unlimited economic potential." Unfortunately that potential has not yet been realized.
13. Sin Hyon Sok, "Juche Revolutionary Cause Continues," *Korea Today*, February 1995, 15.
14. "Keynote Report at International Seminar on the Chuch'e [Juche] Idea in Moscow," FBIS-EAS, February 4, 1996; emphasis added.
15. Evgeny Bazhanov, "A Russian Perspective on Korean Peace and Security," Nautilus Institute Policy Forum, July 28, 1997. Zhirinovsky called North Korea "a country envied even by Russia, which was once the strongest power, and an oasis

for the world." See http://www.nautilus.org/publications/essays/napsnet/forum/1997 (accessed November 10, 2010).

16. Alexandre Y. Mansourov, "In Search of a New Identity: Revival of Traditional Politics and Modernization in Post-Kim Il Sung North Korea," Working Paper No. 1995/3, Department of International Relations, Australian National University, May 1995, 7.

17. The remains of Tangun and his wife were allegedly discovered near Pyongyang on October 2, 1993, and determined by North Korean archeologists to be 5,011 years old. Kim Jong Il oversaw the construction of a mausoleum to be built honoring Tangun as "the father of the nation." *Korea Today*, February 1995, 6.

18. Charles K. Armstrong, *The North Korean Revolution, 1945–1950* (Ithaca, NY: Cornell University Press, 2003), chap. 5.

19. Kim Jong Il, "Respect for Revolutionary Elders Is the Sublime Moral Duty of Revolutionaries," *Rodong Sinmun*, December 25, 1995. Note the phrase "moral duty."

20. Kim Jong Il, *Socialism Is a Science* (Pyongyang: Foreign Languages Publishing House, 1994); originally published in the *Rodong Sinmun* on November 1, 1994.

21. See Chai-sik Chung, "Confucian Tradition and Nationalist Ideology in Korea," in Kenneth M. Wells, ed., *South Korea's Minjung Movement: The Culture and Politics of Dissidence* (Honolulu: University of Hawaii Press, 1995), 67.

22. *Rodong Sinmun*, April 21, 1992, 1.

23. Cited in Ruediger Frank, "The End of Socialism and a Wedding Gift for the Groom? The True Meaning of the Military First Policy," Nautilus Institute, DPRK Briefing Book, December 11, 2003, http://www.nautilus.org/publications/books/dprkbb/transition/Ruediger_Socialism.html (accessed November 14, 2010).

24. Kim Jong Il, *The Songun-Based Revolutionary Line Is a Great Revolutionary Line of Our Era and an Ever-Victorious Banner of Our Revolution* (Pyongyang: Foreign Language House, 2007), 1–2. The essay is based on a talk Kim gave to senior officials of the KWP Central Committee in January 2003.

25. Kim Jong Il, *The Songun-Based Revolutionary Line*, 7.

26. Kim Jong Il, *The Songun-Based Revolutionary Line*, 5.

27. Korean Central News Agency, October 3, 2010.

28. Victor Cha, "The End of History: 'Neojuche Revivalism' and Korean Unification," *Orbis: A Journal of World Affairs* 55, no. 2 (Spring 2011), http://www.fpri.org/orbis/5502.html.

29. Byung-Chul Koh, "'Military-First Politics' and Building a 'Powerful and Prosperous Nation' in North Korea," Nautilus Institute Policy Forum, April 14, 2005, http://www.nautilus.org/publications/essays/napsnet/forum/security/0532AKoh.html.

30. "North Korea Pushing Forward with the Project of Constructing 100,000 Housing Units in Pyongyang," North Korea Economy Watch, November 3, 2011, http://www.nkeconwatch.com/category/policies/2012-goals.

31. See especially Barbara Demick, *Nothing to Envy: Ordinary Lives in North Korea* (New York: Speigel and Grau, 2009) and Stephan Haggard and Marcus Noland, *Witness to Transformation: Refugee Insights into North Korea* (Washington, DC:

Peterson Institute, 2010) for recent reports on North Korean refugees that suggest growing disillusionment with the governing ideology.

32. See for example the collection of underground reportage by North Korean citizens in the journal *Rimjingang*, edited by Japanese journalist Ishimaru Jiro, http://www.asiapress.org/rimjingang.

33. Unique among communist states, North Korea seems never to have moved beyond the "revolutionary" or consolidation stage. See Janos Kornai's classic typology of communism, *The Socialist System: The Political Economy of Communism* (Princeton, NJ: Princeton University Press, 1992).

Chapter Two

The Role and Influence of the Party Apparatus

Ken Gause

The event the Pyongyang watching community had been expecting for nearly three years came to pass on December 17, 2011, at 0830 North Korea time (reportedly) on a train somewhere on the outskirts of the capital. According to the (North) Korean Central News Agency, Kim Jong Il "suffered an advanced acute myocardial infarction, complicated with a serious heart shock." His death brought to an end an era in North Korean politics that began on July 8, 1994, with the death of his father, Kim Il Sung. Nearly fifty hours after the event, the North Korean propaganda apparatus sprung into action, informing the world of Kim's passing and proclaiming Kim Jong Un the "great successor."

What this means for North Korean leadership dynamics going forward is still unclear. Fundamental to answering this question will be the role of the Korean Workers' Party (KWP). Whether real power and authority will be nested inside the KWP or remain something that is intensely personal for the supreme leader will answer the question as to whether the regime will undergo a paradigm shift in how it is ruled.

As with many other communist-ruled countries, North Korea has a party that sits atop the pantheon of its leadership institutions. According to its charter, the Korean Workers' Party guides all state and social organs. The constitution states that "the DPRK shall conduct all activities under the leadership of the Korean Workers' Party."

Despite the rhetoric surrounding its status, in recent years, the role of the party has become a source of contention among Pyongyang watchers. Some contend that it has become irrelevant to the running of the regime. For over a decade since Kim Il Sung's death in 1994, the party was in seeming hibernation, its leading bodies lying dormant and its oversight responsibilities curbed in an era of military-first politics. A Party Congress had not been held since

1980. A Central Committee meeting had not been held since 1993. While there had been rumors of occasional Politburo meetings since the advent of the Kim Jong Il era, none had ever been confirmed. Others argued that even though the government and military had been given more latitude within the regime's troika of power, the party maintained a critical role as a mass organization that exerts control over the population and guides policy.

This debate came to the fore in the summer of 2010 when the Korean (*Chosun*) Central News Agency (KCNA) suddenly announced on June 26 that "the Politburo of the Central Committee would summon a delegates' conference at the beginning of September to elect the leading apparatus of the Workers' Party." The announcement went on to say that the conference was necessary to "reflect the demands for the revolutionary development of the Party, which is facing critical changes in bringing about the strong and prosperous state and *chuche* achievements."

On September 28, 2010, North Korea convened a Party Conference, the third in its history. Over the course of the one-day event, the conference delegates revised the Party Charter and then sanctioned appointments to the Central Committee (increased from 151 to 229), Politburo (increased from 10 to 37), Secretariat (increased from 7 to 11), Central Military Committee (increased from 12 to 19), Central Committee departments, Central Auditing Commission, and Central Control Committee.

The resurrection of the party has continued in the aftermath of Kim Jong Il's death. Although the regime has proclaimed Kim Jong Il as the "eternal head of the party" (still undefined), it has gone to great lengths to tout Kim Jong Un as the new "supreme leader" (*ch'eogo ryo'ngdoja*) and tie his power to the KWP. The party leadership has been on prominent display during the first few months of the new regime. The North Korean media, while paying due deference to military-first policy, has made a point of stressing the leading role of the party. As if to convey this message, a special gathering of the Politburo was convened on December 30 to proclaim Kim Jong Un "supreme commander" (*choson inmin'gun ch'oego*) of the armed forces. At the Fourth Party Conference in April (2012), Kim became the first secretary of the party and chairman of the party's Central Military Committee (CMC).

This chapter will examine the role and influence of the party within the North Korean ruling structure. It will argue that unlike the communist parties of the Soviet Union, Eastern Europe, and China, the Korean Workers' Party is not a vanguard institution. Instead, it is an artifice of the *Suryong*'s ("great leader's") leadership style. If this is the case, what does this portend for the future? Did the resurrection of the party's profile satisfy the requirements for Kim Jong Il succession? Will the party be the center of post–Kim Jong Il leadership configuration? Collectively, who makes up the party leadership, and who among them are closely tied to Kim Jong Un? Finally, what does the party's reemergence say about policy making and the potential for stability in the North Korean regime?

THE KOREAN WORKERS' PARTY UNDER KIM IL SUNG

The North Korean Communist Party was established in 1946 through a merger of the Communist Party and the Nationalist Party. In 1949, it became the Korean Workers' Party. Although it has a familiar organizational structure, the political system and the role of the party in North Korea are considerably different from other socialist countries. To begin with, the KWP is a mass party with a membership of around 3 million, nearly 16 percent of the country's population. If accurate, this means that the Korean Workers' Party has the highest ratio of members of any past or present socialist state.[1]

The unique aspect of the KWP becomes even clearer when one examines its role as a component of the regime. Article 11 of the North Korean Constitution declares, "The DPRK shall conduct all activities under the leadership of the KWP." In addition, Article 46 of the party rules defines the role of the Korean People's Army (KPA) as the party's revolutionary armed forces. On the surface, this seems to mimic the role of communist parties in other socialist countries, such as China and the Soviet Union, both of which played a role in establishing the regime in Pyongyang. But, far from being the vanguard of the working class, the role of the Korean Workers' Party, just as the regime as a whole, is to serve the will of the *Suryong* (leader).

One of the most peculiar features of the North Korean system is the supreme authority of the "leader" in every domain, such as ideology, law, administration, and regulations. For this reason, the North Korean political system is often called "*suryeongje*" ("a leader-dominant system") or "*yuil cheje*" ("a monolithic system").[2] In 1949, Kim Il Sung designated himself *Suryong* and began a campaign to eliminate all opposition to his position as the unbridled leader of the nation. He started to construct the ideological bulwark to support his status within the leadership in the mid-1950s with the unveiling of a Marxist-Leninist model for self-reliance called *juche* (alt. *chuche*), which became the principal ideology for politics, economics, national defense, and foreign policy. By 1956, Kim achieved unchallenged dominance in the Korean Workers' Party, tightly controlling all aspects of both politics and society. This was further inculcated in the late 1960s and early 1970s with the institution of the "*Suryong*'s Monolithic System of Guidance," which was designed to lay the groundwork for the transfer of power from Kim Il Sung to Kim Jong Il. At the Sixth Party Congress in 1980, he proclaimed,

> The whole Party is rallied rock-firm around its Central Committee and knit together in ideology and purpose on the basis of the *Chuche* idea. The Party has no room for any other idea than the *Chuche* idea, and no force can ever break its unity and cohesion based on this idea.

As was made clear by North Korean propaganda, "The *Suryong* is an impeccable brain of the living body, the masses can be endowed with their life in exchange for their loyalty to him, and the party is the nerve center of that living body."

This statement was clearly manifested during the Kim Il Sung era, as most policy making at the national level was realized through official decision-making institutions, which met more or less on a regular basis. At the top of this infrastructure was the party's Political Bureau (Politburo), where senior-level debates were held and Kim's thinking was fleshed out.[3] These decisions were enforced by the Secretariat through the unified *juche* party doctrine and ubiquitous party committee system.

Kim Il Sung placed his stamp on the regime in 1972 with a new constitution, which was designed to make the government more responsive in carrying out party policy. It did this by centralizing all of the administrative duties of the state. The Cabinet, which until then had acted as the supreme executive organ, was divided into guiding and executing functions. This made way for the creation of the Central People's Committee (CPC). Chaired by the president, the CPC was the supreme guiding agency of state sovereignty and policy making.[4] It took over such functions of the former Cabinet and the SPA's Standing Committee as setting state policy for domestic and foreign affairs, guiding national security, and ensuring the observance of the constitution. The Cabinet was renamed the Administrative Council. Led by the prime minister, it became the policy enforcement agency under the supervision of the president and the CPC.

The critical nexus in this new leadership structure was between the CPC and the party. Party policy directives were delivered to the CPC by a joint conference of the Political Bureau and the CPC. Filling the CPC with senior members of the party ensured the relationship between these two bodies. Every member of the KWP's Political Bureau was concurrently a member of the CPC. But in some respects this argument about the party–state relationship is irrelevant. Above both stood the *Suryong*, who was both the general secretary and the president. The 1972 constitution institutionalized these chains of command and provided a means to coordinate the formulation and conduct of policy, which, in the final evaluation, was nothing more than edicts from on high pulsed through the party (where the edicts were recorded and converted into initiatives) to the state and military apparatuses via the CPC–KWP joint conference. The party via its Organization Guidance Department then continued to track and monitor Kim's edicts to ensure their implementation.

THE PARTY AS A CRADLE FOR THE SUCCESSION

It was within this leadership system that Kim Il Sung engineered his succession. Regardless of the prominent role of the president and the CPC, it was the party apparatus that was at the center of the North Korean political regime. This was made clear by the code phrase "Party Center" (*tang chungang*) used by the regime in the 1970s to refer to the heir apparent, Kim Jong Il.[5] Kim Jong Il started his career in the party, his support network was firmly ensconced in the Central Committee apparatus, and his succession took place within the party structure.

Like other communist systems, there is a political regime that exists alongside the ruling apparatus. While the government and the military can take part in the ruling of the country, power is defined and emanates from the political regime. For communist systems, this political regime resides within the Communist Party. It is only through the party apparatus that the heir apparent can learn how to wield power. In 1973 at the Seventh Plenum of the Fifth Central Committee, Kim Jong Il was appointed to the KWP Secretariat with the portfolios for both Propaganda and Agitation, and Organization and Guidance, the two key posts within the party apparatus. The former allowed him to craft the message of the regime, while the latter ensured that the regime would firmly adhere to the notion of Kim family rule and embrace the idea of a dynastic succession.

Ultimately, it was only through the party apparatus that the heir could eventually consolidate his position as the *Suryong* in waiting. At the Sixth Party Congress in 1980, Kim Jong Il moved into the upper echelons of the decision-making apparatus through appointments to the Presidium of the Politburo and the Central Military Committee. Only Kim Jong Il and Kim Il Sung held positions in the KWP's three leadership bodies: Politburo, Secretariat, and Central Military Committee. While Kim Jong Il was officially ranked fifth within the North Korean leadership, his credentials as heir apparent were readily apparent.

As Kim Jong Il inherited more of his father's power and authority, the leadership system changed in important ways. Institutionally, Kim shifted the center of gravity within the party from the Politburo to the Secretariat, his base of power. Decision making on all policies and personnel appointments were transferred to the Party Secretariat Office and specialized departments, while the Politburo was reduced to a rubber stamp for ratification.[6]

LEADERSHIP DYNAMICS UNDER KIM JONG IL: KIM JONG IL REACHES OUTSIDE THE PARTY TO CONSOLIDATE HIS POWER

It is one thing to consolidate one's power as heir apparent in North Korea's *Suryong*-dominant party-state system. It is quite another thing to hold on to that power as the succession moves into its final phase and the heir has to assume more responsibility for running the regime and preparing to assume the role of leader after the passing of his predecessor. In the case of Kim Jong Il, the final phase of the succession began in the early 1990s. During this phase, the regime transformed its operating procedures to prepare for the transfer of power. Kim Jong Il's ruling power began to eclipse that of Kim Il Sung. His situational awareness was further enhanced as he took control of running the day-to-day affairs of the regime. And while Kim Jong Il maintained Kim Il Sung's policies, he began to add his own imprimatur. These aspects of the succession were for the most part contained within the party apparatus.

But for the transfer of power to take place, Kim Jong Il needed to assert his control over the military. This could only be done by revising the North Korean political regime. No longer would the *Suryong* rule through the party.[7] Now he would take a more direct role in ruling the government and military. Only through an undiluted command-and-control system could Kim Jong Il ever hope to garner the respect and assert his guidance to the level of his father. In 1991, Kim was appointed supreme commander of the armed forces. This was a technical violation of the 1972 constitution, which stipulated that this position was intrinsically linked to that of the president, a post still held by Kim Il Sung. This provision was removed during the 1992 revision of the constitution, which also elevated the National Defense Commission (NDC) in status. It was no longer a committee of the CPC, but a free-standing body. In addition, the NDC assumed responsibility for "work on the building of the people's armed forces," which the Administrative Council (Cabinet), directed by the CPC, had been responsible for during the Kim Il Sung era.[8] In 1993, Kim Jong Il became the chairman of the NDC.

The 1992 constitutional revisions, for many Pyongyang watchers, were an indication that the regime dynamics had fundamentally changed. A separate chapter concerning "national security" was introduced as part of the revisions, which highlighted the regime's view that it was entering a new era. The end of the Cold War meant that North Korea lost one of its key patrons in the Soviet Union and its Warsaw Pact support network. Regime survival was now more of a concern in Pyongyang than at any time since the Korean War. As such, the center of gravity had shifted from the party to a more clear division of labor between the party, government, and military, with the military taking on increasing responsibility and influence while the party began to fade into the background.

PARTY'S ROLE FADES IN ERA OF CRISIS MANAGEMENT

After Kim Il Sung's death, this division of labor became more entrenched into the system as Kim Jong Il began to deal with a crumbling economy. It quickly became apparent that the party was not up to the task of dealing with this crisis. In a speech at Kim Il Sung University to party members in December 1996, Kim Jong Il bitterly criticized the party for being debilitated, using terms such as *Noin-dang* ("Elderly Party") and *Songjang-dang* ("Corpse Party"). According to defector reports, Kim even threatened to disband the party during an informal meeting in 1997.[9] He also reportedly castigated the party for "not dealing properly with the food shortages in the country," and contended that he "did not owe anything to the Party."[10] The party's inability to function was manifested in October 1997, when Kim Jong Il bypassed established party rules to assume the mantle of general secretary of the Korean Workers' Party. This was done not through the convening of a plenary meeting of the KWP Central Committee, but through a joint endorsement by the party's Central Military Committee and Central Committee.[11] By eschewing the Central Committee process and not accepting the title of general secretary of the Central Committee, but general secretary of the KWP, Kim placed himself firmly above the party apparatus and gave notice that unlike his father, he would not rule through the party.

If it was not clear before, it became clear during this period that the KWP was no longer functioning as North Korea's central decision-making venue and that the party-led policy-making system had switched to a military-led *songun* ("military-first") politics. Kim Jong Il unleashed military-first politics in an effort to tie himself more closely to the high command. Military-first politics was basically politics for crisis management drawing on the power of the military to stabilize a potentially destabilizing economic situation highlighted by a famine that began in the early 1990s (also known as the Arduous March or the March of Tribulation). It also allowed Kim to create a ruling structure that played to his strengths of micromanagement and close aide politics, while limiting his exposure to the public other than his constant guidance inspections.

PARTY DOMINANCE GIVES WAY TO AN
INCREASING DIVISION OF LABOR

The Tenth Supreme People's Assembly convened in Pyongyang on September 5, 1998. It had three items on its agenda: revise the North Korean Constitution, reelect Kim Jong Il chairman of the National Defense Commission, and appoint officials to posts throughout the government. Although not described as such, the meeting was the ushering in of a new ruling structure—the Kim Jong Il ruling structure.

The revised constitution made Kim Il Sung the "eternal president" (*chusok*) of North Korea, ending speculation on when his son would succeed him to the top state post. Instead, Kim Jong Il chose to continue the pattern begun in 1992 of concentrating authority in the National Defense Commission. The new structure left little doubt that the NDC was Kim's organizational base from which to implement military-first politics. The NDC was elevated to the highest organ of state, and the position of NDC chairman to the highest position in government.

The 1998 "Kim Il Sung Constitution" also weakened the party's command and control over the government and the economy by abolishing the connective ties it had to the Cabinet, namely the presidency and the CPC. Over the next few years leading up to the July 2002 economic reforms, North Korea abolished many of the departments related to the economy within the central party apparatus such as the departments of Agriculture, Light Industry, Finance, Economic Planning, Mechanical Industry, and Construction and Transportation. This was intended to weaken the role of the party to make policy directives and enhance the role of the Cabinet in leading the economy.[12] When Pak Pong Chu assumed the role of premier in 2003, the Cabinet's growing control over economic policy became clear with a number of liberal measures, including the expansion of market activities, trade companies, and small-plot agriculture.

But, while the party had lost some of its mandate for policy formation, it retained a critical, if not leading, role within the North Korean leadership structure. It continued to oversee the development and propagation of the regime's *juche* ideology. This not only tied the party to Kim's evolving personality cult, but it ensured the party's role as a guardian of the principles of the regime. No matter what short-term politics the military might engage in or reform policies the Cabinet might role out, the party was in a position to push back if certain red lines were crossed.

As important as its role as ideological guardian, the party remained the only institution within the regime that could ensure control down to the lowest levels of society. Neither the military, nor the Cabinet, nor the security organs have an organizational structure that can rival that of the party when it comes to penetrating all levels of society.

GETTING THE PARTY STARTED AGAIN

Despite the party's lingering influence and institutional relevance, it remained on the periphery of power until 2005 when the regime began to take steps to reinstitute control following three years of market and economic reforms. Along with the resurrection of the Public Distribution System, new life was breathed into the party's economic oversight bodies. Pak Nam Gi, the former chairman of the State Planning Commission and director of the KWP Heavy Industry Department, began to appear in the North Korean media under a new title, the director of the KWP Planning and Finance Department. While his appointment went largely unnoticed by the Pyongyang watching community, it signaled that the party had begun to take back some of its oversight responsibilities with the aim of suppressing the market and restoring a considerable portion of the planned system.

The party's return as a player on the economic landscape went hand in hand with the regime's efforts to reassert stability. Behind the scenes in the mid-2000s, the North Korean regime was grappling with the consequences of its evolving engagement policy. Initially, the plan had been to open up slowly and in a controlled manner through the isolated economic zones at Sinuiju and Rason. The agreements reached during the inter-Korean summit in 2000, however, held out the real danger of this plan getting out of control. If the strategy was going to work, the country would need to be prepared. This meant instituting control mechanisms from the center and getting rid of those regime elements that could not be trusted in such close proximity with the outside world.

Kim Jong Il looked to his brother-in-law, Jang Song Taek, to carry out the important task of ensuring regime stability as the regime explored avenues to the outside world. In October 2007, according to North Korean sources, Jang was appointed director of the newly reestablished KWP Administrative Department, which had oversight of the internal security apparatus, including the State Security Department, the Ministry of People's Security, the Central Prosecutor's Office, and the Central Court—essentially restoring the portfolio he once held as first vice chairman of the KWP Organization Guidance Department. From an organizational point of view, Jang's appointment made sense, in that Kim, in line with his evolving close aide policy, consolidated the reporting lines for domestic policy in Jang, giving him two of the most critical portfolios tied to regime stability, the economy and internal security.

Not only did Jang now have a strong say in how policy was crafted, but in how it was managed.

With this move, Kim had brought the party back to the center of politics in the regime. But it was not until his stroke in 2008 that it became apparent that much more would have to be done if the regime was going to have to prepare itself for another transfer of power.

LAYING THE FOUNDATION FOR ANOTHER HEREDITARY SUCCESSION

In the months after Kim Jong Il's stroke in August 2008, the regime began to grapple with the implications of his hub-and-spoke leadership model, which is informal in its structure and tied intimately to one man. How would it be possible to pass this model to a new leader who lacked the connections and power that Kim possessed? When Kim's choice of his third son, Kim Jong Un, as his successor became known within leadership circles in 2009, these issues became magnified. Not only was Kim Jong Un in his late twenties, but he had only been involved in regime affairs for a couple of years.

A POLITBURO ANNOUNCEMENT

As Pyongyang watchers began to opine on these issues, the Chosun Central News Agency (KCNA) suddenly announced on June 26, 2010, that "the Politburo of the Central Committee would summon a delegates' conference at the beginning of September to elect the leading apparatus of the Workers' Party." The announcement went on to say that the conference was necessary to "reflect the demands for the revolutionary development of the Party, which is facing critical changes in bringing about the strong and prosperous state and *chuche* achievements."

North Korea had only convened party conferences twice before, in 1958 (to handle the "August Incident")[13] and in 1966 (to create the Secretariat and the position of general secretary). According to the Party Charter, the Central Committee is supposed to convene a Party Congress once every five years. In between congresses, a conference can be summoned to discuss urgent party issues and key policy matters. The two venues share many of the same powers in terms of personnel matters, such as appointing and expelling members from senior party bodies. However, the Party Conference differentiates itself from the Party Congress by not having to report a summary of activities to the Central Committee and the Central Auditing Committee.

But why the sudden focus on the party, which had become moribund since the Sixth Party Congress in 1980? Several theories were raised in Pyongyang watching circles. The first centered on the succession. Ever since Kim Jong Il had assumed the mantle of general secretary in 1997 without convening a meeting of a leading party body, some within the North Korean leadership allegedly questioned his legitimacy as Kim Il Sung's successor. By restoring the party to its dominant position within the regime, an institutional framework would exist for the legitimate transfer of power. Kim's method of rule, the so-called hub and spoke, where he was the center of several formal and informal chains of command, would be nearly impossible to transfer to his son, especially given Kim Jong Un's age and political inexperience. By surrounding his son with powerful and loyal members from his close aide network within the formal party apparatus, Kim Jong Il could enhance Jong Un's chances of surviving a near-term transition. If this were done through a formal party gathering, legitimacy would automatically be conferred on the heir apparent and presumably could not easily be undone after Kim's death.

Another reason for resurrecting the party was related to the regime's plans for developing a strong and prosperous economy by 2012. Whether Kim believed this target was possible or not, there was no escaping the fact that only the party had an apparatus that could reach down to the district and village level. If central planning was going to reach throughout the country, something that only the market forces had so far been able to achieve, the party would have to be the vehicle for delivery. A return to the way in which the economy was run under Kim Il Sung with the party assuming its rightful supervisory function would be necessary.

LEAD-UP TO THE THIRD PARTY CONFERENCE

By early September, delegate elections to the conference were completed and preparations seemed to be finished. Propaganda surrounding the conference was ubiquitous, far exceeding the campaigns associated with the two previous (1958 and 1966) party conferences.

On September 21, Chosun Central Broadcast, North Korea's state-run radio station, announced that the Party Conference would take place on September 28. Asserting that preparations had gone off without a hitch, the conference organizing committee proclaimed that the election of delegates had been completed. And in a show of unanimity and foreshadowing of the proceedings to come, the committee noted that the delegate conferences from around the country had demonstrated their "boundless faith in the Party . . .

and spoke with one mind to select as a Chosun Workers' Party delegate the leader of our Party and our military, great leader Comrade Kim Jong Il."[14]

While the party's resurrection was no doubt imminent, this was still the era of military-first politics. This was made clear on September 27. In its first dispatch on the opening day of the Party Conference, 1 a.m. local time, KCNA announced that the supreme commander of the Korean People's Army, Kim Jong Il, issued Order No. 0051 on promoting the military ranks of commanding officers of the KPA. The order promoted Kim Kyong Hui, Kim Jong Un, Choe Ryong Hae, Hyon Yong Chol, Choe Pu Il, and Kim Kyong Ok to four-star generals.[15] For the first time, Kim Jong Un's name had appeared in the North Korean media.

The timing of the promotions and how they were handled not only made it clear that the upcoming Party Conference would be tied to the succession, but also seemed to highlight the rings of power within the regime.

- *The first ring was the Kim family.* The first two names listed among the promotions were Kim Kyong Hui (Kim Jong Il's sister) and Kim Jong Un (Kim Jong Il's son). The third name, Choe Ryong Hae, was the son of a former defense minister and a longtime aide to the Kim family with close ties to both Kim Jong Il and Jang Song Taek.
- *The second ring was the military.* The fact that the military promotions preceded by one day the appointments of the Party Conference seemed to indicate the continued prominence of the military-first policy and the importance of the KPA to the stability and continuation of the regime.
- *The third ring was the party.* The Party Conference itself was an indication of the importance of the party's role. It was critical for the succession, and the party's revitalization was necessary for the regime's survival beyond Kim Jong Il's death.

In terms of the succession, Kim Jong Il's strategy apparently was to surround his son with patronage networks along three axes so as not to make him vulnerable to any one regent or a collective leadership. Given enough time and skill at power politics, Kim Jong Un could build his own patronage system and ensure his own survival.

THE THIRD PARTY CONFERENCE

On September 28, shortly before noon, the Third Party Conference convened as Kim Jong Il entered the undisclosed assembly hall to the cheers and a standing ovation of the delegates. Walking toward the center of the rostrum, Kim took his seat, which faced the filled auditorium. Behind him was a large, marble statue of Kim Il Sung. In the front row of delegates, one seat in from the right aisle, was Kim Jong Un, who was dressed in a dark Mao suit with a hairstyle reminiscent of photographs of his grandfather taken in the 1940s. Seated to the heir apparent's left was Hyon Chol Hae. Seated to his right were Kim Won Hong (commander of the Military Security Command), Kim Yong Chol (chief of the Reconnaissance General Bureau), and his aunt, Kim Kyong Hui.

Following an opening speech by Kim Yong Nam, the conference was declared open and the delegates stood to sing the "Song of Kim Il Sung." Kim Yong Nam then again took to the podium to deliver a speech regarding the election of Kim Jong Il as KWP general secretary. Kim was followed by VMAR Ri Yong Ho, chief of the General Staff, who delivered a speech in his capacity as a representative of the party organization of the people's army. Several other speakers gave speeches, all expressing their support for the proposal to elect Kim Jong Il as KWP general secretary and praising the leader's past achievements. One hour after Kim Yong Nam's opening speech, the Party Conference unanimously supported the proposal.[16]

REVISING THE PARTY CHARTER

The Party Conference moved to the second item on the agenda, revising the Party Charter.[17] According to the KCNA, the resolution said that present reality called for revising the party rules so that "the KWP might be strengthened in every way and its leadership role further increased." While the revised charter maintained in its preface a reference to the revolutionary principles of Marxism-Leninism,[18] it dropped the phrase "building a communist society" from the description of the party's ultimate goal. Instead, the goal was now to embody the revolutionary cause of *juche* (self-reliance) in the entire society. The Party Conference also took steps to smooth the hereditary transfer of power by increasing the flexibility surrounding the holding of party congresses. The new charter deleted the provision that a party congress had to be held every five years and replaced it with a provision stipulating that the Central Committee only needed to give a six-month notice for an upcoming congress. This change would allow the party more flexibility in dealing with the unfolding demands of the succession without calling the process into question.

Probably more important, the Party Conference attempted to knit together military-first politics and the "Party Center" to create a sustainable leadership that would support the succession. The Central Military Committee was newly defined as "organizing and leading all military operations."[19] Furthermore, the new charter stipulated that the chairman of the committee would be concurrently held by the party's general secretary. This upgrade suggested that the party's military body would become a critical institution from which the heir apparent might consolidate his power, for the move would allow him to control both the party and the military when he eventually became general secretary. Finally, a reference to military-first politics was inserted into the charter, which now read that "the Party will establish military-first politics as a basic political system of socialism."[20] For many Pyongyang watchers, this latter revision validated the transformation in the hierarchy of power from Party-Government-Military that existed under Kim Il Sung to the current Party-Military-Government.

REINVIGORATING THE PARTY APPARATUS

Having completed the revisions to the Party Charter, the conference moved to its last item of business, appointments to central leadership bodies. Key party positions, many of which had been vacant since the Sixth Party Congress, were filled in order to strengthen the KWP leadership capacity and restore the party's status as a collective deliberating and decision-making institution. In particular, appointments were made to the Central Committee (increased from 151 to 229), Politburo (increased from 10 to 37), Secretariat (increased from 7 to 11), Central Military Committee (increased from 12 to 19), Central Committee departments, Central Auditing Commission,[21] and Control Commission.[22]

Politburo

The Politburo Presidium was reconstituted, having been reduced over the years to just Kim Jong Il. Joining Kim were Kim Yong Nam (president of the SPA Presidium), Choe Yong Rim (premier), VMAR Cho Myong Nok (director of the KPA General Political Bureau), and VMAR Ri Yong Ho (chief of the General Staff). The presence of two military officers on the party's highest decision-making body was a clear indicator of Kim Jong Il's strategy to tie the concept of the Party Center to military-first politics. Yong Ho's appointment was particularly interesting since he was believed by many Pyongyang watchers to be serving as a military escort for the heir apparent, much as O Chin U had done for Kim Jong Il.

The appointments to the Politburo did not constitute a generational shift that many had expected. The average age of the thirty-seven members was seventy-four, with twelve being in their eighties. The youngest member was fifty-three. Most of the appointments were drawn from Kim's inner circle of close aides and family members. Kim Kyong Hui was made a full member, while Jang Song Taek became an alternate member, further backing speculation that they would serve as patrons to their nephew. Several of Jang Song Taek's protégés were also made members and alternate members, such as the minister of People's Security Chu Sang Song, the director of the SSD U Tong Chuk, and Choe Ryong Hae, the new KWP secretary for military affairs. Pak Chong Sun, first vice director of the KWP Organization Guidance Department and reportedly one of the facilitators of the Kim Jong Un succession, was also made an alternate member.

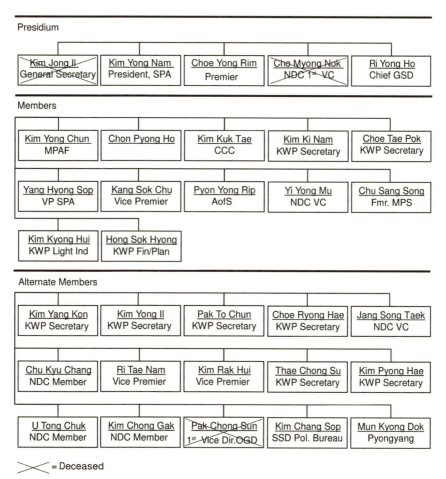

Figure 2.1.   Politburo

Most of the Politburo membership was composed of party secretaries, senior Cabinet officials, and members of the military and security establishment. Ten members of the National Defense Commission were appointed to the Politburo,[23] as were three vice premiers. Key figures tied to the economy (Hong Sok Hyong and Thae Chong Su) and foreign affairs (Kang Sok Chu, Kim Yong Il, and Kim Yang Kon) were also brought into this senior party body in order to inform future deliberations.

Secretariat

The traditional center of Kim Jong Il's power and influence, the Secretariat, had over the years dwindled to seven members, having suffered the deaths of five secretaries since the Twenty-First Plenum of the Sixth Party Congress in 1993. Four holdovers from the previous Secretariat (Kim Jong Il, Kim Ki Nam, Choe Tae Pok, and Hong Sok Hyong) were joined by seven new appointees—four from the provinces and three professional bureaucrats who had for years served in the Central Committee apparatus.

Within this reinvigorated Secretariat, Kim Ki Nam retained the portfolio for propaganda, and Choe Tae Pok continued to oversee international affairs. Kim Yong Il, the director of the KWP International Department, was promoted to support Choe Tae Pok, focusing primarily on China. Kim Yong Gon, the director of the KWP United Front Department, would handle affairs toward the South. The newly minted four-star general Choe Ryong Hae assumed responsibility for military affairs, while Pak To Chun replaced Chon Pyong Ho as secretary for the defense industrial complex. Hong Sok Hyong, Pak Nam Ki's successor as head of finance, and Thae Chong Su split the portfolio for the economy.[24] Finally, Mun Kyong Dok, the youngest member of the Secretariat and a close associate of both Jang Song Taek and Choe Yong Rim, would oversee the day-to-day operations of the capital city.

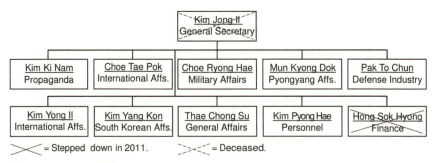

= Stepped down in 2011.   = Deceased.

Figure 2.2.   Secretariat

Central Military Committee

The last public listing of the KWP Central Military Committee was at the Twenty-First Plenum of the Sixth Party Congress in 1993.[25] Of the seventeen members, only six remained at the time of the Third Party Conference. Such first-generation revolutionaries as O Chin U and Choe Kwang had passed away; others had been quietly retired or removed from direct implementation of the party's military policies.

The Third Party Conference dramatically overhauled the Central Military Committee, boosting its membership to nineteen members. The most significant appointments were those of Kim Jong Un and Ri Yong Ho as vice chairmen. Other than membership in the Central Committee, this was the heir apparent's only official title, lending credence to the speculation that the succession was being firmly nested within the party apparatus, but tied to military-first politics.

The other appointments to the Central Military Committee seemed designed to both formalize the regime's control networks within the armed forces, as well as to give Kim Jong Un access to a variety of patronage systems that could assist him in consolidating his power. In terms of operational lines of control, the new membership included the minister of People's Armed Forces (VMAR Kim Yong Chun), chief of the General Staff's Operations Bureau (Gen. Kim Myong Guk), the commanders of the air force and navy (Gen. Yi Pyong Chol and ADM Chong Myong Do), the heads of important special forces units (Lt. Gen. Kim Yong Chol and Col. Gen. Choe Kyong Song), and key members of the General Staff (Gen. Choe Pu Il and Col. Gen. Choe Sang Ryo). Other members held military and security portfolios within the party apparatus, including Gen. Choe Ryong Hae (KWP secretary for military affairs), Chu Kyu Chang (director of the KWP Munitions Industry Department), Jang Song Taek (director of the KWP Administrative Department), and Gen. Kim Kyong Ok (first vice director of the KWP Organization Guidance Department). The four remaining members (Gen. Kim Chong Gak, Gen. Kim Won Hong, Gen. Yun Chong Rin, and Gen. U Tong Chuk) held important security-related portfolios.

Central Committee Apparatus

Over the span of the Kim Jong Il period, the central party apparatus had undergone a variety of changes that were tied to the KWP's overall fortunes. But this evolution was not even across the departments. Those departments for internal party and organizational affairs remained largely untouched and their preeminent status unchanged. These included the departments

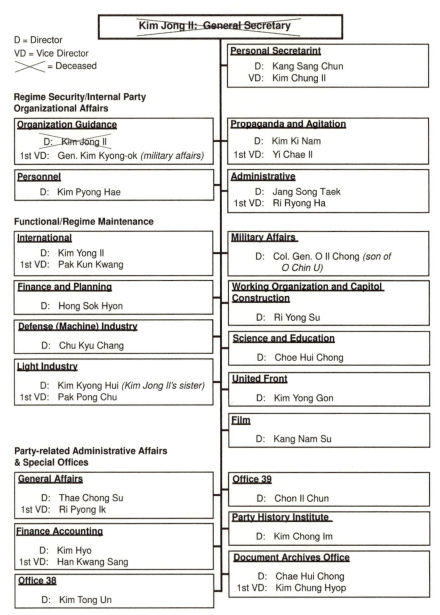

Figure 2.3. Central Committee Apparatus

for Organization and Guidance, Propaganda and Agitation, and Cadre Affairs. Another set of departments that were consistent in their leadership and influence were critical to the running of the regime, both in terms of coordination and surveillance. These included the departments for Military Affairs, Defense Industry (aka Machine Industry), International Affairs, Science and Education, and Light Industry. A final set of consistently present departments included those in charge of party administrative affairs, such as the departments for General Affairs, Finance and Accounting, Party History, and Document Archives.

Another set of departments over the years were reorganized, stood up, and constantly reworked. These include departments related to internal security affairs, South Korean affairs, and economic affairs. As noted earlier, the Administrative Department, which oversees the internal security apparatus, was reestablished in 2006 after having been a part of the Organization Guidance Department since the early 1990s. The United Front Department, while a long-standing and critical department within the central party apparatus, saw its influence rise and fall dramatically over the Kim Jong Il period, being subjected to a major purge in 2006–2007. The Economic Planning and Agricultural Policy departments were abolished around 2002/2003 in a move to give the Cabinet more autonomy and responsibility to handle the economy.

Since 2009, the KWP Central Committee has reorganized its structure by creating a department and removing four others. The Film Department and the Light Industry Industrial Policy Control Department were culled out of other Central Committee departments. Office 38 was folded into Office 39 and then reestablished as a separate entity. The External Liaison Department was relocated under the Cabinet and Office 35, and the Operations Department moved from the Central Committee to the KPA Reconnaissance General Bureau.[26]

The Third Party Conference reflected these changes, as the number of known Central Committee departments declined from approximately twenty-three to twenty. The Civil Defense Department, which had once been led by Jang Song U, was gone. The Financial Planning Department, which had fallen into disgrace when Pak Nam Ki was removed (and allegedly executed), was now under Hong Sak Hyong, a longtime close associate of Kim Jong Il. Kim Ki Nam had returned to his previous post as director of the Propaganda and Agitation Department, filling the post left vacant by the mysterious disappearance of Choe Ik Kyu. Finally, it was apparent that many long-serving cadres had been retired or moved out of the Central Committee apparatus, including Chon Pyong Ho (Defense Industry), Kim Kuk Tae (Cadres), and Ri Ha Il (Military Affairs). Chon and Ri had finally retired, while Kim moved one step closer to retirement with his transfer to head the party's Central Control Committee.[27]

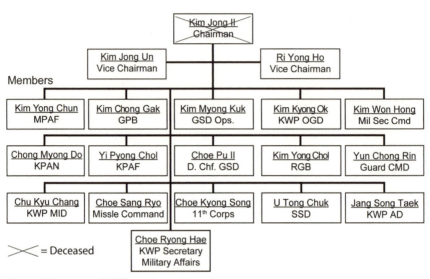

Figure 2.4. Central Military Committee

IMPLICATIONS OF THE THIRD PARTY CONFERENCE

The Third Party Conference was a watershed in modern-day North Korean politics. It formalized a shift in leadership dynamics that had been taking place in the shadows for nearly two years. Elite politics were no longer centered on just one person. Another formal center of power, while in its infancy, was born. In more practical terms, the conference was noteworthy for a variety of reasons.

First, it established the formal ranking of power as the regime moved into the second phase of the succession. North Korean reporting over the course of several events following the conference suggested that Kim Jong Un was ranked fifth within the leadership.[28] In the months that followed, he moved up in the ranks to third in the formal power structure behind Kim Jong Il and Kim Yong Nam.

Second, it reoriented the leadership structure in preparation for the upcoming succession by distributing power from Kim Jong Il's one-man control structure to a collective guidance system based on core groups and loyalists with alternate ties to the Kim family. Instead of the hub-and-spoke architecture of the Kim Jong Il era, where he was the sole lynchpin, key lines of control now run through several members of the Kim family, including Kim Kyong Hui, Jang Song Taek, and even the heir apparent, Kim Jong Un, was reportedly part of the reporting chain for documents seeking his father's signature. How this web of relationships evolves over the coming months and years will largely determine who eventually comes out on top as the real source of power in Pyongyang.

Third, it transferred the focus of military-first (*songun*) politics from the National Defense Commission to the party. Ten members of the NDC were members of the Politburo, and four occupied positions on the party's Central Military Committee. By making Kim Jong Un a vice chairman of the CMC and pulling from the NDC those members with close ties to the heir apparent and giving them additional posts within the party, the Third Party Congress signaled the return of the party as the seat of military decision making.

In the months following the conference, the succession continued apace. Politburo members Cho Myong Nok and Pak Chong Sun died, leaving Pyongyang watchers to wrestle with the implications. On November 23, the campaign to build the legitimacy around Kim Jong Un seemingly began in earnest with the shelling of Yeonpyeong Island, a South Korean island situated along the disputed Northern Limit Line. This provocation increased the tensions on the peninsula and, according to some sources, brought accolades to the heir apparent, who less than an month later was being referred to by *Rodong Sinmun* as "respected general" (*chongyo'nghanu'n taejang*) instead of "young general" (*ch'o'ngnyo'n taejang*).

This apparent nod to military-first politics aside, the party's resurrection proved not to be a fleeting phenomenon. In June 2011, the regime announced the first Politburo meeting since 1993 to discuss Kim Jong Il's trip to China. This appeared to be an indication that the regime viewed the elevation of the party not only as vital to legitimizing the succession, but as part of a fundamental shift in leadership dynamics in North Korea.

THE PARTY UNDER KIM JONG UN

As expected, when Kim Jong Il died, the party apparatus was thrust into the limelight as the new regime configuration began to take shape. The funeral committee announced in the North Korean media harkened back to the period of Kim Il Sung. No longer did NDC members top the list. Instead, the supreme leader's name (Kim Jong Un) was followed by the three members of the Politburo Presidium (Kim Yong Nam, Choe Yong Rim, Ri Yong Ho) and the Politburo membership. Only then did vice chairman of the NDC, O Kuk Yol, who was a Central Committee member but not a member of a party decision-making body, appear.

While the party's resurrection appeared certain, its relationship to the supreme leader remained unclear. The transition of power moved smoothly as the young Kim Jong Un received the title "supreme leader" (*ch'eogo ryo'ngdoja*) and was made (by Politburo proclamation) "supreme commander" (*choson inmin'gun ch'oego*) of the armed forces.[29] While the use of the Politburo, versus a full Central Committee meeting, to announce Kim Jong Un's formal role as head of the armed forces did not detract from his authority, it did highlight the new leader's need to rely on key advisors and established institutional authorities to conduct the regime's business.[30]

That said, with his father's death, Kim Jong Un began receiving reports from all fields, including the national, provincial, and local party organizations.[31] He appeared to control all of the departments of the KWP Central Committee, including the powerful Organization Guidance Department (OGD), which is responsible for reporting on all organizations and cracking down against any factional behavior in the party.[32]

FOURTH PARTY CONFERENCE

At the Fourth Party Conference and Fifth Session of the Twelfth SPA, both held in April 2012, Kim Jong Un received the remaining titles of power. He was named to the newly created posts of first secretary of the Korean Workers' Party and first chairman of the National Defense Commission, leaving his father to assume the eternal posts of general secretary and chairman of the NDC. As was widely expected by the Pyongyang watching community, Kim Jong Un also assumed a seat on the Presidium of the Politburo and became chairman of the Central Military Committee, giving him formal control over the party and military apparatuses.

In addition to bolstering Kim Jong Un's leadership credentials, the Fourth Party Conference continued the reorganization of the individuals around him, presumably in accordance with plans laid down by Kim Jong Il before his death.[33] Personnel moves at the Party Conference highlighted two trends. First, it continued the promotion of individuals close to the Kim family to the highest and most sensitive positions within the regime. Second, it underscored the new leadership's commitment to revitalizing the party as an important instrument of governance during this period of transition. Although characterized as filling vacancies, the regime appeared to replace nearly one-third of the Politburo, many through unannounced retirements or dismissals.[34] The leadership also continued the trend of blurring the distinction between military and security personnel on the one hand and civilian party leaders on the other. By allowing party leaders to assume military ranks, the regime has increased the percentage of officers (military and internal security) in the Politburo to its highest level since the late 1970s.[35]

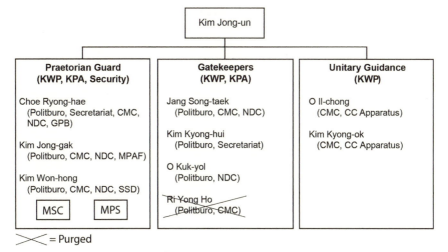

Figure 2.5. Kim Jong Un's Collective Support System

There were a number of officials who apparently gained in status and presumably influence as a result of the April leadership events. Choe Ryong Hae continued his rise. On the eve of the Fourth Party Conference, he was promoted to vice marshal. It was later revealed that he had succeeded Cho Myong Nok as the new director of the General Political Bureau (GPB). His appointments to the Politburo Presidium (elevated from alternate Politburo status) and Central Military Committee (vice chairman) catapulted him past Ri Yong Ho in the formal leadership rankings.[36] As much as any other member of the leadership, Choe is directly associated with Kim Jong Un's strategy to consolidate power. He effectively has become the regime's top military authority after Kim Jong Un.

In addition to Choe, other GPB alumni received promotions. VMAR Kim Jong Gak was made the new minister of People's Armed Forces (MPAF), replacing Kim Yong Chun. Until recently a first vice director of the GPB, Kim is one of the rising stars in the upcoming generation of KPA leaders, as well as a key asset to Kim Jong Un's rise to power. He is also supposedly linked to Jang Song Taek; notably, both of them were removed from the limelight in 2003–2005 and were promoted to high positions in 2007. At the Fourth Party Conference, Kim became a full member of the Politburo.

Gen. Kim Won Hong sprung on the political scene in Pyongyang with the death of Kim Jong Il. At the leadership events in April, he was made director of the State Security Department (aka the Ministry of State Security, the Secret Police), a member of the KWP Politburo and Central Military Committee, and a member of the NDC. As head of the SSD, Kim Won Hong has broad situational awareness in the regime. The State Security Department is

Table 2.1. Additions to and Presumed Removals from KWP Leadership Bodies

	Additions	Presumed Dismissals/ Removals
Politburo		
Presidium	Kim Jong Un (First Secretary)	Kim Jong Il (death)
	Choe Ryong Hae	Cho Myong Nok (death)
Full Members	Jang Song Taek	Jon Pyong Ho (dismissed)
	Kim Jong Gak	
	Pak To Chun	
	Hyon Chol Hae	
	Kim Won Hong	
	Yi Myong-su	
Alternate Members	O Kuk Yol	U Tong Chuk (dismissed)
	Yi Pyong Sam	
	Cho Yon Chun	
Secretariat		
	Kim Jong Un (First Secretary)	
	Kim Kyong Hui	
	Kwak Pom Gi	
Central Military Committee	Kim Jong Un (Chairman)	
	Choe Ryong Hae (Vice Chairman)	
	Hyon Chol Hae	
	Ri Myong Su	
	Kim Rak Gyom	
Central Committee Departments	Kim Yong Chun (Civil Defense?)	Kim Kyong Hui
	Kwak Pom Gi (Finance?)	(replaced)
	Pak Pong Ju (Light Industry)	

one of the regime's chief security and intelligence agencies. Within the formal chain of command, Kim reports to Jang Song Taek in the latter's capacity as KWP director of the Administrative Department.

MOVING FORWARD

Going forward, questions remain as to the role the party will play in the Kim Jong Un era. At the time of this writing, it appears that the party has taken the lead in laying the foundation for a smooth dynastic transfer of power, something many North Korean leaders believe is critical if the regime is to retain its legitimacy. Only time (and North Korean politics) will tell, however, whether the party's efforts will ensure that Kim Jong Un will one day be able to rule as the unchallenged supreme leader.

NOTES

1. The last published membership figures for the KWP date back to the Fourth Party Congress in 1961. The party's current membership is an extrapolation based on Kim Il Sung's speech to the Sixth Party Congress in 1980. See Robert Worden, ed., *North Korea: A Country Study* (Washington, DC: Federal Research Division, 2008).

2. Seong-chang Cheong, "Stalinism and Kimilsungism: A Comparative Analysis of Ideology and Power," *Asian Perspective* 24, no. 1 (2000).

3. After Kim Il Sung's unitary ruling system was established in the late 1960s, the Political Bureau ceased to be a collective consultation body. It became a rubber stamp where only the voices of Kim's loyal supporters were heard. Nevertheless, it remained a body where "constructive opinions" (i.e., those that fit within the boundaries of Kim's own thinking) often broadened Kim's own thinking. Hyon Song-il, *Pukhan-u'i Kukkajo'llyak-kwa P'awo' Ellit'u'* [North Korea's National Strategy and Power Elite] (Seoul: Sunin Publishing, 2006).

4. 1972 DPRK Constitution, Articles 100–106.

5. The term "Party Center" entered the North Korean vernacular at the time of the Eighth Plenum of the Fifth Central Committee in February 1974. Before then, the phrase was rarely used in North Korean mass media. It later became personified as *Rodong Sinmun* increasingly cited the "Party Center" (*tang chungang*) as the brains behind numerous socialist construction guidelines. See "Anti-Japanese Guerrilla Instigation," *Rodong Sinmun*, February 13, 1974. See also Morgan E. Clippinger, "Kim Jong Il in the North Korean Mass Media: A Study of Semi-Esoteric Communication," *Asian Survey* 21, no. 3 (March 1981).

6. Toward the end of the Kim Il Sung period, policy consultation within formal leadership circles became perfunctory, replaced by a reporting mechanism whereby policy drafts were drawn up by each ministry and department and passed directly to Kim Jong Il's office where they were prioritized and, if deemed worthy, passed to Kim Il Sung. The Political Bureau would be convened only to ratify decisions that had already been made by the Kim duopoly.

7. A number of epithets denoting Kim Jong Il's elite status began to appear in the months after his formal designation as heir apparent. It is important to note, however, that Kim Jong Il has never adopted the title "leader" (*Suryong*), which was reserved for his father. In this chapter, the title *Suryong* is used to denote the system within which the leader operates.

8. Kap-sik Kim, "The Suryong's Direct Rule and the Political Regime in North Korea Under Kim Jong-il," *Asian Perspective* 32, no. 3 (2008).

9. *Wolgan Chosun*, April 1997.

10. Jae Jean-suh, "Possibility for WKP to Take Back Role of Decision-making," *Vantage Point* 33, no. 8 (August 2010).

11. The Central Military Committee's ability to endorse Kim Jong Il as general secretary was apparently made possible by a revision to the KWP rules in 1982 in which the CMC was elevated in status equal to that of the Central Committee. Some Pyongyang watchers, however, dispute the fact that since the Central Military Committee was now referred to as the Party Central Military Committee this meant that it

was no longer subordinate to the KWP Central Committee. Regardless of this issue, Kim's assumption of this portfolio seemed to violate Article 24 of the KWP rules, which states that a plenary meeting of the KWP Central Committee should elect the general secretary.

12. Jinwook Choi, "The Changing Party-State System and Outlook for Reform in North Korea," *International Journal of Korean Unification Studies* 18, no. 1 (2009).

13. The August Incident refers to an aborted attempt to oust Kim Il Sung in the mid-1950s and his subsequent purge of the party of key elements of the Soviet and Yunan factions.

14. "Delegates' Conference to Begin Next Week," *Daily NK*, September 21, 2010.

15. Thirty-three other officers were also promoted, including one to colonel general (Ryu Kyong) and six to lieutenant general (Ro Hung Se, Ri Tu Song, Chon Kyong Hak, Kim Kuk Ryong, Hwang Pyong So, and O Il Chong). Within hours, in a separate order, Ri Yong Ho, the chief of the General Staff, was promoted to vice marshal by virtue of NDC Order No. 7.

16. Korean Central Broadcasting Station, September 30, 2010. One day after the event, KCBS carried approximately 1.5 hours of coverage of the Party Conference.

17. The last revisions to the Party Charter took place at the Sixth Party Congress in 1980.

18. However, the description of the party itself was changed from "Marxist-Leninist Party" to "Kim Il Sung Party."

19. The current status of the CMC remains a point of contention among Pyongyang watchers. Some believe that the CMC was placed back under the Central Committee.

20. Workers' Party of Korea [WPK] Charter [*choso'n rodongdang kyuyak*], September 28, 2010, as published in *North Korea Tech*, January 21, 2011.

21. The Central Auditing Commission's new chairman was Kim Chang Su, who was assisted by vice chairman Pak Myong Sun. The membership included Choe Pae Chin, Kim Chol, Sim Chol Ho, O Ryong Il, Kye Yong Sam, Ryu Hyon Sik, Ko Myong Hui, Pang Yong Uk, Chang Chong Chu, Ho Kwang Uk, Chi Tong Sik, Chong Pong Sok, and Choe Kwon Su.

22. The Control Commission was headed by Kim Kuk Tae, the former KWP secretary for Cadres. He was assisted by first vice chairman Chong Myong Hak and vice chairman Ri Tuk Nam. The membership included Cha Kwan Sok, Pak Tok Man, Cha Sun Kil, and Kim Yong Son.

23. Most noticeably, O Kuk Yol was only appointed to the Central Committee, but not the Politburo, raising speculation that his power had been diminished. According to some Pyongyang watchers, O was kept out of the Politburo because he did not fully support the succession. Other Pyongyang watchers contended that his power remained intact along informal channels based on his longtime relationship with Kim Jong Il.

24. Hong Sok Hyong reportedly stepped down as KWP secretary for Finance in 2011.

25. According to Article 27 of the KWP Constitution, the Central Military Committee oversees implementation of the party's military policies, guides development and production of munitions, and has command and control over North Korea's

armed forces. Reportedly, measures regarding command and control of large military units are decided in CMC meetings. Cheong Seong-chang, "The Status and Role of the Central Military Commission in the Kim Jong-il Era," *Vantage Point* 34, no. 11 (November 2011).

26. Ken E. Gause, "The Evolving KWP Central Committee Apparatus in 2011" (unpublished).

27. This chart is based on information from the Ministry of National Unification and interviews conducted by the author. There could be additional, hidden departments that are not represented in this chart.

28. Notably, Kim Jong Il also debuted in the fifth spot in the power rankings after the Sixth Party Congress in 1980.

29. The fact that the Politburo, a body on which Kim Jong Un did not sit, proclaimed him the supreme commander suggested that the regime might be looking to revive a collective institutional process—something not seen since the Kim Il Sung era—as a support mechanism for the young leader.

30. In another move, the Politburo on January 12 issued a "special report" announcing that the late Kim Jong Il's body will be preserved to lie in state at Kumsusan Memorial Palace. It was in this announcement that Kim Jong Il was declared the "eternal party leader," an appellation that was applied to Kim Il Sung in the 1970s and Kim Jong Il in the 1990s.

31. This assumption is based on an analysis of several dozen documents Kim Jong Un has signed that have been released since late December 2011 by the regime's official Korean Central News Agency (KCNA).

32. At the Fourth Party Conference in April 2012, no head of the OGD was announced, leading to speculation that Kim Jong Un, as his father before him, holds this post. Other speculation is that his aunt, Kim Kyong Hui, has assumed the portfolio for organizational affairs with her recent appointment as a party secretary.

33. Before his death, Kim Jong Il allegedly left a last will and testament outlining his goals for the regime after his demise. The executor of that will is rumored to be his sister, Kim Kyong Hui.

34. For the Fourth Party Conference, only appointments were announced in the North Korean media. Dismissals were not publicized, thus complicating efforts to construct comprehensive lists of senior party bodies.

35. This chart is based on a close reading of the funeral list and ceremonies surrounding Kim Jong Il's death, as well as the April 2012 leadership events. It is most likely subject to change if Kim Jong Un is able to consolidate his power. For more information on the analysis behind the chart, see the author's articles in December (2011) and January (2012) on the *Foreign Affairs* and KEI websites.

36. Choe Ryong Hae was made a member of the NDC at the Fifth Session of the Twelfth SPA. He joins Kim Jong Un, Jang Song Taek, Kim Jong Gak, Hyon Chol Hae, Ri Myong Su, and Ju Kyu Chang as the only officials to sit on the Politburo, CMC, and NDC.

Chapter Three

The Roles and Influence of the Military

Terence Roehrig

The armed forces have always played a vital role for states as their guarantor of national security. In addition, the armed forces are often political actors with power and influence that can range from providing input on national security policy and budgets to authority over a broader range of foreign and domestic policy issues or to a full-blown military dictatorship. Some militaries are also significant players in the state economy. In these instances, the military may own and operate factories that produce munitions, small arms, or larger weapons systems for use at home or for export. The armed forces may also engage in other economic activities, both legal and illegal.

The North Korean military, formally the Korean People's Army (KPA) has always played an important role as the guarantor of state security. As is typical of most communist countries, the function of the military is to preserve and defend the state, the party, the revolution, and the people while being largely subservient to the party and its leadership.[1] This was certainly the case in the early years of the Democratic People's Republic of Korea (DPRK) as Kim Il Sung ruled North Korea with a firm hand but did so through the party while imposing a number of measures that ensured the party monitored and guided the military, as it did the rest of North Korean society, to the proper ideological orientation.

As North Korea began its leadership transition from Kim Il Sung to Kim Jong Il, the role of the party began to decline while the status and power of the KPA commenced a slow and steady rise. When the elder Kim died in 1994, Kim Jong Il further increased the stature of the military in an effort to secure the loyalty of the KPA, cement his own grip on an institution that was vital to his hold on power, and supplant what was seen as an increasingly ineffective party.

After Kim Jong Il's health began to deteriorate in fall 2008, North Korea began an accelerated succession process to Kim Jong Il's son, Kim Jong

Un, that appeared to include a resuscitation of the Korean Workers' Party (KWP).[2] The power transition that has followed Kim Jong Il's passing points to a collective leadership of the party and the military where both appear to be working together to ensure a smooth transition. Though Kim Jong Il was firmly in power over the party and military during his rule, Kim Jong Un's precise role as a decision maker within the collective leadership is unclear, and it is likely he does not yet wield the power of his father. Finally, the KPA is also a major economic player in the DPRK system, owning and operating several firms in the industrial, mining, and defense sectors, providing labor for the DPRK economy, and participating in some of the government's illicit activities such as drug trafficking and counterfeit cigarettes.

As North Korea navigates a difficult future of security concerns, economic challenges, and another leadership transition, the role of the KPA in these areas raises some important questions. What role is the KPA likely to play in the future, and how might this impact the current leadership transition? How might an increasing KPA role affect the DPRK's foreign and defense policy? Using the literature on civil-military relations, this chapter examines the role played by the KPA and the impact it has had on North Korean security, politics, and economics. This chapter argues that Kim Jong Il was very adept at elevating the power and stature of the military for his own political purposes while maintaining a fairly tight rein on military power so that the KPA remained largely subservient to his wishes. So long as Kim Jong Il was alive and healthy, these arrangements were likely to hold—the military and its leaders retained their status and privilege in return for loyalty to the Kim regime. With Kim's death and the party's revival, the military and party elites are likely to be the power brokers together for the time being until Kim Jong Un's transition is solidified.

However, Kim Jong Il opened the door and drew the KPA further into politics, and once in, it is not always easy to coax militaries back out of the halls of power. This is particularly so if the military sees chaos and instability looming that may damage its interests, either those of its leadership or the institution as a whole. Though it is unclear what the future holds, the KPA is likely to retain a major role in DPRK security, politics, and economics and may in fact assume a larger role should the ongoing power transition to Kim Jong Un go badly.

CIVIL-MILITARY RELATIONS: THEORY AND THE KPA

An examination of the KPA's role in government and politics is part of a long literature on civil-military relations. National militaries play a fundamental role in maintaining state security. Leaders seek to maintain a military that can deter attack and win the nation's wars. Thus, leaders devote significant amounts of state resources to building military power, even at the expense of other important priorities. At the same time, these militaries have sufficient strength to turn inward and oppress the people they are intended to protect. As one scholar notes,

> since the birth of nation-states, civilians have grappled with the problem of how to subordinate armies to their will. Whether they presided over colonies, newly independent states, or more modern twentieth-century totalitarian, authoritarian, or democratic regimes, political leaders have always had to balance the twin goals of harnessing enough military force to defeat their enemies and ensure that that force not be turned against themselves.[3]

Another author notes, "The military is a tiger with the means to eliminate its master whenever it decides."[4]

A portion of the civil-military relations literature has focused on the best ways to keep the military in its proper position and out of politics.[5] During Kim Il Sung's years in power, he successfully contained KPA influence, ruling through the Korean Worker's Party, and the KPA was largely subservient to his will and that of the party. In 1980 with the formal announcement of Kim Jong Il's transition to succeed his father, speculation was rife that he would not have the credentials and experience for acceptance by party and military leaders. Over the next two decades, Kim Jong Il elevated the stature and power of the military to a major stakeholder in DPRK politics, blurring the boundaries in DPRK civil-military relations.

While Kim Jong Il did much to increase the status of the KPA, it is not entirely clear whether these efforts elevated the KPA to a dominant position in the government or whether most of Kim Jong Il's praises were largely rhetorical and attempts to co-opt the KPA into supporting his regime. It is likely that the KPA was one of a number of competing institutions and that Kim Jong Il remained in charge of them all, though he had to consider their wishes. Moreover, in the transition to Kim Jong Un, it appears that the status of the party is being raised to solidify his rise to power. Finally, has the power of the KPA as an institution become more powerful, or have individual leaders been co-opted to ensure their loyalty and tie them more closely to the fate of the Kim family regime? Given these circumstances, the central issue is the amount of power and influence the KPA wields in North Korean government and politics.

Measuring the type and degree of military influence is a difficult task. Scholars have used several variables to guide these assessments.[6] At the most extreme end is the likelihood or prevalence of coups where the military steps into power to remove an unacceptable civilian regime before either returning to the barracks or choosing to remain in power for an extended period of time. Though North Korea has not experienced a coup, Kim Il Sung and Kim Jong Il feared the possibility and on a few occasions moved to crush suspected centers of opposition. However, the absence of a coup may not necessarily be a good indicator of the degree of military influence in politics and government. A coup may actually signal weakness as the military has no other route to achieve its objectives. Conversely, no coup may be a sign that the military is a very strong player in the system as civilian leaders quickly comply with military wishes so as not to invoke its wrath and tempt the possibility of a coup.[7]

Another important theoretical question is what motivates military leaders to undertake a coup or, more broadly, elect to exert greater political influence. In the past, several reasons have motivated military coups. As expressed in their national security roles, militaries view themselves as the guardians of the country. A breakdown in internal order and stability that civilian authorities are reluctant or unable to control can prompt military leaders to intervene. Military leaders may also intervene if they believe civilian leadership is incompetent or the political process is gridlocked, preventing the system from acting on important economic, security, or political issues. Believing that the state is threatened, military leaders may simply oust what they see as bad leadership, install a new regime, and return to the barracks, or they may choose to remain in power, believing they can do a better job. Moreover, if order is lacking, imposing stability is a task at which most militaries excel. In the end, many military leaders have discovered that solving their country's economic problems was difficult. It is also important to note that the impetus for intervention may come from midcareer officers who carry out a "colonel's coup" because general officers may be viewed as corrupt, linked to the failing civilian leadership, and equally in need of removal. In the end, intervention is always easier if the walls between civil and military leadership are already relatively porous.[8]

Focusing solely on the prevalence of coups provides a surface-level and possibly inaccurate analysis of the degree of military influence in government and politics. Other variables consider a broader view of military influence and are best conceived as a continuum of military control and influence. For example, the military may actually be in control of the political system, as was the case in much of Latin America throughout the 1960s and 1970s along with South Korea and Taiwan. One framework sought to categorize these regimes as moderators, guardians, and rulers.[9] Another study identified military influence in terms of prerogatives or "reserved domains," where civilian authorities grant military leaders autonomy in certain policy areas with the power to veto civilian decisions in return for staying out of politics.[10]

Other measures of military influence assess whether the military is willing to and has publicly opposed civilian/regime policy decisions. If there is a policy dispute between civilians and the military, does one group tend to win these fights more often? Thus, Michael Desch maintains that "the best indicator of the state of civilian control is who prevails when civilian and military preferences diverge."[11] With Kim Jong Il gone, many will watch closely to see if there are indicators pointing to who is prevailing in policy disputes.

While these dimensions provide better granularity for assessing the state of civil-military relations than simply whether or not there have been coups, measuring these types of influence is difficult as well. For example, there may be little disagreement between civilian and military leaders, with relatively straightforward compliance by the armed forces with civilian government dictates suggesting little military influence. However, the lack of outward friction and discord may be a sign of secure civilian control, or it may mask strong military influence since civilian leaders are unwilling or unable to challenge military preferences for fear of the consequences.[12] Moreover, vigorous debate and disagreement between civilian and military sectors can be positive in arriving at good policy decisions.[13]

THREE ROLES OF THE KOREAN PEOPLE'S ARMY

Guarantor of National Security

The chief role of any country's military is that of protector of national security. Since its founding, the KPA has been the defender of the fatherland, the revolution, the people, and the party; its role in national security remains paramount. One of the important issues affecting civil-military relations is the presence of a serious external threat. Outside dangers tend to keep the military occupied and less likely to turn inward to address possible internal threats or to be overly intrusive in politics and government. North Korea faces serious external security challenges and no longer has the same security guarantees it had during the Cold War from its allies. As a result, national security is likely to remain a vital concern, and the KPA will continue to receive a significant share of state resources.

North Korea has one of the largest military forces in the world, ranking fourth in number of personnel behind the United States, China, and India. The military has 1.19 million active-duty personnel with another 600,000 in the reserves and 5.7 million in paramilitary units.[14] With a total population of only 24.5 million, this makes North Korea one of the most militarized societies in the world. Most North Korean men, along with some women, serve in the armed forces, so that a large share of the North Korean population has been in the military, giving them all the common experience of serving the state and the Kim family regime. More importantly, military service provides the government the opportunity to further indoctrinate a large segment of the population in the state's ideology.

The KPA is a unified force made up of ground, naval (Korean People's Navy—KPN), and air components (Korean People's Air Force—KPAF). The ground force component of the KPA is by far the largest, with 1.02 million soldiers on active duty. The KPA maintains a large tank force of 4,060, composed of 3,500 main battle tanks and 560 light tanks.[15] These numbers are offset by the increasing age of the force, outdated technology, and shortages of fuel and spare parts.

The KPA has devoted a significant amount of resources to building up its artillery and multiple rocket launcher systems. Estimates indicate that North Korea has approximately 8,500 self-propelled and towed artillery pieces, along with 5,100 multiple rocket launcher systems.[16] A good number of these are deployed close to the North-South border and are well-protected in hardened, underground facilities or burrowed in nearby hillsides. Given Seoul's proximity to the Demilitarized Zone (DMZ), these artillery and rocket assets give North Korea the ability to inflict punishment on South Korea without sending troops across the border.[17]

Another strength of the KPA is its 200,000 special operations forces. These troops are well trained and disciplined with primary missions of "reconnaissance, establishing a 'Second Front' within the ROK strategic rear, decapitation and disruption of the ROK/US command, control, communication and intelligence structure, neutralisation of ROK and US airbases, and neutralisation of ROK and US missiles and weapons of mass destruction."[18]

The KPAF has a relatively large number of combat aircraft, but of these 620 airplanes, only 69 are the more advanced Soviet model MiG-29s and Su-25s. Most of the air force consists of older Soviet and Chinese models that would struggle against the more modern ROK and U.S. F-15s and F-16s. Along with the rest of the military, the KPAF lacks fuel and spare parts to maintain the fleet, and readiness is questionable given that DPRK pilots train approximately twenty hours or less annually in the air.[19]

Similarly, the KPN has many ships, but only three are frigates, with none in the destroyer class or larger. Most of its navy consists of 383 patrol and coastal combat ships, along with twenty-four mine warfare vessels. The KPN is a brown-water force devoted to coastal defense and lacks advanced targeting and weapons systems. According to the ROK Defense Ministry, the KPN is unlikely to act independently and would operate "in tandem with the ground forces by supporting the deployment of ground forces and by defending coastal areas." Moreover, the North Korean surface fleet has "poor mobility under bad weather conditions and limited operational capabilities at sea."[20]

The KPN does have one major component of the fleet that poses a serious challenge: submarines. The navy has approximately seventy submarines, including twenty-two Romeo-class attack boats and twenty-eight Sang-O class submarines configured for delivering special operations forces, laying mines, and attacking surface ships.[21] North Korea also has over twenty midget submarines, one of which was likely the boat that fired a torpedo on the ROKS *Cheonan*.

Finally, North Korea has devoted considerable effort and resources to its chemical and nuclear weapons programs along with a robust ballistic missile capability. North Korea is believed to have between 2,500 and 5,000 tons of chemical weapons munitions of various types including mustard gas, phosgene, sarin, and V-agents (VM and VX).[22] Chemical weapons are manufactured indigenously and can be delivered with artillery, ballistic missiles, and rockets. Suspicion remains that North Korea may have a biological weapons program, but the extent of these efforts is unclear. The program may be devoted largely to defensive purposes and may be very small scale.[23]

In October 2006, North Korea tested its first nuclear weapon, joining the small club of nuclear weapon states. North Korea conducted a second test on May 25, 2009, and is believed to have between six and ten nuclear devices. Despite DPRK claims, it is not clear that Pyongyang has mastered the difficult technology of miniaturizing a weapon to fit on a ballistic missile. North Korea might also seek to weaponize its nuclear arsenal by developing tactical nuclear artillery shells, but development of these weapons would face the same technology hurdles.[24]

For over four decades, North Korea has worked to build a formidable ballistic missile force. The KPA has approximately six hundred short-range Scud missiles with the range to cover all of South Korea and two hundred Nodong intermediate-range missiles that can reach Japan, along with U.S. bases there. North Korea continues work on the long-range Taepodong missile, which could reach parts of the United States, but has yet to conduct a successful test launch.

The KPA remains a formidable military force with serious conventional capability. However, the quality of some of this capability has been eroding due to aging equipment and technology, along with a lack of spare parts and fuel. Reports also indicate that morale in the KPA is suffering, in part because some soldiers are receiving insufficient rations and are forced to fend for their own food.[25]

A deteriorating conventional capability may be an important motive for the KPA to pursue other, more asymmetric capabilities such as special forces, ballistic missiles, and chemical and nuclear weapons. However, the military balance is not in North Korea's favor, and any large-scale offensive actions are unlikely. Yet, possibly emboldened by the deterrent value of its rudimentary nuclear weapons, North Korea may continue to consider actions such as the *Cheonan* sinking and the shelling of Yeonpyeongdo as a way to utilize its military power without escalating a conflict with Seoul and Washington. South Korea's statements that it will not tolerate further provocations and will "act first, report later" make this a dangerous strategy.

KPA as a Political Actor

Three institutions dominate North Korean politics: the military, the party, and the state. Though all have played and continue to play important roles, their relative position to each other and their power have changed over time. During the early years of Kim Il Sung's rule, the KWP was the central institution, applying the regime's ideology to policy while the KPA held "an honored but subordinate position in North Korean society."[26] Kim Il Sung used the party to control all elements of daily life and, according to one scholar, "fused public and private spheres toward a utopian moral order."[27] To ensure control of the military and party, Kim Il Sung wove a structure that integrated the party and the military by establishing party committees at all command levels of the KPA, placing the military under party guidance, and creating "both vertical and horizontal checks, as well as opportunities for the party to report on and to guide the military."[28]

In the 1960s, Kim Il Sung established the Military Committee in the KWP Central Committee, a group that later became the lead party organization to supervise the KPA. He also introduced political commissars who were respected, high-level party officials placed at multiple levels throughout the military to share power with the respective commanders. Sung Chul Kim notes, "It took the party a long time to successfully incorporate the KPA. The party and the military started as two different institutions in 1945, and the interconnectedness between them ended with the embodiment of each in the other, a situation that, by 1969, left the party in a position of dominance over the military."[29]

Yet the integration cut both ways, creating a system of checks and oversight on both the party and the military so that, McEachern notes, "under Kim Il-sung, the senior levels of the party and military were highly fused. Many senior party members were four-star generals, and the military valued political correctness at least as much as military effectiveness."[30] Finally, Kim Il Sung used purges and promotions to eliminate opposition within the military and to elevate those loyal to the regime.

In 1980, Kim Jong Il was formally presented to the country as the successor to his father and began his slow rise to power, receiving increasingly higher-level positions of responsibility and authority. By the next decade, it was clear that the system was facing some serious difficulties, and significant changes began to occur in DPRK civil-military relations. The KWP was becoming less effective and failing in its ability to advance the regime's economic and ideological goals, a problem that became particularly apparent during the famine of the 1990s. The result was a sharp decline in party morale and the inability to function as the transmitter of policy for the leadership.[31] Moreover, both the party and the military were wrought with factional divides, often forming along generational lines.[32] As McEachern notes, "By the time Kim Jong-il came to power, the party was a fish out of water. Aging officials from a previous era continued to trumpet the importance of applying revolutionary principles to specific policies, but the calls rang increasingly hollow."[33]

Kim Il Sung died on July 8, 1994, and for the next few years, the DPRK faced a savage famine that killed between 600,000 and 1 million, throwing the North Korean political and economic system into crisis.[34] The state and the party struggled to deal with the disaster and corruption along with other antisocietal failings, including crime, black market activities, and smuggling, and illegal migration grew at an alarming rate.[35] Moreover, as food aid came into the country, the KPA was the only institution with the trucks and fuel to distribute the relief, raising the stature of the military even further in the eyes of the people. Military personnel were utilized in construction projects and agriculture, demonstrating to the populace an image that the KPA was effective and working for their interests. Finally, when his father died, Kim Jong Il stood alone as the leader of the DPRK, without his father's credentials as a revolutionary, anti-Japanese guerrilla fighter, or service in the armed forces. Kim Jong Il needed to ensure that the armed forces would support his succession.

Beginning in the 1980s, Kim Jong Il and his father started to separate the military from the KWP and make it more autonomous while elevating the KPA to the same level of power and influence as the party. At the same time, Kim Jong Il needed to bring the KPA firmly under his control. Kim had no formal standing in the military, and his father held the top positions in the state and the party. Consequently, Kim Jong Il received important positions overseeing the armed forces. In 1980, he was appointed first vice chairman of the party's Central Military Commission and a decade later first vice chairman of the National Defense Commission. These positions were followed by elevation to supreme commander of the Armed Forces with a promotion to the rank of vice marshal in 1991 and the following year to the rank of marshal. In

1993, Kim Jong Il received his most important appointment, chairman of the National Defense Commission (NDC).

In 1998, the Supreme People's Assembly amended the constitution to make Kim Il Sung the "eternal president" and designate the NDC as the highest authority over the armed forces and all defense issues. Kim Jong Il was reelected chair of the NDC, which elevated this position to the highest in the government.[36] The most popular government slogan prior to 1998 was "When the party decides, we do it," but this was replaced with "Let us defend to the death the revolutionary command headed by great leader comrade Kim Jong Il."[37] In 2009, the constitution was amended again, and Article 100 made it official that "the chairman of the DPRK National Defense Commission is the Supreme Leader of the DPRK."

After his father's death, Kim Jong Il moved to elevate the position of the military through the promulgation of the "military-first" policy or *songun*.[38] The North Korean media formally acknowledged the start of *songun* on January 1, 1995, when Kim Jong Il visited the 214th Army Unit and praised the exploits of the KPA. During the next five years, Kim visited over 550 military units, commending the KPA for the important role it played.[39] Later statements followed that praised the importance of the military and its central role of protecting the party, the people, and the revolution. For example, in 1999 the *Rodong Sinmun* and *Kulloja* published a joint editorial entitled "WPK's Policy of Giving Priority to [the] Army Is Invincible":

> The mode of give-priority-to-the-army policy is a mode of leadership which solves all problems arising in the revolution and construction on the principle of giving top precedence to the military affairs and pushes ahead with the socialist cause as a whole, putting forward the army as the pillar of the revolution.[40]

These themes are stressed regularly in government pronouncements to proclaim the central position of the military. Military leaders increasingly replaced party members in Kim Jong Il's retinue when conducting "on-the-spot" guidance tours, and more of these activities entailed visits to military institutions.[41] Moreover, more members of the officer corps held important positions in government and party institutions. Finally, the 2009 constitutional revisions elevated *songun* to join *juche* as the central elements of state ideology and included soldiers with workers, farmers, and working intellectuals as the holders of sovereign power.

Though *songun* and other actions elevated the KPA to the status of equal to or slightly above the position of the party and the state, Kim Jong Il also made a concerted effort to control the military. He promoted hundreds of officers to ensure a loyal officer corps while purging others he viewed as a threat to his rule.[42] Moreover, the North Korean regime maintains an extensive and overlapping system of security services within the military, the party, and government that keep close tabs on each other's activities. These security agencies maintain careful surveillance of other groups, and Kim Jong Il had them report directly to him.[43] Concerning the military, Kim Jong Il established three channels of information and received daily reports from the General Staff, the General Political Bureau, and the Political Security Department, with others monitoring the affairs of these three organs and all reporting to Kim.[44] Thus, Daniel Pinkston notes that "the redundancy in the North Korean system ensures control by the elite," and "state security agencies have created almost insurmountable collective-action costs for dissidents hoping to replace the regime." Consequently, "the result is a stable system that has survived well beyond numerous predictions of collapse."[45] This system will likely continue under Kim Jong Un and be even more important for senior DPRK leaders as the transition proceeds, to ensure that all remain committed to a smooth transfer of power in the wake of Kim Jong Il's death.

Military and the Leadership Structure

The organizational diagram of the North Korean political system is complicated but for several decades was simplified by the centrality of Kim Jong Il's power over the government. Ken Gause argues it was a "complicated mosaic of shifting and interlocking, but relatively, simple institutions resting upon the entrenched foundation of one-man dictatorship."[46] With Kim Jong Il's passing, KPA leaders will participate as part of the collective leadership while Kim Jong Un remains the nominal "supreme leader." Within this complex system, the role of the military is embedded with that of the KWP and the state to form a web of competing and overlapping authority.

Within the KWP, the most important decision-making body concerning military affairs is the Central Military Commission (CMC). The CMC is responsible to the party's top body, the Central Committee, and ensures the political control of the KPA and execution of the military policies of the KWP by working through the military's General Political Bureau.[47] According to the KWP Charter (Section 27), "The Military Committee of the Party Central Committee discusses and decides on the party's military policy and methods of its execution; organizes work to strengthen military industries, the people's militia, and all armed forces; and directs the military establishment of the country."[48] In their ascent to power, Kim Jong Il and his son, Kim Jong Un, were given important positions on this committee.

The Supreme People's Assembly first established the CMC in June 1950, but it was disbanded after the Korean War. The organization was resuscitated in 1962 and during most of Kim Il Sung's rule was the chief organization responsible for command and control of the KPA.[49] Though the CMC remains the party's chief institution overseeing the military, overall power shifted to the National Defense Commission in the early 1990s as part of a series of measures to ensure the transition of power from Kim Il Sung to Kim Jong Il.

The National Defense Commission was created in 1972 and was one of six committees that reported to the Central Committee. In May 1990, North Korean officials designated the NDC as an independent commission and elevated the organization to the same level as the Central Committee.[50] Later in the year, authority over the Ministry of People's Armed Forces (MPAF) was transferred to the oversight of the NDC, and Kim Jong Il was appointed the first vice chairman of the NDC followed by his designation as the supreme commander of the KPA.

Kim Jong Il became chairman of the NDC in April 1993, approximately fourteen months prior to his father's death. The NDC is the highest governing body in the state hierarchy and the center of authority for all of North Korea. The NDC controls the MPAF and its associated bureaus. The General Staff Bureau is the one within the MPAF that has direct oversight of the KPA, but another, the General Political Bureau, which also has close ties to the Central Military Commission, is in reality the most powerful of the bureaus within the MPAF.[51] Kim Jong Il's elevation to supreme commander of the KPA further complicated the command structure. Despite this complex array of authorities and positions between the party and the state, Kim Jong Il could issue orders to the KPA or other groups within North Korea and supersede any of these arrangements. In April 2012, prior to the celebration of Kim Il Sung's 100th birthday, the late Kim Jong Il was honored with the titles of General Secretary of the KWP and Chairman of the NDC for eternity while Kim Jong Un became the First Secretary of the Party and the First Chairman of the NDC, now the senior posts in these organizations.

Political Power and the KPA: How Strong Is It?

Measuring a military's political power and influence is difficult in most cases; the presence of coups, civil-military friction, and honoring the military's policy preferences may or may not be clear indicators of a military's actual power in government. As many scholars of civil-military relations point out, military influence can often be the "dog that didn't bark" because civilian leaders may accommodate the wishes of the military before any signs are visible. The task of understanding military influence is even more daunting given the opaque nature of DPRK government and politics. However, it is likely that while the status and influence of the KPA has increased relative to the KWP and other groups, the military under Kim Jong Il was not the dominant player, as he remained the chief political force in North Korea. Yet the precise dimensions of the power balance between Kim Jong Il and the KPA was uncertain.

The status of the KPA received a significant boost based on *songun* and constant praising of the KPA. Moreover, it was apparent that the KPA was an important policy advisor, particularly for foreign and defense policy.[52] The majority of the members of the NDC are military leaders, and several of the party and government organizations, for example the Supreme People's Assembly, have a majority population of KPA officers.[53] In addition, eighteen members of the party's CMC are top-ranking military officers and security chiefs.[54] Kim Jong Il, and now Kim Jong Un, must consider the wishes of these elite military leaders that serve in high-level positions in their services. Yet when asking the question raised by Desch, "Who prevails when civilian and military preferences diverge?" Kim Jong Il was the center of power in the North Korean system and did not always pursue the policy preferences of the military.[55] In addition, the military is one of several institutions that competed for power, and though one of the strongest, it did not appear to dominate over the wishes of Kim Jong Il.

As the power transition to Kim Jong Un unfolds and the party and the military work within the ruling collective, it may be difficult to ascertain in the near term the power balance between these two central institutions. With the dominant presence of Kim Jong Il gone, the working relationship between elites in the military and party and their ability to share power are unclear. Analysts will be watching closely to discern any indicators of the influence exercised by the military and the party.

The elevation of the NDC is often cited as an indication of the military's rise in power. Indeed, Kim Jong Il made it the core institution through which he directed state affairs, and many of its members are military leaders. Yet, while this may be the case, it is not clear this is an indication that the military as an institution received more than rhetorical praise rather than an actual increase in its influence. The military elites on the NDC rose to greater positions of political authority and became more numerous in government and party institutions, but it is uncertain whether they act for the military as an institution or as elites protecting their own interests in the system. Commenting on Kim Jong Il's rule, McEachern noted, "The NDC is better understood as an extension of Kim's inner circle than a broad, deep, and impersonal policy apparatus," and the group is "not an institutional representation of military interests."[56] It may be a combination of both, but it is likely that the military's power and influence as an institution through the NDC is far less than it appears.

KPA as an Economic Player

Finally, the North Korean military also plays an important role in the economy, one that goes beyond what is typical of most military institutions. The

KPA is an owner and entrepreneur while providing free labor in some economic sectors and for public service activities. The KPA and its leaders have
important economic interests in the DPRK economy and work to advance
those interests. However, they are one of several economic players and were
under the control of Kim Jong Il and the NDC.

The DPRK economy continues to struggle, but an area that has done better than most is the defense sector. This area is controlled by the Second
Economic Committee (SEC), but ultimate control of all defense industries
is the NDC. Originally established within the State Administrative Council
in 1993, the SEC was placed under the direction of the National Defense
Commission. The committee is the "single most powerful and influential
economic organization within the DPRK" and is "tasked with all responsibility for planning, financing, production and supplying of military materials for domestic use and foreign sales."[57] These industries produce a variety
of items including small arms, tanks, artillery, rocket launcher systems, and
ballistic missiles. The SEC is independent of the MPAF and KPA, with a
separate budget and control over 134 factories. In addition to these plants,
the SEC also has influence over other non–defense-related industries as its
production orders take priority over other requests, and it can commandeer
these facilities for defense production during wartime. Finally, the SEC
controls over 150 trading companies to facilitate the sale and acquisition of
foreign military equipment.[58]

While the military has its own trading companies, many others exist that
report to other entities but have an impact on the KPA. These firms, known
as the "foreign currency revenue generation base," are expected to produce
goods for export and acquire hard currency for the regime. A portion of
the profits from these trading companies went directly into Kim Jong Il's
personal accounts, which in turn helped to support the budgets for ballistic
missile and nuclear weapons programs along with rewarding KPA and KWP
elites for their loyalty. Those trading companies operated by the KPA have
a particular advantage because the soldiers they employ do not need wages,
providing greater revenue for government or military accounts.[59] These operations are likely to continue to be used to support party and military elites
under Kim Jong Un's tenure.

The KPA, a force of over 1.1 million and a ready pool of manpower, has
also provided labor for a number of other economic sectors, including civil
construction projects such as building electric plants and apartment com-
plexes. Soldiers have often been dispatched to rural areas to assist farmers
with planting and harvesting. However, increasingly, KPA involvement in
agriculture has created discontent in the countryside. Despite the military-
first ideology, many soldiers have seen their rations cut significantly, forcing

them to supplement their own and their family's sources by requisitioning food from peasant farmers. Some members of the KPA are tilling their own plots to offset the shortage of rations, but these efforts are often not able to make up the shortfall. Soldiers are increasingly ignoring any requisition process and seizing or stealing food from farmers. Officers, in turn, are taking food from enlisted personnel, further exacerbating the problem.

The KPA is also heavily involved in mining, an important sector of the North Korean economy that produced 8.3 percent of its GDP and 15.9 percent of its export revenue in 2005. In particular, mineral exports to China increased from $15 million in 2003 to $213 million in 2008. According to a source involved in Sino-DPRK trade, "tighter border patrols by China have made smuggling of stimulant drugs, which had been an underground source of funds for Pyongyang, more difficult. International sanctions have also limited the export of weapons. All North Korea has left is its mining resources."[60] The DPRK has significant amounts of gold, silver, lead, coal, iron, uranium, and copper, among others. However, this sector is operating at only about 30 percent capacity on average and suffers from a lack of modern technology, equipment, and steady supplies of electricity to make the extraction of these resources a profitable industry.[61] Two exceptions are uranium and coal, both areas that have significant KPA involvement. For several decades, the KPA has been involved in uranium production, owning the two major uranium mines. These facilities have operated largely in secret while using advanced equipment and employing workers who receive increased wages and food rations among other bonuses. The importance of uranium to North Korea's nuclear weapons ambitions has made this an important economic and national security venture for the KPA.

Coal mining has also been a sector of significant KPA involvement, but largely due to the military's ability to deliver cheap labor. As noted previously, most of the mining sector is hampered by the lack of modern technology and machinery, and the coal industry is no exception. However, while other minerals must have advanced technology for successful mining, coal can still be mined through a labor-intensive process of "men with shovels" that the KPA can provide. The KPA owns and operates several coal mines, and in addition to revenue generated from the export of coal, the mineral is essential to supporting a power grid that remains a severe vulnerability in the North's economic infrastructure. There appears to be some discontent in the ranks over these projects along with the lack of food these soldiers receive to perform such difficult manual labor.

Finally, there also appears to be KPA involvement with some of the DPRK's well-known illicit economic activities, the chief ones being narcotics trafficking and production of counterfeit cigarettes. Though the KPA does not appear to have significant involvement in either ownership or operation of these ventures, reports indicate that the KPA transports drugs and counterfeit cigarettes on military-owned naval vessels. While the KPA has limited involvement in these activities, the revenue gained helps to support KPA operating budgets, including its nuclear weapons and ballistic missile programs, and provides the funds to reward loyalists in the military and the party.[62]

IMPLICATIONS

There are several implications from this review of the multiple roles played by the KPA. First, the KPA will continue its primary role as protector of the DPRK state, the Kim family regime, the revolution, the party, and the people. North Korea faces a serious security threat from a modern ROK military and the ROK-U.S. alliance, with little confidence in its alliances with China and Russia. Consequently, the KPA and its leaders will remain occupied with their external security environment, helping to mitigate a temptation to intervene in domestic politics. In addition, despite the continued prospects of a deteriorating economy, the military will, for the time being, remain the beneficiary of relatively high levels of defense spending. *Songun* and its rhetoric also contribute to maintaining the DPRK's garrison state, with high levels of mobilization and regime support based on external security threats. All in the DPRK are asked to follow the model of the military: sacrifice for the sake of security and demonstrate loyalty to the leadership, the revolution, and the state. Early pronouncements have indicated that Kim Jong Un will continue the legacies of *songun* and *juche* established by his father and grandfather.

Second, during his rule, Kim Jong Il established himself at the center of North Korean government and politics. Yet Kim's elevation of the military drew them further into the halls of political power, deeper than during the years of Kim Il Sung. Kim Jong Il was able to maintain control of the KPA and channel the organization largely toward his policy priorities. The KPA remains an important player in the political process and now appears to be sharing power with the party. However, in the long run Kim's actions may have been a breach of Juan Linz's admonition that the military is more likely to stay out of politics if the political system it protects functions successfully and if civilians reject "any 'knocking at the barracks door' for armed forces support."[63] Linz was referring to struggling democracies calling in the military, but in North Korea's case, Kim Jong Il's elevation and integration of the military into the highest levels of the government and politics may have set the stage for a future that brings the KPA closer to leadership during some future crisis, should, in their view, civilian leadership fail. With Kim Jong Il gone, it is not certain that the arrangements of a subservient KPA have been sufficiently institutionalized for the military to be content with its current power position. Though the transition of Kim Jong Un is likely to be more stable than many expect, if the transition becomes chaotic, the KPA may decide to step in to protect the state and its own interests.

Finally, the KPA is also an important economic player in the regime. The armed forces of all countries are concerned about the economic livelihood of the state they protect. The military is dependent on economic prosperity and government budgets for the resources to do their job. Military leaders will exert considerable effort to obtain the budgets they believe are necessary to fulfill their core responsibility of protecting the state. However, the KPA has been a participant in the economy far beyond these concerns. Over the years, the KPA has provided labor and transportation for a number of projects and is an owner and entrepreneur both for the interests of individual military leaders and for the KPA as an institution since some of the revenue contributes to KPA operating budgets. This level of involvement raises several important questions.

First, the KPA's extensive involvement in the economy means that it will be affected greatly by any movement toward economic reform. At present, the KPA is opposed to economic reform for fear that it will damage the economic and political interests of its leaders.[64] Yet, if it becomes clear that reform would improve its economic interests without damaging its political power, there may be some room for change, but it is not clear this will ever be the case.

The other important question is the impact of the KPA's economic activities on its readiness as a fighting force. Though difficult to determine the exact extent, it is apparent that a significant share of the KPA is involved in economic tasks that are not consistent with its core function of military training and readiness. The KPA faces serious problems with aging equipment, a lack of fuel and spare parts, and food shortages. It is not clear whether its involvement in the economy is viewed as a necessity to generate income for the survival of the KPA or as a distraction from its primary security role. If segments of KPA leadership ever determine that they are prohibited from fulfilling their core security functions due to economic duties, military leaders may seek a decreased role in the economy.

CONCLUSION

North Korea and the KPA face a daunting and uncertain future. As a military force, the KPA will struggle with a conventional capability that is eroding but place greater reliance on asymmetric capabilities such as nuclear weapons, ballistic missiles, and special operations forces. Maintaining these capabilities will be more difficult with an economy that shows few signs of turning around without serious economic reform, measures that are unlikely in the short term. The biggest wildcard will be the KPA's future role in DPRK politics and government. With Kim Jong Il's death, the future becomes less certain, but so long as the interests of the KPA and its leaders remain secure, they are likely to remain content with the current arrangements. However, should the transition to Kim Jong Un become overly chaotic or the political system become unstable, the possibility of the KPA exerting greater authority to stabilize the situation could increase.

NOTES

I want to thank CDR Quinn Skinner for his research assistance and Nan Li for his helpful comments with this project. However, any errors are my responsibility.

1. Nan Li, ed., *Chinese Civil-Military Relations: The Transformation of the People's Liberation Army* (New York: Routledge, 2006); Dale Herspring and Ivan Volgyes, eds., *Civil-Military Relations in Communist Systems* (Boulder, CO: Westview Press, 1978).

2. Ken Gause, "Leadership Transition in North Korea," *Council on Foreign Relations*, January 2012, http://www.cfr.org/north-korea/leadership-transition-north -korea/p27071?cid=nlc-korea-korea_update-link5-20120117.

3. David Pion-Berlin, "Introduction," in David Pion-Berlin, *Civil-Military Relations in Latin America: New Analytical Perspectives* (Chapel Hill: University of North Carolina Press, 2001), 1.

4. Jei Guk Jeon, "Kim Jong-il's Ride on the Tiger 'KPA': A Two-Pronged Strategy towards the Military," *Korean Journal of Defense Analysis* 11, no. 1 (Summer 1999): 128.

5. Samuel P. Huntington, *The Soldier and the State* (New York: Vintage, 1957); Morris Janowitz, *The Professional Soldier: A Social and Political Portrait* (Glencoe, IL: Free Press, 1960).

6. Michael C. Desch, *Civilian Control of the Military: The Changing Security Environment* (Baltimore, MD: Johns Hopkins University Press, 1999), 1–7.

7. Peter D. Feaver, "Civil-Military Relations," in Nelson W. Polsby, ed., *Annual Review of Political Science*, vol. 2 (Palo Alto, CA: Annual Reviews, 1999), 218.

8. Terence Roehrig, *The Prosecution of Former Military Leaders in Newly Democratic Nations: The Cases of Argentina, Greece, and South Korea* (Jefferson, NC: McFarland, 2002).

9. Eric Nordlinger, *Soldiers in Politics: Military Coups and Governments* (New York: Prentice-Hall, 1977): 21–27.

10. Alfred Stepan, *Rethinking Military Politics: Brazil and the Southern Cone* (Princeton, NJ: Princeton University Press, 1988), 92–127.

11. Desch, *Civilian Control of the Military*, 4.

12. Deborah D. Avant, "Conflicting Indicators of 'Crisis' in American Civil-Military Relations," *Armed Forces and Society* 24, no. 3 (1998): 382–83.

13. Suzanne C. Nielsen, "Civil-Military Relations Theory and Military Effectiveness," *Public Administration and Management* 10, no. 2 (2005): 70.

14. *Military Balance 2011*, International Institute of Strategies Studies (Oxford, UK: IISS, 2011), 249.

15. *Military Balance 2011*, 250.

16. *Military Balance 2011*, 250.

17. Terence Roehrig, "Restraining the Hegemon: North Korea, the United States, and Asymmetric Deterrence," *Pacific Focus* 20, no. 2 (Fall 2005): 45–46.

18. Joseph Bermudez Jr., *The Armed Forces of North Korea* (New York: I. B. Tauris, 2001), 5.

19. *Military Balance 2011*, 251.

20. *ROK 2010 Defense White Paper*, 31, http://www.mnd.go.kr/cms_file/info/mndpaper/2010/2010WhitePaperAll_eng.pdf.

21. *Military Balance 2011*, 250.

22. Bermudez, *The Armed Forces of North Korea*, 226; Jane's Sentinel Security Assessment, "Strategic Weapons Systems—North Korea," January 20, 2011, http://jmsa.janes.com/JDIC/JMSA.

23. Bermudez, *The Armed Forces of North Korea*, 231–35.

24. See Terence Roehrig, "North Korea's Nuclear Weapons Program: Motivations, Strategy, and Doctrine," in Toshi Yoshihara and James Holmes, eds., *Nuclear Strategy in the Second Nuclear Age: Power, Ambition, and the Ultimate Weapon* (Washington, DC: Georgetown University Press, 2012).

25. "N. Korean Military's Morale 'Weakening,'" *Chosun Ilbo*, July 5, 2011, http://english.chosun.com/site/data/html_dir/2011/07/05/2011070500529.html; Kim So Yeol and Cho Jong Ik, "Systematic Embezzlement Causes Food Crisis in Military," *Daily NK*, April 26, 2011, http://www.dailynk.com/english/read.php?cataId=nk00400&num=7617.

26. Kongdan Oh and Ralph C. Hassig, *North Korea through the Looking Glass* (Washington, DC: Brookings Institution, 2000), 106.

27. Patrick McEachern, *Inside the Red Box: North Korea's Post-Totalitarian Politics* (New York: Columbia University Press, 2010), 84.

28. Sung Chull Kim, *North Korea under Kim Jong-il: From Consolidation to Systemic Dissonance* (New York: SUNY Press, 2006), 86.

29. Sung Chull Kim, *North Korea under Kim Jong-il*, 90.

30. McEachern, *Inside the Red Box*, 87.

31. Sung Chull Kim, *North Korea under Kim Jong-il*, 95.

32. Jei Guk Jeon, "Kim Jong-il's Ride on the Tiger 'KPA,'" 128–29.

33. McEachern, *Inside the Red Box*, 85.

34. Stephan Haggard and Marcus Noland, *Famine in North Korea: Markets, Aid, and Reform* (New York: Columbia University Press, 2007).

35. Jei Guk Jeon, "Kim Jong-il's Ride on the Tiger 'KPA,'" 129.

36. Dae-Kyu Yoon, "The Constitution of North Korea: Its Changes and Implications," *Fordham International Law Journal* 27, no. 4 (2003): 1301.

37. Dae-Sook Suh, "Military-First Politics of Kim Jong Il," *Asian Perspective* 26, no. 3 (2002): 161.

38. See Han S. Park, "Military-First Politics (*Songun*): Understanding Kim Jong-il's North Korea," Korea Economic Institute Academic Paper Series, 2008, 118–30.

39. Suh, "Military-First Politics of Kim Jong Il," 151–52.

40. As printed in "WPK's Policy of Giving Priority to Army Is Invincible," *Korean Central News Agency*, June 16, 1999, www.kcna.co.jp.

41. Ken E. Gause, *North Korean Civil-Military Trends: Military First Politics to a Point*, Strategic Studies Institute (September 2006), 7.

42. Suh, "Military-First Politics of Kim Jong-il," 157–58; Gause, *North Korean Civil-Military Trends*, 12–17.

43. McEachern, *Inside the Red Box*, 88.

44. Gause, *North Korean Civil-Military Trends*, 12.

45. Daniel A. Pinkston, "Domestic Politics and Stakeholders in the North Korean Missile Development Program," *Nonproliferation Review*, Summer 2003, 4.

46. Gause, *North Korean Civil-Military Trends*, 3.

47. Bermudez, *Armed Forces of North Korea*, 20; Hassig and Oh, *North Korea through the Looking Glass*, 118.

48. As quoted in "North Korea Leadership Watch: Central Military Commission," January 16, 2011, http://nkleadershipwatch.wordpress.com/the-party/central-military-committee.

49. "North Korea Leadership Watch."

50. Bermudez, *Armed Forces of North Korea*, 21.

51. Oh and Hassig, *North Korea through the Looking Glass*, 118.

52. Gause, *North Korean Civil-Military Trends*, 7.

53. Suh, "Military-First Politics of Kim Jong Il," 157.

54. "Party Military Commission Ascendant in N. Korea," *Chosun Ilbo*, December 22, 2011, http://english.chosun.com/site/data/html_dir/2011122201343.html.

55. McEachern, *Inside the Red Box*, 89–90.

56. McEachern, *Inside the Red Box*, 88–89.

57. Bermudez, *The Armed Forces of North Korea*, 45–46.

58. Bermudez, *The Armed Forces of North Korea*, 44–55.

59. John S. Park, "North Korea, Inc.: Gaining Insights into North Korean Regime Stability from Recent Commercial Activities," U.S. Institute of Peace, April 22, 2009, http://www.usip.org/files/resources/North%20Korea,%20Inc.PDF.

60. Diasuke Nishimura, "N. Korea Lifted Ore Export Limit to Buy Food," *Asahi Shimbun*, February 11, 2010, available at http://www.asahi.com/english/TKY201102090212.html.

61. Edward Yoon, "Status and Future of the North Korean Minerals Sector," *Korean Journal of Defense Analysis* 23, no. 2 (June 2011): 191.

62. See Paul Rexton Kan, Bruce E. Bechtol Jr., and Robert M. Collins, "Criminal Sovereignty: Understanding North Korea's Illicit International Activities," *Strategic Studies Institute*, March 2010; Dick K. Nanto, "North Korean Counterfeiting of U.S. Currency," *CRS Report* #RL 33324, June 12, 2009.

63. Juan J. Linz, *The Breakdown of Democratic Regimes: Crisis, Breakdown, and Reequilibrium* (Baltimore, MD: Johns Hopkins University Press, 1978), 30.

64. Patrick McEachern, "North Korea's Policy Process: Assessing Institutional Policy Preferences," *Asian Survey* 49, no. 3 (May/June 2009): 550–51.

Chapter Four

The Kims' Three Bodies

Toward Understanding Dynastic Succession in North Korea

Bruce Cumings

When Kim Jong Il died on December 17, 2011, I was lucky to be in Singapore. That way I could watch from a salutary distance the froth and nonsense that passed for expert American commentary: How can his callow son expect to grapple with octogenarian leaders in the powerful military—won't there be a *coup*? Then again, Kim Jong Un might "lash out" to prove his toughness to the militarists. Probably Kim's death means "the end of North Korea as we know it," through the unraveling of the regime, or its general collapse. Others worried that such a collapse might require U.S. Marines on Okinawa to swoop in to corral "loose nukes" (one of their key missions for several years). Meanwhile, Obama administration officials fretted about a "power struggle" erupting, something Secretary of State Hillary Clinton frequently mentioned after Kim's stroke three years earlier (even though no evidence of it appeared, then or later). Their model seems to be the USSR after Stalin died, or China after Mao. Utterly ignored is what happened when Kim Il Sung died in 1994: nothing.[1]

On my first visit to North Korea in 1981, I flew in from Beijing and hoped to go out through the Soviet Union, on the Trans-Siberian Railway. Consular officials said I should obtain a visa at the Soviet embassy in Pyongyang. When I duly arrived at its doorstep, a friendly (read KGB) counselor sat me down, offered me cognac, and inquired as to what I might be doing in Pyongyang. More cognac, more discussion, and then he asked what I thought of Kim Jong Il, who had just been officially designated as successor to Kim Il Sung at the Sixth Party Congress in 1980. "Well, he doesn't have his father's charisma," I said. "He's diminutive, pear-shaped, homely. Looks like his mother in fact." "Oh, you Americans," he said, "always thinking about personality. Don't you know they have a bureaucratic bloc behind him, they all rise or fall with him—these people really know how to do this here. You should come back in 2020 and see *his* son take power."

It proved to be the best prediction I've ever heard about this hybrid communist state-cum-dynasty, except that Kim Jong Il's heart attack at the age of sixty-nine merely hastened the succession to Kim Jong Un by a few years. The question is, why are American experts' predictions about the North so bad? It would be one thing if, say, Kim Il Sung had lived to be ninety-nine, finally dying in late 2011. But he died at the age of eighty-two, and just like today, back then experts, pundits, and government officials emitted the same derivative commentary, the same mimetic nonsense.

Newsweek ran a cover story in July 1994 titled "The Headless Beast," which was full of misinformation and, in the end, racism. The U.S. military commander in the South said over and over that the North will "implode or explode," and the imminent collapse of the regime became the CIA's official mantra in the mid-1990s, repeated in congressional testimony by its then-director, John Deutsch. It is well known that Clinton administration officials pledged to construct two light-water reactors for the North as part of the 1994 Framework Agreement, because they thought the DPRK would be gone by the time they came on line, and the South would possess them. A few months before Kim Il Sung's death, I heard a Korean-American scholar tell a university conference crowd in Milwaukee that when Kim died, the people would rise up and overthrow the regime. Instead the masses wept in the streets—just as they did when King Kojong died in 1919, touching off a nationwide uprising against the Japanese.

After his father passed away, Kim Jong Il disappeared, feeding more rumors of power struggles. Actually he was doing what the heir-apparent prince was supposed to do under the ancien régime: mourn his father for three years. By the fiftieth anniversary of the DPRK's founding in 1998, it was clear that Kim Jong Il was in full charge of the country, and he launched their first long-range missile to mark the moment. The 1994 episode also had a prelude, in the many predictions of North Korean collapse after the Berlin Wall fell, and especially after its presumed patron and puppet master, the Soviet Union, came apart in 1991. Nicholas Eberstadt is perhaps the most prominent scholar in Washington to have predicted a North Korean collapse, beginning with an editorial in the *Wall Street Journal* (June 25, 1990) on "The Coming Collapse of North Korea."[2] He elaborated on his reasoning in his subsequent 1999 book, *The End of North Korea* (when a *New York Times* reporter asked John Bolton what the Bush administration's policy was on the DPRK, he strode to his bookshelf and handed him Eberstadt's book: "That's our policy," he said). During a conference at the University of British Columbia in 2009, a leading scholar of Korea told the group, "We all thought the North would collapse." I blurted out, "Not me." But he correctly put his finger on the consensus among scholars. Perhaps this is a normal part of academic life: we all get things wrong from time to time.

What is more daunting—and even frightening—is that bad thinking and bad predictions about the North have lodged at the highest levels of both Democratic and Republican administrations since 1989. The George H. W. Bush administration accepted the collapse scenario after 1989, and Assistant Secretary of Defense Paul Wolfowitz said it again in June 2003—"North Korea is teetering on the brink of collapse." In between we heard Gen. Gary Luck, commander of U.S. forces in Korea, say in 1997, "North Korea will disintegrate, possibly in very short order"; the only question was whether it would implode or explode.[3] In this he was plagiarizing another of our commanders in Korea, Gen. Robert Riscassi, who never tired of saying that Pyongyang would soon "implode or explode" (Riscassi retired in 1992). This ritualistic thinking has even led to scenarios of how to *force* the collapse of the DPRK—which, in my view, is to ask for the next, and even more cata-strophic, Korean War. When does the statute of limitations run out on being systematically wrong?

WHAT IS WRONG WITH THE "COLLAPSE" SCENARIO, AND WHY IT PERSISTS

"North Korea as we know it is over," a knowledgeable Korea scholar who also served in the second Bush administration confidently asserted in the *New York Times*, a mere two days after Kim died, and before it was clear *how* he had died; "Whether it comes apart in the next few weeks or over several months," Victor Cha wrote, "the regime will not be able to hold together after the untimely death of Kim Jong Il." If it somehow managed to persist any-way, it would be because it had become, in effect, "China's next province."[4] Here the argument seems to be that the DPRK has survived only because China does not want it to collapse. There is no question that in recent years North Korea has become heavily dependent on trade with China, and food aid; in 2011 China accounted for more than 53 percent of its total trade.[5] But this is also a direct result of the collapse of trade with South Korea after the advent of the Lee Myung Bak government in 2008; the North's dependency on trade with China was 32 percent at that time, according to IMF figures, while 22 percent was with the South (the Lee government cut off trade in 2010, except through the Kaesong Industrial Zone).

But let's assume that China has been propping up the North. Why did that hardly insignificant assumption not figure into the logic of nearly a quarter century of predictions of the North's coming collapse? Kim Il Sung began his guerrilla career by teaming up with Chinese comrades, even if, as scholars like Han Hong-gu have shown, the "Chinese Communist Party" in Manchukuo was made up of 80 or even 90 percent Koreans. Korean radicals participated in the Northern Expedition and the Canton Commune in the 1920s, the Long March in the 1930s, and contributed tens of thousands of soldiers to the Red Army in the Chinese Civil War. Mao Zedong then bailed Kim's chestnuts out of a very hot fire (the Korean War) in the late fall of 1950. Kim Il Sung was very close to both Mao and his long-term successor, Deng Xiaoping. Why would the current Chinese Communist leaders want a border with the Republic of Korea, with its large military not only being a virtual replica of American military practices, but with 28,000 U.S. troops still in Korea and frequent joint war games directed not just at the North, but at China as well? These are elementary facts that should be known to anyone who claims expertise on the North; furthermore, for the North to become a "province" of China would contradict everything the North has stood for since 1945 (and mimics Syngman Rhee's 1940s propaganda about the North becoming a province of the Soviet Union); notice how, very recently, Pyongyang got so bent out of shape when some scholars in China tried to claim that the ancient Korean kingdom of Koguryo was Chinese.

The "end-of-North-Korea" theme is fundamentally flawed for reasons that can help us understand the DPRK's post–Cold War endurance. Most prognostications of North Korean collapse base North Korean experience on that of the disappeared communist regimes of Europe; they see the DPRK entirely through the lens of Soviet and East European communism and therefore cannot grasp the pragmatic shrewdness of the regime's post–Cold War foreign policy, the desperate survival strategies it is willing to undertake, let alone the anticolonial and revolutionary-nationalist origins of this regime and those in Vietnam and China, yielding no significant break since 1989 in Asian communism.

Repeating the Cold War mantra that Moscow saw everything in the world through the Marxist-Leninist doctrine of "the correlation for forces" ("*sootnoshenie sil*"), Eberstadt argued that this is also the basis of North Korea's global strategy. If so, Pyongyang should have folded its hand and cashed in its chips in 1989; no other state has faced such an incredible array of enemy "forces" and seemingly insurmountable crises since then, with little help from anyone and universal hopes that it simply erase itself and disappear. Here we are more than two decades later, and if you give the DPRK another few years, it will have been in existence for as long as the entirety of the Soviet Union.

More importantly, Professor Cha and Mr. Eberstadt touch on themes of collapse that have framed policy at the highest level. Donald Rumsfeld, secretary of defense in the second Bush administration, knew so astonishingly little about Beijing's relationship with Pyongyang that he actually called for a joint U.S.-China program to topple the North Korean government; more reasonable American officials, on a bipartisan basis, have frequently tried to get Beijing to bring enough pressure on the North to put an end to its nuclear program. Secretary of State Clinton's frequent invocation of "power struggles" in the DPRK apparently derives from a communist model of what happened in the USSR after Stalin died, or in China after Mao died. Quite apart from the leadership stability that followed upon Kim Il Sung's death, Stalin and Mao were very different leaders, with very different agendas, programs, and crimes. Nikita Khrushchev had to denounce Stalinism in his famous 1956 speech if he wanted to continue leading the country, given the tens of millions of Soviet citizens who had perished because of Stalin's rule, with almost everyone having a relative who had died or been relegated to the gulags. Mao was directly responsible for the deaths of tens of millions in the Great Leap Forward famine, and he had supported the Gang of Four—including his wife Jiang Qing—as they terrorized much of the urban population in the Cultural Revolution. After Mao died, they were quickly arrested and put on trial. There is no record in Kim Il Sung's reign of mass violence against whole classes of people; even in the land reform campaign of 1946, landlords were not murdered en masse as they were in China and North Vietnam—and we know this because of a huge archive of captured North Korean documents from 1945 to 1950 that has been open to scholars since 1977.

A NORTH KOREAN "SPRING"?

Since the Tunisian rebellion began the "Arab Spring" in February 2011, many people—especially my students—have asked if something similar might develop in North Korea. It is a reasonable question. The Seoul-based Korea Foundation, which provides much of the funding for Korean studies programs around the world, chose to begin the February 2012 issue of its publication, *Korea Focus*, with an editorial by Kang Chol Hwan that began like this: "North Korea has been paying close attention to developments in Libya because . . . the two dictators are very much alike in their psychotic personalities, their iron grip on power, their hoarding of wealth for their own survival, and the ways they lavish their stooges with benefits to buy their loyalty."[6] If Kim Jong Il before he died, or his son today, were witness to uprisings against their regime, armed foreign intervention bent on regime change under the guise of creating a "no fly zone," and ended up cornered like a rat and tortured to death, everything I wish to get across in this essay would be proved wrong. However, it is Mr. Kang who is wrong.

What the overthrow of Qaddafi proved is that Libya remained a tribal society under the guise of his "Green Revolution." Essentially three countries
under Italian colonialism, King Idris appeared to preside over a single nation
while favoring his tribe until his overthrow in 1969, and then Qaddafi did
the same. Fearing other tribes, Qaddafi did not create a large national army
that would enroll his potential enemies, but a security force with the ultimate
goal of assuring Qaddafi's safety. For many years Libya's oil wealth enabled
Qaddafi to paper over the severe cleavages that remained in the society. As
the Arab Spring spread to eastern Libya, a region always poorly integrated
into Qaddafi's state, U.S. and European powers intervened to provide the
hard power that finally caused his regime to disintegrate and collapse. His
murder proved that at least some sectors of his population hated his guts. At
this writing, Libya's future is anybody's guess—democracy, a new dictatorship, division into three again?

Whatever one thinks of Qaddafi, Kim Jong Il was not psychotic. He commanded the fourth largest army in the world, with few if any signs of disloyalty to the leaders over the past six decades. North Korea has no tribes; perhaps some modest regional differences persist, but Korea had been unified for
a millennium and divided only since 1945. Kim Jong Il certainly rewarded his
friends and acolytes, as every dictator must. But it isn't clear that this signals
a broad disloyalty among the mass of the people. So the Libyan example is a
bad one; it bears little if any relation to what might happen in North Korea.
Nor is it likely that the mass protests stimulated around the world by the Arab
Spring and "Occupy Wall Street" will have much effect on the North.

What Mr. Kang ignores is the civil war that raged intensely from 1945 to
1953 between North and South, and within the South; that war created the
garrison state that has existed ever since and that defines the DPRK, and the
army has only deepened its power under the post–Kim Il Sung *songun* or
"military-first" policy. To imagine that this army is just waiting its chance to
overthrow the Kim family and unite with the South is foolishness. There will
be no "Korean Spring" until the Korean War is finally brought to an end, and
until the two Koreas have reconciled along the path etched out by Kim Dae
Jung and Roh Moo Hyun from 1998 to 2008.

INSIDE THE BELTWAY: ANOTHER WORLD

It is not hard to find similar arguments being made in Washington. As a result
of many researchers plumbing various archives, the democratization of the
South that has enabled a lot of good work on the North, and the large amounts
of information that have poured out about the North since it was forced to

open itself to aid groups and NGOs in the mid-1990s, we have lots of good scholarship on the DPRK. Why, then, does this work not penetrate the upper reaches of either Democratic or Republican administrations? It is because you enter another world inside the Washington Beltway, where partisan calculation or the desire for influence or for a position within a given administration leads to a remarkably narrow and shallow spectrum of opinion.

Shortly after Barack Obama took office, North Korea launched another long-range missile, blew off its second atomic bomb, and greeted the new president with a farrago of nonnegotiable demands: We are a nuclear weapons state! We don't care if you want normal relations with us or not! We want light-water reactors! Get your troops out of the South![7] This was the same Barack Obama who had campaigned on reaching out to the "rogue states" that George W. Bush shunned, and who memorably said at his inauguration that leaders who will "unclench your fist" would find an open hand in Washington. Pyongyang's leaders chose (U.S.) Memorial Day, May 25, to successfully test a three- or four-kiloton atomic bomb, thus silencing claims that their first test of a half-kiloton bomb in October 2006 was a "dud." (Meanwhile, hardly anyone commented on why Pyongyang chose this particular date, but it must amaze people in Pyongyang, who take anniversaries seriously.)

President Obama declared all this to be "a grave threat" to the United States and pushed a resolution through the United Nations Security Council to shadow and possibly intercept North Korean vessels on the high seas. The North then stated that this would be "an act of war" and threatened to respond with "merciless blows"—proffering its fiercest "clenched fist." Somehow the cunning of history had left Barack Obama carrying the water of John Bolton's "Proliferation Security Initiative," no doubt to the delight of former vice president Dick Cheney.

American television rounded up all the usual images of North Korea: frightening soldiers goose-stepping through Pyongyang, a madman at the helm who starves his people, missiles fired "over Japan" (all missile launches are to the east, to take advantage of the earth's rotation); even Hawaii was possibly under risk (Defense Secretary Robert Gates sent special missile-defense batteries to the islands). A few experts sought to point out that the Bush administration, in its peculiar combination of ideological rigidity and haphazard policy, had contrived to hand over the plutonium with which the North made its bombs, but no one wanted to hear it;[8] a seamless, bipartisan Beltway consensus said the North's provocations could never be tolerated—something had to be done.

It did not help that Kim Jong Il could look so sinister when he wanted to, whereas his father's always-smiling visage sometimes made it hard to imagine him shipping enemies off to the gulag or bureaucrats off to the mines. This odd prince perhaps had the face that life rather than nature had given him; like Bush, he had to contend with the knowledge that his fate would have been rather different without Daddy's provenance. But his face was perfect for an American media that loves to front its stories and tales about the North with "Dr. Evil" affixed to the cover. But what do we make of a magazine of record with a world-historical reputation for indefatigable fact-checking, namely *The New Yorker*, advertising a major article on the North under the caption, "How Crazy Is Kim?" Our popular discourse on foreign adversaries has become completely debased; we have a cartoon show playing into the hands of hard-liners, just as it denies the American people the information and knowledge that would enable them to come to reasonable judgments.

How did we arrive at this parody of our long history with Pyongyang? In May 1994 the Koreans dumped 8,000 plutonium fuel rods into cooling ponds, nearly causing Bill Clinton to initiate a second Korean War; luckily Jimmy Carter's intervention brought about a freeze on the North's plutonium facility that lasted eight years. In August 1998 North Korea marked the fiftieth anniversary of the DPRK's founding by testing their first long-range missile, producing another frenzy of ill-informed punditry, and in 2006 they ran a scenario very similar to the one in 2009—testing missiles and their first A-bomb, and choosing American holidays as punctuation (July 4, 2006, was their second long-range missile test; they tested seven short-range missiles again on July 4, 2009). Each episode was followed by more mimetic media tropes: evil communists led by a cognac-swilling nutcase, a rogue regime running amok.

In 1997 the CIA invited outside experts to join a panel of government officials, which concluded that North Korea was likely to collapse within five years. Robert A. Wampler, who obtained this report under the Freedom of Information Act, quoted senior Foreign Service officer David Straub's observation that one expert after another came through the Tokyo embassy in the early 1990s, "pontificating on their prognoses for the inevitable collapse of the North Korean regime, giving odds that allowed Pyongyang anywhere from a few months to perhaps two years before falling."[9] Kim Jong Il, the assembled CIA experts thought, was likely to have just "a brief window of time" to cope with all his difficulties before suffering a probable "hard landing." Without major reform, some "catalyst" would come along "that will lead to collapse." The majority of the group doubted that Kim's regime could persist "beyond five years," yielding a "political implosion." Yet many of them expressed surprise that in spite of the degraded economy and the beginnings of a famine that would soon grow much worse, somehow the "delusionary" (their word) Kim Jong Il "remained firmly in control." Among those outsiders whom the CIA invited to this exercise were academics Kenneth Liebenthal and Robert Ross, AEI's Nicholas Eberstadt, and Daryl Plunk and James Przystup from the Heritage Foundation. No academic experts on North Korea were there (Lieberthal and Ross are China experts), but more surprisingly, neither was anyone from Brookings or the Carnegie Endowment—the liberal anchors of the (remarkably narrow) spectrum of Beltway opinion. Here was the CIA under the Clinton administration reaching out to the right for guidance on "North Korea's coming collapse."

How is it that a long-running crisis, now rather thoroughly known in its admittedly difficult and intricate detail, is reinvented every couple of years with no discernible learning amid the eternal recurrence of the same? As the 1997 report exemplifies, the answer lies not in Pyongyang but in Washington: since the Berlin Wall fell, a Beltway consensus embracing leaders of both parties has adhered to four core axioms: (1) North Korea stands for nothing, has no support from its people, and will soon collapse; (2) American pressure on this regime will either hasten this process (Republicans) or change its behavior (Democrats); (3) if engagement works to get rid of their nukes, fine, but the end goal here, too, is a "velvet" form of regime change, or even a "humanitarian" intervention like the one in Libya; (4) if it doesn't, resorting to military force is justified to stop the North from becoming a nuclear power weapons state. All of these assumptions are false and, in the light of recent history, irrational.

Successive administrations and Beltway pundits get North Korea so wrong because they know next to nothing about its origins, they view it through the lens of Soviet behavior, and they cannot come up with any North Korean interests that they deem worthy of respect. For many, it is an outrage that the regime continues to exist at all (this was the dominant opinion in the Bush administration). But in the end, what difference does this make? In 2004, Nicholas Eberstadt argued that America and its allies should waltz in and, in his Reaganesque flourish, "Tear down this tyranny."[10] At the time, he had excellent backing for such views in Vice President Dick Cheney's entourage, and especially Paul Wolfowitz, John Bolton, and Robert Joseph (director of nonproliferation at the NSC). With the demise of the Bush vision, if one can call it that, enthusiasm for such a course has waned. But it was the preferred policy of hard-liners for several years, amid the internal civil war that shaped Bush's policies toward North Korea—where most meetings turned into raging shouting matches.[11]

THREATS OF WAR, IGNORANCE OF WAR

It will be remembered that the United States put half a million troops into Korea in 1950 who defended the South, invaded the North, and were routed out of there by a joint Sino-Korean army made up mostly of peasants with the barest of resources. The conflict ended in a draw, but as a war, it has never ended: an armistice, yes; a peace treaty, no. Sitting on the National Defense Committee, the most powerful body in the North, are a number of octogenarians who have immediate experience of this terrible war, and burned-in memories of its unrestrained violence. They know this war in their bones and have been ready to fight it again for more than six decades. Yet most well-informed Americans and most high government officials know very little about it, and most of the existing American literature on the Korean War is shot through with error and misunderstanding.[12]

After the 9/11 terrorist attacks, Donald Rumsfeld suggested preemptive nuclear strikes on rogue states,[13] and when it appeared that the invasion of Iraq would move quickly to victory, he demanded revisions in the basic war plan for Korea (called "Operations Plan 5030") and also sought money for new bunker-busting nukes from Congress. The strategy, according to insiders who have read the plan, was "to topple Kim's regime by destabilizing its military forces," so they would overthrow him and thus accomplish a "regime change." The plan was pushed "by many of the same administration hard-liners who advocated regime change in Iraq." Unnamed senior Bush administration officials considered elements of this new plan "so aggressive that they could provoke a war."[14]

It sounds adventurous and ill-advised to say the least, but threatening war is also a bipartisan position and hardly new. On NBC's *Meet the Press* on April 3, 1994, Defense Secretary William Perry said, "We do not want war and will not provoke a war," but if U.S. sanctions "provoke the North Koreans into unleashing a war . . . that is a risk that we're taking."[15] Perry's formulation was careful and precise: he and Ashton Carter Jr. had been studying for many months whether a preemptive strike could be carried out against the Yongbyon plutonium facility without starting the next Korean War; they concluded that it couldn't. By mid-June 1994 the Clinton administration "had devised a plan laying out the first steps the US should take to prepare for war," which included the addition of 10,000 American troops in Korea, dispatching Apache attack helicopters and various other aircraft, and moving in more Bradley Fighting Vehicles.[16] Furthermore, "to make sure Clinton understood both the human and the monetary costs of a war, the Joint Chiefs had summoned all the regional commanders and four star generals in the service to Washington in late May [1994] to discuss Korea and brief the President." According to U.S. commander in Korea Gen. Gary Luck's estimates, he would need as many as 80,000 to 100,000 body bags in the field for the American soldiers who would die in a new Korean war, and Korean troop casualties could reach the hundreds of thousands. Moreover, if the North struck Seoul as expected, "the number of civilian casualties would be staggering." The cost of such a war, Luck predicted, would be at least $500 billion and could top $1 trillion, far higher than the almost $60 billion spent on Desert Storm. If Perry and Carter were right and the North attacked the South after a preemptive strike, the ultimate consequences of that war cannot be known, but might have included American attacks using nuclear weapons: think of it—a nuclear war in the name of nonproliferation. But they seem to have been undaunted by all this, as they continued to publish editorials calling for preemptive strikes against the North during the Bush administration.[17]

Shortly before the fiftieth anniversary of the Korean War armistice in 2003, Perry gave a harrowing interview to the *Washington Post*. "I think we are losing control" of the situation; we are on a "path to war," he said. North Korea might soon have enough nuclear warheads to begin exploding them in tests or exporting them to terrorists. "The nuclear program now underway in North Korea poses an imminent danger of nuclear weapons being detonated in American cities," he charged—an absurdity, in my view, since in retaliation we would turn the North into "a charcoal briquette" (Colin Powell's expression). But Perry had also concluded that Bush just wouldn't enter into serious talks with Pyongyang: "My theory is the reason we don't have a policy on this, and we aren't negotiating, is the president himself. I think he has come to the conclusion that Kim Jong Il is evil and loathsome and it is immoral to negotiate with him." He was correct: Bush possessed a stunning combination of utter ignorance about Korea and visceral hatred for his counterpart in Pyongyang. During his first phone call with Kim Dae Jung, who had won the Nobel Peace Prize in 2000, he cupped the phone and looked at an aide: "Who is this guy?" As for Kim Jong Il, in one meeting Bush exclaimed, "We want him to get rid of his nukes, and if he doesn't . . . we have to get rid of him!"[18] Thus did an insecure, reclusive dictator and an insecure, impulsive foreign affairs naïf hold the peace of the world in their hands.

The Perry-Bush preemptive scenarios utterly disregarded the conflict situation on the Korean Peninsula: we are still technically at war with the North, 1.5 million soldiers are in close proximity along the tense DMZ, and the North has been preparing for the next war ever since the last one ended; it is the world's most remarkable garrison state, with nearly every adult having had military training. The acute danger—which South Korean leaders immediately grasped—was that threatening preemptive strikes on Yongbyon conflated with existing plans for preemption in a crisis initiated by the North, which have been standard operating procedure for the U.S. military for decades. American commanders in the South have long worried about a war accidentally breaking out through a cycle of preemption and counter-preemption. Leaders in Seoul repeatedly sought assurances from

Washington that the North would not be attacked over Seoul's veto. It is my understanding that they never received those assurances. Since the North can destroy Seoul in a matter of hours with some 10,000 artillery guns buried in the mountains north of the capital, one can imagine the extreme consternation that the Bush doctrine caused in Seoul. This, too, is irrationality: there never was a military solution in Korea (as we should have learned in 1953), and there certainly isn't now.

NATIONAL DIGNITY

How might we come to a better understanding of this regime so that our explanations and predictions might improve? We need to make a sincere effort to understand this politics—and when we do, we discover that what began as a rather typical version of postcolonial, anti-imperial revolution in the 1940s rather quickly morphed into a system that drew deeply from the well of Korean political culture. By the 1960s, native political practice had begun to capture and overwhelm this communist system to a degree never before seen in the rest of the world. As the "Arab Spring" developed, some analysts came to understand that the movements of Arab peoples were not just a quest for the democratic rights that we take for granted; they were also a quest for human dignity. So was the North Korean revolution. It was amazing to me when I first visited this country to see the marked difference in body language when Koreans greeted me. They did not bow but looked you in the eye and shook hands. They did not flatter, or dissemble, or give any impression that this encounter was anything but that between equals. One needed to live in South Korea in the 1960s and 1970s to grasp how utterly different this experience was, not just for an American but for all foreigners. It also contradicts the extremes of obeisance that North Koreans exhibit in the presence of their ultimate leader, his statue, or even his photograph, and that our media like to focus on.

Asians, it is often said, hate to lose "face." It is a word better translated as dignity, or honor. In North Korean eyes, the prestige of the nation is bound up with the visage of the leader. On the way in from the airport in 1981, as we sped by various Kim Il Sung billboards, my friendly guide had one solemn admonition: please do not insult our leader. (I hadn't planned to, lest I jeopardize my exit.) The leader's ideology, then and now, was "*juche*," or *chuch'e*, a concept meaning always to put Korea first and above all else in one's mind. Scholar of Korea Gari Ledyard has written that the second character, when joined to the word for nation—*kukch'e*—was used in classical discourse to connote the national face, or dignity. As Ledyard wrote, "The *kukch'e* can be hurt, it can be embarrassed, it can be insulted, it can be sullied. The members of the society must behave in such a way that the *kukch'e* will not be 'lost.' This sense of the word resonates with emotions and ethics that spring from deep sources in the traditional psyche."[19] Anyone who has visited the North will recognize that this idea is still alive and well—too often in overweening pride and grandiose monuments, but at bottom in an insistence on national dignity.

MONARCHY, REVOLUTION, THERMIDOR

The North Korean people have known only millennia of monarchy and a century of dictatorship—Japanese from 1910 to 1945, where in the late stages of colonial rule Koreans had to worship the (Japanese) emperor, and the hegemony of the Kim family for the past sixty-seven years. We can begin with monarchy, then an anticolonial revolution, and finally that odd term, *thermidor*, that Crane Brinton and others used to describe the reaction against the French Revolution.

Korean culture is steeped in the ceremony, ritual, literature, poetry, lore, and gossip of royal families—and especially which son would succeed the king. Many did so at a young age. The greatest of kings, Sejong, under whom the unique Korean alphabet was promulgated, took office in 1418 at the age of twenty-one, assisted by the regency of his father. Like Kim Jong Un, he was the third son; the eldest son was banished from Seoul for rudeness, and the middle son became a Buddhist monk. Kim Jong Nam, Kim Jong Il's first son, embarrassed everyone by getting caught entering Japan under a pseudonym (hoping to visit Disneyland, it is said) and prefers to reside in Macao, the gambling capital of the world. Virtually nothing is known about the middle son, and neither appeared at their father's funeral.

The penultimate Korean king, Kojong, was a mere eleven when he took the throne in 1864, guided by his father—a powerful regent known as the Taewôn'gun—until he reached maturity. During his regency, the father reenergized the dominant ideology (neo-Confucianism), practiced a strict seclusion policy against several empires knocking at the Korean door, and fought both France (1866) and the United States (1871) in serious wars; two years later the new Meiji leadership in Japan came very close to invading Korea. This was the Hermit Kingdom at its height, and *kukch'e* was a particularly prominent concept under the Taewôn'gun's exclusionary foreign policy. But when Kojong came of age, he sought modern reforms, signed unequal treaties opening Korea to commerce, and tried to play the imperial powers off against each other. It worked for a quarter century, and then it didn't; opening

up merely staved off the eventual and predictable end—the obliteration of
Korean sovereignty in 1910. At the Revolutionary Museum in Pyongyang,
fronted by a sixty-foot statue of Kim Il Sung, visitors witness a paean of
praise to the Taewôn'gun, stone monuments from his era meant to ward off
foreign barbarians, and breast-beating tributes to Korean "victories" against
the French and the Americans. After 1989, Kim Jong Il opined many times
that communism had fallen in the West because of the dilution and erosion
of ideological purity, a formulation that the Taewôn'gun's neo-Confucian
scribes would have liked.

THE KIM MONARCHY

Kim Jong Il told Secretary of State Madeleine Albright, when she met with
him in Pyongyang in October 2000, that he found the Thai monarchy quite
interesting. The Thai king is different than, say, the British royal house in
genuinely being revered by his people, with laws against insulting him (the
British, to the contrary, take delight in mocking the royal family). Thailand
has swung between constitutional monarchy and military coups, but the king
abides. A more salient example, perhaps, was Kim Il Sung's close relationship with Prince Norodom Sihanouk. They were very close friends, more than
any other foreign figure for Kim it seems, and of course he set up a big villa
near Pyongyang for Sihanouk during his long exile. The latter was (and still
is) one of the most knowledgeable leaders in the world; I still remember seeing him at a press conference in Beijing after he had gone into exile, and some
American reporter asked him about "the state of freedom" in Cambodia under
Pol Pot. Sihanouk let out a high-pitched giggle, and said in a polite way that
the question itself was an absurdity. Whatever Americans might think, both
Sihanouk and Kim were generally revered by their people. And, I suppose, it
takes one king to know another.

   North Korea is a bundle of contradictions, because its leaders are preg-
nant with ideas that can't really be voiced in our time. Karl Marx was famously opaque on what the nuts and bolts of a communist political system
might look like, so Lenin filled that vacuum with "the dictatorship of the
proletariat," which became the dictatorship of the Politburo; even so, Lenin
and his successor Stalin provided no reliable guidance on the mechanisms
of leadership transition. Pyongyang has filled that vacuum with monarchical
succession, but cannot say so because it smacks of feudalism. The North's
philosophy of rule bears close resemblance to what Koreans traditionally
said about their kings—or what Hegel said about the German monarch—but
they cannot admit that, either.

Belief in bloodlines and genealogy is as old as the hills in Korea, and while the North's scribes spill a lot of ink about the perfect bloodlines of the Kim family, that was clearly a big stretch when it came to Kim Jong Il, who knew from his first moments of consciousness that he could never live up to his father—and so did everybody else. Belief in ethnic purity and homogeneity is a staple of Korean culture in North and South, but it smacks of racism to non-Koreans, and modern science has completely debunked it (Korean DNA is most similar to Japanese and Mongolian DNA, yet all anyone on either side of the East Sea emphasizes is Korean and Japanese *difference*). It is entirely predictable, based on ancient Korean political practice, that sooner or later the scribes would declare Kim Il Sung's bloodline to be the purest and best of all. When we read a recent account of Hegel's theory of the monarch, the resonance with North Korea's ideology is marked. As Eli Diamond put it, "The general intention of Hegel's justification of the hereditary monarchical principle is to provide an institutional corrective to a purely liberal standpoint. . . . The immovable unity of the state is embodied in the undivided unity of the monarch's rule, in contrast to the insuperable division of civil society." Diamond goes on to say that "the monarch is a *subjectivity* that makes decisions that are to a large extent arbitrary, in a way that is tolerable to citizens, since it is done from a perspective beyond the political fray. . . . This moment of arbitrary decision is necessary, because there are always various possible ways of looking at any practical matter, and opposed opinions on these matters can create deep divisions within government. At the same time, as belonging to the well-informed thinking will of the monarch, these decisions will not be wholly arbitrary and devoid of human reason."[20]

Marxist-Leninist ideology has been converted to a native doctrine in the DPRK, "*juche*," or *chuch'e*, which began as a predictable form of anti-colonial nationalism, generally translated as self-reliance but meaning a withdrawal from the world economy and attempts at independent development. But it slowly evolved into an idealist metaphysic that bears close resemblance to Korean neo-Confucian doctrines and, again, to Hegel's philosophical idealism. Or as high-level defector Hwang Jang Yop put it simply, the two Kims "turned Stalinism and Marxism-Leninism on their heads by reverting to Confucian notions."[21] To put the matter slightly differently than Hwang did, North Korea has turned Marx on his head—or put Hegel back on his feet—by arguing that "ideas determine everything."

It is not clear that anyone, including Hegel himself, quite understood what he meant by the constant invocation of the term "subjectivity,"[22] but that is the usual dictionary definition of *chuch'e* in South Korea and Japan. And further, "the organic unity of the powers of the state itself implies that it is *one single mind* which both firmly establishes the universal and also brings it into its determinate actuality and carries it out." With this, and especially with his endless emphasis on "mind" ("the nation state is mind in its substantive rationality"), and the identification of "one single mind" with the monarch,[23] Hegel merely expresses a mid-nineteenth-century German version of an ancient Korean truth.

In his "Philosophical Rebuttal of Buddhism and Taoism,"[24] the famous philosopher and architect of fourteenth-century Chosôn reforms Chông To-jôn wrote, "The mind combines principle and material force to become master of the body. . . . [Principle] is also received by the mind and becomes virtue. . . . Principle is truly embodied on our minds." In the same discourse, Kwôn Kûn wrote, "Only after one is able to embody humanity, make complete the virtue of his mind, and constantly maintain without fail the principle with which he is born, can he be called human without being embarrassed."

The human condition is none other than *virtue*, embodied in *mind* (conceived organically as brain, heart, and body integrated); virtue-in-mind is what makes us different from animals. Not only that, but it is the "cause by which material force comes into existence"! Now if we make the "postmodern" stipulation that we are all subjective creatures (not objective rational actors), and that therefore we construct our own realities and call them things like books, then Chông To-jôn does seem to be saying that humans create their universe—but not just any human, only those humans who, through long study, have cultivated the virtues that are the sine qua non of having the capability to judge, to decide, to lead, to teach, and thus to create. At the apex, of course, is the monarch, a perfected human being, "the supreme mind of the nation," and woe be it to the person who challenges his authority or denies that he can walk on water.

Just like Korean philosophers, Hegel overcomes the difficulty of deciding *who* should be king by relying on bloodlines; for practical political reasons, he thought, the monarch's accession to the throne has to be hereditary: "It is the hereditary principle of succession that guarantees this unmoved quality, the *majesty* of the monarch. An elected head of state, and hence the state itself, is associated with one political perspective to the exclusion of others, and generally turns the state on its head, compromising the majesty of the monarch by grounding the sovereign's legitimacy in the attitudes and opinions of the masses, rather than having the sovereign be self-grounded and the source of the rights of the people."[25]

It was none other than Karl Marx who cut his intellectual teeth by ripping these justifications for monarchy to shreds, and he no doubt flips in his grave to hear the monarchical Koreans call themselves communists. "Hegel thinks he has proven," Marx wrote in 1843, "that the subjectivity of the state, sovereignty, the monarch, is 'essentially characterized as *this* individual, in abstraction from all his other characteristics, and this individual is raised to the dignity of monarch in an immediate, natural fashion, i.e., through his birth in the course of nature.' Sovereignty, monarchial dignity, would thus be born. The *body* of the monarch determines his dignity. . . . Birth would determine the quality of the monarch as it determines the quality of cattle. Hegel has demonstrated that the monarch must be born, which no one questions, but not that birth makes one a monarch." Or, to put the point simply, for Marx, if a man becomes monarch by birth, this "can as little be made into a metaphysical truth as can the Immaculate Conception of Mary." And even more simply: "The body of [the King's] son is the reproduction of his own body, the creation of a royal body."[26] Because of the emperor system in Japan and the monarchy in Korea, Hegel's thought was always influential on scholars in both countries; indeed, An Ho-sang, the education minister under the First Republic in the South, had studied Hegelian philosophy in prewar Germany and was a lifelong exponent of his own idiosyncratic version of *chuch'e*.

A SINGLE, THIN STRAND OF THE PAST

In his book *Splendid Monarchy*, Tak Fujitani shows in engrossing detail how the post-1868 Meiji elite invented what came to be known as Japanese tradition, as part of a newly engineered centralization of power in Tokyo amid a multitude of mostly independent domains. It was a self-conscious design to build a modern nation and weld a mostly peasant society to the new idea that they were part of something called "Japan," and to create a new and potent nationalism. In the course of this argument, he remarks that "believability can be engineered by dominant groups."[27] North Korea's entire history is testimony to this truth.

Japan's parcelized sovereignty was not a problem in Korea, in that almost everything important had been centralized in Seoul for centuries, and millennia of kings and queens had come and gone, creating a vast cultural panorama of ruling practice, royal stories, poetry, lore, and gossip. By contrast, in Japan the emperor was "taken out of the cupboard and dusted off"; for most inhabitants of these four islands, he had not been an important figure: one emperor was murdered in exile, another escaped to a remote island hidden "under a load of dried fish," and so on. No one could ever say that about Korean monarchs, and when the last effective king died in 1919, Kojong's place in the heart of his people detonated the March First Movement against the Japanese, the touchstone of Korean nationalism ever since.

Fujitani makes the important point that this is a modern politics, not "feudal" as Maruyama Masao had written; the emperor system was not part of an incomplete or backward modernity, but was a form of modernity itself;[28] think, for example, of the British monarchy. However much Americans may find the North Korean regime loathsome, it too is a form of modernity. The Japanese emperor is also presumed to represent an immortal, perfect, unsullied monarchy tracing back to the mists of time, having neither youth nor old age, only health and no disease, representing "the immutability of the political order." The Japanese, suffused in neo-Confucian doctrine just like Koreans, underlined the benevolence, beneficence, and even love of the emperor: "There is nothing better for the well-being of the state than to make the people love the ruler," one scribe wrote. An intimacy between ruler and ruled should be cultivated, thus "to make it unbearable to part from the ruler." The male royal gaze even becomes "motherly," as soldiers during the Pacific War took comfort in the "loving, forgiving, all-embracing" imperial image.[29] Then the ruler's family becomes an object of worship too, to insinuate power into the living room, so to speak (and the bedroom: when is the princess ever going to produce a son?, etc.). The family is the core building block of the state, the ruling family its symbol, its gendered model, and also the alter ego of the citizenry, the charismatic object of attention, curiosity, gossip—Princess Diana was the epitome of all of this (and the North Koreans put out a postage stamp with her face on it). Think also of the global media attention to Prince William's recent wedding—it nicely illustrated Bagehot's observation in 1867 that "a princely marriage is the brilliant edition of a universal fact, and as such, it rivets mankind."[30]

The venerable city of Kyoto, Fujitani wrote, was the singular core place in Japan that "embodied the authentic history, that single and thin strand out of the past that the regime certified as significant." For North Korea, the single, thin strand was the establishment of Manchukuo as a second Korea, on the bitterly redolent date of March 1, 1932, and the resistance it immediately spawned, symbolized by their ubiquitous revolutionary opera, *The Sea of Blood*. The North Korean elite draw a straight line from 1932 down to the present; this founding moment is also the fount of their legitimacy, the original source from which all honor and power flows. Historians who point out that this moment is saturated with myth and exaggeration are right, but they miss Fujitani's point about how power engineers its own myths. But think also, for example, about Kim Il Sung's decadelong fight against the Japanese in the bitterest imaginable conditions, as compared to Castro's attack on the Moncada Barracks, or John F. Kennedy's heroism in saving much of the crew of his PT 109: the North had much more to work with, much more with which to make myths. But what is amazing about this regime, seemingly, is that they prefer myths and lies to what would be an eminently useful truth. Perhaps they learned too well something that historians tend to forget: power chooses its own history, its own heroes, and the sacred truths that serve its purposes; what actually happened makes little difference to engineered believability.

All modern states privilege one kind of history and engage in the erasure of others and the subjugation of alternatives; it's just that North Korea does it so obviously, with barely any attempt to conceal its intent, and with what appears to be a morbid fear of alternative histories; much of its propaganda would insult the intelligence of a ten-year-old. Partly this is because it is, of course, a solipsistic dictatorship, but also because modern Korea has been divided since 1945, with a top-to-bottom set of histories, alternatives, and erasures in the South—and because Koreans take history so seriously; to become "history" in the curious American sense, of oblivion and irrelevance, is to imagine the disappearance of one's self and its connection to parents, ancestors, and progeny—a rupture in the "great chain of being" that promises permanent, irreparable oblivion.

In a reversal of Michel Foucault's influential idea that modern power is both ubiquitous and hidden, such that people surveil themselves, he noted that Napoleon's face "loom[ed] over everything with a single gaze which no detail, however minute, can escape." His gaze was so strong as "to render useless both the eagle and the sun."[31] The emperor's gaze carries immanent power: the people see the emperor, and he sees them—he is watching them, he embodies correct behavior, he expects their correct behavior—and thus the awesome and also unnerving sight of hundreds of thousands of people marching through Pyongyang, or playing intricate card games in unison at the 150,000-seat Kim Il Sung stadium. It is almost unnecessary to point out that Kim Il Sung's gaze is the first thing babies see when they are born, the face on the wall of every home when babies are made, and the last face seen by the dying. Like Maruyama, however, Foucault assumes that Napoleon is part of the "ancient" fabric of France, whereas Fujitani sees this, too, as another instance of modern forms of power.

On the last page of his book, Fujitani asks why, in spite of the demystification of all these things, people still believe in the dominant national narratives, even though they are entirely modern constructs (in Japan, North Korea, or anywhere else). Why does your quarter say "In God We Trust"? This did not exist on coinage before 1874, and was made into the U.S. national motto very recently—in 1956, as part and parcel of the Cold War. Yet it is made to seem eternal—and believed to be eternal among certain Christian groups, namely, the idea (which never occurred to the Founding Fathers) that the United States is, first of all, a Christian nation. Take a close look at your dollar bill—it says *novus ordo seclorum*: a new order for the ages, a quintessential idea of the Founding Fathers. Here was a new, exceptional nation that, in John Quincy Adams' words, made the world's monarchies tremble. (He also said, famously, that Americans do not go abroad in search of monsters to destroy. Yet that's all we have done since 1950—and not very effectively.)

THINK ABOUT WHAT WE SEE

To know that the North Korean regime is unlikely to collapse anytime soon, we don't need an exegesis on Korean and Japanese monarchical history. We just need to observe the leadership stability that followed on the death of Kim Il Sung, and the symbolism of Kim Jong Il's funeral procession on a wintery January day. Kim Jong Il's brother-in-law, Jang Song Taek, walked behind Kim Jong Un; Jang, sixty-five, has long been entrusted with command of the most sensitive security agencies. Behind him was Kim Ki-nam, a man in his eighties who was a close associate of Kim Il Sung. Three generations walking solemnly alongside the vintage mid-1970s armored Lincoln Continental carrying the coffin of Kim Jong Il, and strolling on the other side of the limousine, top commanders of the military in what has to be modern history's most amazing garrison state, with the fourth largest army in the world.

On the grandson's birthday, January 8, 2012 (his birth year still seems to be a secret, but it was 1983 or 1984), Pyongyang television ran an hour-long documentary bathing him in every North Korean virtue and identifying him with every salient place or monument visited by Kim Il Sung, but especially White Head Mountain (Baekdusan), the vast volcanic peak on the Sino-Korean border, mythical fount of the Korean people, site of some of Kim's anti-Japanese guerrilla battles in the 1930s, and purported birthplace of Kim Jong Il in 1942. Most interesting, however, was Jong Un's body language: tall, hefty, grinning, pressing the flesh, already a politician, a hearty individual seemingly at home with his sudden role as "beloved successor." Erased was the dour, dyspeptic, cynical, and ill-at-ease Kim Jong Il, swaddled in a puffed-up ski jacket, his face hidden behind enormous sunglasses. Most important, in visage and personal style, Jong Un is the spitting image of his grandfather when he came to power in the late 1940s, even to the point of shaving his sideburns up high (the documentary pointedly featured photos of Kim Il Sung with the same haircut). It is as if the DNA passed uncontaminated through son to grandson—and no doubt that is what the regime wants its people to believe.

These rituals were markedly similar to those when Kim Il Sung died, but it will be interesting to see if Kim Jong Un follows the same three-year mourning ritual—so far he has not, visiting military units and appearing publicly elsewhere. Certainly it is in his interest to lay low and gain experience, while the seasoned old guard runs the country. Furthermore, with American and

South Korean presidential elections later in 2012 (the current Korean president, a hard-liner whom the North loathes, cannot run again), top leader Hu Jintao stepping down in China, and Putin's political dominance now less of a certainty in Russia, biding one's time is smart. But Jong Un has unquestionably (if instantly) become the face of the regime, one much more agreeable to the public than Kim Jong Il's.

Still, my Soviet informant was right and I was wrong about the significance of bodily appearances: regardless of what he looks like, the king can do no wrong—he can even shoot several eagles on his first golf round (as Kim Jong Il's acolytes claimed). In a classic book, *The King's Two Bodies*, Ernst Kantorowicz wrote that there were two kings: the frail, human, and mortal vessel who happens to be king, and the eternal king who endures forever as the symbol of the monarchy. The latter is a superhuman presence, an absolutely perfect body representing the God-king, maintained through the centuries as an archetype of the exquisite leader. In death the body natural disappears, but the soul of the God-king passes on to the next king. In Pyongyang this translated into Kim Il Sung's "seed" bringing forth his first son, Jong Il, continuing the perfect bloodlines that his scribes never tire of applauding—and now, a fortiori, Jong Un. The family line thus becomes immortal, explaining why Kim Il Sung was not just president for life but remained president of the DPRK in his afterlife.

The Koreans thus made the dead Kim Il Sung president for eternity, all imperfections erased, and now his elaborate mausoleum is the most important edifice in the country. His own body has now morphed into three. But Jong Un's mimetic face, one imagines, will make the population quickly forget about Kim Jong Il, whose seventeen-year reign was one of flood, drought, famine, the effective collapse of the economy, and mass starvation leading to hundreds of thousands of deaths—the time of troubles expected to follow on the death of the dynastic founder. Kim had one singular, if dubious achievement: the acquisition of nuclear weapons. (But here a lot of credit goes also to the ignorantly provocative "Bush doctrine," which listed the DPRK along with Iraq and Iran not just as an "axis of evil," but as targets for preemptive attack.)

CONCLUSION: UNDERSTANDING DIFFERENCE

By virtue of my wife's position at the University of Virginia, we live in one of ten campus "pavilions" designed by Thomas Jefferson nearly two hundred years ago. Here is one hallowed ground that is not "history," that typically American term for the obliterated, beside-the-point past. He is still "Mr. Jefferson" to everyone, and to hear people talk, he often seems "perfect"—but the brick shed where slaves kept their tools still sits in our garden. In early 2012, a museum in Washington and the curators at his Monticello home both opened exhibitions devoted to exploring the grandest of American contradictions, that between a slavery that lasted so far into the modern world, and the brilliant author of these indelible words: "We hold these truths to be self-evident: that all men are created equal." Jefferson aimed squarely at the ubiquitous political form in the world—the "Divine Right of Kings"—in announcing a new nation, founded on principles of equality and democracy. Then he journeyed home to his Monticello slaves. We human beings all, consciously or not, live within our complicated and contested history and search for a usable past.

North Korea is thus a modern form of monarchy, realized in a highly nationalistic, postcolonial state. Americans have such trouble understanding this because most have not subjected their own liberal assumptions and beliefs, their own subjectivity, to a thorough inquiry and self-criticism. "The social unity expressed in the 'body of the despot,'" Fredric Jameson pointed out, is political, but also analogous to various religious practices. That the favored modern practice of former colonies should be embodied nationalism (the resistance leader's body, the body politic, the national body) is also entirely predictable. But the Western Left (let alone liberals) utterly fails to understand "the immense Utopian appeal of nationalism"; its morbid qualities are easily grasped, but its healthy qualities for the collective and for the tight unity that postcolonial leaders crave, are denied.[32] When you add to postcolonial nationalism Korea's centuries of royal succession and neo-Confucian philosophy, it might be possible to understand North Korea as an unusual but predictable combination of monarchy, anti-imperial nationalism, and Korean political culture.

We who live in Western liberal society have our subconscious automatically (if imperfectly) produced from birth, and we take for granted the relatively stable societies that we join as adults, so that we do what is expected without necessarily thinking about it. Civil society is thus internalized and reproduced, as an outcome of centuries of Western political practice. The creation of such habits, however, the spontaneous production of good citizens and good workers, loyal subjects who are also afforded the opportunity of disloyalty, appears as an opaque mystery where it does not exist—how can social exchange be so open, so fluid, so simultaneously orderly and threatening even to the powers, and yet so stable? "The ways by which people advance toward dignity and enlightenment in government," George F. Kennan wrote, "are things that constitute the deepest and most intimate processes of national life. There is nothing less understandable to foreigners, nothing in which foreign influence can do less good." It is our blindness, our hidden complex of unexamined assumptions, that constitutes the core of Kim hating—what makes him simultaneously so laughable, so impudent, and so outrageous; we revile him, while he thumbs his nose at us and our values and gets away with it. We have proved over seven decades that we do not understand North Korea, cannot predict its behavior, and cannot do anything about it—however much we would like to. We can do something about our prejudices.

What is entirely predictable, in my view, is that North Koreans will welcome the only handsome face of authority that all but the most elderly Koreans have known, the founder of the country, the "fatherly leader," now reincarnated. He may not yet be thirty, but if my Soviet interlocutor was right (and he has been for three decades), we are going to see Kim Jong Un's face for a long, long time.

NOTES

1. The idea for this chapter began with an 1,800-word editorial that I did for *Le Monde Diplomatique* in January 2012.

2. See his "The Coming Collapse of North Korea," *Wall Street Journal*, June 25, 1990.

3. Naewoe Press, *North Korea: Uneasy, Shaky Kim Jong-il Regime* (Seoul: ROK Government, 1997), 143.

4. Victor Cha, "China's Newest Province," *New York Times*, December 19, 2011.

5. www.businessweek.com/news/2012-01-17/north-korea-trade-rebounds-on -growing-partnership-with-china.html.

6. Kang Chol Hwan, "Three Preconditions for North Korea's Democratization," *Chosun Ilbo*, October 25, 2011, reprinted in *Korea Focus*, February 2012.

7. Korean Central News Agency, April 5 and 24, May 4, 2009.

8. On May 28, 2009, I was interviewed for more than thirty minutes by CNN's "Anderson Cooper 360," but the only clip they used was the few seconds where I said Kim Jong Il wasn't crazy—giving "the other side of the story" after a retired American general had said he clearly was.

9. Robert A. Wampler introduced the collection with his essay, "North Korea's Collapse? The End Is Near—Maybe," October 26, 2006. I am part of Dr. Wampler's declassification project at the National Security Archive and appreciate his making these documents available to me. The CIA's January 21, 1998, report (about the 1997 conference) is titled, "Exploring the Implications of Alternative North Korean Endgames: Results from a Discussion Panel on Continuing Coexistence between North and South Korea," which is mostly declassified except for some redacted names.

10. Eberstadt, "Tear Down This Tyranny," *Weekly Standard*, November 29, 2004.

11. The best account of the knock-down, drag-out internal struggles is Mike Chinoy, *Meltdown: The Inside Story of the North Korean Nuclear Crisis* (New York: St.

Martin's, 2008). Chinoy's deeply informed book exemplifies the ideal that investigative journalism is the first draft of history.

12. I argue this point at some length in *The Korean War: A History* (New York: Random House Modern Library, 2010).

13. Chinoy, *Meltdown*, 68.

14. Bruce B. Auster and Kevin Whitelaw, "Pentagon Plan 5030, A New Blueprint for Facing Down North Korea," *U.S. News and World Report*, July 21, 2003; see also Chinoy, *Meltdown*, 234.

15. Quoted in the *Chicago Tribune*, April 4, 1994.

16. Susan Rosegrant in collaboration with Michael D. Watkins, "Carrots, Sticks, and Question Marks: Negotiating the North Korean Nuclear Crisis" (Harvard University, John F. Kennedy School of Government, 1995), 2, 33–35.

17. Rosegrant and Watkins, "Carrots, Sticks, and Question Marks," 34–35. See also Chinoy, *Meltdown*, 279.

18. Chinoy, *Meltdown*, 50, 298.

19. Gari Keith Ledyard, contribution to Koreanstudies@koreaweb.ws, February 12, 2002.

20. Eli Diamond, "Hegel's Defence of Constitutional Monarchy and its Relevance within the Post-national State," *Animus* 9 (2004), www.swgc.mun.ca/animusDiamond, pp. 115–16.

21. Bradley Martin, *Under the Loving Care of the Fatherly Leader* (New York: St. Martin's Griffin, 2007), 259.

22. For example, this passage from Hegel's *Philosophy of Right*: "This is also what is required of the activity of the individual will, which 'consists in canceling the contradiction between subjectivity and objectivity and in translating its ends from the subjective determination into an objective one, while at the same time remaining *with itself* in this objectivity.'" In Diamond, "Hegel's Defence," 115.

23. *Hegel's Philosophy of Right*, trans. T. M. Knox (London: Oxford University Press, 1967), pp. 185–87, 212, 289.

24. Translation by John Duncan, in Peter H. Lee, ed., with Donald Baker, Yongho Ch'oe, Hugh H. W. Kang, and Han-Kyo Kim, *Sourcebook of Korean Civilization*, vol. 1 (New York: Columbia University Press, 1993), 454–58, 461.

25. Quoted in Diamond, "Hegel's Defence," 117.

26. Karl Marx, "Notes for a Critique of Hegel's Philosophy of Right," 1843, www.marxists.org/archive/marx/works/1843/critique-hpr/ch02.htm.

27. Tak Fujitani, *Splendid Monarchy: Power and Pageantry in Modern Japan* (Berkeley: University of California Press, 1998), 103, citing Pierre Bourdieu.

28. Fujitani, *Splendid Monarchy*, 26–27.

29. Fujitani, *Splendid Monarchy*, 156, 161, 171.

30. Quoted in Fujitani, *Splendid Monarchy*, 163.

31. Foucault quoted in Fujitani, *Splendid Monarchy*, 144.

32. Fredric Jameson, *The Political Unconscious* (Ithaca, NY: Cornell University Press, 1981), 295–96, 298; see also Ernst Kantorowicz, *The King's Two Bodies* (Princeton, NJ: Princeton University Press, 1957), 4–14. For an excellent analysis of the nature of the North Korean regime, see Heonik Kwon, "North Korea's Politics of Longing," *Japan Focus*, April 2009.

Chapter Five

North Korea after Kim Jong Il

Victor Cha and Nicholas Anderson

Academic and expert conferences have proliferated in recent months analyzing the meaning of the Arab Spring and the death of Kim Jong Il for Asia. The final verdict of most every analyst who discussed the North Korea case is that revolution akin to what took place in Tunisia, Egypt, and other places is impossible. They argue that the regime's stability in the aftermath of the events in the Middle East and Kim's death is an "old question" that was answered in the 1990s when the DPRK (Democratic People's Republic of Korea) faced the most critical challenge of its life, and survived. The death of Kim Il Sung, the collapse of the Soviet Union, the drastic cuts in patron aid from China, and the onset of famine that killed thousands all constituted the ultimate test of DPRK stability, and the regime staggered on through it all. Thus, these scholars and intelligence analysts argue that the Arab Spring and the dynastic succession to Kim Jong Un have little relevance for DPRK stability. The scholarly literature tends to support this assessment. Scholars have argued that the late Kim Jong Il had effectively "coup-proofed" himself through an elaborate system of patronage, bribery, and draconian rule.[1] The only way his rule could have ended was as it did—through a massive heart attack and sudden death, not through revolution.

This may be true, but the phenomenal events that have taken place in the Middle East and North Africa have shown us two things. First, in spite of all the reasons for thinking that things won't change, they could, and quite suddenly. And second, the mere existence of variables that could spell the collapse of an authoritarian regime tells us nothing about when or if that collapse could happen. Among the ruins of collapsed dictatorships in Libya, Egypt, and Tunisia, experts have picked out causes that have long been in existence, yet they cannot explain why they led to collapse in 2011 as opposed to decades earlier. Dictators who have fallen in the tumultuous protests of the Arab

Spring, Saleh of Yemen, Ben Ali of Tunisia, Mubarak of Egypt, and Qaddafi of Libya, had each been in power longer than Kim Jong Il had in North Korea. Can we simply assume that events in the Middle East in combination with the death of Kim Jong Il have no bearing on the North Korean regime?

To dismiss the relevance of these two major events by saying the 1990s constituted the critical case test of DPRK stability is to answer an old question with an old answer. We argue that the 1990s crisis and the situation today should not be viewed as two discrete time periods, but as a continuum—a continuum during which Pyongyang may have survived, but in its crisis, it set off divisive processes in DPRK politics and society that have taken root and are now over twenty years in development. Exogenous shocks like the Arab Spring and the death of Kim Jong Il may have less direct material impact on the DPRK like the crisis of the 1990s, but it comes at a time when North Korean society is a far cry from its monolithic state over two decades ago. We argue that political and social dynamics since the 1990s crisis have been moving in opposite directions, and that this gap is only being widened by the leadership transition from Kim Jong Il to his son. Ironically we should pay less attention to scholars and experts who dismiss the Arab Spring's relevance and more attention to the late Kim Jong Il's actions in the aftermath of the Middle East tumult—these do not look like the actions of a leader confident that his worst days were left behind some twenty years ago. Do the post–Kim Jong Il rulers in North Korea, led by the "Great Successor" Kim Jong Un, fear their own version of an Arab Spring?

THE CAUSES

Answering the question of the Arab Spring's meaning for North Korea necessitates getting down to the root causes of popular revolutions and uprisings. The events that took place and continue to take place across the Middle East and North Africa since early 2011 are historic in their scope and scale. The dramatic self-immolation of Mohamed Bouazizi, a frustrated and humiliated twenty-six-year-old vegetable vendor in Tunisia, set off the greatest movement for political change the region has seen since the fall of the Ottoman Empire some ninety years ago. In the months that have followed, men, women, and children—individuals young and old—have risen up to challenge their governments in the face of violence and even death. From Tunisia it spread to Algeria. And then to Libya. And from Libya on to Egypt. Within a few months, nearly every single state in the region, in one way or another, had to deal with popular uprisings of some sort. And the reverberations didn't end at the edge of the desert. The Chinese government reportedly firewalled their Internet against searches of "Egypt," "Jasmine Revolution," and "Arab Spring." And in North Korea, orders were given to ban all public gatherings. On the surface, Bouazizi's dramatic suicide was the immediate cause, but there were obviously much larger forces at work that turned this single event into a mass movement. The causes for the Arab Spring can be divided at least five ways: modernization theories, development gap theories, demographic theories, contagion theories, and regime-type theories.

One collection of possible explanations falls under what political scientists refer to as "modernization theory."[2] What this body of work argues is that the process of human development brought about by socioeconomic modernization leads to increased levels of desire for, movement toward, and eventual sustenance of democratic forms of government. What is generally seen across societies, whether they are Arab, Asian, African, or American, is that the process of modernization brings with it similar traits. Things such as urbanization, the rise of literacy rates and education levels, civic organizations, a more secular public sphere, market-type economies, the emergence of a property-owning middle class, and the temperance of class divisions tend to accompany societal modernization. With these developments, individuals tend to think less about where they are getting their next meal, and more about how their government is performing. Put simply, when wealth increases and individuals begin to develop, they are implicitly given a stake in the system. Once citizens get a taste of a better life, their expectations and demands grow exponentially faster. The body of literature, though, isn't a coherent whole, as there is some contention over whether modernization actually leads to the *initiation* of democratization, or whether it simply aids in its *consolidation*, post-transition.[3] But the unifying idea is that these economic, social, and political changes take place simultaneously and are mutually reinforcing, and that the causal arrow generally runs from development to democracy. Thus, from this perspective, it was not popularly held notions of dire poverty and other such grievances that set the Arab Spring in motion. Rather, it was, at least in part, minimal levels of empowerment through socioeconomic development.[4]

Modernization is measured by looking at levels of individual wealth in societies. Though an imperfect measure, what is generally found is that societies with higher levels of individual wealth, unless of course they are primarily oil-exporting petro-states, will be more prone to movements toward democracy. It is not the wealth per se that leads to mass movements, but the factors listed above, such as health and education, which tend to accompany this wealth and lead populations to demand political change. Though there is no consensus here, most cite figures of approximately $7,000 per capita GDP as the socioeconomic level of development beyond which a country is increasingly likely to transition to democracy, and $1,000 as the level below which a transition is highly unlikely.[5]

Tunisia, for example, is in fact a surprisingly modern society, with the average Tunisian making nearly $3,800 in 2010. While this may not seem like a lot to developed-world audiences, it is significantly more than the average Chinese, Indian, or Indonesian, as well as eighty or so other countries in the world. The UN Human Development Index, which combines measures of health, education, and income, puts Tunisia in the 68th percentile in the world, a full ten points above the regional average. Egypt displayed similar characteristics, though less starkly than Tunisia. In Egypt, the average individual made $2,270 in 2010, and while that doesn't put it in the class of Luxembourg ($105,044), it is also not with Burundi ($160). With regard to its human development, Egypt sits at the 62nd percentile, which is still well above the regional average. In Libya, too, we see a relatively modern society. Its per capita GDP of $9,714 is artificially inflated by the fact that the country derives nearly 60 percent of its GDP from oil exports, but a good portion of this does seem to trickle downward. Its human development rating is in the 75th percentile, significantly higher than Tunisia, Egypt, and most other regional states, and its life expectancy is seventy-five years. Syrian society exhibits similar tendencies, with a per capita level of wealth at about $2,500 and a human development ranking at just below the 60th percentile. But in some of the cases the modernization theory seems to reach its limits. For instance, in 2010 the average Yemeni made just over $1,000, and its Human Development Index rating is at about the 40th percentile, nearly twenty percentage points below the regional average.[6] So it seems there must be more at play here.

Rather than focusing on the individual, some look at broad societal economic development as a possible catalyst of unrest.[7] If growth in the overall economy occurs in a rapid fashion, it often outpaces the political institutions that make up the society and can lead to instability. This phenomenon is akin to what the late Harvard political scientist Samuel Huntington referred to as a "development gap": people's aspirations increase at a faster rate than the government is able to meet them. Their "wants" begin to form faster than they can be satisfied.[8] What really distinguishes this idea from the modernization theory is that rather than economic, social, and political changes taking place simultaneously, they in fact run on their own trajectories, and this creates tension which can lead to upheaval. There is some evidence of this in a number of the Arab Spring countries, as the past decade has been marked by steady economic growth but stagnant authoritarianism.

In Libya, for instance, the economy has grown at an average of just over 4 percent per year, peaking at 13 percent in 2003, with only modest increases in its population. Tunisia, too, has grown at an average rate of 4.5 percent per year over the past ten years, adding only about 10 percent to its total population during that time. Yemen as well, believe it or not, has averaged just under 4.5 percent growth per year since 2000, but has seen more substantial population growth numbers. Syria and Egypt also have had growth rates averaging consistently above 4 percent, but their more rapid population growth has taken some of the force from this increased economic power.[9] GDP per capita growth—which captures the effects of population growth—mirrors these developments. Since the year 2000, Egypt experienced a 31 percent increase in its real GDP per capita. Over the same period, Libya's was just under 20 percent, and Syria's just shy of 23 percent. Tunisia, over the past decade, has seen its GDP per capita increase by a full 41 percent, with Yemen trailing quite well behind the rest with just 12 percent growth.[10] And yet while there may be some variation in growth levels among these countries, what they all share in common is political stagnation at the highest levels, something referred to as "authoritarian entrenchment."[11] Saleh of Yemen has been in power since 1990, Ben Ali of Tunisia since 1987, Mubarak of Egypt since 1981, and Qaddafi of Libya since 1979. Bashar al-Assad in Syria took power in 2000, but he inherited the throne from his father, Hafez, who ruled the country for twenty-nine years. In 2010, these five states had either a 6 or a 7 out of 7 (7 is the lowest freedom; 1 is the highest) according to Freedom House's Freedom in the World Index and were all labeled "Not Free."[12] The steady growth of their economies during the 2000s essentially meant that the people began to outgrow their governments.

Another group of theories looks at the demographic makeup of a society.[13] The younger a population is and the less it is employed, the higher are the chances for civil unrest. It is easy to imagine how hundreds of thousands, or even millions of un- or underemployed, disaffected youth can lead to trouble for a government in relatively short order. And in many cases this is what was seen in the Arab Spring, with some referring to what happened in the region as a "youthquake."[14]

Yemen is perhaps the quintessential example of this theory at work. Its median age is just 18 years,[15] and its unemployment rate, the last time it was officially measured (which, tellingly, was 2003), was 35 percent. Libya also seems to fit the bill. Half of the population in the country is under 24.5 years, with an unemployment rate of a whopping 30 percent. Tunisia, too, had a fairly high unemployment rate of 14 percent in 2010, and a median age of 30 years, still significantly lower than developed countries like the United States (37 years), Canada (41 years), and Japan (44 years). Egypt, as well, has a fairly young population, half being under 24.3 years. Yet its unemployment rate is surprisingly low, at just under 10 percent. And Syria also has a relatively young population, with a median age of 21.9 years, but a surprisingly low unemployment rate of its own, floating at just over 8 percent.[16] And so, the sort of hit-and-miss nature of the "youthquake" hypothesis points to the possibility of still more factors making their presence felt.

Getting beyond the internal, structural factors in these societies, there are powerful arguments for external factors as having contributed to the new "Arab Revolt." One such example is what Huntington referred to as "snow-balling," or what commentators have been calling "contagion" effects.[17] A man in Egypt was said to have set himself alight after the inspiration of his Tunisian comrade. Then Facebook groups started popping up all over the region and the world, claiming, "We are all Egyptians now!" The inspiration effect of one country's struggle on another is unquestionable. But how does this happen? In the modern era, the rise of rapid communications technology and the twenty-four-hour news cycle ensures that in all but the most repressive regimes, information is ubiquitous. Although the press in individual countries may be harshly repressed, social media such as Facebook, Twitter, YouTube, and SMS messaging ensures that dictators can no longer plug every leak.

In Tunisia, for instance, 91.8 percent of its 10.6 million people have mobile phones, and 33 percent have Internet access, the highest in North Africa. Similarly in Egypt, 64.7 percent have cell phones, and about 25 percent are Internet users. In Libya, 76 percent have cell phones, and in Yemen, 34 percent. In Syria, too, 37 percent have mobile phones, and just under 20 percent use the Internet regularly.[18] Though some of these numbers may seem small compared to the developed West, they were certainly enough for all of us to see personal footage from inside these movements on the news on a nightly basis. The relatively high literacy rates in these countries, moreover, acts as a force multiplier for these types of media. In Libya it is 89 percent, in Syria 84, in Tunisia 78, in Egypt 66, and even in Yemen, 62. This means that the potential for spread is all the greater. While a literacy rate of 62 percent may not seem all that impressive, it must be remembered that a number of sub-Saharan African states have rates that are less than half that.[19] Through these media, individuals can share information, organize protests, and post pictures and videos online for all to see. But perhaps more important than these new, Internet- and handheld-based social media is the good old television.[20] In the Arab Spring, this is what some referred to as the "Al Jazeera Effect."[21] Libyans saw coverage of the Tunisian revolt on Al Jazeera, which, in part, encouraged them to rise up, followed similarly by Egypt, then by Yemen, and so on. And the relative ubiquity of televisions in society facilitated this effect. In Yemen, for instance, there are at least thirty-four televisions for every one hundred inhabitants. In Egypt there are twenty-four. Syria boasts nineteen, Libya fourteen.[22] Again, while these numbers may not seem all that impressive for the average American (where there are seventy-four TVs for every one hundred people), it is worth remembering that in the world's most impoverished societies, such as Eritrea (0.02/100), Chad (0.1/100), and Tanzania (0.28/100), television is basically nonexistent for the vast majority of the population.[23] And rather than literacy, in the case of the Al Jazeera effect, the force multiplier was the fact that Arabic (the language of Al Jazeera) is widely spoken in at least twenty-eight countries worldwide, basically all situated in the Middle East and North Africa. In this way, protest among Arab states was "contagious," in that it went from one, to the other, to the other, until even the Chinese and the North Koreans began to get nervous.

A final important causal factor has to do with the type of regime in charge of the country.[24] It can be argued that regime types which allow some freedoms in the name of economic growth or as a steam valve for popular dissatisfaction are more liable to face upheaval among their people. It is this type of "soft authoritarianism" that opens up the classic modernizing dictator's dilemma: leaders may allow some freedoms to keep growth rates up, but in doing so they sow the seeds of their own destruction as they lose control of the population.

In Tunisia, this was most certainly the case. According to the Economist Intelligence Unit (EIU) Democracy Index, its civil liberties are rated 3.2 out of 10, and its political culture 5.6, but its electoral process is given a zero. Freedom House echoes these figures, giving the country a 5 out of 7 (higher) for civil liberties but a 7 out of 7 (lower) for political rights. We see similar trends in Egypt. The EIU gives it 5 out of 10 for political culture and 3.5 for civil liberties, but only 0.8 for its electoral process.

Similarly, Egypt is given a 5 (higher) for civil liberties, but a 6 (lower) for its political rights by Freedom House. According to the EIU, Libya scores an impressive 5 of 10 for political culture, but zero for its electoral process. And according to Freedom House, Yemen as well has greater civil liberties (5) than its political rights (6). And finally, in Syria, though political culture is ranked 5.6 out of 10, its electoral process rating is also zero. Freedom House again agrees here, giving Syria a lower political rights ranking (7) than its civil liberties (6).[25] And according to the World Bank, not one of these countries has had a "voice and accountability" ranking greater than the 15th percentile in the past three years, with some (Libya, Syria) barely breaking the 5th percentile.[26] The difference of one or two points on a 0 to 10 (EIU) or 7 to 1 (Freedom House) scale may not seem like much, but it likely proved just enough to set the process of revolt in motion. And so in sum, there appears to be an inherent contradiction in the sort of liberalizing authoritarianism seen in many of these Middle Eastern states. In many cases the people were free to choose their own jobs, their own religions, and even their own civil society organizations, but not their own leaders. And this taste of freedom they have been given seems to have set off a ravenous hunger, which may not be satiated until all of the dictators are gone.

ARAB SPRING IN PYONGYANG?

There are five potential variables—individual socioeconomic development, broader rates of growth, demographics, contagion effects, and regime type—that could bring the Arab Spring to a post–Kim Jong Il North Korea. Do we see the possibility for change in the DPRK from any of these? Not really. There is no development gap in North Korea. Wealth accumulation and economic growth have not been apparent. Rather than modernizing and growing, the society has seen little development. Traversing the streets of Pyongyang, one is struck by how the city skyline and streets, though neatly maintained, have not really seen any development since the 1960s. Not just the architecture, but the public phone booths, trolley cars, street lamps, and other fixtures all look over forty years old. The economy has been contracting. GDP growth, when it was not contracting in the 1990s, has trudged along at unimpressive rates. Per capita gross national income, moreover, has been

Table 5.1.   Economic Growth in the DPRK, 1990–2009

	Per Capita GNI ($US)	GDP Growth (% change)
1990	1,146	−4.3
1991	1,115	−4.4
1992	1,013	−7.1
1993	969	−4.5
1994	992	−2.1
1995	1,034	−4.4
1996	989	−3.4
1997	811	−6.5
1998	573	−0.9
1999	714	6.1
2000	757	0.4
2001	706	3.8
2002	762	1.2
2003	818	1.8
2004	914	2.1
2005	1,056	3.8
2006	1,108	−1.0
2007	1,152	−1.2
2008	1,056	3.1
2009	960	−0.9

Source: The Bank of Korea (2011).

decreasing over the past two decades from $1,146 in 1990 to as low as $573 in 1998, and reaching $960 in 2009—still a net decrease from two decades earlier.

Other signs of a modernizing consumer-oriented society are just not present. Life expectancy is 67.4 years, down from 70.2 years in 1990.[27] One-third of the population is undernourished.[28] Given this state, the people of North Korea do not entertain notions of demanding a new political leadership that can improve their lifestyles. What French philosopher Baron de Montesquieu once referred to as the "spiral of expectations" is absent in North Korea. Such rising expectations only come with a degree of hope, which is nonexistent. Instead, the people are preoccupied with survival, finding their next meal, and staying warm in the depths of winter.

North Korea does have a relatively young and literate population, two important variables for the Arab Spring.[29] The median age is 32.9 years, and literacy rates are near 100 percent.[30] But the likelihood of a "youthquake" is remote. Contrary to what many may think, the North's poor economic performance does not translate into widespread idle and unemployed youth susceptible to lashing out at the government. As a communist economy, first of all, there is technically no unemployment rate, as everyone works for the state. Of course, given that the state cannot pay the workers for months at a time, this population would by any reasonable definition be considered unemployed. But this does not lead to idleness, because most workdays are spent devising coping mechanisms to subsist. The average factory worker at a state-owned enterprise might choose not to continue to work at the factory because he is not getting paid, but he will not quit his job. Instead, he will report to work in the morning, punch the time clock, and then bribe the foreman to allow him to spend the day trying to catch fish or forage for scrap metal that he can sell on the black market. Aside from these coping mechanisms to occupy their time, all young males are gainfully employed for up to twelve years in the military. The DPRK has a military conscription system where service in the army is between five and twelve years, service in the navy five to ten, and in the air force three to four years—by a very wide margin the longest service terms in the entire world.[31] Thereafter, all are obligated to compulsory part-time service until forty and must serve in the Worker/Peasant Red Guard until sixty.[32] This system is set up ostensibly to keep the military strong, but it also serves the purpose of keeping young men harnessed and off the streets. Finally, leisure time in North Korean society, to the extent it exists, is largely spent in ideological indoctrination. There is no idle time when one is serving the "Dear Leader" or "great successor." After school, for example, students will march with their work units to the square in front of Kim Il Sung's mausoleum to practice performances for the spring festival, or they will be in sessions reading about the greatness of Kim Il Sung thought. There do not appear to be objective indicators of an impending youthquake in North Korea anytime soon.

What about a contagion effect? Can news of what happened in the Middle East and North Africa spread to the DPRK? Could a demonstration effect occur where North Koreans do not necessarily identify with the frustrations of a Tunisian street merchant, but where they simply learn of the fact that popular protest is a mode of expressing needs and effecting change? One of the major priorities of human rights NGOs (nongovernmental organizations) on North Korea in the aftermath of the Arab Spring was to try to get as much information as possible into the country about the unprecedented events. After the 2010 artillery shelling of Yeonpyeong Island, the ROK (Republic of Korea) military sent nearly 3 million leaflets into North Korea describing the Arab Spring. Another method entailed flying hot air balloons from islets off the west coast of the peninsula into North Korea. Packages attached to these balloons carried money, food, and newspaper reports about events in the Middle East. If the winds blew in the desired direction, these balloons would land in the North and disseminate information that burst the bubble of tightly controlled information the regime seeks to maintain. But these launches are small scale when it comes to educating an entire population. Moreover, they put North Koreans at great risk if they are caught with these materials by state authorities. Human rights–based and reform-advocacy radio broadcasting NGOs, such as Radio Free Asia, Radio Free Chosun, and NK Reform Radio, also broadcast news of the events in the Middle East into North Korea on a daily basis. But the signals for these broadcasts are often well jammed by the DPRK authorities, and most North Koreans don't have access to the kinds of radios that can pick them up anyway. In order for there to be a contagion effect, you need high literacy rates and social media, or a somewhat free press. In North Korea's case, you clearly have the former but neither of the latter. There is no access to the World Wide Web from within the country, and the only Internet that exists is an "intranet" that connects to tightly controlled government websites. There is only one Twitter and one Facebook account in the whole country (set up by the government). All of North Korea's television stations are state run, with no regional or inter-Korean "Al Jazeera"-type networks. And based on the latest statistics, there are only about five TVs for every one hundred North Koreans.[33] There is no foreign travel, and domestic travel is severely restricted. And it is safe to say that the average North Korean is oblivious to the plethora of personal media and entertainment devices that have become staples in our lives. When I (Cha) traveled to Pyongyang in 2007, I was allowed to keep my iPod, largely because the airport security personnel did not know what the device was. I assured them it could not be used as a communications device within the country (there is no wireless Internet) and that it had only music and videos on it.

The two most interesting recent developments in this regard have been the introduction of cell phones into the country and the opening of a new computer lab at the Pyongyang University of Science and Technology (PUST). In late 2002, the North Koreans introduced cell phones into the country for the exclusive use of the elites in Pyongyang. But in 2004 it banned them after an explosion at the Ryongchon train station looked uncomfortably close to an assassination attempt on Kim Jong Il's leadership train which had passed through the station hours earlier. In the rubble of the blast, officials found what looked to be evidence of a cell phone detonated bomb. In 2008 the Egyptian company Orascom won an exclusive contract worth $400 million to provide cell phones in North Korea.[34] The first year of operation in 2009 started with 70,000 units. There are about 500,000 units now in Pyongyang, but this only represents about 1.8 percent of the population, and the phones do not have the capacity to dial outside of the country.

PUST was opened in October 2010 through the efforts of evangelical Christian Americans and a combination of academic, Christian, and corporate world funders in South Korea.[35] The facility features 160 computers for which a select group of university students are being trained. The use of these computers, however, is heavily restricted to these select students whose job is to glean information from the Internet useful to the state. By comparison, Tunisia had nearly 40 percent of its population conversant with the Internet.[36] This level of exposure to outside information in North Korea is minuscule when compared with that of the Arab countries.

North Korea remains the hardest of hard authoritarian regimes in the world. Unlike South Korea in the 1980s, which shifted to a soft authoritarian model with a burgeoning middle class that eventually demanded its political freedoms in 1987, the North has resisted all change. Those who visit Pyongyang come out claiming that life does not look so bad. People walk freely in the streets without omnipresent military patrols. Society seems very orderly. There are no urban homeless visible. A recent CNN broadcast from Pyongyang showed city dwellers attending a street carnival, eating cotton candy, and texting on their cell phones. These episodic reports, however, misportray a terribly restricted society with draconian controls on all liberties. North Korea still ranks 7 out of 7 (lowest possible score) on Freedom House's Freedom in the World Index, and it has therefore earned the odious title "the Worst of the Worst" for its political rights and civil liberties record.[37] It sits dead last of 167 countries on the EIU's democracy index.[38] It is in the 0th percentile for the World Bank's Voice and Accountability Index and is ranked 196 out of 196 countries in the Freedom of the Press Index.[39] What is astonishing about these rankings is not the absence of movement to a softer form of authoritarianism, necessitated by the need for economic reform, but that the regime has consistently maintained such controls decade after decade with no letting up whatsoever. This persistence stems not from a lack of understanding that some liberalization is necessary for economic reform, but from the Kim regime's conscious choice to prize political control over anything else. This puts the Kim regime in a class of authoritarianism of its own.

Creating political change at home often requires outside resources and a vibrant expatriate community with a political agenda to push for change, according to respected scholars of political diasporas.[40] While it is the average people on the ground that spark mass movements for political change, it is often exiled elites, who fled the country in search of educational and employment opportunities, that support such movements and eventually come back to rebuild and lead their countries.[41] The obvious example from the Arab Spring would be the Egyptian Mohamed ElBaradei, the former IAEA director general who came back to run in Egypt's 2012 general elections.

But there is no real dissident exile community for North Korea like we see with Egypt, Iran, and other cases. Defectors from North Korea show anger toward their former prison guards or toward corrupt bureaucrats, but this surprisingly does not aggregate into an anger to expel the Kim leadership. A July 2008 survey of refugees in Seoul, for example, found that 75 percent had no negative sentiment to then-leader Kim Jong Il.[42] Kang Chol Hwan, the defector who wrote the famous book *Aquariums of Pyongyang*, detailing his life and escape from a North Korean gulag, displayed anger in his writing toward the guards in his camp but not toward Kim Il Sung. A National Geographic documentary, *Inside North Korea*, followed an eye doctor around the country who did cataract surgeries for ailing citizens.[43] After thousands of surgeries, upon having their bandages removed every single patient joyously and immediately thanked Kim Il Sung and Kim Jong Il for their renewed eyesight, not the doctor. Even the news of Kim Jong Il's 2008 stroke elicited empathy rather than anger from defectors:

> [I don't know] whether I should reveal my sadness over Kim Jong-il's health. . . . He is still our Dear Leader. It is the people who work with him and give him false reports who are bad. When I hear about his on-the-spot guidance and eating humble meals, I believe he cares for the people.[44]

This is not to say that dissident movements started by North Korean defectors are wholly absent. The Committee for the Democratization of North Korea (CDNK), Fighters for a Free North Korea (FFNK), and the Citizens' Alliance for North Korean Human Rights are examples of NGOs devoted to creating political change in the North, but relative to other cases, these movements are small and do not pose a direct threat to the regime.

There are several reasons for the lack of a politically active exile community. First, the recent migrants out of North Korea are almost all female and are leaving the country purely for economic reasons.[45] Some 75 percent of recent defectors are from the northern Hamgyong provinces, which is the worst economically hit area of North Korea. Women therefore leave the country purely as an economic coping mechanism to survive rather than to act out political ambitions against the regime. Furthermore, because they most often leave husbands and children behind who wait for much-needed support in the form of food, money, and medicine, these female defectors are unlikely to become political activists and put their families at risk. Prior to the 1990s, the flow of refugees might have been more liable to protest, as it was constituted of male political elites and military officers who left for ideological reasons or because they were accused of committing state crimes. The numbers of these, however, were fairly small (607 total between 1949 and 1989), compared with the recent wave (nearing 20,000 currently resettled in South Korea).[46]

Second, defectors from North Korea have significant enough difficulties adjusting to life outside of the North that preclude the luxury of entertaining ideas about promoting political change in their former home country. Life in South Korea, where many of these defectors resettle, is fast paced and often filled with social challenges, including disadvantages due to lack of education, physical diminutiveness compared to well-fed southerners, and social discrimination in terms of jobs and marriage. Many northerners are engrossed with meeting these challenges, as well as paying off brokers' charges as high as $6,000 for their successful escape to a life that is different, undoubtedly free, but challenging nonetheless. For this reason, many northerners still self-identify, according to defector interviews, as North Korean rather than "Korean" or "South Korean" even after living many years in the ROK. They still feel a sense of pride about their former homeland, and though they are fully cognizant of its shortfalls, most say that if they had to do it all over again, they would still be happy to have been born in the North.[47]

THE REGIME'S CEAUŞESCU/QADDAFI MOMENT

By all of our political science metrics, the DPRK shows no potential to have an Arab Spring. But then why has the regime seemed so worried? Why did the North Korean regime stifle the inflow of all news regarding events in Libya, Egypt, Tunisia, and Syria? Why did they amass tanks and troops in urban centers as a precaution against public gatherings? Why did Pyongyang issue a personal directive in February 2011 to organize a special mobile riot squad of one hundred strong in each provincial office of the Ministry for People's Security? Why did it bolster surveillance of all organizations on university campuses and in residential areas? Why did the government issue a countrywide inventorying of all computers, cell phones, flash drives, and MP3 players among the elite population? Why did they crack down on all public assembly even to the extent of removing dividers in restaurants to prevent unseen gatherings? Why did they threaten to fire artillery on NGO balloons from offshore South Korean islets carrying news of the Arab Spring into North Korea?[48]

Indeed there seems to be a significant gap between what theories of revolution tell us and what the gut instincts of the regime elite tell them. The regime's actions reflect a sense of vulnerability. For Kim Jong Un, the stark fact is that dictators who held power much longer than his father—like Qaddafi of Libya, Mubarak of Egypt, Ben Ali of Tunisia, and others—all have fallen from power, or have been hanging on by their fingernails. This must have sent a chilling message. The fact that all of the political science indicators for revolution were in existence but dormant in the Middle East and North Africa till now must give Kim little comfort about the absence of any such indicators in his own country. The main lesson of the Arab Spring is that authoritarian regimes, no matter how sturdy they look, are all inherently unstable. Or as George Kennan put it, they bear within them "the seeds of [their] own decay."[49] They maintain control through the silence of people's fears, but they also cultivate deep anger beneath the surface. Once the fear dissipates, the anger boils to the surface and can be sparked by any event akin to a Tunisian police officer slapping the face of a street merchant. The late North Korean leader Kim Jong Il admitted to Hyundai founder Chung Ju Yung to having dreams where he was stoned to death in the public square by his people.[50] What the Dear Leader feared was his "Ceaușescu moment" (which can now also be understood as a "Qaddafi moment"). Condoleezza Rice explained this at a 2011 meeting at the Bush Presidential Center in Dallas, Texas, as the moment when the Romanian dictator went out into the streets to quell protests by declaring all the positive things his rule had done for the people. A quieted crowd, once fearful of the leader, listened. Then after a pause, one elderly woman in the crowd yelled out, "Liar!" and others joined in the chant, replacing their fear of the dictator with anger against him. Ceaușescu was subsequently executed in the streets of Târgoviște, Romania. Kim thus must have felt like he was living on borrowed time. A collapsing domino of dictators, many who were personal friends of his and his father's, became the larger context in which the regime was trying to execute a dynastic succession of power to a twenty-something-year-old unprepared young man.

The new North Korean leader must be paranoid about the Arab Spring because he watched fellow dictators lose control in the context of dramatic changes in their own societies, and he has his own challenges stemming from a changing North Korean society. In the early to mid-nineties, as the famine in North Korea kicked into full gear, a process of change emerged which has carried on according to its own "sorcerer's apprentice" logic. To deal with the dilapidated economy, the collapsing public food distribution system, and the masses of starving North Koreans, the authorities began to turn a blind eye to market activities in society. In search of food and opportunity, North Koreans began risking life and limb to cross the border with China by the thousands. Aid agencies such as the World Food Programme and NGOs poured into the North. These experiences, among others, fundamentally altered average North Koreans' frame of reference. The things they have seen and experienced can't be erased or reversed. And so while the regime may be attempting to harden its control from on high, these minimal tastes of freedom experienced by North Koreans make that inherently difficult.

There are two forces at work here in diametrically opposed ways: marketization and ideological reification. After the 2002 economic reforms allowed for some markets to spring up in the North, the society changed permanently. These reforms, which lifted price controls and introduced market mechanisms, were initiated not because of a newfound love for liberalization, but because the public distribution system (PDS) had broken down and the government was essentially telling the citizens to fend for themselves. Markets opened everywhere, and society permanently changed after that. Even with the government's reinstitution of the ration system and crackdown on market activity, citizens refused to rely solely on the government, and according to defectors, the majority of North Korean citizens today rely on the markets for some significant portion of their weekly food, goods, and a wide range of other products. Farmers meet their production quotas and then sell their best produce in the market. Or factory workers at the Kaesong Industrial Complex save their desserts (Choco-pies) from the cafeteria lunch and sell them on the black market. A 2008 study by distinguished Korea scholars Stephan Haggard and Marcus Noland found that more than two-thirds of defectors admitted that half or more of their income came from private business practices.[51] Greater than 50 percent of former urban residents in the DPRK reported that they purchased as much as 75 percent of their food from the market. These numbers were reported, moreover, when the government was in the midst of a crackdown on markets and was aiming to reinstitute the PDS. These markets have become a fixture of life in North Korea that is virtually impossible now to uproot.

Markets create entrepreneurship. And entrepreneurship creates an individualist way of thinking that is alien to the government. This change is slow and incremental, but it affects a good part of the population and is growing every day in a quiet but potent way. The change was evident in the way the people responded to the government's effort to crack down definitively on marketization by instituting a currency redenomination in 2009. This redenomination wiped out the hard work of many families who could exchange only a fraction of their household savings for the new currency. People reacted not with typical obedience out of fear, but with anger and despair. Some committed suicide. Others fought with police who tried to close down the local market. Still others defiantly burned the currency in the public square. The greatest vulnerability for a regime like North Korea is when a population loses its fear of the government. Once the fear is gone, all that is left is the anger.

NEO*JUCHE*'S IDEOLOGICAL RIGIDITY

The inescapable dilemma for Pyongyang is that its political institutions cannot adjust to the changing realities in North Korean society. It can take short-term measures to dampen the anger. After the botched currency redenomination measure, for example, Pyongyang tried to adjust by raising the ceiling on the amount of old currency that citizens could exchange. They also shot the seventy-six-year-old Planning and Finance Department director in public as the scapegoat for the policy mistake. But in the longer term, North Korean political institutions and ideology are growing more rigid, not more flexible, as the leadership undergoes the third dynastic passing of power within the Kim family.

Neo*juche* revivalism is in many ways the worst possible ideology that the regime could follow in parallel with the society's marketization. *Juche*, which is commonly translated as "self-reliance," "independence," or "noninterference," is North Korea's official ideology and, in many ways, its state religion.[52] During the early Cold War years, when the North was as its best, *juche* was held up as the justification for its success (though it was in large part massive amounts of aid and trade from China and the Soviet Union). In the early post–Cold War years, the North Korean leadership moved away from *juche* ideology as it put forth more militaristic forms of ideology and experimented with economic reform. In more recent years, with the North's persistent failures and the need to find a new ideology for the post–Kim Jong Il era, there has been a return to early Cold War *juche* orthodoxy—what we call neo*juche* revivalism. The ideology's emphasis on reliving the Cold War glory days through mass mobilization and collectivist thought is, in fact, the complete opposite direction from that in which society is moving. And yet the government cannot adjust its course because (1) it needs a new ideology that has a positive vision for a new leader (and the only positive vision the state ever experienced was early Cold War *juche*), and (2) it attributes the past poor performance of the state over the last two decades not to Kim Jong Il but to the "mistakes" of allowing experimentation with reform that "polluted" the ideology. Another lesson that Pyongyang learned from the Arab Spring was that this new neoconservative *juche* ideology must be implemented without giving up its nuclear weapons. The example of Libya made clear to North Koreans that Qaddafi's decision to give up his nuclear programs to the United States was an utter mistake; precisely because he no longer had these capabilities, NATO and the United States were at liberty to take military actions against him.[53] And he met his end, like Ceauşescu, bloody and battered on the streets of the country he had ruled for so many years.

This confluence of forces gives rise to a ticking time bomb or a train wreck in slow motion, whatever metaphor you prefer. A dead dictator, a rushed succession process to a young and inexperienced son, and an evolving ideology that moves the country backward, not forward. Meanwhile, society is incrementally moving in a different direction from North Korea's past, in large part sparked by the economic failures of the government. One might call this a North Korean version of Samuel Huntington's development gap. Rather than economic growth outpacing static political institutions in an unstable, democratizing society, you have a growing gap between a rigidifying ideology and a slowly changing society in North Korea. A single event—akin to a botched government measure by the new leader or a severe nationwide crackdown on markets—could spark a process that would force the post–Kim Jong Il leadership out of control. A young and inexperienced dictator, taking the throne after the sudden death of his father, could fail spectacularly to cope with this ideology–society gap. Whatever the case may be, it seems likely that new regional leaders, including the United States, China, and South Korea, who take the reins of power in 2012 will be faced with fundamental discontinuities in North Korea before they leave office.

The North Korean regime's fears about the Arab Spring also presumably derive from an understanding of the role social media played in those countries, and the realization that the recent baby steps the DPRK made into acquiring cell phones and accessing the Internet have the potential to puncture the hermetically sealed information bubble around the country. Recent North Korean ventures are modest by comparison with the Middle East states, so there is little chance of a technology-driven contagion effect today. Indeed, the regime sees these technology instruments as enhancing the state's power, not weakening it. But their introduction creates a slippery slope for the regime with regard to information penetration. The Internet, for example, is like marketization. Once a society is exposed to it even a little, the conveniences associated with it become a fixture of life that is very difficult to uproot. North Korea is ironically a country that desperately needs the Internet—its citizens are not allowed to travel overseas, and yet the country wants information from the outside world cheaply and without a lot of interaction. Access to the Web handsomely meets these needs. In 2003, the DPRK set up their official website, uriminzokkiri.com, hosted on a server in Shanghai, and in 2010 the government joined Twitter and Facebook. The government wanted to carefully restrict all use of the Web, but then they realized that the Internet allowed access to information instantaneously and costlessly, without having to send anyone abroad to get it. Moreover, the government realized that greatly restricting international access to their websites undercut the purposes of trying to attract foreign direct investment. In meeting these needs, the government started walking down the slippery slope, gradually relaxing restrictions. Now there are twelve web domains and about 1,000 government and nongovernment users of the Internet, albeit greatly censored, in North Korea.[54] Some users must be fairly sophisticated given reports about hacking attempts on ROK and U.S. government sites originating from within North Korea. The PUST project is another step down the slippery slope, as it teaches some of Pyongyang's best and brightest youth how to use the Internet. While this is limited to only a handful of carefully selected students who are monitored at all times as they download information useful to the state, the basic fact remains that there are youth in North Korea who know how to surf the Web and will someday gain access to a South Korean or Chinese computer that is not monitored. Cell phones followed a similar trajectory. The government reintroduced them to the country after the 2004 Ryongchon train blast with a contract with the Egyptian company Orascom. The purpose of introducing these devices was to serve the state. Phones would enable better communication among the elite and another means of coordination and control among security services. In 2009, 70,000 units were introduced for the elite, but this turned into nearly 500,000 phones by April 2011, and predictions are they could go as high as 1 million units by 2012. These phones cannot call outside the country, but they do give a broader portion of the population familiarity with phones, texting features, and web access. Moreover, there are an estimated 1,000 phones smuggled in from China with prepaid SIM cards. With these phones, North Koreans near the Chinese border can call within the DPRK and to China, and reportedly as far as Seoul. Again, these are small steps, carefully controlled by the government, and do not come near replicating the use of social media in other parts of the world. But the Internet and cell phones are truly a slippery slope for the regime. They quickly become fixtures of life, and a new generation of North Koreans will be literate in these technologies.

Finally, the North Korean leadership evinces a growing discomfort with the way the fight for freedom in distant Arab states reverberates internationally. Analysts talk about a new wave of democratization and hypothesize whether it will move to Asia. This raises concerns about international recognition of human rights abuses in the DPRK. As late as 2004, it was fair to say that outside of the human rights movement, the global community did not acknowledge the plight of the North Korean people. Among the many other causes around which the world organized, North Korea was notably absent. But thanks in large part to efforts by the United States, this is no longer the case. Both Presidents Bush and Obama have succeeded in connecting the cause of the North Korean people with the global American agenda of promoting freedom and human dignity. Bush in particular was the first U.S. president to appoint a congressionally mandated special envoy for human rights abuses in North Korea. He was the first U.S. president to make a statement protesting China's refoulement of North Korean refugees and to allow for a refugee resettlement program for North Koreans in the United States. Bush also invited the first North Korean defectors into the Oval Office, including Kang Chol Hwan, the gulag survivor and author. The meeting was a private one not listed on the president's official schedule. But afterward, the decision was made to release only one picture of the meeting to the Associated Press with a simple caption saying the president welcomes Mr. Kang to the Oval Office. The picture spread like wildfire around the world. It did not spur human rights protests within North Korea because the government did not allow the picture into the country, but it did create an international contagion effect. The world suddenly was awakened to the abuses inside North Korea. Newspaper editorials in Asia questioned why their governments did not have a North Korean human rights envoy, or why their leaders had not read *Aquariums of Pyongyang* like Bush had done. G8 countries put the issue on their agenda and released statements condemning the government's atrocities against its people. Obama maintained U.S. focus on this issue under his administration such that in May 2011, the DPRK for the first time allowed a visit by the U.S. human rights envoy, Ambassador Robert King. In short, how the DPRK runs its country is now under the magnifying glass more than ever before. And the Arab Spring only highlights how tenuous an authoritarian regime's control can be, and how the breakdown of this control can capture the imagination and support of the free world.

Skeptics might argue that our speculation about the regime's paranoia is not borne out by the history of the regime's stability. The fact is, skeptics would argue, there have been no instances of coups or domestic instability in the North over the past fifty years like we have seen in South Korea, for example, with two military coups in 1961 and 1979 that overthrew standing governments. The people are too weak, and the military and state controls are simply too strong for anything untoward to happen to Kim. However, if we quickly peruse the history, domestic disturbances are not exactly unknown occurrences in the North. These have taken place within the military, between the military and the citizens, and even against the leadership. In 1981, there were reports of armed clashes between soldiers and workers in the industrial center of Chongjin on the eastern coast of the country that left as many as five hundred dead. In 1983, there were Soviet-based reports of similar clashes in Sinuiju. In 1985, there were reports of a massacre of hundreds of civilians in Hamhung over food. In 1990, a small group of students at the elite Kim Il Sung University reportedly were arrested and tortured for organizing pro-tests. In January 1992, there were reports of a failed attempt by officers in the State Security Department's bodyguard bureau to stage a coup preventing Kim Jong Il from assuming the position as commander of the KPA. In April 1992, rumors surfaced that thirty officers were executed for a failed plot to assassinate Kim Jong Il. In March 1993, thirty officers of the VII Corps headquarters stationed in Hamhung tried unsuccessfully to stage a rebellion against their superiors. In 1995, upset with Pyongyang's decision not to ship food to the Hamgyong provinces, senior officers of the VI Corps stationed in Chongjin sought to take control of a university, a communications center, Chongjin port, and missile installations and reportedly planned to team up with VII Corps in Hamhung to oppose the government. In December 1996, leaflets were found in front of Kim Il Sung mausoleum criticizing the costs of the mausoleum when citizens were starving. In 1997, a statue of Kim Il Sung was found vandalized and reports of antiregime graffiti were found. In March 1998, there was a report of a failed assassination attempt by one of Kim's bodyguards. In late 2001 to early 2002, there were reports of another failed assassination attempt on Kim by one of his bodyguards. In February 2004, in what is widely viewed as a failed assassination attempt, two parked trains filled with ammonium nitrate and fuel exploded at Ryongchon station near the border with China killing 170 people several hours after Kim Jong Il's train passed through the station returning from a trip to China. In 2005, a video surfaced online that showed a nervous youth hanging a banner under a bridge in rural North Korea which denounced Kim Jong Il in bright red letters and was signed by the "Freedom Youth League." In December 2007, when the government decided to ban market activity for women under the age of fifty (by far the most important group in the markets), protests sprang up in Chongjin within months, with female participants reportedly calling out, "If you do not let us trade, give us rations!" and "If you have no rice to give us, let us trade!"[55] In 2009, families committed suicide over the government's surprise currency redenomination measure which wiped out their life savings. In Hamhung, people burned the old currency in protest, and fights broke out in markets where police officers tried unsuccessfully to close them down. Anti–Kim Jong Il graffiti was found in alleyways.

And the list goes on. It is hard to confirm the severity of these incidents because no one inside the country can report on them. It is also impossible to know whether these reports represent the entirety of dissent within the North or only the tip of the iceberg. Most of the reports of dissent occurred in the 1990s after Kim Il Sung's death and during the famine years. But we do not know if the dissent has disappeared or if the government has just gotten better at stifling news of it. It is clear, however, that internal dissent is not unheard of, despite the draconian controls of the DPRK system. It has emerged in the past. It can emerge again.

But who would be North Korea's Bouazizi, sparking an Arab Spring–type uprising? Two possible sources of discontent might be the "selectorate" and the urban poor. The "selectorate" refers to the elite in North Korean society—party members, military officers, and government bureaucrats who have benefited from the regime's rule.[56] Their support is co-opted by the state through the promise of benefits doled out by the leadership. They are the most loyal, ranging in number from 200 to 5,000 according to different estimates. And to retain their loyalty, they are showered with benefits, such as highly coveted employment positions, desirable residences, plentiful and high-quality foods, and access to highly coveted items such as red meat, liquor, and other imported goods. In many cases, elites are even given lavish gifts, such as luxury cars, jewelry, and electronics—and even wives.[57] In 2005, after we had achieved the Six-Party joint statement, we heard that Kim Kye Gwan, the DPRK lead negotiator, was given a new Mercedes Benz sedan. Some scholars claim that the Kim regime "coup-proofed" itself by prioritizing the bribing of these officials over any broader economic performance metrics for the state.[58] But this loyalty lasts only as long as the regime can continue the handouts, and the government's capacity in this regard, under Kim Jong Un, is increasingly shrinking. The cumulative effect of years of UN sanctions on luxury goods, the continued decline in the economy, and the inability of China to forever backstop the regime will take its toll, making the circle of the selectorate smaller and smaller. Favorites will have to be chosen to receive the shrinking handouts, leaving some disaffected. A leadership transition from Kim Jong Il to Kim Jong Un, moreover, promises even more disaffection in the party and military as the new Kim will have to choose his inner circle to be his basis of leadership, which will send ripples throughout the selectorate, giving opportunities to some, but more ominously, taking opportunities away from others.

Moreover, as neo*juche* ideology puts more strain on the economy, the segment of society that will feel the pain is the urban poor. When the DPRK undertook economic reforms in 2002 that lifted price controls, the resulting inflation badly hurt salaried urban populations who suffered increases in their cost of living. While farmers could offset this with the higher prices they enjoyed from the sale of their own produce in the black market, urban workers faced a double whammy—higher prices and delayed salary disbursements from the government. The result is a potentially unhappy population in cities that are literate, educated, and may have more knowledge of the outside world than most others in the country. Moreover, they identify with the system because they once benefited from it, which may give them cause to regain those advantages. And they probably have cell phones.

CONCLUSION

In sum, the leading causes that seem to have sparked protests across the Arab world are conspicuously absent in North Korea. Socioeconomic modernization, spiraling expectations, contagion effects, demographics, and regime-type factors are all either nonexistent or are severely hampered by other phenomena unique to the DPRK. The lack of a politically motivated diaspora community is a similarly discouraging prospect. And yet the Kim family seems to lack the confidence in their regime that many outside observers and experts hold. The events that have taken place across the Middle East and North Africa over the past year have given us all an important lesson in humility—you simply never know with certainty what is going to happen, or when. And this lesson should be well heeded in the case of North Korea. While according to the above-mentioned metrics, all looks calm in the Hermit Kingdom, there are underlying factors that could potentially spell the end for the Kim dynasty. The combination of tectonic, bottom-up societal shifts counteracted by rigid, top-down repression efforts is creating a tension in the North that could give way someday soon, creating a political earthquake in the country. And the forces unleashed by spreading modern technology seem to only exacerbate these ongoing trends.

The lessons of the Arab Spring and their implications for North Korea carry broader lessons about authoritarian governments the world around. Despite the apparent solidity of many of the world's relatively successful authoritarian regimes, there are often tensions simmering below the surface that can be unleashed without prior notice. The increasing interconnectedness of the world we inhabit makes controlling populations and information increasingly difficult, and this is not a welcome prospect for autocrats. One way or another, it is far from clear that what appears to be the latest "wave of democratization" has reached its crest. And if it can happen in Yemen, among the world's poorest and least developed societies, it can seemingly happen anywhere—perhaps even North Korea.

NOTES

An earlier, shorter version of this chapter was published by the authors as "A North Korean Spring?" *Washington Quarterly* 35, no. 1 (January 2012): 7–24. Segments reprinted by permission of the publisher (Taylor & Francis Ltd., http://www.tandf online.com).

1. Daniel Byman and Jennifer Lind, "Pyongyang's Survival Strategy: Tools of Authoritarian Control in North Korea," *International Security* 35, no. 1 (Summer 2010): 44–74.

2. Seymour Martin Lipset, "Some Social Requisites of Democracy: Economic Development and Political Legitimacy," *American Political Science Review* 53, no. 1 (March 1959): 69–105; Seymour Martin Lipset, "The Social Requisites of Democracy Revisited: 1993 Presidential Address," *American Sociological Review* 59, no. 1 (February 1994): 1–22; Ronald Inglehart and Christian Welzel, "How Development Leads to Democracy: What We Know about Modernization," *Foreign Affairs* 88, no. 2 (March/April 2009): 33–41; Christian Welzel, "Theories of Democratization," *Worldvaluessurvey.org*, 2009, pp. 80–81, 86–88, http://www.worldvaluessurvey.org/ wvs/articles/folder_published/publication_579/files/OUP_Ch06.pdf (accessed June 16, 2010); Larry Diamond, "Economic Development and Democracy Reconsidered," *American Behavioral Scientist* 35, no. 4/5 (March/June 1992): 450–99; Stephan Haggard and Robert R. Kaufmann, "The Political Economy of Democratic Transitions," *Comparative Politics* 29, no. 3 (1997): 263–83; Ross E. Burkhart and Michael S. Lewis-Beck, "Comparative Democracy: The Economic Development Thesis," *American Political Science Review* 88, no. 4 (December 1994): 903–10.

3. For an argument on the "initiation" side, see Carles Boix and Susan C. Stokes, "Endogenous Democratization," *World Politics* 55, no. 4 (July 2003): 517–49. For an argument on the "maintenance" side, see Adam Prezworski and Fernando Limongi, "Modernization: Theories and Facts," *World Politics* 49, no. 2 (January 1997): 155–83.

4. Eric Goldstein, "A Middle-Class Revolution," *Foreignpolicy.com*, January 18, 2011, http://www.foreignpolicy.com/articles/2011/01/18/a_middle_class _revolution?page=full (accessed May 10, 2011); David Brooks, "The Forty Percent Nation," NYTimes.com, February 5, 2011, http://www.nytimes.com/2011/02/06/ opinion/06brooks.html (accessed May 10, 2011).

5. Diamond, "Economic Development," 467; Francis Fukuyama, *The End of History and the Last Man* (New York: Free Press, 2006), 344; Prezworski and Limongi, "Modernization," 160; Boix and Stokes, "Endogenous Democratization," 522.

6. GDP per capita figures and life expectancy from Worldbank.org, 2011, http://data.worldbank.org (accessed May 10, 2011); Human Development ratings from UNDP.org, 2011, http://hdr.undp.org/en (accessed May 10, 2011); Oil export revenue figure from IMF.org, 2011, http://www.imf.org/external/pubs/ft/weo/2011/01/weodata/index.aspx (accessed May 10, 2011).

7. Francis Fukuyama, "Is China Next?" *Wall Street Journal*, March 12, 2011, http://online.wsj.com (accessed May 10, 2011).

8. Samuel Huntington, *Political Order in Changing Societies*, 2nd ed. (New Haven, CT: Yale University Press, 2006), 53–56.

9. IMF.org, 2011, http://www.imf.org/external/pubs/ft/weo/2011/01/weodata/index.aspx (accessed May 10, 2011).

10. All real GDP per capita figures from IMF.org, 2011.

11. Steven Levitsky and Lucan A. Way, "Elections without Democracy: The Rise of Competitive Authoritarianism," *Journal of Democracy* 13, no. 2 (April 2002): 51–65.

12. "Freedom in the World 2011," Freedomhouse.org, 2011, http://www.freedomhouse.org/template.cfm?page=594 (accessed May 10, 2011).

13. Ellen Knickmeyer, "The Arab World's Youth Army," Foreignpolicy.com, January 27, 2011, http://www.foreignpolicy.com/articles/2011/01/27/the_arab_world_s_youth_army (accessed May 10, 2011).

14. Bobby Ghosh, "Rap, Rage, and Revolution: Inside the Arab Youth Quake," Time.com, February 17, 2011, http://www.time.com/time/world/article/0,8599,2049808,00.html (accessed May 10, 2011).

15. Median age shows the distribution of age in a population. It essentially divides a population into two equal halves; half being older than the given age and half being younger. And so in the case of Yemen, half of its population is eighteen or younger, the other half being eighteen and older.

16. All demographic and employment figures from CIA.org, 2011, https://www.cia.gov/library/publications/the-world-factbook (accessed May 10, 2011).

17. Samuel Huntington, *The Third Wave: Democratization in the Late Twentieth Century* (Norman: University of Oklahoma Press, 1993), 33, 100–108.

18. Cell phone and Internet penetration data from CIA.org, 2011.

19. All literacy data from "World Bank Open Data," Worldbank.org, 2011.

20. On this, see Jon B. Alterman, "The Revolution Will Not Be Tweeted," *Washington Quarterly* 34, no. 4 (Fall 2011): 103–16.

21. Hugh Miles, "The Al Jazeera Effect," Foreignpolicy.com, February 8, 2011, http://www.foreignpolicy.com/articles/2011/02/08/the_al_jazeera_effect (accessed June 8, 2011).

22. "ICT Indicators," *Arab Information and Communications Technology Organization*, 2008, http://www.aicto.org/index.php?id=432&L=0 (accessed June 8, 2011).

23. "Televisions per capita by country," Nationmaster.com, 2011, http://www.nationmaster.com/graph/med_tel_percap-media-televisions-per-capita (accessed June 8, 2011).

24. Paul R. Pillar, "How Does a Ruler Stay in Power?" Nationalinterest.org, April 7, 2011, http://nationalinterest.org/blog/autocracy/how-does-ruler-stay-power-5133 (accessed May 10, 2011).

25. All EIU data from "Economist Intelligence Unit Democracy Index 2010: Democracy in Retreat," EIU.com, 2011, http://graphics.eiu.com/PDF/Democracy _Index_2010_web.pdf (accessed May 10, 2011).

26. "World Bank World Governance Indicators," Worldbank.org, 2011, http:// info.worldbank.org/governance/wgi/index.asp (accessed May 10, 2011).

27. "World Bank Open Data," Worldbank.org, 2011.

28. UNDP.org, 2011.

29. Stephanie Schwartz, "Youth and the 'Arab Spring,'" USIP.org, 2011, http:// www.usip.org/publications/youth-and-the-arab-spring (accessed October 26, 2011); Knickmeyer, "The Arab World's Youth Army"; Ghosh, "Rap, Rage, and Revolution."

30. *The CIA World Factbook*, 2011, https://www.cia.gov/library/publications/the -world-factbook/index.html (accessed October 26, 2011).

31. The next-closest military service terms are in Vietnam (24–48 months), Chad (36 months), Egypt (12–36 months), and Venezuela (30 months). See CIA.gov, 2011; *The Military Balance, 2011* (London, UK: Routledge, 2011).

32. *The Military Balance*, 249.

33. Nationmaster.com, 2011.

34. "Orascom Signs Mobile Phone Deal with North Korea," NYTimes.com, November 15, 2008, http://www.nytimes.com/2008/12/15/technology/15iht-orascom.4.18698 081.html (accessed June 7, 2011).

35. Bill Powell, "The Capitalist Who Loves North Korea," *Fortune*, September 15, 2009, http://money.cnn.com (accessed June 7, 2011).

36. CIA.org, 2011.

37. Freedomhouse.org, 2011.

38. EIU.com, 2011.

39. "World Governance Indicators," Worldbank.org, 2011; "Freedom of the Press 2011," Freedomhouse.org, 2011, http://freedomhouse.org/template.cfm?page=668 (accessed June 7, 2011).

40. Yossi Shain, "Mexican-American Diaspora's Impact on Mexico" *Political Science Quarterly* 114, no. 4 (Winter 1999–2000); 661–91.

41. "Arab States Look to Diaspora to Rebuild," Albabwa.com, October 16, 2011, http://www.albawaba.com/arab-states-look-diaspora-they-rebuild-397074 (accessed October 26, 2011).

42. *Survey of 297 NK defectors* (Seoul: Institute for Peace and Unification studies, Seoul National University, July 24, 2008); cited in Kyung-Ae Park, "People's Exit, Regime Stability, and North Korean Diplomacy," in Kyung-Ae Park, ed., *New Challenges of North Korean Foreign Policy* (New York: Palgrave MacMillan, 2009), 52.

43. *Inside North Korea*, directed by Peter Yost (US: National Geographic Television, 2007).

44. Andrew Salmon, "North Koreans Escape Freedom but Still Hold Kim Jong Il Dear," *Times of London*, May 29, 2009; cited in Kyung-Ae Park, *New Challenges*, 52.

45. On this, see Kyung-Ae Park, "People's Exit in North Korea: New Threat to Regime Stability?" *Pacific Focus* 25, no. 2 (Summer 2010): 257–75.

46. "Number of N. Korean Defectors in S. Korea Tops 21,000," *Yonhap News*, May 14, 2011, http://english.yonhapnews.co.kr (June 4, 2011); "Settlement Support for Dislocated North Koreans," Republic of Korea Ministry of Unification, 2011, http://eng.unikorea.go.kr/eng/default.jsp?pgname=AFFhumanitarian_settlement (accessed June 7, 2011).

47. Kyung-Ae Park, "People's Exit in North Korea."

48. Park Hyeong Jung, "How Can We Move North Korea?" unpublished paper for the fourth Korea Institute for National Unification-U.S. Institute of Peace Washington Workshop, March 10, 2011; "NK Tightens IT Gadget Control to Block Outside Info," *Korea Herald*, April 1, 2011.

49. X (George F. Kennan), "The Sources of Soviet Conduct," *Foreign Affairs* 25, no. 4 (July 1947): 580.

50. "Kim Jong-il 'Has Nightmares of Being Stoned by His People,'" *Chosun Ilbo*, March 28, 2011, http://english.chosun.com/site/data/html_dir/2011/03/28/2011032801124.html (accessed June 7, 2011).

51. Yoonok Chang, Stephan Haggard, and Marcus Noland, "Exit Polls: Refugee Assessments of North Korea's Transition," *Journal of Comparative Economics* 37, no. 1 (March 2009): 144–50.

52. For more, see Han S. Park, "Military-First (*Songun*) Politics: Implications for External Policies," in Kyung-Ae Park, ed., *New Challenges of North Korean Foreign Policy* (New York: Palgrave Macmillan, 2009), 89–109.

53. "DPRK Foreign Ministry Spokesman Denounces U.S. Military Attack on Libya," March 22, 2011, http://www.krld.pl/krld/czytelniateksty/biuletyny//129%20-%20DPRK%20Foreign%20Ministry%20Spokesman%20Denounces.pdf.

54. Nina Hachigian, "The Internet and Power in One-Party East Asian States," *Washington Quarterly* 25, no. 3 (2002): 41–58; Ko Kyungmin, Heejin Lee, and Seungkwon Jang, "The Internet Dilemma and Control Policy," *Korean Journal of Defense Analyses* 21, no. 3 (2009): 279–95; "North Korea Takes to Twitter and You-Tube," *New York Times*, August 16, 2010.

55. Andrei Lankov, "Pyongyang Strikes Back: North Korean Policies of 2002–2008 and Attempts to Reverse 'De-Stalinization from Below,'" *Asia Policy*, no. 8 (July 2009): 61–62.

56. Daniel Byman and Jennifer Lind, "Pyongyang's Survival Strategy: Tools of Authoritarian Control in North Korea," *International Security* 35, no. 1 (Summer 2010): 44–74.

57. Byman and Lind, "Pyongyang's Survival Strategy," 60–64.

58. Sheena Greitens, "Succession and Stability in North Korea," *CSIS Korea Platform*, January 23, 2012, http://csis.org/files/publication/120123_KoreaPlatform_SheenaGreitens.pdf (accessed January 27, 2012).

Part II

PROSPECTS FOR THE
NORTH KOREAN ECONOMY

Chapter Six

Western Aid

The Missing Link for North Korea's Economic Revival?

Nicholas Eberstadt

As the leadership of the Democratic People's Republic of Korea (hereafter DPRK, or North Korea) looks to the future, economic development figures centrally in its officially proclaimed agenda. This year, as it has done every year since the start of the new century, the government's canonical Joint New Year Editorial in 2012 stressed the imperative of economic construction, broadly outlining the sorts of improvements that are to be achieved over the remainder of the current calendar year, intoning, "We must vigorously launch an all-out drive to implement our Party's grand strategy for achieving prosperity," while of course lauding the DPRK's "significant achievements" to date in "building the country into an economic giant in the 21st century."[1]

But economic growth and development has in fact taken on a whole new importance in North Korean policy, one that extends beyond rhetoric. In January 2011, for the first time in over two decades, Pyongyang formally unveiled a new multiyear economic plan: a ten-year "strategy plan for economic development" under a newly formed State General Bureau for Economic Development. The new economic plan is intended not only to meet the DPRK's longstanding objective of becoming a "powerful and prosperous country" (*kangsong taeguk*) by 2012 (the one hundredth anniversary of the birth of Kim Il Sung), but also to promote North Korea to the ranks of the "advanced countries in 2020."[2]

Details on the new ten-year economic plan are as yet sketchy. South Korean analysts report that the plan envisions massive amounts of new investment in North Korea: up to $100 billion, by some of these accounts.[3] (Gossip within the business community in China puts the price tag even higher: according to some of these sources, $200 billion or more.) But even if the investment target is more modest than such rumors suggest, North Korea will be counting on more than just domestic capital accumulation to secure this funding. It will have to rely upon major inflows of capital from abroad.

Evidently, North Korea's ten-year plan envisions attracting sizeable sums of private capital from abroad to help finance the country's new development goals. Pyongyang has established a State Development Bank for channeling foreign funds into state projects, as well as a "North Korea Taepung International Investment Group" (based in China and formally headed by an ethnic Korean of Chinese citizenship) to scout for international funding sources for this bank. Further, in the year before his death, North Korea's supreme leader Kim Jong Il himself made several trips to China, with a key objective in these visits reportedly being to secure financial backing for new DPRK projects. DPRK policy makers, however, have more than just private funding in mind when they consider potential sources of capital from abroad. Overseas economic assistance presumably will figure centrally in North Korea's future economic plans, just as it has in the past.

No less than eliciting domestic economic revival and development, commanding large and steady transfers of economic aid from abroad has been an abiding priority of the DPRK government. In Pyongyang's official narrative, indeed, these two quantities are instrumentally and inseparably related. By this official narrative, North Korea's economic woes after the end of the Cold War were the direct consequence of the loss of economic assistance and (subsidized) trade from the erstwhile Soviet Bloc. By that same narrative, North Korea's economy continues to suffer largely as a result of America's "hostile policy" of economic sanctions—which limit not only trade, but also aid, for the DPRK.

In the era of Seoul's "Sunshine Policy" and Washington's "Perry Process," Western diplomats and their North Korean counterparts seriously discussed the prospect of a $10 billion payment to Pyongyang by Japan in the event of a comprehensive settlement of the nuclear and other security issues under discussion in the late 1990s and early 2000s.[4] Though the Sunshine Policy and the Perry Process are dead, the vision of a $10 billion aid payment from Japan may still be very much alive in the eyes of North Korean policy makers—to say nothing of additional and continuing transfers from other Western countries (and perhaps additional benefits accruing not from aid, but from the opening of certain essentially closed foreign markets in Western countries).

Leave aside for the moment the likelihood of a major and sustained upsurge in Western aid for North Korea, or the conditions under which such aid commitments might be arranged: if such an upsurge were to occur, could this lead to an economic florescence in the DPRK? Could Western aid flows be the key to jump-starting the North Korean economy? North Korean officialdom is keenly aware of the massive economic assistance the United

States provided to South Korea in its poor and hungry years after the Korean War; South Korea, of course, subsequently entered into a sustained spurt of dazzling growth that transformed the country into a society enjoying Western levels of affluence and productivity. Could massive Western aid spark the same sort of transformation for the DPRK?

To address this set of questions comprehensively, it is necessary to examine a number of separate but related issues: (1) the record of North Korea's economic performance in recent decades; (2) the relationship between DPRK policies and practices and the country's economic performance; (3) the international record of Western aid's influence on economic growth and development; (4) the rationale or logic behind current DPRK policies and practices bearing on economic performance; (5) the history of U.S. aid to, and economic development in, South Korea; and (6) some of the prerequisites for sustained economic growth (and aid effectiveness) of the DPRK. We will examine these issues in sequence in the following pages.

THE DPRK'S ECONOMIC PERFORMANCE
OVER THE PAST GENERATION

There is no way to state this diplomatically: the DPRK's economic record over the past two decades has been abysmal, among the very worst of any population on the planet.

The DPRK was founded in 1948, and although this important fact has been widely forgotten, the North Korean central planning system functioned tolerably well for about a generation after its inception. Indeed, the North Korean economy appears to have outperformed its South Korean competitor for several decades; there is reason to believe that both per capita output and per capita exports were higher in the North than South as late as 1970.[5] But in the 1970s and 1980s, the North Korean economy veered off toward stagnation while South Korea's soared—and since the Soviet collapse, the North Korean economy suffered a catastrophic slump from which it has yet to recover fully.

Reliable data on North Korea's economic and social trends are, of course, notoriously scarce. It may suffice, however, to consider this single fact to assess the overall performance of the DPRK economy in the post-Soviet era: North Korea is the only literate and urbanized society in history to have undergone a famine in peacetime.[6] And the Great North Korean Hunger of the 1990s was not a once-only event, attributable to natural disaster or force majeure; quite the contrary, it reflected fundamental new structural realities for the DPRK economic system. From the mid-1990s to this day, North Korea has relied on "temporary" international emergency humanitarian food aid donations—but on a permanent basis (the latest appeal being issued in early 2011[7]). Evidently, North Korea has lost its capacity for feeding its own people (by growing food domestically or purchasing it from abroad). The DPRK is the only once-industrialized society in economic history to have "accomplished" such a fateful retrogression.

Virtually the only uninterrupted economic time series data related to the DPRK's economic performance come from "mirror statistics": purchases and sales of merchandise as reported by a country's trading partners. These are by no means free from flaw, but to the extent they can be trusted, they depict North Korea as an economy that has not only been falling behind, but perhaps falling backward, over the past generation.

Figures 6.1 and 6.2 provide a glimpse of North Korea's relative export performance in 1980 and 2007 (the last year before today's ongoing global economic crisis), based on estimates of per capita merchandise exports in current U.S. dollars drawn from the World Bank.

In 1980, North Korea's per capita merchandise exports ranked next to Turkey's and were only a bit lower than the average for what the World Bank calls "Lower Middle Income Economies." In 1980, the DPRK's per capita exports were over twice as high as China's, six times those of Bangladesh, and over twenty times higher than in Cambodia; that year, in fact, North Korea's per capita merchandise exports were still comparable to (even slightly higher than) the average for developing economies in East Asia.

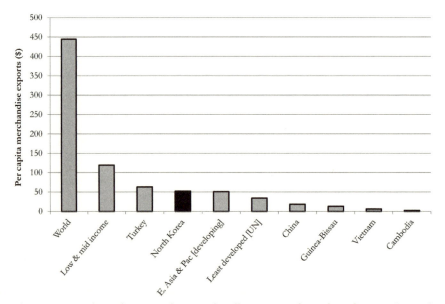

Figure 6.1. Estimated per Capita Merchandise Exports for Selected Countries and Regions: 1980 (current USD)

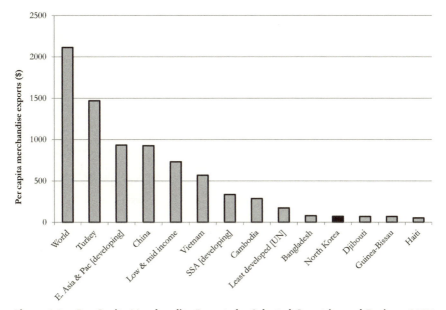

Figure 6.2.   Per Capita Merchandise Exports for Selected Countries and Regions: 2007 (current USD)

By 2007, North Korea's per capita exports were just one-twentieth of Turkey's, less than a tenth of China's, and barely a quarter of Cambodia's. They were also less than a quarter of the average for developing sub-Saharan economies, and less than half the average for the UN's classification of "least developed countries" (the world's most perennially distressed economies). Although North Korea's estimated level of per capita merchandise exports was slightly higher than the average for developing economies in East Asia back in 1980, by 2007 the average for the East Asian developing states was over thirteen times higher than for North Korea. By 2007, North Korea's "neighbors" in per capita merchandise exports were no longer the likes of Turkey, but instead countries like Guinea Bissau, Djibouti, and Bangladesh (although Bangladesh's estimated per capita exports were somewhat higher than North Korea's).

In nominal terms (current, unadjusted U.S. dollars), North Korea's per capita merchandise exports grew by less than 40 percent between 1980 and 2007—meaning that if inflation were taken into account, the DPRK's per capita export level would have been significantly lower in 2007 than nearly three decades earlier. In a world exploding with trade and trade opportunities, North Korea's capacity to generate revenues from merchandise exports has diminished markedly.[8] And in a world where the composition of international trade is constantly evolving as a result of increasing income levels and technological innovation, North Korea's export structure appears to be locked in a time warp: today the country relies for most of its legitimate reported export earnings on the very same half dozen relatively low-tech commodity groupings as a generation ago (sea products; textiles and clothing; iron and steel; and cement, gold, and magnesite clinker).[9]

North Korean authorities maintain that their international trade performance is seriously impaired by America's "hostile policy" toward their government.[10] It certainly is true that the DPRK faces a thicket of restrictions—some of them executive orders, some of them federal laws—that erect barriers or impose outright prohibitions on US–DPRK trade and finance.[11] In recent years Japan and South Korea have also restricted or curtailed various aspects of their commercial relations with the DPRK, a repercussion of increasing nuclear tensions and other security issues involving North Korea. But the fact of the matter is that most OECD (Organisation for Economic Cooperation and Development) countries do not impose any systematic restrictions on commerce with the DPRK—and those other countries offer a huge and steadily expanding market for exports for would-be exporters, including North Korea. In 1980, that OECD import market (excluding the United States, ROK, and Japan) purchased over $1 trillion in goods from abroad (in current U.S. dollars); by 2000 that market had grown to $3.2 trillion, and by 2007 it had reached $6.8 trillion. Over this same period, however, North Korea's share of the aforementioned OECD markets steadily and precipitously dropped: from 0.03 percent in 1980 to 0.01 percent in 2000, to a mere 0.002 percent in 2007 (see table 6.1).

It is worth noting, furthermore, that the nominal value of North Korean exports to these countries was only slightly higher in 2000 than it had been twenty years earlier—and was almost 50 percent lower in 2007 than in 1980. Adjusting for intervening price changes, real DPRK exports to this group of countries would have been about 30 percent lower in 2000 than in 1980—and about 70 percent lower in 2007 than in 1980. Real per capita exports, for their part, would have been about half as high in 2000 as in 1980—and almost 80 percent lower in 2007 than in 1980. To judge by these numbers, a "hostile

Table 6.1. Estimated North Korean Exports to OECD Markets (excluding South Korea, the United States, and Japan), 1980–2007 (current US$)

	1980	*2000*	*2007*
OECD total imports from DPRK	$330,719,598	$349,825,364	$177,110,376
Imports from DPRK as percentage of total OECD imports	0.0310%	0.0109%	0.0026%

Source: United Nations Commodity Trade Statistics Database (UN COMTRADE), http://comtrade.un.org (accessed March 2011).

policy" by the United States and/or her Asian treaty allies can hardly explain North Korea's dismal international economic performance over the past three decades. Quite the contrary: these data would suggest instead that a steadily and sharply diminishing capability to generate export revenues under competitive world market conditions has in fact been the norm for the North Korean economy over the past generation—and the bilateral trade relationships in which North Korea has registered rising real per capita export earnings over time are the exceptions that require explanation. Closer examination indicates that such exceptions are governed by politics rather than economics; that is to say, they are explained by a political determination on the part of given trade partners to subsidize their commerce with Pyongyang (viz. China and South Korea, the latter especially during the "Sunshine Era").

Human resources underpin a country's potential for economic performance, which then in turn affects the evolving quality and stock of a nation's "human capital." International estimates of key social indicators, to the extent these can be deemed reliable, likewise indicate long-term stagnation, if not outright retrogression, in human capital stock for the DPRK. The U.S. Census Bureau's analysis of the DPRK's 1993 and 2008 censuses, for example, suggests that life expectancy in North Korea was lower in 2007 than it had been in 1993.[12] Very few other contemporary economies could claim the same.

WHY HAS THE DPRK ECONOMY PERFORMED SO BADLY OVER THE PAST GENERATION?

In a world and time where long-term economic progress is the norm, how are we to understand the woeful aberration of prolonged economic failure for the contemporary DPRK?[13]

The explanation cannot lie in the "Korean-ness" of the DPRK, or analogous "cultural" hypotheses. The economic record of the Korean population just across the DMZ attests to this. Between 1980 and 2007, South Korea's nominal per capita exports rose over sixteenfold (see figure 6.3); over those same years, real per capita GDP in the ROK more than quadrupled (from $5,544 to $25,021 in constant 2005 international dollars).[14] By the same token, between 1993 and 2007, a period over which North Korea's life expectancy is estimated to have fallen, South Korea's life expectancy at birth is reckoned to have jumped by five and a half years.[15] If anything, the strikingly discordant performance of the North and South Korean economies over the past generation should prompt us to ask just how a people so obviously capable of economic success were organized and managed into "achieving" sustained and catastrophic economic failure in the DPRK.

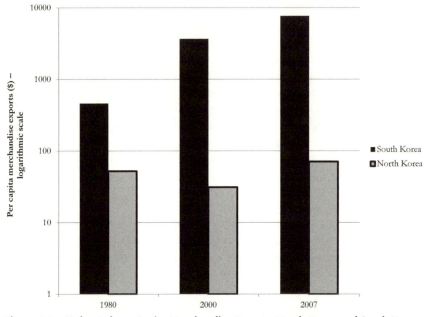

Figure 6.3.   Estimated per Capita Merchandise Exports: North Korea and South Korea, 1980–2007

Another hypothesis might be that North Korea was subject to communist central economic planning and that central economic planning always fails. Such an answer might seem plausible in the aftermath of the collapse of the Soviet empire, but the suggestion is challenged by both theory and fact. In terms of theory, Nobel Economics Laureate Friedrich Hayek and his mentor Ludwig von Mises demonstrated in the 1920s and 1930s that central planning systems suffered from an irresolvable "socialist calculation problem," that is, an inability to determine scarcity relationships for the purpose of allocating resources efficiently.[16] But this insight by the Austrian school merely criticized centrally planned systems for mounting inefficiencies and unnecessarily heightened costs, rather than for sharp and prolonged economic decline. From the empirical standpoint, estimates by eminent Western economic historians suggest that the Soviet Bloc economies and Mao-era China did in fact experience considerable and long-term material advances,[17] even if their "total factor productivity" suffered, and their command mobilization and technical innovation forced output up for many successive decades. Furthermore, the DPRK itself seems to have achieved a considerable measure of material progress under its first generation of command planning—successfully effecting a forced-pace transformation from an agrarian to an industrial and from a rural to an urban economy, not only reattaining prewar or colonial levels of per capita output for key agricultural and industrial output, but far exceeding them.

A third hypothesis, perhaps the most plausible on its face, would be that a socialist Asian economy that had been heavily dependent upon Soviet Bloc aid and (subsidized) trade should suffer serious long-term adjustment problems if those erstwhile economic ties were suddenly sundered, as with the sudden and widely unexpected collapse of Soviet and Eastern European socialism. Yet disruptive as they clearly were, such economic shocks need not consign former beneficiary states to long-term economic distress. Vietnam provides an "existence proof" of this. Like the DPRK, Vietnam was heavily dependent upon Soviet economic ties in 1990—then, just as with the DPRK, those ties suddenly evaporated. But Vietnam neither starved nor tumbled into long-term economic decline. According to World Bank estimates, Vietnam's per capita GDP was in fact over 150 percent higher in 2007 than it had been in 1990 ($2,455 versus $902, using constant 2005 international dollars); for their part, Vietnamese per capita merchandise exports, in nominal dollar terms, were over fifteen times higher in 2007 than they had been seventeen years earlier.[18] (One may argue of course that Vietnam benefitted from highly positive "neighborhood effects," situated as it is in economically dynamic Southeast Asia—but the same argument should also obtain for the DPRK, given its land borders with China and South Korea.)

The DPRK's conspicuous economic failure, then, must be explained not in the failings of the Korean population, or the generic economic shortcomings of command socialism, or even the disruptive reverberations of the Soviet Bloc collapse on a heavily dependent socialist economy, but instead in terms of the particularities of "socialism with Korean characteristics" as it evolved in the DPRK over the past generation—what North Korean officialdom terms "our own style of socialism" (*urisik sahoejuui*). North Korea's current "own style of socialism" is a grotesquely deformed mutation of the initial DPRK command planning system, from which it fatefully devolved over time. Simply stated, the quality of Pyongyang's economic policies and practices are distinctly more hostile to growth and development nowadays than they were thirty or even forty years ago.

What are the particular factors contributing to modern North Korea's disastrous economic record? We can identify some of the more obvious elements succinctly below.

Breakdown of the DPRK Statistical System

The DPRK is notoriously secretive: it has never published a statistical yearbook, and it only episodically releases even the most mundane statistical tidbits about social conditions or economic performance. There are reasons, furthermore, to suspect that some of those data that have been released are heavily doctored or even falsified. This may not be just a matter of deceiving the outside world. Since the early 1970s, there have been continuing signs that the DPRK statistical apparatus was becoming increasingly incapable of transmitting accurate and comprehensive information to the country's decision makers—a critical danger for any centrally planned system.[19]

Breakdown of the DPRK Central Planning Apparatus

The North Korean economic planning system remains opaque to outsiders, but there are indications that the process has become increasingly compartmentalized, irregular, and ad hoc since the early 1970s, and that it may have ceased to function in a systematic, long-range manner altogether since then, i.e. after the end of the last completed plan (1993). Professor Mitsuhiko Kimura terms the current North Korean approach "planning without plans."[20]

Hypermilitarization of the National Economy

In the early 1970s, in the classic study of North Korean communism, Robert Scalapino and Chong-Sik Lee described the DPRK as "perhaps the most highly militarized society in the world today."[21] In the years that followed, North Korea's policy tilted to an ever higher degree of militarization—full-throttle militarization, without respite. By the late 1980s, according to analysis of the DPRK's own demographic statistics, the country was supporting a cadre of over 1.2 million noncivilian males: over 6 percent of the national population, a mobilization equivalent to America's in the year 1943.[22] If North Korea is operating on something like a total-war footing, it is allocating an enormous share of its resources to the defense sector and the allied defense industries. Under such circumstances, there is likely to be an extraordinary and continuing drain of potentially productive resources into activities that produce little or no economic "value added." A total-war footing may have limited long-term economic consequences if the mobilization is for relatively short period periods of time,[23] but North Korea's hypermilitarization has been in progress for almost four decades.

Relentless War against the Consumer Sector

All Soviet-type economies have unnaturally small consumer sectors, but North Korea's tiny consumer sector is strangely compressed, even by the standards of Stalinist planning. Even before the hypermilitarization of the 1970s, the estimated share of the consumer sector within the DPRK economy was much lower than for counterpart economies within the Soviet Bloc.[24] Extreme suppression of the consumer sector inhibits productivity and growth by reducing the consumption of goods and services contributing to "human capital," and by eliminating the sort of "inducement goods" whose attractiveness would otherwise be motivating workers to earn and save money.

Demonetization of the National Economy

Complex modern economies cannot function efficiently on a barter basis. Nevertheless, money has played an amazingly limited role in the DPRK's economic activities over the past generation. In the late 1980s, the DPRK's wage bill apparently amounted to only a third of its "net material product," and therefore to far less than a third of its GNP.[25] Even for a communist economy, this was a remarkably low ratio—one that presumably declined still further over the 1990s. With the July 2002 economic measures, Pyongyang effectively reintroduced money into its consumer sector—a welcome event—but that sector accounts for only a small share of the overall national economy. And in any event, with the "currency reform" of late 2009, North Korea's government has once again resumed its campaign to suppress the role of domestic currency in the allocation of goods and services.

Lack of Financial Intermediation

As has by now been well established in the economics literature, financial intermediation (banking, credit markets, etc.) plays a direct and positive role in the growth and development of national economies. North Korea has virtually no officially approved mechanisms for such intermediation in its domestic economy.

Defiant Nonpayment of International Debts

The DPRK has been in virtual default on its Western loans since the mid-1970s. Although many other debtor governments from low-income areas have experienced performance problems on their loans over the past generation, Pyongyang has adopted an almost uniquely pugnacious and hostile posture of nonrepayment toward its creditors. Consequently, the DPRK's international credit rating is approximately zero. (It is worth noting, incidentally, that North Korea's stance on foreign debt to Western countries does not seem to betoken a particular "anti-imperialist" animus; Cold War era archives from erstwhile Soviet Bloc states now reveal that Pyongyang likewise routinely refused to repay the principal and often the interest on its loans from fraternal socialist governments during the 1950s, 1960s, and 1970s.[26])

Allergy to Licit International Trade

Despite huge and steadily expanding opportunities to earn export revenues from commercial import markets around the world, North Korea has exerted virtually no effort at penetrating or cultivating these lucrative markets over the past generation. To the extent that Pyongyang's policies have been concerned with generating export revenue, much of the DPRK's energies have been concentrated on securing streams of illicit or even criminal revenue. The fact that North Korea has come to engage regularly in international drug trafficking, currency counterfeiting, insurance fraud rackets, and other "Soprano state"[27] activities is by now well established and beyond debate. This "highwayman" approach toward international trade and finance is largely informed by Pyongyang's continuing apprehension about what it terms "ideological and cultural infiltration" (about which more later)—but it assures the marginalization of North Korea in the international economy.

Exceptionally Inhospitable Institutional Landscape

Although Soviet-type economies are always characterized by a problematic "business climate," the North Korean setting is perhaps uniquely unfavorable for spontaneous economic activity or independent enterprise. Some of the factors worth mentioning are (a) pervasive restrictions against and penalties on private initiative for both individuals and enterprise—recent "reforms" notwithstanding; (b) highly opaque and unpredictable application of existing economic measures, regulations, and laws toward DPRK citizens; (c) often severe extralegal intervention in the business activities of the domestic population; (d) unattractive economic legislation governing foreign enterprises; (e) lack of consistency between existing legislation and actual government decisions concerning foreign business activities; and (f) pervasive government opposition to the generation and/or repatriation of profits by foreign businesses.

When one considers this imposing array of economically wasteful—or positively destructive—policies and practices, the explanation for North Korea's prolonged and severe economic decline becomes clear enough. North Korea's political economy is the proximate explanation for the country's current precarious economic straits—no additional external or internal factors need be adduced to explain this dismal record.[28]

WESTERN AID, AID RECIPIENTS' POLICIES, AND ECONOMIC GROWTH

Western governments have directly (through their own bilateral aid organizations) or indirectly (through multilateral organizations and international financial institutes like the World Bank, IMF, ABD, UNDP, etc.) transferred the inflation-adjusted equivalent of well over $2 trillion to recipient states over the past half century.[29] Perhaps curiously, given the staggering scale of these ongoing transfers, there is no consensus in the economics literature on the macroeconomic impact of development assistance on economic growth in recipient societies. Some studies identify strong positive benefits from development assistance, while others do not detect any appreciable impact on growth—the difference largely having to do with the countries, and time horizons, under consideration.[30]

However, that paradox seems to be resolved by disaggregation of recipient states according to the criteria of "policy and institutional environment" (or perhaps to put it another way, business climate). Over the past decade and a half, a series of pathbreaking studies by economists at the World Bank have convincingly demonstrated that the growth effects of aid depend critically on the quality of institutions and policies in the countries to which these aid transfers flow.[31] This research conforms with the commonsensical a priori notion that additional resources placed in the hand of any given government will permit that government to pursue its own objectives more easily—with economic consequences depending crucially upon the government's objectives and intentions.

Figure 6.4 summarizes the findings of this research. In general, a more auspicious policy environment tends to elicit more economic growth from aid than a less favorable policy environment. But two more specific findings here are worth emphasizing in particular. First, aid can actually have a *negative* impact on growth when recipient states have poor institutional and policy environments. Second, and no less important, the negative impact of aid in economies with poor policies is actually *greater* when the volume of aid is *larger*.

What does this all mean hypothetically for Western aid to the DPRK and its prospective impact on economic growth in that country? As we just saw in the preceding pages, the DPRK has established an absolutely horrific "institutional and policy environment" regarding economic performance over the past generation. But this is not just a qualitative assertion; it is corroborated quantitatively by the reckoning of such indices as the annual "Index of Economic Freedom" compiled by the *Wall Street Journal* and the Heritage

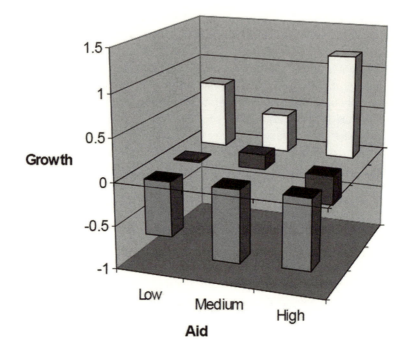

■ Bad Policy ■ Medium Policy □ Good Policy

Figure 6.4.   Economic Growth, Foreign Aid, and Recipient Country Policy: World Bank Estimates

Foundation—an index which may be taken as a rough proxy for what economic researchers refer to as "institutional and policy environment."

Figure 6.5 shows North Korea's performance in the Index of Economic Freedom in relation to selected other countries. It is clear that "top grades" are not necessary for very rapid sustained growth: China, for example, has been a world leader in economic growth rates over the past fifteen years, yet its ranking on this Index is no more than mediocre. The same is true for Vietnam. North Korea, however, is in a league of its own: near the very bottom of the table, and losing score over time. North Korea, indeed, is consistently far below Zimbabwe in its ranking on the Index for Economic Freedom. Given the famously destructive nature of the Zimbabwean governments' economic policies and practices in the late Mugabe era, this should give pause.

As it happens, furthermore, North Korea is not a "low aid" state. To the contrary, since the end of the Cold War era, Pyongyang has managed to procure enormous sums of economic assistance from the West. Between 1995 and 2007, North Korea received well over $1 billion in concessional eco-

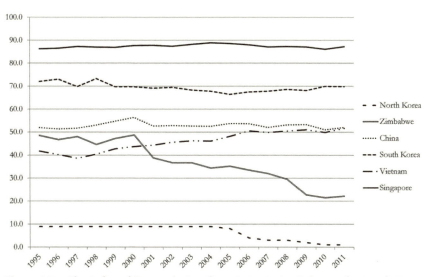

Figure 6.5. The Index of Economic Freedom, 1995–2011: Estimates for North Korea and Selected Countries

nomic transfers from the United States (see table 6.2). Over those same years, it obtained over $4 billion in publicly acknowledged economic aid from South Korea (see table 6.3). Together, this amounts to nearly $5 billion—and that total excludes considerable additional aid from other Western sources (including the World Food Programme, the Japanese government, etc.)—to say nothing about aid from China and sub rosa payments to the North from the "Sunshine era" South Korean government (such as the initially secret $500 million transfer that was instrumental in securing the historic North–South summit of June 2000).

One way of understanding how important Western aid has been to the operations of the North Korean economy over the past decade and a half is to compare estimates of Western aid inflows to estimates of merchandise export revenues to assay the dimension of "aid dependence" for the North Korean economy. To go by estimates in tables 6.2 and 6.3, and the estimates of DPRK licit merchandise export revenues from the World Bank from table 6.4, North Korea's "aid dependence" on America and South Korea in relation to merchandise export earnings was about 34 percent over the 1995–2007 period—that is to say, for every $100 in merchandise export revenues it was thought to tally, it received $34 in aid from South Korea and the United States. Compare this to the situation in sub-Saharan Africa: between 1995 and 2007, the ratio of official development assistance (ODA) to merchandise export revenue for that region was estimated by the World Bank at 17.6 percent—barely half the corresponding figure for North Korea (see table 6.5)!

Table 6.2. U.S. Economic Assistance to North Korea, 1995–2010 (current US$)

Calendar or Fiscal Year (FY)	Food Aid (per FY) Metric Tons	Commodity Value ($ million)	KEDO Assistance (per calendar year; $ million)	Six-Party Talks–Related Assistance (per FY; $ million) Fuel Oil	Nuclear Disablement	Medical Supplies & Other (per FY; $ million)	Total ($ million)
1995	0	$0.00	$9.50	—	—	$0.20	$9.70
1996	19,500	$8.30	$22.00	—	—	$0.00	$30.30
1997	177,000	$52.40	$25.00	—	—	$5.00	$82.40
1998	200,000	$72.90	$50.00	—	—	$0.00	$122.90
1999	695,194	$222.10	$65.10	—	—	$0.00	$287.20
2000	265,000	$74.30	$64.40	—	—	$0.00	$138.70
2001	350,000	$58.07	$74.90	—	—	$0.00	$132.97
2002	207,000	$50.40	$90.50	—	—	$0.00	$140.90
2003	40,200	$25.48	$2.30	—	—	$0.00	$27.78
2004	110,000	$36.30	$0.00	—	—	$0.10	$36.40
2005	25,000	$5.70	—	—	—	—	$5.70
2006	0	$0.00	—	—	—	$0.00	$0.00
2007	0	$0.00	—	$25.00	$20.00	$0.10	$45.10
2008	148,270	$93.70	—	$106.00	—	$0.00	$199.70
2009	21,000	$7.10	—	$15.00	—	$4.00	$26.10
2010	—	—	—	—	—	—	$0.00
Total	**2,258,164**	**$706.75**	**$403.70**	**$146.00**	**$20.00**	**$9.40**	**$1,285.85**

Source: Compiled by CRS from USAID, U.S. Department of Agriculture, State Department, KEDO (Korean Peninsula Energy Development Organization).

Table 6.3. South Korean Aid to North Korea, 1991–2008 (current millions of US$)

Year	Total Assistance	Total Humanitarian	Food Aid	Fertilizer	Assistance through NGOs	Road & Rail	Mt. Kumgang Tours	Aid to ROK Business	Kaesong Industrial Complex	Family Reunions	Other
1991	0										
1992	0.71									0.71	
1995	236.60		236.60								
1996	12.89		3.76		3.07						6.06
1997	20.05				20.05						
1998	14.29				14.26					0.01	0.02
1999	28.88			28.53						0.35	
2000	180.99	163.10	76.69	83.42	2.99	12.89		0.44		2.75	1.81
2001	196.86	90.29	14.68	49.47	26.14	69.60	34.86	0.83		1.20	0.08
2002	278.71	175.37	84.63	66.60	24.14	53.50	26.71	2.20		20.56	0.37
2003	370.84	256.93	159.21	70.13	27.59	94.09	5.03	10.66		3.47	0.66
2004	340.35	196.31	98.25	84.46	13.60	96.55	6.20	27.78	6.00	3.68	3.83
2005	636.38	357.26	193.79	123.44	40.03	193.17	0.01	28.62	25.65	16.67	15.00
2006	483.83	226.65	10.65	125.66	90.34	93.06	1.28	50.16	80.75	15.91	16.02
2007	770.31	395.71	157.34	103.49	134.88	68.33	0.50	60.95	82.89	30.80	131.13
2008	209.56	54.11	3.91	0	50.20	14.38	1.52	9.79	52.22	19.00	58.54
Total	**3,784.29**	**2,221.99**	**1,039.51**	**735.19**	**447.29**	**695.57**	**76.11**	**191.45**	**247.50**	**115.12**	**236.55**

Source: As appearing in Dick K. Nanto and Emma Chanlett-Avery, "North Korea: Economic Leverage and Policy Analysis," CRS Report RL32493, January 22, 2010.

Table 6.4.   Estimated Merchandise Exports by North Korea, 1995–2007 (current US$)

Year	Merchandise Exports (current US$)
1995	$959,000,000
1996	$909,000,000
1997	$1,098,000,000
1998	$651,000,000
1999	$637,000,000
2000	$708,000,000
2001	$826,000,000
2002	$1,008,000,000
2003	$1,066,000,000
2004	$1,278,000,000
2005	$1,338,000,000
2006	$1,465,000,000
2007	$1,685,000,000
Total DPRK exports	$13,628,000,000
Total aid from United States and South Korea to North Korea, 1995–2007	$4,634,070,000
US–South Korea aid as % of North Korea exports	34%

Source: World Development Indicators, World Bank, 2011.

Table 6.5.   Merchandise Exports from, and Development Assistance to, Sub-Saharan Africa, 1995–2007 (current US$)

Year	Merchandise Exports	Official Development Assistance	Development Assistance as Percent of Exports
1995	$75,607,885,249.31	$18,682,550,000	24.71%
1996	$85,159,112,455.24	$16,426,060,000	19.29%
1997	$86,126,221,378.22	$14,939,390,000	17.35%
1998	$71,779,320,891.69	$14,500,950,000	20.20%
1999	$78,437,784,336.49	$13,259,640,000	16.90%
2000	$93,405,605,655.86	$13,067,110,000	13.99%
2001	$87,996,818,493.25	$14,278,840,000	16.23%
2002	$93,295,280,266.11	$19,321,950,000	20.71%
2003	$114,000,905,855.49	$24,965,080,000	21.90%
2004	$153,447,607,266.99	$26,536,210,000	17.29%
2005	$191,452,018,443.66	$32,797,100,000	17.13%
2006	$225,853,439,780.69	$40,872,100,000	18.10%
2007	$266,848,080,389.39	$35,747,920,000	13.40%
Total	**$1,623,410,080,462.39**	**$285,394,900,000**	**17.58%**

Source: World Development Indicators, World Bank, 2011.

While admittedly aid from the United States and the ROK to North Korea may not correspond exactly to the OECD's definition of "development assistance" (utilized in World Bank estimates of ODA flows to sub-Saharan Africa), the point remains clear nonetheless—North Korea is an extremely aid-dependent economy, even by comparison with the notoriously aid-dependent economies of contemporary sub-Saharan Africa. And as we have already seen, North Korea's "policy environment" has been virtually inimical to economic growth. The confluence of a poisonous domestic policy environment and high inflows of Western aid, to go by recent economic research, should in theory set back economic growth substantially—perhaps even more, indeed, than those poisonous policies would do on their own, unfinanced by assistance from abroad. This theoretical result, indeed, seems to be the real-life tale of Western aid and "development" as it unfolded in the DPRK over the past decade and a half.

The World Bank researchers who uncovered the aforementioned relationship between development aid, policy environment, and economic growth came to argue strongly in favor of what they called "selectivity" in the disbursal of foreign aid over what they called "conditionality." *Conditionality* is a term of art employed by aid donors to refer to the changes in policy and behavior they would require of beneficiary governments in order to obtain grants and subsidized loans. These World Bank researchers, however, concluded that such promises were essentially worthless—or at very best, highly unreliable. Once a recipient cashed the check, there was little the donor could do to enforce the implicit contract. These researchers instead advocated a "selectivity" approach—by which they mean financing countries that had *already* demonstrated their credibility by embracing sensible and pragmatic policy regimens *before* the aid subventions came under consideration.

By the criterion of selectivity, the DPRK today is clearly not a promising candidate for development aid. To put the matter more plainly, it is one of the *least* promising candidates on the planet at the moment. North Korea has virtually the lowest ranking on the globe for the Index of Economic Freedom—and remarkable as this may sound, its ranking has actually fallen over the past decade and a half.

To be sure, the DPRK has attempted a number of halfhearted experiments in economic innovation over the past generation or so—the September 1984 "Joint Venture Law," the Rajin-Sonbong "special economic zone" established in 1991, the July 2002 "Measures for the Strengthening of the National Economy," the September 2002 "Special Administrative Zone" decreed in Sinuiju, and others—but all of these were ultimately abandoned, either quietly discarded as failures or explicitly acknowledged as such. No serious effort at what might be considered to qualify as "economic reform" in Western countries—or even in socialist states such as China and Vietnam—has ever been broached in Pyongyang. Indeed, *reform* remains an absolutely impermissible word in the official DPRK lexicon—with regard to the North Korean system, that is. In 1998, the DPRK's party daily, *Rodong Sinmun*, declared that as "we have incessantly improved and are still improving economic management in our own style under the principle of *juche*, for us there is nothing to reform."[32] To this very day, North Korea's official news service, KCNA, has never used the word *reform* in conjunction with any contemporary North Korean practice or policy.

In consequence, and by no surprise, despite the enormous aid flows that have piled into Pyongyang's state coffers over the past decade and a half, the country has remained economically destitute and permanently on the brink of famine. One might go so far as to suggest that foreign aid inflows have been the *enabling condition* that has permitted the perpetuation of such economically devastating policies by the DPRK regime; absent those subsidies, after all, how could the North Korean government possibly have afforded to maintain such predictably destructive policies and practices?

THE LOGIC OF THE DPRK'S POLITICAL ECONOMY

In a sense, "fixing" the afflictions of the North Korean economy looks like a very simple proposition: all that would be necessary would be to cease imposing some or all of the positively costly or positively destructive state policies and practices enumerated just above. But it would be a mistake for us to ignore the degree to which North Korea's aberrant and seemingly dysfunctional economic policy regimen today is actually a result of conscious purpose, deliberate design, and considered official effort. There is deeply embedded *regime logic* in the DPRK's tangential and precarious relationship with the world economy. And far from being irrational, it is based on careful and coolheaded calculations about regime survival.

Ideological and Cultural Infiltration

Pyongyang's remarkably poor long-term performance in the advanced economies' huge markets is no accident. Rather, it is a direct consequence of official DPRK policy and doctrine, most particularly Pyongyang's concept of "ideological and cultural infiltration" (sometimes also termed "ideological and cultural poisoning"). Official North Korean pronouncements relentlessly decry the dangers of this phenomenon, characterized as a technique by which outsiders attempt to undermine the foundations of established communist states. A classic declamation will give the flavor of the general argument:

> It is the imperialist's old trick to carry out ideological and cultural infiltration prior to their launching of an aggression openly. Their bourgeois ideology and culture are reactionary toxins to paralyze people's ideological consciousness. Through such infiltration, they try to paralyze the independent consciousness of other nations and make them spineless. At the same time, they work to create illusions about capitalism and promote lifestyles among them based on the law of the jungle, in an attempt to induce the collapse of socialist and progressive nations. The ideological and cultural infiltration is their silent, crafty and villainous method of aggression, intervention and domination. . . .
>
> Through "economic exchange" and personnel interchange programs too, the imperialists are pushing their infiltration. . . . Exchange and cooperation activities in the economic and cultural fields have been on the rise since the beginning of the new century. The imperialists are making use of these activities as an important lever to push the infiltration of bourgeois ideology and culture. . . .
>
> The imperialists' ideological and cultural infiltration, if tolerated, will lead to the collapse and degeneration of society, to disorder and chaos, and even to the loss of the gains of the revolution. The collapse of socialism in the 20th Century—and the revival of capitalism in its place—in some countries gave us the serious lesson that social deterioration begins with ideological degeneration and confusion on the ideological front throws every other front of society into chaos and, consequently, all the gains of the revolution go down the drain eventually.[33]

DPRK party lecture notes published in South Korea late in 2002 put the point more succinctly:

> *The capitalist's ideological and cultural infiltration will never cease, and the struggle against it will continue, as long as the imperialists continue to exist in the world.* . . .
>
> The great leader, Kim Jong Il, pointed out the following: "Today, the imperialist and reactionaries are tenaciously scheming to blow the wind of bourgeois liberalism into us." . . .
>
> People will ideologically degenerate and weaken; cracks will develop in our socialist ideological position; and, in the end, our socialism will helplessly collapse. A case in point is the bitter lesson drawn from the miserable situations of the former Soviet Union and Eastern European countries.[34]

Note that both of these disquisitions appeared *after* Pyongyang had announced its heralded July 2002 economic measures (widely misreported in the West as "reforms").

Economic exchange with the capitalist world, in other words, is explicitly and officially regarded by Pyongyang as a process that unleashes powerful, unpredictable, and subversive forces—forces which ultimately erode the authority of socialist states. Viewed from this perspective, North Korea's record of trade performance vis-à-vis the advanced market economies is not a record of failure—that is, failure to integrate into the world economy—but rather a mark of *success* in the effective containment of a potentially lethal security threat.[35]

It is true that official directives from Pyongyang have from time to time discussed the desirability of significantly increasing the DPRK's volume of international trade. Against such comments, North Korea's extraordinary and continuing weakness in export performance may seem especially curious, insofar as it would be—at least in theory—so very easy to redress. But Pyongyang's conspicuous neglect of the revenue potential from trade with advanced market economies is not to be explained away as a prolonged fit of absentmindedness. Instead it speaks to fundamental and abiding calculations in Pyongyang's strategy for state survival.[36]

MILITARY-FIRST POLITICS

If staying out of the poisonous embrace of the world economy is viewed as an imperative for state survival by DPRK leadership, a corollary question about state survival inevitably arises: how then to generate sufficient international resources to forestall economic collapse? To date, Pyongyang's answer has been to make nonmarket transactions. The DPRK has always pursued an "aid-seeking" international economic strategy, but in the post–Soviet Bloc era, the particulars of that approach have perforce mutated. In the era of the "strong and prosperous state," North Korea's main tactics for generating international resources are viewed through the prism of the current state campaign for "military-first politics" (*songun chongch'i*).

Like the concept of "ideological and cultural infiltration," the theory and recommended practice of military-first politics have received a tremendous amount of airtime in the North Korean media over the past decade. Two exegeses may clarify some of the economic implications of this doctrine.

As a long, official analysis in March 2003 instructed, it was a renewed emphasis on military development that enabled North Korea to conclude its "Arduous March" and to step onto the pathway to power and prosperity:

Today, the peoples' struggle for their nation's independent development and prosperity is waged in an environment different from that of the last century.

In building a state in our era, it is essential to beef up the main force of the nation and fortify the revolutionary base, and, in this regard, it is most important to build up powerful military might. In today's world, without powerful military might, no country can . . . achieve development and prosperity.

During . . . "the Arduous March" in our history, great Comrade Kim Jong Il firmly believed that the destiny of the people and the future of the revolution hinged on the barrel of a gun, and that we could break through the difficulties and lead the revolution to victory only by depending on the Army. . . . Through the arduous practice in which the Army was put to the fore and the unheard-of trials were overcome, the revolutionary philosophy that the barrel of a gun was precisely the revolution and the barrel of a gun was precisely the victory of socialism was originated. . . .

Our theory on the construction of a powerful state . . . is the embodiment of the profound truth that the base of national strength is military might, and [that] the dignity and might of a country hinges on the barrel of a gun. . . . In a powerful state, the defense industry takes a leading and key position in the economy. . . .

Today, by firmly adhering to the principle of putting prime effort into the defense industry and, based on this, by developing the overall economy ceaselessly, our party is brilliantly resolving the issue of consolidating the national strength of a powerful state.[37]

And how exactly does military power conduce to prosperity? The answer was strongly hinted at in a statement the previous month:

A country's development and the placement of importance on the military are linked as one. . . .

Once we lay the foundations for a powerful *self-sustaining national defense industry*, we will be able to rejuvenate all economic fields, to include light industry and agriculture and enhance the quality of the people's lives.[38]

This is a fascinating, and revealing, formulation. In most of the world today, a country's defense outlays are regarded as a weight that must be shouldered by the value-adding sectors of the national economy—hence the phrase "military burden." North Korean leadership, however, evidently entertains the concept of a "self-sustaining" defense sector, implying that Pyongyang views its military activities as *generating* resources, and not simply absorbing them. In effect, in the enunciated view of North Korean leadership, the DPRK's military sector is the key not only to unlocking the resources necessary to finance its own considerable needs, but to financing the recovery of the rest of the national economy as well.

It does not require a great deal of imagination to spell out the operational details of this approach. While forswearing any appreciable export revenues from legitimate commerce with advanced market economies, North Korean policy today seems to be banking on the possibility of financing state survival by exporting *strategic insecurity* to the rest of the world. In part, such dividends are derived from exports of merchandise, such as missile sales, or international transfers of WMD technology. But these revenues also depend heavily on what might be described as an export of services, or, in this case, military extortion services—might we better call them "revenue-sensitive threat reduction services"?—based upon Pyongyang's nuclear development and ballistic missile programs.

The export of strategic insecurity, in its different components, can arguably be said to explain much of the upsurge in North Korea's unexplained surfeit of imports over commercial export revenues since 1998, especially to the extent that Western aid policies in recent years can be described as appeasement motivated.[39] In an important tactical sense, that approach has enjoyed success, as it has facilitated state survival under imposing constraints. But the territory demarcated by "ideological and cultural infiltration" on one side, and military-first politics on the other, is also quite clearly a sort of no-man's land, an inherently unstable niche in which survival is utterly contingent, and sustained development utterly unlikely.

THE QUEST FOR AN UNCONDITIONAL
KOREAN UNIFICATION

A third keystone to the architecture and behavior of the North Korean state is its abiding insistence that it is the sole legitimate government in the Korean Peninsula—and its apparent intention to effectuate an ultimate Korean unification on Pyongyang's own uncontested terms.

The DPRK Constitution lays claim to the entirety of the Korean Peninsula (cf. Article 9),[40] and the preamble to the charter of the DPRK Korea Workers' Party expressly calls for

> the revolutionary goals of national liberation and the people's democracy on the entire area of the country, with the ultimate goal of the indoctrination of the entire society with *Juche* philosophy.[41]

It is true, of course, that South Korea's constitution likewise lays claim to the entirety of the Korean Peninsula and its adjacent islands (Article 3)[42]—but South Korea has not actively attempted to promote unification on its own terms for decades. North Korea's commitment to unconditional unification, by contrast, is far from merely symbolic and vestigial. The only "South Korean" mission officially permitted in Pyongyang today, for example, is the "Anti-Imperialist National Democratic Front" (AINDF)—a fictitious construct that purports to be the voice of a revolutionary underground in the South dedicated to overthrowing the current dictatorship that controls southern Korea, in order to join their northern compatriots under the benevolent care of Kim Jong Un.[43] Further, consider this declaration by the late General Jo Myong Rok, then vice chairman of the DPRK National Defense Commission and the highest-ranking North Korean official ever to visit Washington, at a dinner in his honor at the U.S. State Department in October 2000:

> Chairman Kim Jong Il of the DPRK's National Defense Commission will certainly make the very important political decision to turn the current bilateral relations of confrontation and hostility into the new relationship of friendship and cooperation and goodwill, if and when the Democratic People's Republic of Korea and our leadership is assured, is given the strong and concrete security assurances from the United States for the state sovereignty and *the territorial integrity of the Democratic People's Republic of Korea.*[44]

When one recalls what Pyongyang regards as the territory of the DPRK (see the DPRK Constitution and the WPK charter's preamble above), General Jo's remarks to his American audience underscored the fact that North Korea's claim to dominion over South Korea remained an absolutely central concern to North Korean policy makers.

North Korea's preoccupation—obsession is not too strong a term—with unconditional peninsular reunification has a number of practical corollaries. The most important of these is the North Korean war-footing economy and the DPRK's nuclear and ballistic weapons development programs—which are evidently regarded as the regime's most viable tools for promoting its own vision of unification—or at the very least, the regime's most effective tools for competing for unification against South Korea. (Given its ideology, it may even be that DPRK leadership would regard any North Korean government that did not embrace hypermilitarization and WMD buildup as fundamentally unserious about Korean unification.)

FOREIGN AID AND ECONOMIC "TAKEOFF": THE SOUTH KOREAN EXAMPLE

In the prevailing narrative on the postwar institution of development assistance, South Korea is always adduced as one of the prime "success stories" underscoring the potentialities of economic aid.[45] South Korea, after all, was a desperately poor country after partition, it absorbed large inflows of U.S. aid, and it is now an affluent Western society—an aid giver itself these days. (No doubt this narrative has made a deep impression on North Korean policy makers as well: to judge by official North Korean commentary, Pyongyang's position is that U.S. economic assistance is what made South Korea rich.) The actual story of the interplay between aid and development in South Korea, however, is a bit more complex, and interesting, than today's narratives suggest.

Between 1946 and 1961, exclusive of its Korean War help, the United States provided the Republic of Korea with $5 billion (in current dollars) of direct grants. This was a fantastic sum of money, probably equivalent to nearly a tenth of ROK GDP over that period. How did these transfers affect South Korea's material prospects?

Viewed in very broad terms, the impact of these enormous concessional transfers on the South Korean prospect can be described by two generalizations. On the one hand, one may be reasonably certain that these massive donations permitted the survival of the state; even in retrospect, it is difficult to imagine how the Republic of Korea would have sustained itself against domestic collapse or external aggression during those years without vast outside help. On the other hand, it evidently did not coincide with recovery to prepartition levels of per capita output, much less spark an immediate economic "takeoff."

The ROK's "First Republic"—the regime of Syngman Rhee (1948–1960)—was, in the estimate of both his contemporary critics and some of his close personal advisors, quite content to treat U.S. aid essentially as an ongoing program of external relief. Some analysts have even termed Rhee's policies as "aid maximizing": in effect, designed to require large and continuing inflows from its American ally to redress the precarious fiscal and financial conditions they engendered. Needless to say, such a strategy would not be predicted to excite rapid economic growth. In underwriting it, the United States seems to have purchased the possibility of rapid development in South Korea at a future date, even as its aid effectively precluded that possibility at the time.

Rapid economic growth in South Korea in the 1960s was directly related to U.S. foreign aid, albeit in a somewhat unexpected manner, for South Korea's transition to outward-oriented growth was a consequence of a warning by Washington that it would be *terminating* its programs for Seoul.

By the late 1950s, the Eisenhower administration had become expressly displeased by what it saw as the Korean government's unhealthy dependence on and unseemly interest in U.S. aid. (Eisenhower is alleged to have complained about "pouring aid down a rat hole," the "rat hole" being South Korea.) The incoming Kennedy administration shared the sentiment; its top policy makers questioned the aid arrangements they inherited in Korea—

under which the ROK was, among other things, America's single greatest recipient of foreign assistance. With the military coup in 1961, the Kennedy administration's displeasure with Seoul increased further.

The new U.S. Agency for International Development's response to Seoul's politics and economics was unambiguous—and completely unexpected by the recipient regime. Late in 1962 and early in 1963, the Park Chung Hee government was informed by Washington that an irreversible decision had been reached: although security assistance would continue, U.S. economic assistance would be terminated in an orderly but deliberate manner and would be phased out entirely by the second half of the 1960s.

This fact—central to any understanding of subsequent South Korean policies, yet seldom discussed in the development assistance literature—was nicely captured at the time by a front-page story in the *New York Times*:

> The United States has quietly decided to reduce economic grants to South Korea, a country whose economy is mainly based on such assistance. The decision was taken considerably before the current political struggle between the military regime and civilian leaders. . . .
>
> Leading South Korean officials have been told privately to expect reduced aid. For months they decided not to believe what Washington said, but now some of them believe it, and in the words of one American, are in a "dither" about it. Washington has decided it can no longer underwrite all the shortcomings of the South Korean economy. . . . Any future government, civilian or military, will find the flow of United States grants thinner and more carefully controlled.[46]

It is easy to see why planners in Seoul would have been in a "dither" about this news. At the time, economic assistance from Washington was the principal vehicle for financing the operation of their state—in fact, those monies accounted for more than half of all the funds the central government raised. Radical adjustments in fiscal and economic policy would be required to compensate for this impending loss of revenue. The response to this American challenge was the package of "reforms" implemented between 1963 and 1966, which launched the rapid and sustained economic transformation that propelled the South Korean economy to where it is today. Washington's unwelcome announcement thus seems to have served as the proximate stimulus for the Park regime's decision to embark on an export-oriented development strategy.

North Korea, as it happens, was not the only (or perhaps even the first) of the Korean states to exhibit a "mendicant mentality" toward foreign aid: that stinging phrase was used by American policy makers to describe their counterparts in Seoul before the mid-1960s. And in any event, for a variety of reasons, American aid to Seoul did not cease as threatened but continued on into the 1970s. But it was the credible announcement of the end of that aid that impelled South Korean policy makers to embark upon the "bold switchover" (to borrow a phrase Pyongyang deploys in a quite different context) in economic policies that ultimately led to that country's economic ascent and enrichment.

WHAT WOULD A GENUINE REFORM AND OPENING LOOK LIKE FOR NORTH KOREA?

Instead of sketching out the full contours of a DPRK transition to sustainable export-led growth, it may serve our purposes here to outline some possible "indicators" of serious economic reform in North Korea if and when that process is truly under way. In particular, we should dwell on three essential and inextricably linked features of any North Korean economic reform worthy of the name: an outward opening itself, military demobilization, and normalization of relations with the ROK.

Economic Opening

If Pyongyang were to embark upon a genuine move toward an economic opening, what initial signs would outsiders be able to see? Some of these might include (1) meaningful departure from old economic themes, and new dialogue about economic issues, in DPRK propaganda and guidance organs; (2) doctrinal reorientation regarding the treatment of profit-generating transactions in official DPRK pronouncements—and especially profits involving transactions with foreign concerns; (3) an attempt on the part of the DPRK to settle its longstanding international debt default problems; (4) a move toward greater economic transparency, for instance, the publication of economic and social statistics describing the North Korean domestic situation; and (5) serious attempts to promulgate a legal framework for potential foreign investors that might assist in attracting profit-seeking overseas entrepreneurs to North Korean soil. Although some observers may see glimmers of conditions (1) and (2), none of these "blinker lights" are flashing brightly and consistently in North Korea today.

Military Demobilization

Military demobilization would represent a critical aspect of a North Korean program for "reform" and "opening" insofar as (a) a dismantling of

Pyongyang's WMD programs would indicate that North Korean leadership was committed to earning its living from activities other than international military extortion, and (b) reallocation of resources from the hypertrophied military to the civilian sectors would permit much more potentially productive economic activity in the DPRK.

To date, of course, there is little evidence that North Korea has ever, at any point in its more than five decades of existence, voluntarily abjured any new instrument of military force that might possibly lie within its grasp. (Today, indeed, such a renunciation would seem fundamentally inconsistent with the state's established policies of *kangsong taeguk* and "military-first politics.") Moreover, North Korea's commitment to developing weapons of mass destruction has been implicitly and explicitly reaffirmed repeatedly since the resumption of the North Korean nuclear drama in late 2002, and even during the period of "Six-Party Talks" that commenced in 2003.

Normalization of DPRK–ROK Relations

The DPRK cannot execute a successful economic opening unless it demobilizes, and it cannot demobilize unless it comes to terms with the right of the Republic to coexist with it on the Korean Peninsula. Consequently, one important and indeed indispensable marker of movement toward reform and opening would be a change in North Korea's official stance concerning the legitimacy of the ROK.

If North Korea were to evidence a new attitude toward the legitimacy of the ROK, the indications of this change would be direct and unmistakable: its highest figures and its official media would simply disclose that they were prepared to accept the existence of the South Korean state, that they recognized the ROK's right to conduct its own foreign policy, and that they respected (even if respectfully disagreeing with) Seoul's decision to maintain a military alliance with the United States.

CONCLUSION

In the preceding pages we have emphasized the strong elements of continuity in DPRK economic policy. Powerful and pervasive as these are, they should not prevent us from noting important changes on the North Korean political and economic scene today—including at least a few new and heretofore uncharacteristic departures from previous received practices.

The most momentous of these changes, of course, was perforce the December 2011 death of DPRK supreme leader Kim Jong Il. His successor and son,

Kim Jong Un, is (at least for now) the world's youngest head of state. Much remains unclear about the country's new leadership, including how stable the new configuration will prove to be and whether it will be willing to deviate from the orthodoxies laid down by his father—and if so, how far.

Yet even before the death of Kim Jong Il, a number of recent changes bespoke an admittedly limited measure of pragmatic experimentation, testing the boundaries of the politically acceptable in the hope of generating techno-logical and economic dividends. The DPRK, for example, has begun to make a few accommodations with the global information revolution: activating its country domain name (".kp") on the Internet through ICANN; permitting the Associated Press to open an office in Pyongyang; and—perhaps most signifi-cantly—authorizing the Egyptian telecom company Orascom to set up a do-mestic mobile phone network which has attracted over 1 million subscribers to date. North Korea has also permitted the launching of a privately financed educational facility, the Pyongyang University of Science and Technology, in which North Korean students are trained exclusively in English and exclu-sively by foreigners, and are given access to global Internet connections. And in June 2011, North Korea inaugurated a special economic zone with China on two small islands in the Yalu near the Chinese city of Dandong; there are suggestions that Pyongyang is considering the use of Chinese rather than North Korean commercial and business law on this territory.

Whatever these changes may signify, they will provide—at least for the time being—some additional arguments for proponents of Western aid to North Korea: for now it may be said that Western economic assistance may be allocated to support the glimmerings of "reform" in the DPRK. Indeed, Western proponents of economic engagement with the DPRK can have it both ways: aid may be applied in the hope of fomenting liberalization in North Korea, or alternatively for fear that North Korea will resort to danger-ous and destabilizing international behavior unless propitiated.

Thus in the months or years ahead, it is not only plausible but likely that the issue of economic assistance to the DPRK will return to the agenda for policy makers in Washington, Seoul, Tokyo, and other Western capitals. So, to return to the theme of this chapter, is effective international economic as-sistance to the DPRK conceivable?

The answer to this question depends upon one's definition of "effective." Clearly, international humanitarian aid has not been effective, at least to date: despite a decade and a half of these charitable inflows, North Korea remains on the verge of another eruption of mass hunger. Security aid will remain utterly ineffective so long as the objectives of the DPRK govern-ment remain diametrically opposed to those of the prospective donor states. And absent a "bold switchover" in DPRK priorities and policies, development aid is most unlikely to promote what Western donors understand "development" to entail.

There is one way, however, in which international economic assistance to the real existing North Korean regime can indeed be effective: this is in helping the North Korean government stay in power, resist system-threatening reform, and augment its military capabilities to threaten both its own population and populations abroad. The point here is not just that international Western aid *could* be effective in such an effort: for nearly two decades—since the end of the Cold War—this is exactly what international economic aid to the DPRK *has* done.

NOTES

The author would like to thank Philip I. Levy, Apoorva Shah, and Dale Swartz of the American Enterprise Institute and Marcus Noland of the Peterson Institute for International Economics for valuable comments on earlier versions of this work. The usual caveats apply. The author can be contacted at eberstadt@aei.org.

1. Korea Central News Agency [hereafter KCNA] (Pyongyang), "Joint New Year Editorial," January 1, 2012, http://www.kcna.co.jp/index-e.htm (accessed March 5, 2012).

2. KCNA (Pyongyang), "State General Bureau for Economic Development to Be Established," January 15, 2011.

3. Yonhap News Agency (Seoul), "N. Korea Draws up 10-Year Development Plan: State Media," January 15, 2011; see also "Daepung International Investment Group Established in North Korea: Goals for Economic Development from 2010 to 2020 Set," *NK Briefs* (Seoul: Institute of Far Eastern Studies), October 13, 2011, http://ifes.kyungnam.ac.kr/eng/FRM/FRM_0101V.aspx?code=FRM111013_0001.

4. The $10 billion figure did not come entirely out of thin air—it was a population-scaled, exchange-rate- and inflation-adjusted number based on Japan's economic assistance to South Korea in 1965, when relations between the two countries normalized.

5. For a detailed recounting and analysis of this saga, see Nicholas Eberstadt, *Policy and Economic Performance in Divided Korea during the Cold War Era: 1945–1991* (Washington, DC: AEI Press, 2010).

6. Pyongyang has never divulged the toll of the Great North Korean Hunger of the 1990s; some Western demographers, nevertheless, have speculated that the total count of excess deaths may have run on the order of 600,000 to 1,000,000—or roughly 3 to 5 percent of the country's population at the time. Cf. Daniel Goodkind and Loraine West, "The North Korean Famine and Its Demographic Impact," *Population and Development Review* 27, no. 2 (June 2001): 219–38. For comprehensive treatments, see Stephan Haggard and Marcus Noland, *Famine in North Korea: Markets, Aid and Reform* (New York: Columbia University Press, 2007), and also Andrew S. Natsios,

The Great North Korean Famine: Famine, Politics and Foreign Policy (Washington, DC: Institute of Peace Press, 2001).

7. Cf. "North Korea Desperate for Food Aid," *Korea Herald*, April 3, 2011, http://www.koreaherald.com/national/Detail.jsp?newsMLId=20110403000248.

8. If we use the US Producer Price Index as the deflator (an arguably appropriate metric), dollar-denominated price levels would have been 89 percent higher in 2007 than in 1980—implying that per capita North Korean merchandise export revenues would have fallen by more than a fourth over that period. PPI data derived from U.S. Bureau of the Census, *Statistical Abstract of the United States 2010*, http://www.census.gov/prod/2011pubs/11statab/prices.pdf (accessed March 2, 2012).

9. Note that mirror statistics, depending as they do upon voluntary reporting by a country's trade partners, can only illuminate North Korea's licit trade. Illicit trade—counterfeiting, drug trafficking, proliferation of nuclear goods and services, and the like—may figure importantly in North Korea's current international trade export profile, but we have no way of tracking such transactions with any precision.

10. In the decade since April 2001, KCNA has published over 530 news items and editorials denouncing the "U.S. hostile policy" toward the DPRK—or roughly one a week.

11. As of 2010, according to the U.S. Congressional Research Service, a total of thirty-two separate legislative and executive strictures against commercial and financial relations with the DPRK were on the books, all but one of which (an executive order on state-sponsored terrorism) were being enforced. Dianne E. Rennack, "North Korea: Legislative Basis for U.S. Economic Sanctions," Congressional Research Service Report R41438, October 29, 2010.

12. U.S. Census Bureau International Data Base, http://www.census.gov/ipc/www/idb (accessed March 1, 2012).

13. This section draws upon Nicholas Eberstadt, *The North Korean Economy between Crisis and Catastrophe* (New Brunswick, NJ: Transaction Publishers, 2007), chap. 9.

14. World Bank, *World Development Indicators 2011*, http://data.worldbank.org/data-catalog/world-development-indicators (accessed March 1, 2012).

15. U.S. Census Bureau International Data Base, http://www.census.gov/ipc/www/idb (accessed March 1, 2012).

16. Cf. Ludwig Von Mises, *Socialism* (New Haven, CT: Yale University Press, 1951); Friedrich A. Hayek, *The Fatal Conceit* (Chicago: University of Chicago Press, 1989).

17. See Angus Maddison, *Monitoring the World Economy: 1820–1992* (Paris: OECD, 1995), and subsequent updates of this work. By Maddison's estimates, for example, per capita output in the USSR rose from US$1,386 (in 1990 Geary-Khamis dollars) in 1929 to US$7,032 in 1989—a fivefold increase over six decades, implying an average growth rate of 2.7 percent per year over that period; by Maddison's estimates, even Maoist China managed to double its per capita output between 1950 and 1975, rising from US$614 to US$1,250, implying a long-term per capita growth rate of nearly 3 percent per annum.

18. World Bank, *World Development Indicators 2011*, http://data.worldbank.org/data-catalog/world-development-indicators (accessed March 2, 2012).

19. Pyongyang's 1999 "Law on Socialist Economic Planning" can be seen as an implicit acknowledgement that the statistical apparatus necessary for centrally planning had effectively broken down; for a full evaluation of available DPRK statistics, and details of earlier signs of trouble in the DPRK statistical system, see Eberstadt, *The North Korean Economy*, chap. 1.

20. Mitsuhiko Kimura, "A Planned Economy without Planning: Su-ryong's North Korea," Discussion Paper F-081, Faculty of Economics, Tezukayama University, 1994.

21. Robert A. Scalapino and Chong-Sik Lee, *Communism in Korea* (Berkeley: University of California Press, 1972), 2:919.

22. Cf. Nicholas Eberstadt and Judith Banister, "Military Buildup in the DPRK: Some New Indications from North Korean Data," *Asian Survey* 31, no. 11 (November 1991): 1095–1115.

23. See Alan S. Milward, *War, Economy, Society: 1939–1945* (Berkeley: University of California Press, 1977).

24. Eberstadt, *Policy and Economic Performance*.

25. Eberstadt, *Policy and Economic Performance*.

26. For background here, consult the translated Soviet Bloc archives of the North Korea International Documentation Project, an initiative promoted by the Woodrow Wilson International Center for Scholars' Cold War International History Project, http://www.wilsoncenter.org/index.cfm?topic_id=230972&fuseaction=topics.home.

27. See Sheena E. Chestnut, "The 'Soprano State'? North Korean Involvement in Criminal Activity and Implications for International Security," Stanford University Honors Thesis, May 20, 2005, and David L. Asher, "Pressuring Kim Jong Il: The North Korean Illicit Activities Initiative, 2001–2006," in David L. Asher, Victor D. Comras, and Patrick M. Cronin, *Pressure: Coercive Economic Statecraft and U.S. National Security* (Washington, DC: Center for New American Security, 2011); on North Korea's insurance fraud racket, see Blaine Harden, "Global Insurance Fraud by North Korea Outlined: Government Has Collected Millions of Dollars on Large, Suspicious Claims," *Washington Post*, June 18, 2009.

28. For additional analysis and quantitative assessments regarding the failure of the North Korean economy, see the important work by Marcus Noland of the Institute for International Economics, especially Marcus Noland, *Avoiding the Apocalypse: The Future of the Two Koreas* (Washington, DC: Institute for International Economics, 2000), and Haggard and Noland, *Famine in North Korea*.

29. William Easterly and Tobias Pfuetze, "Where Does the Money Go? Best and Worst Practices in Foreign Aid," Brookings Global Economy and Development Working Paper No. 21, June 2008.

30. Cf. Carole Adelman and Nicholas Eberstadt, "Foreign Aid: What Works and What Doesn't," *AEI Development Policy Outlook*, October 2008, http://www.aei.org/outlook/28842.

31. See, for example, David Dollar and Lant Pritchett, *Assessing Aid: What Works, What Doesn't, and Why* (New York: Oxford University Press, 1998); Craig Burnside and David Dollar, "Aid, Policies and Growth," *American Economic Review* 90, no. 4 (September 2000): 847–68; Craig Burnside and David Dollar, "Aid, Policies and Growth: Revisiting the Evidence," World Bank Policy Research Working Paper no. 3251, March 2004.

32. *Rodong Sinmun*, September 17, 1998.

33. *Rodong Sinmun*, April 20, 2003.

34. Reprinted in *Chosun Ilbo* (Seoul), December 20, 2002; emphasis added.

35. Moreover, it is worth recalling that the DPRK's public misgivings about "ideological and cultural infiltration" are long standing, almost precisely paralleling the state's record of minimal export outreach to advanced market economies over the past generation. North Korean leadership had been highlighting the dangers of that tendency for at least a decade *before* the final collapse of the Soviet Union. In 1981, for example, Kim Il Sung was urging North Korea's "workers and trade union members" to "combat the ideological and cultural infiltration of the imperialists and their subversive moves and sabotage."

36. Additional characteristic features of the DPRK's "own style of socialism" can likewise be understood as components of this same survival strategy: among these, the demonetization of the domestic economy, the repression of the consumer sector, and the suppression of financial intermediation, all of which reduce the economic influence and political power of nonstate actors within North Korea and reduce the risk of "ideological and cultural poisoning."

37. *Rodong Sinmun*, April 3, 2003.

38. *Rodong Sinmun*, March 21, 2003; emphasis added.

39. Even ostensibly humanitarian food aid transfers to North Korea are informed by the reality of military extortion; think, in particular, of the 1999 "inspection fee" (as Pyongyang called it) of 600,000 tons of U.S. food aid via WFP channels for access to the alleged underground nuclear site at Kumchang-ri, or, more generally, whether the opaque rules under which food relief is administered in the DPRK would be tolerated by the international donor community in any other setting.

40. For an electronically accessible translation of the DPRK Constitution, see http://www1.korea-np.co.jp/pk/061st_issue/98091708.htm.

41. As translated in Sung-yoon Lee, "Engaging North Korea: The Clouded Legacy of North Korea's Sunshine Policy," *AEI Asian Outlook*, no. 2 (April 2010): 5, http://www.aei.org/docLib/2AOLeeApril2010-g.pdf (accessed March 7, 2012).

42. Cf. the ROK Constitution, http://english.ccourt.go.kr/home/att_file/download/Constitution_of_the_Republic_of_Korea.pdf.

43. For an example of the viewpoint attributed to this AINDF, see for example this portion of a longer AINDF letter to Kim Jong Il, as reported by KCNA, October 10, 2010:

> The Central Committee of the AINDF will cherish the unshakable faith that the reunification of the country and the dignity and prosperity of the nation depend on trusting and following you as the Heaven and consolidate as firm as a rock the organizational and ideological unity of the ranks based on the *juche* idea and the *songun* idea, causing the hot wind of worship for you and supporting *songun* to sweep all over south Korea.

44. As transcribed and translated in the Department of State archives, http://usinfo.org/wf-archive/2000/001011/epf302.htm (accessed March 5, 2012); emphasis added.

45. This section draws upon Eberstadt, *Policy and Economic Performance*.

46. A. M. Rosenthal, "U.S. Will Cut Aid to South Koreans," *New York Times*, April 4, 1963, 1.

Chapter Seven

Future Strategies for Economic Engagement with North Korea

Bradley Babson

North Korea's economic isolationism has deep roots in Korean history, post–Korean War political philosophy and national identity, and contemporary political realism both at home and in its international relations. Principles of economic efficiency and welfare distribution that derive from Western economic thought and experience with balancing the roles of governments and markets, and that have been institutionalized in the global economic system, have not figured significantly in North Korean economic policy or strategy for becoming a "strong and prosperous" nation. It is thus not surprising that North Korea remains among the last of the nations of the world to join the International Monetary Fund, World Bank, and World Trade Organization. Indeed, contact between North Korean economic officials and these core institutions of the global economic order has been hesitant and sporadic at best over the years, reflecting both North Korean ambivalence about the costs and benefits of joining this club, and equally an ambivalence among the larger shareholders—the United States, Japan, and Europe—about accepting North Korean participation in this system without first attending to their unresolved security and political concerns. The challenges of North Korea's global economic integration are thus inextricably linked with the political challenges of the transformation of North Korea's domestic political economy and its relations with its neighbors and with the international community at large. Following the death of Kim Jong Il, these challenges have taken on a new urgency for stable regime succession and economic improvements that will be important for future regime legitimacy. While the risks are higher than ever before, there is now unprecedented opportunity for fresh consideration of policy changes that could dramatically alter future North Korean economic prospects and external economic relations.

The present situation needs to be understood in the context of transformations that have been taking place within North Korea and the evolution
of external economic and political engagement experiences since the early
1990s. These have set in motion dynamics of change that are compelling
North Korea toward a future where markets play a larger role than in the past
and which requires a deepening of external economic integration. The path
of future integration of the North Korean economy with the global economic
system is however uncertain and could evolve in a number of different ways.
This path will depend on policy choices made by the North Korean leadership and policy choices made by those countries with most at stake in North
Korea's external economic and political relations, especially South Korea,
China, the United States, Japan, and Russia. The Six-Party framework for
negotiations over North Korea's nuclear future is thus also highly relevant
for shaping a commonly shared vision and coherence in policies for defining
a path for North Korea's economic future.

HISTORICAL PERSPECTIVES

North Korea's historical image as a "Hermit Kingdom" has roots in Korea's
historical geographical position caught between two large powers—China
and Japan—and the psychology built from centuries of experiences of being
a "shrimp among the whales" and seeking refuge from unwanted external
influences in isolation and self-reliance. This orientation was reinforced by
the policies North Korea adopted following the era of Japanese occupation
and the Korean War that were formalized in Kim Il Sung's *juche* political
philosophical justification for national independence and self-reliance.[1]
While South Korea, starting with the Park Chung Hee government, has
pursued national development through opening up to the outside world
and aggressive outward-oriented economic development policies that have
evolved over time, North Korea has sought external economic relations
principally to maintain political and subsidized economic ties with its Soviet and Chinese sponsors, improve relations with South Korea, and obtain
foreign exchange, technology, aid, and commodities (such as food and
oil) that it considers essential for regime survival, not for robust national
economic development. Efforts to shelter the North Korean people from
outside influences have been a hallmark of North Korean management of
its external economic relations for decades.

Trade as a percentage of GDP dropped from about 20 percent in 1990
before the collapse of the Soviet Union to 12 percent in 2000, reflecting the
impact of the trade shock on the North Korean economy that was a major

factor contributing to the famine of the mid-1990s. By 2008, trade had recovered to about the 20 percent level, but the primary trading partners had shifted dramatically from communist Europe to China and South Korea. Even so, this ratio is very low compared to estimates of what would be expected if the North Korean economy were functioning as a fully developed market economy with open trade with the international community.[2]

While expanding economic relations with South Korea under the "Sunshine Policy" era from 1998 to 2008 and a rapidly growing economic relationship between China and North Korea during this same period account for much of the shift in trade patterns, the role of economic sanctions imposed by the United States historically, and then much more widely by the UN Security Council after the missile and nuclear tests of 2006, have also been important factors limiting North Korean trade with the international community as a whole. One important by-product of sanctions is the disincentive for North Korea to adopt open and transparent practices as it attempts to expand trade and obtain foreign exchange. Masking both illegitimate and legitimate trade by setting up shell companies to avoid detection of sanctioned firms, using barter trade or cash rather than banks for business transactions, and forcing overseas diplomatic offices to engage in clandestine moneymaking practices have become the norm rather than the exception in the way North Korea conducts international economic activities around the world beyond the special economic ties that North Korea has developed with South Korea and China.

Thus the low level of trade as a percentage of GDP, high concentration of trade with neighboring countries, and nontransparent business practices, along with North Korea's reluctance to pursue economic interdependence rooted in its isolationist political philosophy and primacy of concern for regime survival, together constitute the starting point for consideration of future strategies for integration of the North Korean economy in the global economy.

Another historical factor affecting North Korea's economic future is the inevitable need to accommodate the growing role of markets. North Korea now faces the twin realities that all of its external trading partners are market economies, and the domestic economy is irreversibly a mixed economy that comprises both state-directed and market-based activities. The virtual abandonment of socialist economic management principles as the primary organizing mechanism for the economies of China and the former Soviet Union has left North Korea isolated in a way that was not of its own choosing. It has to learn how to be a successful player in other countries' market economies if it is going to be integrated in the regional and global economy. This requires an investment in learning how market economies work and how to engage with them effectively on a commercial rather than political basis governed by transparent business practices and the rule of law. Also, North

Korea's continuing unwillingness to embrace transition to market mechanisms domestically in a robust way and its halting off-again, on-again, and
so far unsuccessful efforts to squash the role of markets and reassert socialist
economic management practices[3] have left it stymied in a dual trap of its own
devising. It no longer receives the benefits of a functioning socialist management system, and it has not yet created the conditions to benefit fully from a
functioning market economy, leaving it stuck in both a poverty trap and an
economic management system trap. This dilemma poses a major policy challenge to the leadership as it seeks a path for an economically viable future.
It also poses a challenge to potential external economic partners in devising
economic engagement policies with North Korea that can produce significant
and sustainable economic development outcomes.[4]

ASSESSMENT OF THE CURRENT SITUATION

By now, the North Korean leadership knows that significantly expanding
foreign trade and foreign investment is needed to achieve the economic development that the country needs to remain a viable country in the medium
to long term, regardless of progress in dealing with the military and other
security challenges facing the country. However, the current North Korean
economic situation is fragile and disorganized, which constrains the policy
choices available to the leadership.[5] It is defined by (a) continuing fragmentation of economic interests inside the country which militate against
rational management of the economy, (b) a financial system that cannot
efficiently mobilize and allocate domestic resources for investment, (c) an
external environment not conducive to mobilization of foreign capital for
investment (with the possible exception of China), and (d) a lack of commitment to pursuing economic reforms that would embrace the important
role for markets and an outward-oriented economic development policy.
Present policy is focused on domestic productivity improvements through
technology advances and mass mobilization campaigns, import substitution, appealing for international food aid, taking administrative measures
to improve capacity for planning and management of hoped-for foreign
investment, and seeking ways to obtain foreign exchange needed to finance
critical imports for the military and "court economy."[6] The overarching
goal appears to be to shore up support for the regime in a sensitive political
transition period where there are also real stresses on food security for the
population, due in part to adverse weather factors but more importantly to
failure to reform the economic system. Following the death of Kim Jong

Il late in 2011, the 2012 New Year's editorial outlining policies for the emerging regime led by Kim Yong Un emphasizes continuity with the Kim Jong Il era, but at the same time recognizes the urgency of dealing with the food situation and the priority of delivering improvements in the economy overall. The need to focus on building domestic support for the political transition can be expected to foster pragmatic attention by the leadership group to the economic challenges facing North Korea, and this increases the possibility of consideration of new policy options.

A notable development in 2010–2011 was increased dependence on trade and investment relations with China, as economic relations between the two Koreas have been scaled back, combined with the continued impact of sanctions on North Korea's ability to engage in normal international trade and the reluctance of South Korea and the international community to provide food assistance on any significant scale to help offset the structural gap in food supply. The expanding economic relationship with China is driven not just by political factors, but significantly by commercial ones, reflecting economic interests of local governments and enterprises in bordering provinces. This could have significant impact on the process of economic integration in this region if North Korea is successful in attracting more investment and adopts more businesslike practices in investment approvals and management of joint ventures and trade, as seems to be the intention from recent organizational changes and initiatives. The expanding economic relationship with China is also supporting the growth of market economic activity in North Korea, but the dynamics are complex because of the need to mitigate the considerable risks for stakeholders on both sides of the border in an opaque nexus of investment and trade relationships, underdeveloped market mechanisms, and rent seeking, where normal and reliable business practices and financial settlements are still a dream, not a reality.[7]

The failure of the currency reforms of late 2009 and efforts to curtail the role of markets and reassert the socialist economic management model in early 2010 have revealed that the North Korean economic system is being directed by a combination of ideology, ignorance, and seeking ways to centralize control over foreign exchange inflows, with scant attention to external advice, even from the Chinese, or appreciation of the potential value of markets in stimulating production and increasing efficiency of distribution of goods and services. The lack of ability to control inflation reinforces a perception that there seems to be little understanding or appetite to address policies and institutional changes needed for effective macroeconomic management and supervision of the financial system. It is in this context that recent initiatives to increase foreign investment and trade need to be assessed.

ASSESSMENT OF RECENT INITIATIVES TO INCREASE
FOREIGN INVESTMENT AND TRADE

The North Korean leadership's recognition of the need to get serious about increasing foreign investment and expanding trade especially with China can been seen in a series of actions taken in 2010 and 2011:

- The establishment of a State Development Bank was announced in March 2010 to provide investment in major projects and according to the Korea Central News Agency "will have advanced banking rules and system for transactions with international monetary organizations and commercial banks." Notably, the Board of Directors is made up of representatives from the National Defense Commission, the Korea Asia-Pacific Peace Committee, the Ministry of Finance, and the Korea Taepung International Investment Group.[8]
- The Joint Venture and Investment Commission was established in July 2010 with ministerial status in the Cabinet to oversee approvals of foreign invested projects and undertake investment promotion activities. This office is intended to facilitate processing of foreign investment project proposals throughout the country with the exception of the Kaesong Industrial Zone.
- A ten-year economic development plan was adopted by the government in early 2011 that includes a commitment to shift from an aid-dependent relationship with China to an economic partnership.[9] Subsequently, announcements have been made of the establishment of the Rason Economic and Trade Zone in the eastern border region and the Hwanggumpyong and Wihwa Islands Special Economic Zone in the western border region. Rules governing these zones on the China border are more liberal than those governing the Kaesong Industrial Zone, including permitting use of Chinese currency for transactions; allowance for establishment of independent and joint banks; permission to lease, lend, or bequeath land to relatives within a contracted period of time; and freedom of access to cell phones and the Internet.[10] In developing these zones, North Korea appears also to be looking to Hong Kong and Singapore as models for openness and international transport respectively, and not relying solely on mainland Chinese firms' experience. It is noteworthy that the chair of the North Korean side in the DPRK-China Joint Guidance Committee for Economic Zones is Jang Song Taek, Kim Jong Il's brother-in-law and vice chairman of the National Defense Commission.[11]
- North Korea is also pressing China to sign a double taxation avoidance agreement and has already signed similar accords with Egypt and eleven other countries as a way to attract foreign investment.[12]

- North Korea's Taepung International Investment Group with close ties to the Kim family and the Korean Workers' Party is aggressively seeking to attract foreign investment, in both open and clandestine ways to avoid U.S. economic sanctions.
- Educational activities have increased, notably with North Korean economic officials responsible for international investment and trade increasing interactions with Chinese counterparts, attending courses offered by the Choson Exchange, and participating in a first-ever informal study tour of the U.S. economy in March 2011.
- A visit to Pyongyang to evaluate North Korea's legal framework for accepting foreign investment in June 2011 concluded that it appears to resemble China's legal regime: investment projects are categorized into encouraged, permitted, restricted, and prohibited categories; there is a defined process for review and approval of projects; operations and governance of North Korean corporate bodies are set out in law; and domestic and foreign arbitration is the primary mechanism for resolving commercial disputes between North Korea and foreign parties.[13]
- North Korea's relationship with the Egyptian company Orascom Telecom continues to expand following the visit of the company's president early in 2011. Orascom has invested not only in the cell phone telecommunications field, but also the construction and financial sectors, signaling a diversifying relationship based on commercial principles.[14]
- As a result of a sluggish international response to North Korea's appeals for food aid in the first half of 2011, North Korea increasingly recognizes it will need to trade for food rather than seek aid for food. This is a significant driver for stimulating a more creative and expansive foreign trade effort. In addition to the China market where barter trade for rice is commonplace, efforts to trade military equipment for rice with Myanmar, and more recently mining and hydropower expertise for rice and other agricultural products with Cambodia,[15] represent rational North Korean responses to these incentives, even if military sales are sanctioned and at least one shipment to Myanmar was effectively blocked by intensive American surveillance of sanctioned trade activities. North Korea's shortage of foreign exchange coupled with rising food prices have also prompted another rational shift from importing rice to lost-cost corn and beans from China this past year.[16]

These examples of recent initiatives demonstrate that the North Korean leadership is indeed serious in its intent to seek increased foreign investment and expanded trade. The concentration on developing the already expansive economic relationship with China and pursuing clandestine trade in sanctioned military equipment illustrate the impact on North Korean economic decision making and practices by the policies that are being pursued by both the United States and the Lee Myung Bak administration in South Korea that seek to force changes in North Korea's political behavior by economic pressure and sanctions.

Thus from the perspective of eventual integration of North Korea into the global economic system, these recent developments contain both positive and negative aspects. The positive ones are the seemingly genuine efforts to create an administrative and legal framework for a policy of expanding international economic relations, and in particular making North Korea a more attractive and less risky environment for investment. How well this plays on the two Chinese border fronts remains to be seen, as North Korean behavior in business relations does not have a good reputation, and there is considerable skepticism even in China about the willingness of North Korean partners to deal fairly and openly in business transactions. Nevertheless, it is clear that North Koreans have been doing their homework about what kinds of legal and other incentives are important to attract foreign investment in today's world, and these for now have the full support of the leadership, at least in the carefully delineated territories of the approved enterprise zones.

On the other hand, it is equally clear that North Korea is pursuing a distinctly circumscribed policy of opening up to foreign investment and trade. One characterization of this approach is "controlled capitalism,"[17] which seeks to keep the general population at bay and in the dark but permits the benefits of low wages and North Korean incentives for investment to generate income that will accrue to the controlling elite and not the general public. Indeed, the effort to reinforce centralized control over inflow of foreign exchange and relations with foreign partners can be viewed as seeking to maintain the long-standing political economy structure wherein wealth is concentrated in the elite through control over resources and rent seeking, together with patronage practices that sustain support for the regime. Trade along the China border in recent years has enriched and emboldened a new political economy where traders take risks and gain rewards that are outside the traditional ways of managing and controlling access to resources and which have stimulated the growth of the market economy inside North Korea despite periodic efforts by the government to suppress the markets.

How the new enterprise zones in Rason and the Hwanggumpyong and Wihwa islands evolve will have important longer-term consequences for stimulating sustainable economic growth and for meeting the leadership's stated goal of improving the livelihoods of ordinary North Koreans. They could evolve as enclave economies with little meaningful overflow impact on the rest of the economy, or they could empower a new class of entrepreneurs in North Korea operating within an expanded space that embraces and reinforces commercial norms and stimulates the building of backward linkages to small and medium-size enterprises in the people's economy inside and outside these zones that would leverage the impact of investments in the zones on the lives of ordinary North Koreans. Thus the implementation of these new enterprise zone initiatives on the China border will have potentially significant consequences for the integration of the North Korean economy more widely with the global economy.

ASSESSMENT OF SOUTH KOREAN– NORTH KOREAN ECONOMIC RELATIONS

The "Sunshine Policy" that guided South Korean economic engagement with North Korea from 1998 to 2008 produced significant results, especially after the June 2000 summit between the two Korean leaders. Total trade rose from $333 million in 1999 to $1.8 billion in 2008. Of this, processing-on-commission trade quadrupled during the period, reaching $410 million in 2008, while economic cooperation projects, including the Mt. Kumgang and Kaesong initiatives, reached $1.7 billion. Noncommercial trade grew from $97 million in 1999 to $422 million in 2006 before declining after the North Korean missile and nuclear tests that year.[18] While UN sanctions were introduced in 2006 on military-related trade with North Korea and luxury goods, these had little impact on inter-Korean economic engagement, which was based mainly on commercial and humanitarian interests. Transfers linked to the Korean Energy Development Organization (KEDO) dropped sharply after 2002 reflecting the abandonment of the light-water reactor project following the escalation in tensions over the North Korean nuclear program.

While the decade of the "Sunshine Policy" led to expansion and diversification of South Korean economic engagement with the North, its impact on the economic system has been mixed. Greater contact between Koreans in joint projects and exchanges linked to economic cooperation have exposed more North Koreans to the economic realities of South Korea and contributed to knowledge building about economic management and business practices that have helped South Korea achieve its own economic successes. But the potential impact of South Korean knowledge on the North Korean economy has been muted by North Korean apprehensions about the consequences of opening up too much to South Korea and thus resistance to proposals for education and training programs led by South Korean economic experts. This ambivalence in wanting both to expand and control inter-Korean economic contacts reflects a deep resistance to South Korean interests in change processes within North Korea.

There are six major criticisms that can be made about the conduct of South Korean economic engagement with the North in this period from the perspective of impacts on transformation of the economy and the North's eventual integration with the global economy: (1) the practices of providing up-front gifts and under-the-table cash payments to obtain concessions from North Korea have reinforced wrong behaviors and not helped the North Koreans to learn to conduct business transparently and in line with international norms; (2) providing food and fertilizer aid on a government-to-government basis has propped up the North Korean elite patronage system and public distribution system and has not aided the growth of market mechanisms; (3) the processing-on-commission trade also reinforces the status quo by using state trading companies and the siphoning of foreign exchange earnings to maintain the disconnect of prices, costs, and revenues for enterprises in the North Korean system engaged in production for foreign markets; (4) the business model used in the Kaesong Industrial Zone is limited in that it does not provide more opportunities for North Korean enterprises to learn market-based management practices, for example by permitting joint ventures and North Korean firms to participate; (5) acceptance of a policy of not paying employees directly also limits motivation to improve productivity and the evolution of a more flexible labor market within North Korea; and (6) there has been little stimulation of backward linkages of inter-Korean economic projects to the local North Korean economy and incentives for small and medium-size firms to provide inputs or services to foreign-invested projects.[19]

While the administration of President Lee Myung Bak recognized at the outset the importance of pursuing more businesslike conduct of inter-Korean economic relations, the political and military tensions that have grown since 2008 have overshadowed the economic relationship, and little progress has been made in restructuring this relationship to have a more positive impact on the economic transformation and development of North Korea or its integration with the global economy. The decision to curtail fertilizer and rice shipments has added pressure on North Korea to seek alternative sources of food to meet its structural deficit, which has been reflected in continued growth in the North Korean economic relationship with China and its efforts to reach out for barter trade with other rice-producing countries. The resilience, however, of the Kaesong economic cooperation venture in the face of deteriorating inter-Korean relations, especially after the sinking of the *Cheonan* incident, reveals that the mutual benefits and interdependence that has been built up in the Kaesong initiative has significance.[20] This is an important lesson that growing economic interdependence between the two Koreas can promote stability on the peninsula and at the same time reinforce

North Korean commitment to attending to business rather than just politics as it pursues its own national interests.

ASSESSMENT OF SANCTIONS

Economic sanctions have been a factor affecting the evolution of the North Korean economy since the end of the Korean war, by constraining access to foreign investment and trade on a global basis, providing incentives for the North Koreans to pursue clandestine and illicit means of earning foreign exchange needed to purchase high-priority imports, and reinforcing the justification domestically for the *juche* policy of self-reliance. A general assessment of the long-term impact of sanctions is that they have contributed to the distortions that limit North Korea's ability to pursue its natural comparative advantages in the international economy and that underlie internal inefficiencies in resource allocation choices. These limitations and distortions have contributed to the poverty trap dilemma that North Korea faces. While implementation experience with sanctions imposed on North Korea has been mixed, and China is pursuing a policy of selective and minimalist compliance with UN sanctions imposed after the 2006 missile and nuclear tests, there is no doubt that sanctions affect the overall climate of doing business with North Korea. For nonstate actors, including private sector foreign investors and banks providing financial services for normal commercial transactions, sanctions or the threat of sanctions raises risk perceptions and costs of business. From this perspective, the recent policy of the United States in pursuing "smart sanctions" targeting specific firms, banks, and individuals can be expected to have repercussions on nonsanctioned international economic engagement activities and not simply on the economic interests of the "military economy" and "court economy" that are the targets of the sanctions.

In addition, sanctions have contributed to the growth of dependence of the North Korean economy on trade and investment from South Korea and China, which since the nuclear test of 2006 now overwhelmingly dominate North Korea's external economic relations.[21] These countries have reasons of their own to pursue economic engagement regardless of the international sanctions regime. Even if ties with these two countries enable the North Korean economy to avoid total isolation and collapse, any future objective of integrating North Korea into the global economy as a normal country will require eventual lifting of sanctions.

Removal of economic sanctions has been an explicit objective of North Korean negotiations with the United States, South Korea, and aligned

countries since the early 1990s, and conversely, the United States in particular has followed a dual-pronged strategy of tightening economic sanctions and offering incentives for expanded economic engagement as tools to
influence North Korean decision making with regard to its nuclear, missile,
and conventional weapons programs.[22] The conjoining of political/security
negotiations and the incentives of removing sanctions and offering economic inducements has been a primary dynamic of both bilateral and multilateral negotiations with North Korea since the Agreed Framework. But it is
also important to recognize that neither removing sanctions alone nor providing inducements such as heavy fuel oil or spare parts for conventional
energy generation plants, as was agreed during Phase 2 of the Six-Party
Talks in 2007 and 2008, would be sufficient to provide the real economic
benefits that will be needed to meet the objective of North Korea becoming
a prosperous nation. This will require more comprehensive efforts to address the challenges of the transition gap, poverty trap, and dysfunctional
aspects of the patronage system. These will all need to be overcome to
transform the North Korean economy sufficiently to become more efficient
and productive, more fully integrated in the global economy, and following
a sustainable economic growth path that will significantly improve the lives
of the North Korean people, not just the elite group in Pyongyang.

IMMEDIATE ISSUES FOR ENCOURAGING ECONOMIC
TRANSFORMATION AND ADVANCING INTEGRATION
IN THE GLOBAL ECONOMY

The objectives of economic engagement with North Korea are not the same
for South Korea, China, and the United States. All have sought to advance
their own interests through the ways they have chosen to engage with North
Korea.[23] As a result, the impacts on the North Korean economy have been
contradictory, and it is not surprising that the transformation of the economic
system has been incoherent and that prospects for meaningful integration in
the global economy are very limited. At the same time, the willingness to
engage, even if the objectives and modalities differ, has contributed to the
avoidance of economic and regime collapse and the high risks of instability
and hardship that would accompany such an eventuality. Acknowledging the
transformations that have already occurred and the dynamics of change in the
North Korean economy, and taking into account the lessons of experience,
what is needed in the next phase of economic engagement with North Korea

is more economic rationality in negotiations to resolve outstanding security and political concerns, more clarity and consensus of vision about a desirable direction of future transformation of the economy and its integration in the regional and global economies, and more agreement on the modalities and priorities for engagement with North Korea that can help realize this vision. Now that North Korea is confronting the challenges for stable leadership succession and performance posed by the death of Kim Jong Il, and with the experience of dramatic failures of regressive economic reform efforts in 2010, the time is ripe to consider how to proceed with these new directions for economic engagement.

ECONOMIC RATIONALITY AND NEGOTIATIONS ON SECURITY AND POLITICAL ISSUES

In both bilateral and multilateral negotiations with North Korea, the question arises of how to frame economic rewards that will reinforce and not undermine the process of reaching political and security agreements. This involves both the content of any economic package that is linked to the negotiations and the sequencing of actions that are tied to progress on the political agenda. Several principles should guide future negotiations:

- Economic rewards should have a genuinely positive benefit for the North Korean economy and reinforce the process of integration with the global economy, such as investments that increase productivity, removal of obstacles to commercial trade, and assistance to improve economic management and public reporting of economic and financial statistics.
- Cash and in-kind transfers that serve to prop up the status quo patronage system or inhibit the role of markets should be avoided.
- Economic benefits should be progressively sequenced so that there are positive incentives for moving along a multistage process of implementing the political and security measures.
- Economic rewards should be provided and implemented in a transparent way and results measured.

In designing future economic packages linked to political negotiations, economic experts should be involved. Track 2 meetings of experts to share information and perspectives can help build consensus and reduce risks of complications arising in the implementation phase.

CLARIFYING A SHARED VISION FOR NORTH KOREA'S FUTURE ECONOMY AND IMPLICATIONS FOR MODALITIES OF ENGAGEMENT

Two critical challenges that need to be addressed are how the North Korean leadership and economic management team will redefine the North Korean vision of what kind of economic future they aspire to work toward, and how North Korea's neighbors and the international community more generally will align their economic engagement with a vision that all can support. The current course of "controlled capitalism" needs to be reframed to include linkages to domestic as well as international markets and institutional reforms in the financial system and economic management.

The first challenge requires internal debates among North Korean policy makers. The opportunities for external engagement to influence these internal debates are twofold. One is to use knowledge engagement to provide information and perspectives from the experiences and advice of other countries that can improve the quality of these internal debates. Study tours and educational opportunities both within North Korea and abroad can contribute to such engagement. The willingness of the North Korean authorities to send multiple delegations of officials to China and a delegation of economic officials for a study tour of the U.S. economy in 2011 indicates growing receptiveness to such informal knowledge exchange that is beneficial for clarifying understandings and contributing to internal policy discussions. Objective assessments of the North Korean economic situation and policy advice, such as can be provided by international financial institutions (IFIs), could also contribute to the learning process and have a positive impact on future policy making.

The other opportunity for external engagement to influence internal policy debates is to provide positive inducements to reduce fears of unacceptable consequences of change and risk perceptions among decision makers. Recent acceleration of economic contacts and dialogue between North Korean and Chinese officials both in Beijing and in the border areas illustrates the potential importance of such inducements at this juncture. The announcement of the establishment of two new economic zones in Rason and the Hwanggumpyong and Wihwa islands and the creation of a joint guidance committee are evidence of the impact that is possible. There is also an opportunity to realign South Korean inducements in ways that will have a more positive systemic impact on the North Korean economy and its future integration not only with the South Korean economy but also with the global economy as the two Koreas work to repair their currently frayed relations.

The second challenge requires commitment among North Korea's economic partners to align more closely their bilateral economic engagement policies and to work more actively with multilateral mechanisms to support the economic transformation process. The IFIs and United Nations Development Program (UNDP) can play useful roles in both shaping a broader international consensus and in helping to coordinate multilateral and bilateral engagement.[24] A practical first step would be to encourage North Korea to invite the International Monetary Fund and World Bank to undertake a collaborative fact finding study of the North Korean economy and provide an assessment report that can serve as a common platform for more informed and coherent discussions of what kinds of policies and engagement activities would have the most benefit in supporting a transformation process that can be broadly agreed to be desirable. This could be initiated within the framework of a resumption of the Six-Party Talks process or a successor process of discussing how to move forward on the agenda set forth in the 2005 Joint Statement that North Korea has confirmed it continues to endorse.

There are four core elements to a future vision for the North Korean economy that will need to be addressed. The first is acceptance that the North Korean economy is in fact a mixed economy, with both state-directed and market economy features; that efforts to return to a more pure socialist model of economic management have failed and that further efforts in this direction will be resisted both by the North Korean people and by North Korea's major external economic partners; and that the way forward will require taking measures to improve economic management so that the benefits to the economy of more market-based activities can be realized. While the recent acquiescence to the return of markets signals some appreciation of this reality, there is no visible sign yet that the regime leadership is ready to embrace a policy of moving toward a market economy and managing a planned transition process. Thus a high priority for engagement is on the motivation to adopt this policy posture, confronting old-fashioned socialist mind-sets still at work in the Workers' Party and military, and reducing fears of inability to manage and control a transition process. At a micro level, economic engagement activities can be designed more carefully to reinforce the expansion of market-based business practices and not buttress the status quo. This is particularly true for inter-Korean economic engagement. For example, future expansion of the Kaesong Industrial Zone could allow for multiple business models with North Korean enterprises, more flexible hiring and pay arrangements, and promotion of backward linkages to the North Korean economy based on commercial principles.

A second element that is closely linked to the first is the need to reduce fragmentation of the North Korean economy to more efficiently utilize resources available for national development, enable effective macroeconomic management, and improve the coordination of external economic activities and the process of deepening integration with the global economy. Reports of changes that give the National Defense Commission more systemic supervision of financial resources in the party and guidance to the Cabinet are one sign that the leadership may see the need for more systemic integration of economic management. The October 2010 meeting of the Workers' Party and the restructuring of the party's leadership may have an impact on the course of future policy, but ideological and practical considerations still appear to be in conflict. Increased frequency of on-site economic inspection and guidance visits by Premier Choe Young-rim in 2011 suggests that the Cabinet is now being asked to play a more visible leadership role.[25] While foreign influence over the inner dynamics of the leadership circle is highly circumscribed, knowledge engagement with lower-level officials in the Cabinet and informal engagement with the senior officials in the party, military, and first family can introduce new thinking into internal discussions and help reinforce the positive potential of more coherent direction of the entire economic system. Recent Chinese engagement seems to have moved in this direction. One potentially positive role for sanctions that target military weapons programs and specific enterprises and individuals operating outside the supervision of the Cabinet is to reinforce the external view that reducing fragmentation and subjecting actors in the economy to more policy control and transparent supervision is a desirable direction for the future transformation of the economic system. A particularly important role for the IFIs would be to address these integration issues from an objective perspective, especially in public finance administration, banking supervision and control over external finances including foreign debt and national vulnerabilities in money laundering, and macroeconomic management. These are all issues that must be addressed if North Korea is to deepen over time its integration in the global economy.

A third element of a vision for the future is finding a way out of the poverty trap and putting the economy on a path of sustainable economic growth. This involves not just moving toward a more effective economic management system addressing issues related to price liberalization, asset ownership, and labor market flexibility, but also mobilizing capital domestically and abroad, prioritizing investments to have the most beneficial impact on economic development, upgrading technologies to increase productivity, pursuing enterprise reforms and stimulation of small and medium-size enterprises, and significantly expanding foreign trade following an outward-oriented economic development strategy. Balancing the roles of aid, trade, and foreign investment will be important issues for foreign engagement requiring a common framework and coordinated policies. Resolving North Korea's outstanding external debt will also need to be addressed to improve creditworthiness. The roles of the UNDP and IFIs can be valuable mechanisms for building consensus with the North Korean authorities on economic development strategy and fostering the coordination needed both among North Korea's external partners and internally among domestic stakeholders.

Starting down the road of coordinated economic development engagement with North Korea will require progress in overcoming the critical security and political issues that dominate the current policies of economic engagement with North Korea. But informal exchanges of views among economic experts and building capacity to manage economic development activities in keeping with international norms are ways to advance confidence building and collaborative working relationships. Also, focusing on areas where common agreement is feasible can help propel the process forward. For example, the policies articulated in the January 1, 2012, New Year's editorial of addressing the "burning issue" of food; promoting development of light industries, power supply, mining and transport; improving the welfare of the North Korean people; and seeking productivity improvements through advances in science and technology are all areas where seeking cooperative engagement seems possible. Recent efforts by North Korea to promote foreign investment and facilitate decision making on projects signal the readiness of the North Korean government to engage with foreigners as political conditions and risk perceptions of investors move in more positive directions conducive to expanding external engagement in foreign trade and investment. While at the moment, most eyes are on China, the possibilities for a more broadly based foreign engagement in North Korean economic development projects should be on the horizon of a desirable future.

The fourth element of a future vision for North Korean economic transformation is the restructuring of military assets and manpower if political and security negotiations lead to resolving conflicts that would allow North Korea to shift away from military-first politics and the need for enemies to justify regime legitimacy. Release of these resources could spur economic production and amplify the progress that can be made through moving toward a market economy and pursuing an economic development strategy that is more outward oriented. Here, too, sanctions play a role in reducing the benefits of relying on a military economy for economic as well as security reasons. Successful experience with the Kaesong Industrial Zone and pursuing expansion of export-oriented investment on the Korean border and development of the new zones along the China border can encourage the North Korean leadership to see the benefits of redeploying manpower to more economically and socially beneficial activities.

LONGER-TERM ISSUES AND STRATEGIES FOR INTEGRATION WITH THE GLOBAL ECONOMY

Membership in International Economic Organizations

Sooner or later the issue of North Korean membership in the IFIs and eventually the World Trade Organization will need to be addressed if North Korea is going to become fully integrated in the global economy. While these organizations can provide training, policy advice, technical assistance, and even some grant funding before membership (if the governing bodies of these organizations determine that it is in their interests to do so), access to the full range of financial and other services that these organizations provide can only come with membership. Also, North Korea's future economic partners in trade, foreign investment, and possible official development assistance will expect North Korea to accede to the requirements of membership and normalize its place in the international financial community. It is a legal requirement that membership in the International Monetary Fund (IMF) precede membership in the World Bank and its constituent organs: the International Bank for Reconstruction and Development (IBRD), the International Development Association (IDA), the International Finance Corporation (IFC), the Multilateral Insurance Guarantee Agency (MIGA), and the International Center for Settlement of Investment Disputes (ICSID). Membership in the Asian Development Bank (ADB) legally requires prior membership in the United Nations Economic and Social Council for Asia and the Pacific (ESCAP). North Korea already is a member of ESCAP and other UN economic organs, but the larger shareholders of the ADB will most likely require that North Korea join the IMF first, as for the World Bank.

Membership in the IFIs comes with both privileges and responsibilities, and while North Korea has expressed interest in the past in exploring the possibility of seeking membership, it so far has balked at the requirements for transparent reporting of statistical information on its economy and financial system, review and assessment of its economic management performance that comes with the requirement of routine surveillance and Article IV consultations, and the prospect of conditionality attached to possible funding. Overcoming these inhibitions on the North Korean side will be necessary before any membership process can proceed. More importantly, membership requires that existing members vote to accept new members. As a practical matter, North Korea would need the political support to join the IFIs from the largest shareholders, notably the United States, Japan, and European countries in addition to China, in order to obtain the votes needed. Thus the timing of future membership will be governed not only by technical readiness considerations, but more significantly by political judgments made both by North Korea and the major shareholders of these organizations. For this reason, the issue of support for North Korean membership in the IFIs can be expected to be linked to the political negotiations regarding North Korea's future relations with these countries and resolution of both security concerns and progress toward a peace accord to replace the Armistice Agreement, as well as reaching a common vision for North Korea's economic future as a member of the international community and participation in the global economy.

Membership in the World Trade Organization (WTO) is a complicated process that requires extensive negotiations over a protracted period of time. For North Korea, an appropriate strategy would be to pursue building blocks toward eventual membership. In addition to receiving technical advice and assistance from the IFIs, UNDP, and other UN development agencies on specific issues needing to be addressed and consultations with other countries to learn from their experiences with WTO accession, the experience of negotiating bilateral and multilateral trade agreements could be useful intermediate steps, as was the case with Vietnam. Such negotiations could be initiated in parallel with steps to remove economic sanctions by the international community and especially the United States, once the political environment is conducive to this form of cooperation.

Regional Economic Integration

There are a variety of ways in which pursuing regional economic integration would be consistent with the goal of North Korea's integration in the global economy.

The Tumen River Commission, established in 1995 to coordinate subregional economic cooperation among China, Russia, Mongolia, North Korea, and South Korea, is likely to have renewed vigor following the announcement of the establishment of the Rason and the Hwanggumpyong and Wihwa island economic zones. For Rason, in particular, the opportunity to develop a regional transport hub and support services looks finally likely to become a reality. North Korea withdrew from the Tumen River Commission several years ago; thus rejoining should be encouraged.

Other priority areas where North Korea could benefit from Northeast Asian regional economic cooperation would be in energy, transport (especially rail), and exploitation of minerals, including rare earths.[26] Such regional cooperation could be pursued through the Tumen River Commission framework or from new cooperation mechanisms established for specific purposes. If there is an improvement in North Korea–Japanese relations, such regional cooperation would be significantly enhanced. Also, if regional cooperation in these sectors involves private sector partners and not just governments, the process of integrating North Korea in the regional economy as it evolves would be accelerated as political factors would become less critical than commercial ones in providing models and incentives for North Korea to adopt internationally acceptable business practices.

As a by-product of the Association of Southeast Asian Nations (ASEAN) plus 3 regional economic cooperation activities, there has been in recent years a determined effort to increase coordinated economic research and policy dialogue among the three large economies of Northeast Asia—China, Japan, and South Korea—despite historical tensions in the relations among these countries. Trade and investment have dominated this agenda, but it has proved a model for expanding trilateral economic coordination that could have important long-term consequences not only regionally, but globally. While North Korea has not participated in these activities, one way to promote deepening integration of North Korea in the regional and global economy would be to use a model of incentives and cooperation based on the way the European Commission has approached the inclusion of Eastern European countries in transitions to market economies following the collapse of the Soviet Union. In this case, "joining the club" requires policy and institutional developments—especially in the financial and legal systems—to conform to standards established for all members of the European Union. While similar to the WTO accession process, this type of neighborly cooperation and incentives to gain access to markets and preferential treatments could provide a vehicle for technical cooperation and longer-term expansion of trade and investment in a variety of sectors, following principles of natural comparative advantage.

North Korea already participates in the ASEAN-sponsored Asian Regional Forum on security cooperation. North Korea also has important if presently limited economic ties with most ASEAN countries and is actively seeking to expand trade with them. With the possible exception of Myanmar, where North Korean weapons appear to be used for barter trade for rice, North Korean trade with other ASEAN countries appears to be primarily commercial and involve nonsanctioned commodities. Thus promoting trade and investment relations with ASEAN countries would seem to be a viable arena for integrating North Korea into the regional and global economy. Inviting North Korea to participate in the expanded group that discusses economic cooperation under ASEAN auspices would be worth pursuing, and including North Korea in the future in regional trade agreements would be another vehicle for providing incentives for North Korea to meet regional and international norms for expanded commercial relations.

Unification of the Korean Peninsula

The aspiration for eventual unification that exists in both Koreas cannot be ignored in considering future strategies for integrating North Korea in the global economy. While there are various scenarios about how unification might eventually occur, any process of unification will necessarily have to deal with the integration of what are now two very different economic systems: one highly integrated in the global economy and one hardly integrated at all. The only feasible trajectory is that the North Korean economy evolves in ways that are increasingly compatible with the South Korean economy, whether unification comes gradually in a managed way over time, or whether it comes abruptly from a breakdown of the North Korean regime for whatever reason. North Korea's socialist economic management model has proven to be unsustainable and definitely not exportable to South Korea or elsewhere. Thus any progress that can be made in moving the North Korean economy toward deeper integration with the world economy would be compatible with unification aspirations, and in fact this can be an important motivator for efforts to accelerate the process of North Korean integration in the global economy.

Nevertheless, because inter-Korean relations at the present time are dominated by political and not just commercial drivers, the way in which inter-Korean economic relations are handled can have both positive and negative impacts on the process of integrating North Korean in the global economy. In the past, as discussed earlier in this chapter, South Korean economic engagement practices have both propped up the status quo socialist system in the North and reinforced expectations and behaviors that are not compatible with the goal of facilitating transformation of the North Korean economy in ways that increase the role of markets and foster businesslike conduct. As the two Koreas work to repair their presently badly frayed relations, reshaping the conduct of inter-Korean economic cooperation should be given high priority. It is noteworthy that the rules governing the new enterprise zones on North Korea's China border are considerably more liberal than the arrangements in place for the Kaesong Industrial Zone, so one place to start would be discussions focused on changes to the Kaesong model when plans to proceed with further expansion become politically feasible to pursue. Similarly, negotiations on the future of the Mt. Kumgang resort area should aim to advance normal commercial arrangements. In the longer term, expanded inter-Korean economic cooperation can aim to assist North Korean integration in the global economy by combining South Korea's management and marketing skills with North Korean low-cost manufacturing. Korean partnerships can leverage the comparative advantages for both Koreas to their mutual benefit. Also, cooperation on regional economic projects, such as in energy and transport, can accelerate integration of the two economies and integration of North Korea into the regional and global economy, while also paving the way for the eventual unification of increasingly compatible systems.

CONCLUSION

North Korea's economic future is closely tethered to decisions affecting both the future of the domestic political economy and North Korea's external relations. While there are some positive indicators of progress in internal North Korean thinking and actions seen through recent initiatives, there is still much room for improvement, and these initiatives are not likely to achieve their intended results without greater commitment to systemic economic reforms and institution building by the North Korean leadership. The political transition in North Korea following the death of Kim Jong Il could lead to greater openness to consider new directions for economic policies, and thus any initial steps that may be taken should be positively reinforced. North Korea's principal economic partners—South Korea, China, and the United States— are also presently pursuing contradictory policies of economic engagement that complicate both North Korean policy making and international coordination, making it harder to achieve the goals that these parties are seeking. The challenge today is to reach a common vision that North Korea's economic future must be linked to continuing transformation of the economic management system, adopting an outward-oriented economic development strategy, and becoming increasingly integrated in the global economy. If such a vision were to be accepted, there are many modalities available both in the short and the longer term to assist North Korea in going down this path. Without reaching such a common vision and willingness to resolve the political issues that inhibit wholehearted international economic engagement with North Korea, North Korea is likely to be consigned to a confused and unguided process of continuing change with uncertain outcomes politically and economically.

NOTES

1. For a full discussion of these historical perspectives, see Bruce Cumings, *Korea's Place in the Sun: A Modern History* (New York: Norton, 1997), 19–85.

2. Marcus Noland has estimated that the natural share of total trade in North Korean GDP should be 70 percent. Marcus Noland, *Avoiding the Apocalypse: The Future of the Two Koreas* (Washington, DC: Institute for International Economics, 2000), 262.

3. Push back by the population to the currency reform and market closings of late 2009 and early 2010 revealed that people are no longer always willing to acquiesce to abusive policy directives from the top. This is a significant development and one reason for the increased attention to the goal of improving the lives of ordinary people and developing consumer products in the 2011 New Year's editorial tied to the goal of becoming a "strong and prosperous" country by 2012.

4. William Brown, "Engaging and Transforming North Korea's Economy," *Joint U.S.-Korea Academic Studies* 21 (2011): 136.

5. This section draws from Bradley Babson, "Evaluation and Prospect of the North Korean Economy," *EXIM North Korea Economic Review*, April 2011, 71–74.

6. Fragmentation of the North Korean economic system is frequently characterized by differentiating between the "people's economy" controlled by the Cabinet, the "military economy" controlled by the Korean People's Army, and the "court economy" controlled by Kim Jong Il's family and the Korean Workers' Party. Deok Ryong Yoon and Bradley Babson, "Understanding North Korea's Economic Crisis," *Asian Economic Papers* 1, no. 3 (2002): 69–89.

7. For detailed discussion of Chinese experience with investment and trade with North Korea, see Drew Thompson, *Silent Partners: Chinese Joint Ventures in North Korea* (Washington, DC: Johns Hopkins School of Advanced International Studies, 2011); and Stephan Haggard, Jennifer Lee, and Marcus Noland, "Integration in the Absence of Institutions: China-North Korea Cross-Border Exchange," Working Paper Series WP-11-13 (Washington, DC: Peterson Institute for International Economics, August 2011).

8. "DPRK Launches State Development Bank," *Xinhua*, March 10, 2010.

9. "Politics Comes before Economy for North Korea," *Global Times*, June 19, 2011.

10. "Pyongyang Promises Chinese Investors the Moon," *JoongAng Daily*, June 24, 2011.

11. Korea Central News Service, June 9, 2011.

12. "North Korea Pushing to Sign Double Taxation Avoidance Deal with China," *Korea Herald*, June 6, 2011.

13. For details, see Peter Morely, "Legal Framework for Foreign Direct Investment in the Democratic People's Republic of Korea," *Choson Exchange*, 2011.

14. *North Korea Brief 421* (Seoul: Institute for Far Eastern Studies, Kyungnam University, June 25, 2011).

15. "North Korea Wants to Buy Cambodian Rice, Invest in Mining," NKnews .org, July 27, 2011.

16. "Lack of Foreign Cash Forces North Korea to Buy More Corn, Less Rice," Yonhap News Agency, August 14, 2011.

17. Andrei Lankov, "North Korea Special Economic Zones," eastasiaforum.org, July 16, 2011.

18. Data are from KOTRA as presented in Doowon Lee, "Estimating the Potential Size of Inter-Korean Economic Cooperation," *Joint U.S.-Korea Academic Studies* 21 (2011): 155.

19. One interesting exception to this overall negative assessment has been the impact of Choco Pies on the economic behavior of North Korean workers at South Korean factories in Kaesong. As many as nine pies are given to each worker every day, and instead of consuming these snacks, they are sold in the black markets of North Korea at high prices, giving the workers a direct source of income and triggering demands for more. *Dong-A Ilbo*, November 21, 2011.

20. The Ministry of Unification reported that trade between the two Koreas shrank more that 14 percent during the year following the sinking of the ship *Cheonan*, from June to May. General trade and processing-on-commission trade dropped 76 percent, while at the same time trade via the Kaesong Industrial Zone increased by 24 percent. *Yonhap*, July 3, 2011.

21. Marcus Noland and Stephan Haggard, "North Korea's Economic Development and External Relations," *Korea's Economy 2008*, vol. 24 (2008): 89–90.

22. A good summary of experience with sanctions is "Congressional Research Service Memorandum to Hon. Richard G. Lugar on Implementation of U.N. Security Council Resolution 1874," October 8, 2010.

23. This section builds on Bradley Babson, "Transforming the North Korean Economy and Implications for Future Engagement Strategies," a paper prepared for the 2010 Symposium on Inter-Korean Cooperation and Development: Fishing for Cooperation and Netting for Development, Washington, DC, Johns Hopkins School of Advanced International Studies and Korea Maritime Institute.

24. For a detailed discussion of potential IFI roles, see Bradley Babson, "The International Financial Institutions and the DPRK: Prospects and Constraints," *North Pacific Policy Papers*, no. 9 (2000); Bradley Babson, "Visualizing a North Korean Bold Switchover: International Financial Institutions and Economic Development in the DPRK," *Asia Policy* 2 (2006); and Bradley Babson, "Realistic Expectations of the Future Roles of the IFI's on the Korean Peninsula," *Korea's Economy 2008*, vol. 24 (2008): 106–13.

25. "Premier Choe-Yong Rim Is Making Unprecedented but Vigorous Economic Inspections," *North Korea Brief 423* (Seoul: Institute for Far Eastern Studies, Kyungnam University, July 12, 2011).

26. The Nautilus Institute and the Economic Research Institute for Northeast Asia (ERINA) have produced numerous studies on the potential for regional cooperation in energy and transport in particular. Recently, renewed attention has been given to the prospects for a gas pipeline from Russia to South Korea over North Korean territory that could have far-reaching implications for engaging North Korea in regional energy cooperation.

Part III

NORTH KOREAN SOCIETY
AND CULTURE IN TRANSITION

Chapter Eight

Low-Profile Capitalism

The Emergence of the New Merchant/Entrepreneurial Class in Post-Famine North Korea

Andrei Lankov

The last fifteen years have been a time of profound change for North Korean society. Probably it was as dramatic as the transformation that has happened in China since the start of Chinese reform in the late 1970s.

North Korea of the Kim Il Sung era was a society where many defining features of Soviet Stalinism were taken to extremes. Private economic activities, while not completely absent, were controlled and suppressed to an extent unheard of elsewhere in the communist bloc. Monetary incentives played a surprisingly minimal role in the economic life of the country, since distribution was far more important than retail trade. Agriculture was controlled by the state to a nearly unprecedented extent (suffice it to say that private plots in villages could not exceed one hundred square meters).[1]

However, everything changed in the last decade or two. After the collapse of the Soviet Union and the communist bloc, North Korea suddenly lost access to subsidized trade with and aid from other communist countries. This triggered a massive economic crisis, which led to a disastrous famine, with 600,000 to 900,000 people dead. The state public distribution system collapsed, never to recover completely. And old state-run industries largely came to a standstill.

In order to survive in the new situation, the North Korean populace began to look for coping strategies. One can say that essentially in the last fifteen to twenty years, the common people of the North rediscovered capitalism—or rather created a fairly complex capitalist economy from scratch. The late Kim Jong Il's North Korea can be seen as a kind of grand (and completely unintended) historical experiment. A society where the suppression of capitalist activity for a long time was exceptionally thorough suddenly began to redevelop capitalism, and to do so with remarkable speed.[2]

Inevitably the emergence of a capitalist market economy implies the emergence of capitalists—of a new class of entrepreneurs, merchants, and commercial operators. The present study concentrates on this new social group (or rather an array of interconnected social groups). We will discuss the origins of the North Korean new rich, the types of business activities they are engaged in, their social role, and their political views. The inner subdivisions of the emergent North Korean bourgeoisie will also be discussed briefly.

Since the North Korean media remain silent about deep social changes unfolding in the country, by far the most important source of information is interviews with refugees who have left the North and now reside in South Korea and China. Currently there are some 23,000 North Koreans living in South Korea. Former entrepreneurs and market operators seem to be over-represented in this group.[3]

The present chapter is based on manifold interviews with defectors (some few dozen such interviews have been conducted by the present author in the last two years as a part of a few research projects). Interviews provide a fascinating window into the daily lives of the North Koreans, even though reliance on such primary material also has some limits and biases which must be clearly stated.

First, the vast majority of interviewees come from the northern part of the DPRK. This reflects the current composition of the refugee community in South Korea, which in turn reflects the relative ease of escape for the inhabitants of the borderland regions. At the same time, it is known that the northern provinces of the country have been largely neglected by the government since the mid-1990s. This means that these areas do not receive much food and other daily necessities from the state, so therefore one should expect market activity to be more pronounced there. Second, the geographic proximity of these regions to China is also important. China looms large in the world of North Korea's new private business, so geographic proximity and long-term cross-border connections do matter. Third, these areas, being remote, have escaped the gaze of the authorities—to some extent, at least. Therefore, the locals might be less harassed when they engage in market activities.

So one would have good reason to suspect that the areas we deal with in the present study tend to be more active when it comes to commercial activity of any kind. Nonetheless one should not be excessively skeptical and discard the experience and conditions of the northern areas as atypical or marginal. Many of our informants have traveled extensively across North Korea. And they claim that the level of commercial activity does not differ much across the country. So, one might surmise that the situation in the borderland areas is more or less representative of the entire country, with the exception of the capital city of Pyongyang. Nonetheless, this chapter concentrates largely on the developments in the regions along the border, and this should be kept in mind.

THE ORIGINS OF THE NEW ENTREPRENEURS

There seem to be four major groups that comprise North Korea's new entrepreneurial class.

The first group consists of high-level officials, often with close connections to the ruling Kim family. Since the late 1990s, these people have begun to foray into the world of private business. Technically they are top managers or CEOs of state-run companies, but in most cases this appears to be a fiction. In the final count these people run their companies as if they are owners, generating significant gain for themselves. In most cases the companies in question are so-called "foreign-exchange earning companies" (hence FEEC), which exist under the auspices of different government and military agencies.[4]

Unfortunately this upper tier of North Korea's new entrepreneurial class is beyond the reach of the average researcher. Only a handful of such people (usually of less significance) have ever fled the North. So finding and interviewing them is prohibitively difficult. So, in this chapter we concentrate on small-scale businesses.

The second group includes private operators who also have connections with FEECs. However, unlike the bigwigs mentioned above, these people usually begin as independent entrepreneurs. Once they amass enough capital, they use bribing and/or personal connections to get a managerial position in some FEEC. This position tends to be much more profitable (and to some extent more secure) than that of an independent business operator, since FEECs have much government backing and in some cases a formal monopoly in some kinds of goods (like pine mushrooms, gold dust, and wild ginseng).

This group can be described as private entrepreneurs who have chosen to describe (or should we say "disguise") themselves as state employees. Apart from FEEC operators, this group includes other businesspeople—like owners/managers of restaurants or fishing enterprises. With very few exceptions, the state-run restaurant industry collapsed in 1996–1997. Nowadays a majority of restaurants are owned privately, but are still officially considered to be state property. The existence of this group creates an interesting phenomenon of a pseudo-state company, which will be dealt with at some length in this presentation.

The third group includes large-scale businessmen who do not pretend to be managers of government enterprises. Some do wholesale trade, while others provide a number of services to the general populace. For example, some of them deal with money transfers, both domestic and international (including, importantly enough, money that refugees from the South send to their relatives in the North). Others deal with money exchange or the provision of private loans. The same group also includes some owners of private workshops, which are rather common nowadays (small-scale production of garments, footwear, and the like).

The fourth group includes small vendors who are engaged in the private economy largely in order to survive. Unlike large-scale entrepreneurs of the above-mentioned groups, these people seldom if ever hire permanent staff. Their use of credit is also rather limited; these people are essentially a petit bourgeoisie, in the classical Marxist sense of the word.

THE ORIGIN OF THEIR BUSINESSES

Most North Korean businessmen launched their businesses in the early to mid-1990s in the midst of social disruption created by the so-called Arduous March (this is how the North Korean famine of 1996–1999 is referred to in official North Korean parlance, and in Korean generally). In most cases the decision to start private business operations was the result of grave economic circumstances.

The case of A1 (female, 35) might be seen as typical. A1 was a schoolteacher, but in the early 1990s, when the food situation began to deteriorate fast, visiting relatives from China suggested that she should buy some dry fish for resale to China. The said relatives became her first business partners. A1 traveled to a fishing village and bought some fish for resale. She discovered that in merely a few days, she made more money than she would earn as a schoolteacher in a year. From that time onward, she became a full-time merchant.

A2 (female, 29) was a schoolteacher as well. After she married into a family that had connections with a local tobacco factory, she decided to start her own tobacco workshop. She used her in-laws' money to buy primitive equipment (made and sold by private artisans) and start her workshop. She bought tobacco leaves from local farmers. The paper and packaging materials were bought locally at the market; packaging materials were imported from China, while cigarette paper was either Chinese or stolen from a local tobacco factory. A2 hired a few teenage girls to operate the equipment used to produce cigarettes. Five years later, she had a monthly income of 500 to 700 USD, which made her quite rich by North Korean standards.

There are many other examples, but the two above are important in one regard: one of the major challenges every aspiring entrepreneur faces in the

North is how to get start-up capital. This is often emphasized by the refugees themselves. A10 (female, 34), a rather successful businesswoman herself, puts it bluntly: "People, who really do not have money, they make a living by moving pushcarts. People like me, people who trade, always have money." A11 (female, 65), far less successful, agrees: "Only if there is start-up capital, one can trade. If one has no such money, trade is impossible."

It seems to be impossible to acquire credit; private providers of loans do exist, but a moneylender granting credit to somebody with little experience and no business is seemingly rare. Therefore start-up capital is usually acquired in one of two ways. First, it can be provided by relatives overseas, overwhelmingly in China. Many North Koreans, especially in the northern part of the country, have relatives in China. Taking into account the difference in income levels between China and North Korea, we should not be surprised that Chinese relatives are often willing to provide some start-up capital to their North Korean relations. In some cases money comes as a gift, but it seems that more frequently, this is essentially a mutually beneficial investment.

Another way is to use some connections with existing government industry. Technically officials and managers are banned from partaking in private commercial activities. This ban seems to be generally respected, but it does not prevent them from actively doing business by proxy (using wives, in-laws, siblings, and the like). Usually in such cases, these new businesses can use state-owned resources which are appropriated (not to say stolen) by managers. Official connections also help to ensure the security of the business.

Many businesspeople, especially the more successful, come from families with official connections to the old system. Kim Il Sung's North Korea had a clear-cut hierarchy of hereditary groups, membership being defined by an individual's origin (*songbun*)—or, to be more precise, by the political behavior of his or her direct male ancestors in the 1940s and 1950s. The descendants of war heroes, officials (those who never fell out of favor with the Great or Dear Leader), Christian activists, and the like were privileged. Conversely, descendants and relatives of defectors to the South, clerks in the colonial administration, and political and common criminals were discriminated against.[5]

The arrival of capitalism in the North did not completely reverse this system: as has been mentioned above, the people with official connections have tended to have serious advantages. Nonetheless, in the new system, the groups hitherto discriminated against have had the opportunity to better their lives.

Those in especially advantageous positions were people who had a personal connection with China. In the past, these people were seen as somewhat suspicious, but from the mid-1990s onward, they discovered themselves to be in an advantaged position. Their relations in China not only provided them with start-up capital but also helped them with procurement of goods to be moved to the North for processing or resale. This was especially important because China plays a major role in the new North Korean business world. Most of the most profitable businesses usually involve either resale of Chinese products or purchasing goods which are in high demand in China and then reselling them in China.

Of especial importance are the so-called *hwagyo* (*huaqiao*), citizens of the People's Republic of China who have permanent right to reside in the North. Their numbers are estimated to be between 5,000 and 10,000 (no exact statistics are available), and they seem to be by far the largest, or perhaps the only group of foreign citizens who are allowed to reside in North Korea indefinitely while earning income as regular employees of North Korean enterprise. Most of them are descendants of ethnic Chinese who moved to what is now North Korea from the late nineteenth century onward. In the past, hwagyo were barely tolerated by the North Korean authorities, which would have preferred to squeeze these foreigners out of the country. In spite of many forms of discrimination, ethnic Chinese stubbornly refused to consider leaving. This stubbornness had largely economic explanations—until at least the mid-1980s, China was lagging behind North Korea in terms of income and living standards.

The position of the hwagyo changed dramatically after the early 1980s when they were given the right to visit their relatives in China, more or less as they liked. This made the hwagyo the only group whose members could travel overseas, all but freely. They immediately took advantage of the new situation and began to move goods for resale across the border. The closed nature of North Korea's economy meant that large profits could be made by those few who had access to markets outside the country. Hwagyo made most of this advantage in the years that followed the collapse of Kim Il Sung's state economy. Therefore, by around 1990, being hwagyo became synonymous with being rich. A2 said, "Of course they are rich; if you are a hwagyo you cannot be poor. My parents told me that back in the '70s they were poor, but such [poor] hwagyo are difficult to find now."

There was one group though that has been a net loser as a result of the recent transition—families who returned from Japan in the 1960s, when some 93,000 ethnic Koreans moved to the "Socialist Motherland." Until the late 1980s, these people were both discriminated against and privileged. On one hand, they were carefully watched by the security police and were not eligible to hold high-level jobs; on the other hand, a steady stream of money transfers from their families in Japan meant that they lived very affluently by the standards of North Korea.[6] Money transfers began to dry up in the late 1980s, since those relatives who once knew the returnees began to die out.

The younger generation was much less inclined to spend their hard-earned yen on their uncles or second cousins who once proved to be too credulous and took North Korean propaganda at face value. But one might expect that such people would do what people with Chinese connections have successfully done: use money from their relatives as the start-up capital in launching a business. However, this didn't happen. As my informants agree almost unanimously, returnees are seldom involved with new business and generally speaking do not fare well in the new situation.

It would be wrong to describe the economic crisis and disintegration of Kim Il Sung–style socialism as a great leveler, but it seems that some members of hitherto discriminated against social groups have successfully used their skills, industriousness, and shrewdness to improve their lot dramatically. Under the old system, such an improvement would have been impossible, as A12 (female, 40) put it: "Under Kim Il Sung, *songbun* was very important; it decided everything. Under Kim Jong Il things are different; your family background still matters, but money nowadays is more important than social background."

PRIVATE BUSINESS: ITS TYPES

It seems that—at least in the areas under consideration—the most common types of business involve wholesale and retail trade. As we have mentioned above, connections with China are decisive. North Korean market vendors largely sell goods which are imported from China—consumption and household items, cosmetics, garments, footwear, bicycles, construction materials, and so forth. A considerable number of the goods offered for resale in the North Korean market are also available for resale in China.

The major export items include seafood, medical herbs, and scrap metal. There is also a large (by North Korean standards, that is) export of mineral resources, such as coal, iron ore, and gold dust, but this trade is usually handled by the government agencies, though private business in the above-mentioned guise of FEECs might play a role as well.

The business of A3 (male, 43) seems to be rather typical for a small quasi-state FEEC. A3 made good money through smuggling and running small quasi-state operations (including a large restaurant). He used the money earned in this way to bribe officials in the WPK Central Committee to secure rights to restart a small abandoned gold mine. Officially the gold mine was owned by the state (or rather by the WPK, since it was a part of a party-controlled FEEC). But in actuality, A3 and his business partners paid an agreed-upon amount of money to their superiors and could use the rest of the revenues as they pleased. This quasi-tax generally amounted to 40 percent of the revenue of the mine. The gold was sold privately to Chinese merchants. Money was used to pay salaries to a few dozen workers, as well as to pay for equipment and raw materials. A3 was left with some 2,000 USD a month—a very substantial income by the North Korean standard.

A different case of a private enterprise that was disguised as a government one was run by A7 (female, 54). Together with her friends, A7 operated a restaurant. Technically, the restaurant was a state property, owned and managed by the local government. But for all practical purposes it was a private enterprise. Its co-owners (largely middle-aged women) paid a fixed amount of money to the local administration. The remaining part of the revenue was used to run the restaurant, to pay workers, to buy foodstuffs, and occasionally to provide police and other officials with "presents" and bribes. The restaurant was located near a major railway station, so it had a large turnover of patrons and was quite profitable. A7 made 300 to 500 USD a month; however a combination of bad luck, bad managerial decisions, and the consequences of the 2009 currency reform resulted in the bankruptcy of this venture. A3, as we have mentioned above, also ran a quasi-state restaurant at some point in his career.

The explosive growth of private commerce also led to the emergence of privately owned infrastructure that meets the demand of private entrepreneurs and their businesses. Wholesalers and some retailers need to travel frequently, and they also need to move their goods around. This has, predictably, led to the emergence of private inns, where they can stay for a night, canteens where they can eat, and private buses and truck companies which can be used for moving their goods around.

A4 (male, 47), together with a number of business partners, runs one such freight company. It has seven trucks, all of which were imported from China. All the trucks are registered to different government agencies, as if they were the property of the agencies themselves, but actually the trucks have nothing to do with these agencies. The company owners pay regular contributions to the cadres who agreed to participate in the registration scheme. The trucks are usually used to move salt from the seacoast where it is produced to the wholesale markets in inner North Korea. Sometimes the company also transports sugar and cement stolen by workers from still operational cement factories (of which there are only a few). In private conversations, A4 expressed his surprise about the skill of workers who managed to move 50 kg of cement from their workplace without getting in trouble.

Bona fide production exists as well. A5 (female, 40) once was an engineer at a state factory. In the mid-1990s, in the days of the economic crisis, she began trading in secondhand Chinese dresses—largely in order to survive.

She made good money (thanks to her connection with relatives in China), so she switched to garment production. By 2005, A5 was running a number of workshops that employed a few dozen women.

They made copies of Chinese garments using Chinese cloth, zippers, and buttons. Some of the materials were smuggled across the border, while another part was purchased legally, mostly from a large market in the city of Rason (a special economic zone that can be visited by Chinese merchants almost freely). Interestingly, A5 technically remained an employee of a nonfunctioning state factory from which she was absent for months on end. She had to pay for the privilege of missing work and indoctrination sessions, deducting some $40 as her monthly "donation." This is an impressive sum if compared with her official salary of merely $2. This type of arrangement seems to be very common for the North Korean "new rich" who overwhelmingly are employees of state enterprises.

The necessity of Chinese connections and the instability of North Korea's currency ensures a constant demand for money changing, which in North Korean market parlance is known as *ton changsa* (literally "money trade"). It is usually combined with money lending business. Money lending business is important because no official banking institution would ever grant a loan to a private business. Since risks are high, interest rates are exorbitant by normal standards. A13 (female, 29) and A6, both involved with money lending and currency exchange, say that 10 to 15 percent interest *per month* are seen as the norm (a decade ago the average interest rate was significantly higher).

For any money lender, it is vital to ensure that loans are paid back. In some postcommunist countries at the early (fairly violent) stages of transition to a market economy, lenders used connections with the criminal underworld to collect debt. Interestingly, in North Korea, the normal way to ensure repayment seems to be to maintain good relations with the police and authorities. For a fee, policemen will ensure that an outstanding debt will be repaid. Unlike many other postcommunist countries, North Korea has not developed serious problems with violent criminal gangs. It appears that amid the disruption and chaos of the 1990s, the North Korean state has successfully maintained its monopoly on the use of violence.

A6 (male, 51) is a good example of a successful money changer cum lender. Reputedly he is the most successful in his city. A6 began his business in the mid-1990s. Initially his business involved smuggling goods to China and wholesale business, but then he switched to money changing. It helped that A6 was once a semiprofessional Taekwondo fighter. So he could rely on his former fellow team members as his enforcers. But his cozy relations with police are more important. Tellingly, A6's house has an illegal power supply cable which connects it with the local headquarters of the political police. The headquarters usually have a round-the-clock supply of electricity. So A6 can use a refrigerator and other power-hungry household appliances (even an air conditioner).

Strictly speaking, all of the above activities are illegal, so every single North Korean businessperson can be sent to jail at any time in full accordance with the letter of North Korean law. However, most such activities have been passively tolerated by the North Korean authorities. At the same time there are types of businesses which are not likely to be tolerated by the state. These risky types of business also tend to be especially profitable.

Predictably, one such business is smuggling. The most common items include herbal remedies, deer meat, and pine mushrooms. Theoretically such items can be sold only by state agencies, but since the trade is highly profitable, a number of private operators sell such prohibited merchandise to China. Smuggling usually requires good connections with border guards, but establishing such connections is not that difficult since border guards are not well paid. A professional smuggler (a Chinese citizen, based in China) in 2009 told the present author that in the vicinity of the city of Dandong, at that time it would cost around 300 USD to move a boatload of merchandise across the border, with no questions asked by the authorities.

Between 1997 and 2007, antiques were among the major items smuggled. Koryo-era ceramics were especially popular and highly profitable. Other items of the Koryo and Choson periods were widely sold as well. The source of antiques was largely areas around Kaesong, the capital of the Koryo dynasty. Local farmers, in spite of warnings and threats from the authorities, were more than willing to dig up graves, searching for anything of value. But informants tell me that the great boom in the antiques trade ended a few years ago. It seems that all easily identifiable archeological sites have already been robbed, so the supply has declined dramatically. There are, interestingly enough, rumors about illegal workshops which still produce fakes of Koryo and Choson antiques. Personally, I have come across indirect evidence of the existence of such workshops only once. One of my North Korean informants mentioned that his friend, a cabinetmaker, produces imitations of antique furniture that "look very ancient and sell for very good money" (he did not state that the imitations are sold as fake Choson-era furniture, but this seems to be a highly likely presumption).[7]

A sad and worrying development in recent years is the emergence of the private drug trade in the North. In the past, the sale of illicit drugs was usually conducted by North Korean government agencies. There is good reason to believe that the scale of this government-sponsored operation has decreased considerably in recent years—as was admitted by the U.S. State Department in March 2011. However, to a very large extent, the government's drug-related activities have been replaced by similar operations conducted by private businesses (one can see this "privatization" of drug dealing as a curious reflection of the general trend of changes in the North Korean economy and society).[8]

Most of these privately produced drugs are amphetamines (known colloquially as "ice"). The chemicals are smuggled from China in order to be processed in labs in the borderland areas of North Korea. My informants say that it is easier to process drugs in North Korea because the law enforcement there is lax, and the police are remarkably corrupt, so the production (with its telltale smell) can be hid easier. Indeed, in many if not all cases, this activity is done with the involvement of the local police and government authorities. But unlike earlier years, the revenue from drug sales is said to go to the pockets of individual drug dealers and their official supporters, not to the coffers of the North Korean state. The produced crystal meth is partially smuggled to China, but from around 2005, there has been a dramatic increase in the domestic use of illicit drugs, hitherto almost unknown inside North Korea.[9]

THE LIFESTYLE OF THE NEW RICH

All of the above-mentioned activities are illegal, so many of the new rich, especially those who are old enough to remember the days of high Kimilsungism in the 1970s, deliberately keep a low profile and try not to attract much attention by the authorities. A8 (male, 49) seems to be typical in this regard. His business was seriously illegal: he used Chinese mobile phones to provide the North Koreans with opportunities to talk to family members who had moved to China or South Korea (an activity that equals espionage and might be punished by death). So he was very careful not to stand out. He did not even buy a motorbike, using an old bicycle instead.

However, A8's cautiousness is not typical of the new rich. Nowadays one can see a lot of conspicuous consumption in North Korea, where the average official figure is misleading—virtually no North Korean family survives on the official wage alone. A North Korean female refugee told this author, "Until 2005, all but officials lived similar lives. But after 2005, everybody can see the difference between rich and poor." [A11] Perhaps the change is difficult to associate with just one year, but on balance she seems to be correct—some five to seven years ago, the new rich ceased to hide their wealth, and the gap between rich and poor in North Korea began to widen fast.

The official monthly wage in North Korea is between 2,000 and 5,000 NK won, which under the current market exchange rate is roughly equivalent to merely $1 to $2. The average monthly income is actually higher—thanks to the nearly universal involvement with the unofficial economy—and seems to be close to $15 if the black market exchange rate is used for calculations. As we have seen, the businesspeople earn much more—a few hundred or even a few thousand dollars a month.

It is no surprise that the new rich enjoy consumption. Overseas travel is out of the question (it is permissible only for top businesspeople related to the upper elite and/or the ruling Kim family), and domestic travel does not seem to be very popular. Nonetheless, the new rich frequent restaurants where a good meal will cost roughly as much as the average North Korean family makes in a week or two. In recent years, Pyongyang went through a minor restaurant boom, and it was largely brought about by the new bourgeoisie and its conspicuous consumption habits.

The new rich buy houses—even the above-mentioned A8, in spite of his extreme caution, was not an exception. Technically, the sale of real estate is illegal, but in the past two decades, North Koreans have developed many techniques that allow the circumvention of these measures with ease. Usually the sale of the real estate is documented as a "home swap": two families swap their houses, even though one house is much better than the other (very similar to a trick that was employed in the Soviet Union in the 1960s and 1970s). Newly bought houses are renovated, often at great expense. Even in small cities, one can find skilled workers whose major income is derived from remodeling the houses and apartments of the new rich. The necessary construction materials are imported from China, and the interior design seemingly follows the current conventions of the Chinese wealthy class.

The successful entrepreneurs buy all kinds of household appliances: flat-screen TVs, computers, large fridges, and motorbikes. Even private cars have begun to appear, though in most cases successful businessmen prefer to register their used Toyotas and Hondas as the property of some state agency (it attracts less attention and also helps to sort out problems with greater ease).

Surprisingly, many people in the countryside still buy fridges, even though these contraptions are unusable most of the time, due to a highly unreliable electricity supply. I have frequently come across North Koreans who have boasted of the fridge they own, only to admit immediately that they do not have electricity to switch it on. To my perplexed question of why they spent so much money on such a useless device, my interlocutors would usually reply that a fridge was an important and even practically useful status symbol. An affluent household nowadays is expected to own a fridge, even if the absence of electricity means that it is actually used as a bookshelf (as was the case with one of my North Korean acquaintances). A fridge is an important sign of business success in the North Korea of 2011.

Indeed, even Pyongyang, let alone smaller cities, has a very unreliable supply of electricity. Large batteries and small power generators are a help, but only to a certain extent. Batteries are enough to run a TV or a DVD player, but power-hungry air conditioners and fridges need a constant supply of electricity that is not readily available.

At first glance, a small power generator appears to be the solution, but this is not really the case. Such generators are often imported from China and are easily come by in the North, but they are not reliable, they consume a lot of expensive fuel, and, last but not least, they are very noisy, which makes continuous use highly problematic. So, even though many rich North Korean families have such generators, they are usually only used on special occasions.

The seemingly exotic practice of electricity theft (or should we say "backdoor purchase"?) is mentioned frequently and seems to be widespread. A North Korean of wealthy means makes a deal with a manager of the local power grid, and then an illegal power cable connects the entrepreneur's house with a power grid substation or military base (military installations are usually supplied with electricity even when the common customers are switched off). We have already mentioned a more exotic variety of the same deal, with the local political police HQ being a source of illicit energy supply for a well-connected businessman.

A9 (male, 52) lived in a rich neighborhood in a borderland North Korean city. The neighborhood consisted of half a dozen households who around 2007 made an illegal deal with a manager of the power grid. Each family pays the equivalent of $7 and has round-the-clock access to an unlimited electricity supply. All these houses boast air conditioners, a supreme luxury in the countryside.

SOME SPECULATIVE REMARKS ABOUT THE FUTURE

What will happen to these people? What is their role in the future of North Korea? Ostensibly, there seem to be reasons to be optimistic. The rising merchant classes in Europe of the seventeenth and eighteenth centuries eventually destroyed feudal monarchies and the entire ancien régime. So why shouldn't we expect a similar fate for the Kim regime, which has a surprising amount in common with the states of premodern Europe?

This indeed might happen; the growth of the private economy is slowly eroding the authority and control of the government and concurrently is bringing dangerous ideas to North Koreans. Businesspeople themselves see the state and its officials as a swarm of parasites (frankly, this feeling seems to be mutual). The seemingly unstoppable growth of private entrepreneur-ship creates an environment where uncensored and unauthorized information about the outside world spreads with great ease—and, as it has been argued countless times, in order to ensure stability, the North Korean regime has to maintain a very strict information isolation. Last but not least, the very exis-tence and power of the new enterprises demonstrates that the state is not the only natural provider of jobs and income, that one does not need an official interference to make a living.

So, does it mean that new North Korean entrepreneurs are a revolution-ary force? Perhaps, but there is an interesting twist which makes me slightly skeptical about such a statement. If a North Korean revolution comes, it is likely to be followed by unification with (or rather absorption by) the South; the allure of the rich and free South is seemingly irresistible. However, if this were to happen, the future of North Korean nascent businesses would not be rosy. It is telling that in the countries of the former communist bloc surpris-ingly few bosses of communist-era black/gray market businesses managed to adjust to the new, "regular" capitalist environment.

In North Korea, their peers are likely to fare even worse, since they will have to compete with the capital and expertise of South Korean businesses. Paradoxically, the long-term interests of the emerging North Korean business class might even coincide with that of the Kim regime and its officials—even though now they see one another as swarms of parasites. Unlike common people in the North, both groups—officials and entrepreneurs—have an inter-est in maintaining a separate North Korean state. Unification with the South is bound to spell disaster for both groups.

A person who is now running a couple of small shops might eventually, if North Korean capitalism continues uninterrupted growth, become an owner of a supermarket chain. If unification comes, such a person would be lucky to survive the competition with the South Korean retail giants and keep the few corner shops he or she had.

However, an alliance between the regime and the newly emerged North Korean entrepreneurial class does not seem likely; neither officials nor mar-ket operators are that farsighted, and their mutual distrust is too great. On top of that, the activity of the North Korean markets makes a great contribu-tion toward eroding what is left of Kim Il Sung's once formidable "national Stalinist" state. This is probably good news for the vast majority of North Koreans who are likely to benefit from the collapse of the regime and pos-sible unification with the South.

NOTES

This work was supported by the National Research Foundation of Korea Grant funded by the Korean Government (NRF-2010-330-B00187).

1. According to a 1998 law, the maximum size of the kitchen gardens is limited to thirty pyŏng for farmers and ten pyŏng for industrial workers. See the law cited in Pak Il Su, *Konan-ŭi haeggun ihu kaein soyugwon pyŏnhwa-e kwanhan yŏngu* [A Study of Changes in the Individual Ownership System after the "Arduous March"] (Seoul: Kyŏngnam Taehakkyo Pukhan Taehagwon, 2006), 57.

Some published sources, however, insist that the size of private plots can reach fifty pyŏng; see Im Su Ho, *Kyehwaek-kwa sijangŭi kongjon: Pukhanŭi kyŏngjae kaehyŏk-kwa ch'aejae byŏnhwa chŏnmang* [Coexistence of Planning and Market: Prospects for Economic Reform and System Change in North Korea] (Seoul: Samsung Economic Research Institute, 2008), 105.

2. For some description of the spontaneous growth of the markets, see Yi Young-hun, "Pukhan-ŭi chesaengjŏk sojanghwa-wa kyŏngje kaehyŏk-ŭi chŏngae [The Spontaneous Marketization and Development of North Korean Economic Reform]," *T'ongil munje yŏngu* 17, no. 2 (2005); Andrei Lankov and Kim Seok-hyang, "North Korean Market Vendors: The Rise of Grassroots Capitalists in a Post-Stalinist Society," *Pacific Affairs* 81, no. 1 (2008).

Of special importance is the recent publication of Marcus Noland and Stephen Haggard, *Witness to Transformation: Refugee Insights into North Korea* (Washington, DC: Peterson Institute for International Economics, 2011).

The best and most comprehensive study of North Korea's unofficial economy is a recently published book by Yang Mun-su, *Pukhan-ŭi sijanghwa* [Marketization of North Korea] (Seoul: Hanul, 2010).

3. For a detailed general review of the refugee population, see *Pukhan It'al chumin-ŭi Yihae* [Understanding the Refugees from North Korea] (Seoul: Naum-ŭi chip, 2009). The most current statistics on the refugees population is available on the Ministry of Unification website, unikorea.go.kr.

4. For a general overview of the FEEC, see Pak Hyon-chung, "Pukhan-eso 1990 nyŏndae chŏngkwŏn kikwan-ŭi sangŏpchŏk hwaldong-kwa sichang hwaktae [The Growth of Markets and Commercial Activity of the State-Owned Companies in North Korea of the 1990s]," *T'ongil munje yŏngu* 20, no.1 (2011).

5. The best description of the *songbun* system in English can be found in Helen-Louise Hunter, *Kim Il-song's North Korea* (Westport, CT: Praeger, 1999), 31–35.

6. For the background of this massive repatriation, see the recent research by Tess Morris-Suzuki, *Exodus to North Korea: Shadows from Japan's Cold War* (Lanham, MD: Rowman & Littlefield, 2007).

7. For more information on the large-scale smuggling of antiques from North Korea, see an interesting series of investigative articles that were published in the *Kookmin Ilbo* daily in March–April 2005 (issues of March 27, March 29, April 3, April 5, April 10, April 12, and April 17).

8. In March 2011, the U.S. State Department issued a statement saying that "North Korea seems to have largely ended state-sponsored drug trafficking but private groups are smuggling methamphetamine across the border with China." See "US Says N.Korea's State Drug Trafficking on Wane," AFP, March 4, 2011.

9. The private production of drugs was frequently mentioned by many interviewees. In the last two or three years, the reports about drug smuggling to China began to appear frequently. For example, see "China Cracks Ring Smuggling Drugs from N.Korea," Reuters, June 4, 2011.

Research on the problems can be found at the Brooking Institution website: Yong-an Zhang, "Drug Trafficking from North Korea: Implications for Chinese Policy," Brookings Institution, http://www.brookings.edu/articles/2010/1203_china_drug_trafficking_zhang.aspx (accessed November 15, 2011).

Chapter Nine

"Cultural Pollution" from the South?

Woo Young Lee and Jungmin Seo

The steady and broad penetration of Korean popular culture, or the "Korean Wave" (*hallyu*), into the global cultural market symbolizes a type of South Korean soft power beyond the manufacturing of industrious semiconductors and automobiles. Korean popular music, often referred to as K-pop, has become so popular and fashionable among younger Japanese that conservative and nationalist organizations in Japan have staged anti-K-pop demonstrations against TV stations that favor airing Korean soap dramas and K-pop music videos.[1] Despite repetitive efforts by Chinese authorities to curb the overflooding of Korean films and music into Chinese TV stations, the Korean Wave is now an integral part of Chinese pop culture. Most recently, the Korean Wave is making its way beyond regional boundaries while enthralling young populations in Southeast Asia, Europe, Latin America, and the rest of the world. Yet the question addressed in this chapter is whether the Korean Wave can reach and influence South Korea's closest but toughest neighbor, North Korea.

THE KOREAN WAVE IN NORTH KOREA

According to recent news reports and interviews with North Korean refugees and Korean Chinese, the Korean Wave in North Korea seems to be much more than just the hobby of deviant youngsters. Watching Korean films and television soap operas ("dramas") via the Internet has become fashionable among the young population in the North. For instance, *Iris* and *Athena*, the two biggest hit television dramas in South Korea in 2010, were popular among North Koreans even before the airing of the final episode of the TV series in the South.[2] In addition to dramas, many South Korean television programs are also popular. For instance, VCDs of *muhandojon* (Unlimited Challenge), *1bak 2il* (One Night, Two Days), and *bungeoppang* (Doubles) are the ones North Korean parents desperately seek for their children, even through illegal street vendors if necessary.[3] At the same time, many South Korean television entertainers are becoming as famous in North Korea as they are in the South. In North Korea, one particularly popular South Korean entertainer, "Kungmin MC" (National MC), has even attained the nickname, "the MC of the Korean Peninsula," for his inter-Korean fame.[4] North Korean teens are particularly susceptible to the Korean Wave. Some of the children from the wealthy families of Pyongyang are willing to pay up to twenty U.S. dollars to receive private lessons to learn the fashionable dances of *Sonyosi-dae* (Girls' Generation), which many consider to be the most popular singing girl group in East Asia.[5]

The South's pop culture has been infused into North Korean society since the early 2000s via smuggled CDs and DVDs. Thanks to the development of new media, South Korean pop music and television dramas are circulated in the form of MP3 players, USB, and memory chips in cellular phones. In particular, cellular phones are the most popular medium since North Korean teens can listen and watch music videos and dramas on the street, although phones will be seized if noticed by public security personnel.[6]

It is also important to note the emergence of merchants that make money by circulating the Korean Wave. Despite the high risk of being arrested and imprisoned, a growing number of merchants engage in this dangerous business to meet the constant demands of North Korean society. Most importantly, underground VCD rental shops are the primary means of circulating the Korean Wave. While a massive amount of CDs and VCDs come from China, these rental shops make a hefty amount of money by renting a VCD for 1,000 North Korean won (approximately 30 U.S. cents each).[7] According to the numerous testimonies of North Korean refugees, television sets and video players are regarded as the most desirable luxury items for the *nouveau riche*. For these few, well-off members of North Korean society, Chinese or South Korean cultural items are much more popular than North Korean media products.[8] At the same time, the increasing availability of Chinese cellular phones near border villages since 2000 has also contributed to the influx of the Korean Wave into North Korean society.[9]

The growth of the various circulation routes for the Korean Wave into North Korea has been made possible through the expanding rudimentary markets across the country since the food crisis of the late 1990s. Naturally, unofficial networks and communication channels blossomed. For instance, to pass Korean Wave CDs and DVDs throughout North Korean society, there should be trustworthy networks among acquaintances and friends in order to avoid harsh punishments by North Korean censoring authorities. Or conversely, stable unofficial networks emerge through repeated transactions among friends, merchants, and smugglers.[10] Recent interviews even indicate that North Korean censors are also participating in these networks to make extra income.[11] Figure 9.1 is a rough sketch of how Korean Wave visual media are being circulated in North Korea.

In addition to the circulation of South Korean visual media via smuggling and unofficial networks, a number of North Korean families are watching South Korean television and radio programs through television sets that are modified to watch channels blocked by North Korean authorities. Families living around the North Korea–China border are usually able to gain access to Chinese television programs. Surprisingly, it is estimated that more than 60 percent of these families are watching South Korean soap dramas that are frequently aired on Chinese local television stations. North Korean residents living south of Pyongyang can access South Korean television channels directly.[12] Though there is no reliable study regarding the number of North Korean families exposed to South Korean television channels, a recent survey of North Korean refugees in South Korea found that roughly 38.8 percent of respondents replied that they had watched South Korean television programs via television sets. Furthermore, about 15.2 percent of them testified that they watched South Korean broadcasting regularly.[13]

The ubiquity of the Korean Wave in North Korea is certainly more than the passive acceptance of "corrupted," entertaining television programs from the South. Many North Korean residents that are exposed to the Korean Wave tend to imitate behaviors, speech patterns, and fashions appearing on South Korean TV programs; some even desperately buy South Korean products and decorate their homes according to the styles set by fashion trends in the South.[14] A Korean Chinese who frequently visits North Korea for business said, "Some young North Koreans asked me to produce South Korean actors' and actresses' attires while bringing pictures from South Korean soap dramas. Some kids from cadre families requested to bring them from South Korea when I said that producing them was impossible."[15] Though North Korean authorities have tried to keep out vulgar, capitalistic culture by implementing a "mosquito net theory," a complete block of the inflow of new culture through increasing contacts with the outside world seems impossible. Despite the draconian laws that make watching South Korean cultural media illegal, South Korean movies and TV dramas are becoming more and more popular among North Koreans, even among elites who are supposed to uphold the North Korean system.

While surviving the 1990s famine and the crisis of the governance system in North Korea and being exposed to South Korean culture via various

Diffusion routes via sales

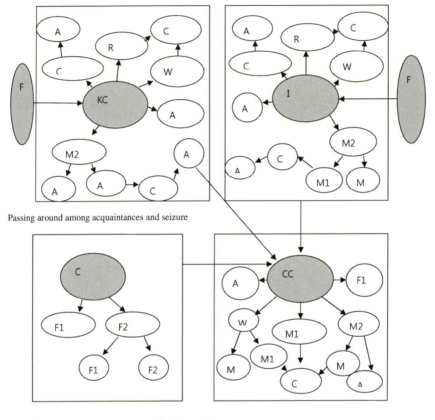

Passing around among acquaintances and seizure

A: Acquaintances
C: Consumers
M1: Merchants
M2: Mediators
R: Rental Business
CC: Censors/Cadres

KC: Korean Chinese
F: Foreign Suppliers
F1: Family members
F2: Friends
I: Importers

Figure 9.1.   The Structure of Circulation and Diffusion of South Korean Visual Media in North Korea. *Source:* **Dong-Wan Kang and Jung-Ran Park, "Distribution Channels and Influences of South Korean Visual Media in North Korea,"** *Unification Policy Studies* **(*tongil chongchaek yonsu*) 19, no. 2 (2010): 129.**

Table 9.1.   Did South Korean Dramas Influence Your Decision to Escape North Korea? (N = 90)

Answer	% (number)
Yes, very much	13.2% (12)
Yes	71.5% (65)
Maybe	8.8% (8)
No	5.5% (5)

channels, North Koreans have lost their faith, to a dangerous degree, in the official culture and official discourses. It is not unusual to hear a story about North Korean children laughing during class when they are told about "ragged and hungry South Korean children."[16] Tables 9.1 and 9.2 present the results of an unpublished survey conducted by Woo Young Lee, which confirms that exposure to South Korean soap dramas has meaningfully influenced the decision of North Korean refugees to leave their country.

Overall, it is undeniable that South Korean popular culture is penetrating quickly into the everyday lives of North Korean residents. However, the pivotal point to watch in this new phenomenon is how growing access to the South's popular culture will impact the North Korean sociopolitical system in general. On the one hand, we can easily conclude that North Korean social control is not working as comprehensively as it had prior to the economic/ food crisis of the 1990s. The tone and nuance of the majority of news articles and policy reports on the invasion of South Korean popular culture into North Korean society has supported this perspective. Yet extremely few have discussed the expansion of unofficial culture in North Korea as a potential independent variable that could significantly change the North Korean sociopolitical system.

Of course, treating popular culture as a direct factor of system/regime change is very risky since we do not yet have a well-structured theoretical framework. Furthermore, interpreting South Korean pop music in Pyongyang as a signal of regime change would be an extremely naive form of wishful thinking. Hence, our approach to this issue will take a cautious step—interpreting the expansion of South Korean popular culture in North Korea as a sign of emerging unofficial/private realms in North Korean society.

Table 9.2.   Amount of Exposure to South Korean Dramas

	Yes, Very Much	Yes	Maybe	No	Not at All
Once	2.3% (2)	13% (12)		3.35% (3)	
Twice	2.3% (2)	7.8% (7)	5.6% (5)	2.3% (2)	
Three times	2.3% (2)	13% (12)	3.35% (3)		
More than four times	6.7% (6)	38% (34)			

OFFICIAL/UNOFFICIAL CULTURE IN NORTH KOREA

Culture and art in communist states cannot be separated from the ruling communist party's intention to tightly control public discourses and symbols. Even in reforming China, which is rapidly adapting itself to the neoliberal global order, no private enterprise is allowed in the sphere of discourse and image-making businesses, such as broadcasting, radio, publishing, filmmaking, and music. North Korea is no exception; its policies toward popular culture, literature, and art follow communist cultural doctrine faithfully. In principle, the Ministry of Culture under the State Council and the Department of Culture and Arts in the North Korean Labor Party govern and supervise the cultural realm of North Korea. Yet in actuality, power is exercised by two party institutions, the Department of Culture and Arts and the Department of Propaganda. Furthermore, the recently deceased leader, Kim Jong Il, was frequently involved in designing cultural policies even before he became the sole leader of North Korea.

If we accept the commonsensical perspective that cultural management is pivotal in the social stability of a communist society, North Korea must have been very successful in this realm considering the longevity of the regime. In the late 1960s, when the Partisan Group was consolidating the Kim dynasty, Anti-Japanese Revolutionary Literature (*hangil hyongmyong munhak* and *suryong hyongsang munhak*) played an indispensable role in justifying the establishment of the dynasty. Since the party initiated the Campaign to Learn from Unsung Heroes (*sumun yongung ddara baeugi undong*) at the Sixth Party Congress in 1980, literary works promoting heroism in everyday life have been promoted. In the age of the military-first policy (*songun chongch'i*), art and literature of military heroism flourished.

Although there have been significant changes and transitions in the contents and methods of official culture in North Korea, its fundamental nature has been consistent: imbuing loyalty toward the leader, devotion to the party, and conviction in North Korean–style socialism to the populace in North Korea. While forcing North Koreans to internalize collectivist values, North Korean cultural policies dubbed all the official culture with anti-imperialism and anticapitalism rhetoric. In the meantime, a strong social control system and national seclusion policies have eliminated any room outside of official culture.

Considering the relatively stable and consistent cultural policies and their successful implementation from the beginning of the republic until the beginning of the economic/food crisis of the 1990s, "cultural pollution," which is introduced in the beginning of this chapter, can easily be characterized as revolutionary. A close reading of recent official North Korean literature, however, shows that there have been important discursive changes even in the realm of official culture, which can be interpreted as a slow blurring of the distinction between official and unofficial realms of North Korean culture. Let us introduce a few examples below:

"Sanjun, I thought that you are a man. But, I heard that you are just a henpecked husband. A man who used to drive a tank shouldn't do that. You've got to win, just like me, whether right or wrong."[17]

"Company management is just about production cost and profit. Whether the country will gain profit or lose? All workers in factories and companies should consider this first."[18]

"Quite a few Party and economic leaders criticized Comrade Sangmin for following anti-Party elements and introducing a revisionist economic theory, Libermanism. However, I did not want to see Comrade Sangmin in such a one-dimensional perspective. I did not think that it (Comrade Sangmin's policy) was based on Eastern European revisionism which is a messy company management method. Rather, I thought that it (his policy) stems from his burning passion to increase fertilizer production through better company management."[19]

"We have to earn foreign currency. With foreign currency, we can buy miscella-neous resources to normalize the operation of production across the country."[20]

The excerpts introduced above directly challenge time-honored North Korean revolutionary literary tradition as they legitimize public attitudes toward outright pragmatism in which performance precedes procedure. While the first two emphasize and praise an attitude toward achieving goals regardless of the legitimacy of methods, the latter two indicate proactive endorsement of pursuing profits and hard currency, which would be betraying *juche* principles such as self-reliance. Let's read a few more excerpts from recent North Korean novels that show newly emerging cultural trends.

"Please my dear. . . . Let's decorate our house better. Ok will be discharged and return home. . . . Then, we have to marry her off. Take a look at other houses please."[21]

"In the meanwhile, father made a number of business trips abroad. He used to bring nothing from business trips but a few leftover candies from the plane for his daughter. Since Yonghae knew her father well, she assumed that her father had entirely forgotten her request for a shaver. Nevertheless, when the father heard that Yonghae would be making a business trip to the place where her husband, Chunghae, works, he gave a luxurious shaver to her as a gift for her husband. Yonghae was rather surprised than pleased. Chunghae touched the shaver curiously. 'Bring it to me.' Yonghae took the shaver and explained how to use it . . . switch, battery, how to dissemble, to clean it. . . . Then, she turned it on. The shaver pleasantly ran with a smooth sound."[22]

"Duk-jun Yoon observed that girl with an old man's curiosity. Though her face and figure were conspicuously beautiful, it was her outfit that attracted everyone's attention. The bright dress perfectly fit with spring weather, shining high heels, a fedora-like hat that often appears in foreign movies, a bag with a golden chain in her hand. . . . In short, her outfit was like it just came out from a foreign movie. Duk-jun Yoon has no knowledge about women's dress, especially about the quality of fashionable dresses among women. Yet, through the jealous faces of many girls passing by that girl, he could assume that the quality and style of her costume was splendid."[23]

In the three extracts above, it is striking to observe outright endorsement of desire for material affluence and yearning for foreign culture. Showing interest in appearance of clothing and housing seems to be accepted as a natural desire. Especially interesting is that the narrators above regard foreignness and foreign goods as criteria of being good and beautiful. At the same time, as also shown in earlier excerpts, the backgrounds and situations of these stories, which proactively reflect new values and ideas, are closely related to family, romance, or private affairs. In other words, North Korean official literature also recognizes the expanding private realms that are becoming the source of new narratives.

North Korean novels have to go through rigorous censorship since they still play a pivotal role as a propaganda tool for the party. Hence, it would be difficult to argue that the new trends appearing in the novels quoted above are accurately representing private discourses of contemporary North Korean society. Yet it is noticeable that heterogeneous values and norms, which do not belong to the orthodox official discourses of North Korea, are becoming conspicuously frequent in recent North Korean novels. Indeed, a novel quoted above, *Desire* by Mun Chang Kim, is broadly recognized as a textbook for reformers and is known for the heated controversies it generated during its publication process. These nonconventional novelists who write reform-oriented stories are not participating in the 415 Creating Corps (*changjakddan*).[24] In some sense, a space for nonofficial discourses is emerging in the North Korean literary field in spite of tight censorship.

We can speculate as to why the official culture in North Korea is transforming and why elements of unofficial culture have become conspicuous even among government-managed cultural productions. The collapse of the formal ration system after the food crisis paved the way for the surge of unofficial culture. The ration system not only governed the distribution of grains but also played the critical role of combining social constituents in a single official organization. Nevertheless, the collapse of the ration system also weakened the integrity of work units, and North Korean residents started to move around freely, seeking basic necessities including grains. Furthermore, the 7.1 Measure unwittingly allowed for the development of various private realms in society by activating local markets that exist without official control mechanisms.

The expansion of individual agricultural lots and commercial activities activated the private economy. Through that process, traditional family relations became safety networks and, at the same time, strengthened private communication channels, just as Chinese society had witnessed three decades earlier.[25] At the same time, the emergence of rich individuals through rampant governmental corruption and their relationship with powerful bureaucrats also weakened the overall legitimacy of North Korean official culture. Increased commercial activities also produced social spaces for leisure, such as billiard rooms and game rooms. Those new spaces would produce new leisure activities and culture that have played an important role in creating unofficial culture.

The emergence of a new generation can be seen as another important factor for the burgeoning unofficial culture in North Korea. Here, we define the "new generation" in North Korea as the young population that grew up after North Korean industrialization in the 1960s. Compared to their parents who experienced the Korean War and the mass-mobilized industrialization up until the 1960s, they tend to embrace pragmatic economism, an individualistic value system, an absence of unification fever, and practical career choices. For this generation, the traumatic experience of the food crisis in the 1990s furthered their unorthodox perspectives on the economy, as well as on career and unification, while strengthening their belief that financial and economic stability in their career path is the most important value.

The collapse of the public education system after the food crisis is another important factor. During the critical period of the late 1990s, when only around 10 percent of middle school students could attend school and many teachers had to abandon classrooms to feed their families,[26] reproduction of official culture through public education was virtually impossible in many parts of North Korea. On the contrary, a few nouveau riche who accumulated wealth through corruption or the burgeoning markets are contributing to the emergence of a private educational market, such as piano and accordion lessons.[27]

Among all these contributing factors, the influx of new information can be regarded as the most important factor that has weakened the official culture. North Korea is not only experiencing a collapsing agricultural sector but also the breakdown of manufacturing structures. Therefore, many basic commodities are being imported from China. Importation of Chinese goods through official and unofficial routes is naturally accompanied by an influx of novel information. At the same time, expanding transaction between North and South Korea is another source of new information. Though strictly controlled, the transfusion of South Korean culture through the over 10,000 South Koreans that visit North Korea (other than Kaesong Industrial Park and Kumgang Mountains) cannot be easily ignored—as South Korean visitors have reported, some hotels that are popular among South Korean visitors started to serve southern-style spicy foods, and female laborers in the Kaesong Industrial Park tend to follow South Korean–style cosmetics. With this, we can begin to contextualize the fast infiltration of South Korean popular culture into North Korean society. As described in the first section of this chapter, the penetration of visual mediums greatly contributed to the circulation of the Korean Wave, while, at the same time, vitiating official culture.

INTERPRETING CULTURAL POLLUTION IN NORTH KOREA

Many North Korean refugees have testified to the widespread cynicism in North Korean society against the Kim Jong Il regime's empty slogans and rhetoric of anti-imperialism and military-first politics. Yet we do not have a well-structured theoretical framework to interpret a logical sequence from political cynicism to formation of antiregime culture and, finally, to political transition. On the contrary, thinkers like Vaclav Havel and Lisa Wedeen suggest that widespread cynicism is an intended consequence of authoritarian rulers, as "living a lie" in a system of strictly ritualized truth by a dictatorial regime is the most essential element of the domination by an authoritarian regime in everyday life.[28] Hence, overinterpretation of refugees' testimonies would repeat the mistake of wishful thinking that occurred in 1994 when numerous scholars predicted the collapse of the Kim dynasty following Kim Il Sung's death.[29] Instead of making the argument that Girls' Generation will destroy the late Kim Jong Il's regime, we would like to cautiously suggest that the changing relationship between official culture and unofficial culture is the most important implication for the introduction of the Korean Wave and other foreign cultures into North Korean society.

Regardless of the strength of official culture, unofficial culture always exists as a part of official culture. A subculture like juvenile culture with its unique language patterns and rebellious values is a good example. Yet not all unofficial culture or subcultures are resisting against the dominating culture. As a number of cultural theorists argue, our tendency to define anything unorthodox as counterhegemonic, resistance, or rebellion is nothing but the "romance of

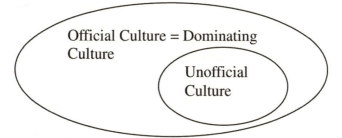

Figure 9.2. Official and Unofficial Culture in North Korea before the 1990s

resistance,"[30] which ignores the reality that the forms and contents of resistance are predetermined by the dominating culture's design.[31] A meticulous study of the Stalinist era attests to this aspect by showing how seemingly discontent individuals under a totalitarian regime had to borrow Stalinist concepts and tenets to criticize the ossified dictatorship.[32] Hence, within a closed system with successful ideological indoctrination, unofficial culture or subcultures are an integral part of domination as shown in figure 9.2.

Nevertheless, what if a totalitarian regime, which has long been successful in maintaining ideological/cultural integrity, fails to keep up with cultural sanitation against the influx of undesirable foreign culture? As indicated in the section above, the North Korean regime had few measures to maintain its closed system since it had to expand interactions with South Korea and China to overcome unprecedented economic hardship since the 1990s and had to tolerate the influx of taste, information, and aesthetic sensitivities from abroad, especially from the South. Then, the transformation of unofficial culture in North Korea in the last two decades is the direct consequence of North Korea's unprecedented contact with the outside world. This is because new elements of North Korean unofficial culture are not integral parts of the official culture but are deeply contradictory to it. From this aspect, we can see that North Korean unofficial culture might be transforming into a "counterculture" which could directly challenge the ruling ideology of North Korea (see figure 9.3).

Figure 9.3. A Conjecture on Official and Unofficial Culture in North Korea after the 1990s

Despite the numerous signs of an emerging counterculture in North Korea, we definitely need further evidence to verify it. A full-fledged counterculture needs a well-defined social space and networks through which cultural production, circulation, and diffusion can be done without state interference. Burgeoning rural markets and urban black markets are producing private realms based on off-state economic transactions and communications. Yet they are too fragmented and localized to produce a countrywide private sphere. A counterculture also needs a carrier group that reproduces and promotes new values and perspectives. A number of North Korean residents such as construction workers, doctors, traders, and waitresses have rich overseas experiences and are constructing distinctive everyday lifestyles. Nevertheless, there is no hard evidence that this unique population is homogeneous in terms of cultural, political, or ideological orientation.

Above all, the most important condition for a powerful counterculture in North Korea is the conjunction of deepening social contradictions and emerging new values. Economic hardship does not automatically produce antiregime movements. Discontent and dissatisfaction cannot evolve into a counterculture unless a relatively coherent interpretation is given to those who are enduring economic and political hardships. In other words, it would be important to observe whether newly available information through the Korean Wave or new cultural sensitivities that are emerging in North Korean official/unofficial culture can be used as a prism through which to see and interpret the current North Korean sociopolitical and economic situation.

NOTES

1. http://english.hani.co.kr/arti/english_edition/e_entertainment/491009.html.

2. *Korea Times*, June 24, 2011.

3. *Choson Ilbo*, August 29, 2011.

4. *Korea Times*, June 24, 2011.

5. *Seoul Sinmun*, August 17, 2011.

6. *Daily NK*, August 17, 2011.

7. *Choson Ilbo*, June 30, 2011.

8. Interview with a North Korean, August 18, 2010.

9. Interview with a North Korean refugee, October 31, 2004.

10. Woo Young Lee, "The Possibility of the Construction of Private Discourses in North Korea [*Pukhan chaje nae sajok tamnon hyongsong ui kanungsong*]," in *A Study on North Korean Urban Residents' Private Realms* [*Pukhan tosi chumin ui sajok yongyok yonsu*] (Seoul: Hanul Academy 2008), 167.

11. Dong-Wan Kang and Jung-Ran Park, "Distribution Channels and Influences of South Korean Visual Media in North Korea," *Unification Policy Studies* [*tongil chongchaek yonsu*] 19, no. 2 (2010).

12. Chu-chol Lee, "Current State of North Korean Residents' Exposure to South Korean Broadcasting," paper presented at the Korean Logistics Forum, August 18, 2011.

13. Chu-chol Lee, "Current State of North Korean Residents' Exposure."

14. *Maeil Kyongje Sinmun*, January 25, 2011.

15. *Joongang Ilbo*, March 26, 2011.

16. Interview with a North Korean refugee, August 2011.

17. Ro Chongbom, "My Wife's Hope [Anhae ui sowon]," *Korean Literature* [*Choson Munhak*], August 2006.

18. Kim Munchang, *Desire* [*Yolmang*] (Pyongyang: Munhak Yesul Chonghap Chulpansa, 1999).

19. Paek Namryong, *One Thousand-li of East Sea* [*Tonghae cholli*] (Pyongyang: Pyongyang Chulpansa, 1996).

20. Kim, *Desire*.

21. Chang Son-Hong, "Their Happiness," *Choson Munhak* (Korean Literature), July 2006.

22. Park Ryong-Un, *Young Captin* [*cholmun sonjang*] (Pyongyang: Kumsung Chongnyon Chulpansa, 2006).

23. Yong-hak Choi, *Our House* [*uri ui jip*] (Pyongyang: munhak yesul chulpansa, 2005).

24. Some might argue that official discourses are embracing "pragmatism" in the name of "pragmatic socialism" (*silli sahoejuui*), and stories such as *Desire* are representations of this new official ideology. Nevertheless, literary works that are introduced here do not belong to this new official ideology since pragmatic socialism still focuses on ideology in the struggles between ideology and pragmatic interests.

25. In some places, the collective farms distributed land to individuals or small groups so that they could solve the food crisis independently. Interview with a North Korean refugee February 28, 2006.

26. Interviews with North Korean refugees, October 31, 2005; August 18, 2010.

27. Teachers who could not receive regular salaries during the economic crisis started to participate in private education. Interviews with North Korean refugees March 22, 2006; November 6, 2005.

28. Vaclav Havel, *Living in Truth: Twenty-Two Essays Published on the Occasion of the Award of the Erasmus Prize to Vaclav Havel*, ed. Jan Vladislav (London: Faber & Faber, 1987); Lisa Wedeen, *Ambiguities of Domination: Politics, Rhetoric, and Symbol in Contemporary Syria* (Chicago: University of Chicago Press, 1999).

29. Bruce Cumings, "Why Didn't North Korea Collapse, and Why Did So Many Influential Americans Think It Would?", paper prepared for the conference, "Why Didn't Communism Collapse?" Dartmouth College, Hanover, NH, May 25–26, 2007.

30. Lila Abu-Lughod, "The Romance of Resistance: Tracing Transformations of Power through Bedouin Women," *American Ethnologist* 17, no. 1 (1990).

31. Timothy Mitchell, "Everyday Metaphors of Power," *Theory and Society* 19 (1990).

32. Jochen Hellbeck, "Fashioning the Stalinist Soul: The Diary of Stepan Podlubnyi, 1931–1939," in Sheila Fitzpatrick, ed., *Stalinism: New Directions* (New York: Routledge, 2000).

Part IV

FOREIGN RELATIONS
IN THE TRANSITION ERA

Chapter Ten

Changes and Continuities in Pyongyang's China Policy

Liu Ming

2010 and 2011 were two unusual years for North Korea. Kim Jong Il visited China three times within twelve months, in May and August 2010 and May 2011. The ruling Workers' Party of Korea (WPK) convened a conference of delegates in September 2010, almost forty-four years after it held its previous one in 1966. This party conference informally designated Kim Jong Il's third son, Kim Jong Un, as vice chairman of the WPK Central Military Commission and Kim Jong Il's heir, and elected members and alternate members of the party's Central Committee, launching a new era of power transition in Pyongyang. In addition to these domestic developments in North Korea, 2010 was a year marked by unfortunate events for the South Korean people, including the sinking of a navy corvette *Cheonan* in March that left forty-six sailors dead. A joint investigation team claimed that the sinking was caused by the North, and in November, North Korea shelled Yeonpyeong Island, located near the disputed Northern Limit Line (NLL), killing two soldiers and two civilians.

An assessment of North Korea's China policy must be set in historical context to identify some key characteristics, logics of change, and basic principles. Over the last sixty years, China and North Korea have weathered great changes in their domestic politics and international environment, over the course of which their relations have unavoidably fluctuated. At least six factors have shaped North Korea's China policy: its interests related to Sino-Soviet competition and ideological disputes, China and the Soviet Union's respective attitudes toward North Korea's growing demand for economic assistance, China's capacity to assist North Korea in the economic and military realms, the impact of Chinese and North Korean domestic politics, the tense situation on the Korean Peninsula, and North Korea's new policy toward the South.

Based on North Korea's diplomatic orientation, we may find that its China policy has been based on not pure friendship but on its own interests in response to China's foreign and domestic policy and Chinese attitudes toward Pyongyang. North Korea's China policy has largely been just a passive response, but on some occasions, North Korea has taken an upper hand in the development of the relationship, leading China into a direction favorable to North Korean interests. In dealing with Beijing or Moscow, North Korea strongly maintained its independence, and both China and the Soviet Union respected this nationalistic stance.[1]

This chapter will trace the historical development of North Korea–China ties since the Korean War and offer some evaluations of the dynamic factors behind North Korea's policy adjustments toward China.

PYONGYANG'S CHINA POLICY IN THE COLD WAR ERA: FROM DISTRUST TO INTERDEPENDENCE

North Korea's relations with China in the Cold War era can be roughly divided into five periods, characterized by reluctantly war-bound comrade-in-arms relations (1950–1956), close political and economic ties (1957–1968), ideologically contentious and distrustful relations (1968–1971), limited resumption of amicable ties (1971–1979), and reservation toward China's reform and opening, while maintaining symbolic political relations with some minimum level of economic interdependence (1979–1992).

It appears to many North Korea observers that China and North Korea maintained cordial relations during the Cold War.[2] This is not completely true. Declassified archives and historical reinterpretations of the Korean War and the 1953–1992 period indicate that North Korea's leader Kim Il Sung held a suspicious attitude toward Chinese leaders as early as the beginning of the Korean War. Kim did not want China to dispatch its forces to North Korea when the war had turned unfavorable to Pyongyang, fearing that a long-term Chinese presence could weaken his power and Pyongyang's independence.[3]

As Chinese marshal Peng Dehuai led the Chinese People's Volunteers into the North, Kim Il Sung did not want Peng to command the DPRK People's Army after UN forces crossed the 38th parallel into North Korea in September 1950. Kim's position created feelings of distrust in the Sino–North Korean relationship that intermittently lasted the entire war period. China recalled its ambassador and did not dispatch a new ambassador until January of 1955, a move that clearly reflected the degree of tension in the relationship.

China–North Korea relations remained distant after the end of the Korean War. According to a Soviet diplomat's report, Chinese premier Zhou Enlai largely rebuffed the North Korean ambassador during receptions at the DPRK embassy in Beijing, and North Korean leaders showed ignorance of the inferior conditions at the Chinese People's Volunteers bases in North Korea.[4]

The socialist camp remained united in appearance, and China still felt obliged to help North Korea recover its economy. During Kim Il Sung's visit to China in 1953, Beijing proposed the Economic and Cultural Cooperation Agreement and another six agreements, in which China offered 8 trillion RMB in assistance for the period 1954–1957 and rendered gratis the 7.29 trillion RMB costs incurred over the three years of war. In 1954 and 1955, China provided 130,000 tons and 150,000 tons of grain, respectively, to the North.

Kim Il Sung's purging campaign against the Yanan faction within the WPK in 1956 became the greatest source of Chinese animosity. The high-level officials in this faction were originally middle-level officers of the Communist Party of China (CPC)'s Eighth and New Fourth Armies in the civil war who were deployed for the Korean War at the request of Kim Il Sung.[5] Kim's campaign was launched after the "August Incident" in 1956 following the Twentieth Party Congress of the Soviet Communist Party, where General Secretary Nikita Khrushchev delivered a secret speech denouncing Joseph Stalin. During Kim Il Sung's visit to Moscow in June 1956, Soviet faction leader Pak Chang Ok, Choe Chang Ik, and other leading members of the Yanan faction planned to attack Kim Il Sung at the plenum of the Central Committee for building a personality cult and distorting the "Leninist principle of collective leadership." A sharp conflict occurred between the Yanan faction and Kim's supporters at the plenum meeting on August 30 and 31. The Yanan faction was finally defeated, and their core members escaped to China.

The Soviet Union expressed its concern over the incident and its willingness to consult with China, but declined to intervene. Seeing the Soviet's softening attitude, Kim decided to divert his main attack on the Yanan faction. Members of the faction who failed to escape were arrested and sent to prison camps. Kim Il Sung's actions infuriated Mao Zedong. In September 1956, a joint Soviet-Chinese delegation led by Peng Dehuai and the Soviet senior statesman Mikoyan went to Pyongyang. The delegation talked with Kim Il Sung twice to "instruct" him to cease the purges and reinstate the leaders of the Yanan and Soviet factions.[6] Kim conceded at the time but continued to suppress the faction members, causing more people to flee to China.

The Soviet-Chinese intervention was a major insult for Kim Il Sung,[7] and China–North Korea relations stagnated to historic lows from September 1956 to the first half of 1957. Beijing put aside Pyongyang's requested assistance of 50 million RMB in loans, and Mao Zedong in private talks with Soviet ambassador P. F. Yudin placed Kim Il Sung within the ranks of such leaders as Josip Broz Tito and Imre Nagy.[8] North Korea canceled Kim Il Sung's planned trip to China for the Eighth CPC Congress as well as the DPRK vice premier's visit to Beijing. North Korean leaders repeatedly complained to Soviet diplomats about the Chinese ambassador's unfriendly attitude.[9]

The riots in Poland and Hungary in 1956 may be regarded as a turning point in China–North Korea and China–Soviet Union relations. Mao Zedong's positive views on the role of the Soviet Union as leader of the socialist camp began to change. Mao criticized Khrushchev's reconciliation policy toward the United States and other Western countries, calling it a policy of surrender. North Korea's weight increased ostensibly on Chinese strategic calculations. From June 1957, Mao Zedong's attitude toward North Korea seemed to warm up. During North Korean vice premier Kim Il's visit to China from September to October, China exported such vital materials as coal, sulfur, raw rubber, and cotton to the DPRK to support its economic revitalization.

Noticing the subtle changes in Beijing–Moscow relations, Kim Il Sung engaged in frank discussions with Mao about the suppression of opposition forces in the Korean Workers' Party. On the sidelines of a meeting in Moscow in November 1957, Mao Zedong expressed regret to Kim Il Sung for China's intervention in North Korean domestic affairs in 1956. Mao thus recognized Pyongyang's independent status.

China–North Korea relations entered a period of climax in 1958. North Korea launched the Chollima Movement, apparently modeled after China's "Great Leap Forward" and "People's Communes," and shifted to conservatism in the socialist construction. China offered more economic assistance and various raw materials to North Korea, including support for the construction of several hydropower stations and many factories.[10]

As the policy differences between Moscow and Beijing deepened and began to surface in late 1959, Kim Il Sung appeared to initially side with Moscow given the large amounts of Soviet industrial assistance to North Korea. Although the DPRK began to join China in criticizing Soviet revisionism in Sino–North Korean bilateral talks from 1960, Kim Il Sung's tilt to Beijing remained ambivalent given North Korea's economic dependence on Soviet aid. Following secret talks with Khrushchev in Moscow in May 1959, Kim Il Sung in a closed-door meeting angrily accused China of its intention to turn North Korea into a Chinese colony.[11] At the World Communist Party Conference in October 1960, North Korea did not support China's position against Soviet ideology; neither did North Korea align with the Soviet Union to criticize China.[12]

North Korea's foreign policy environment was also shaped by Pyongyang's own independence philosophy and China's active engagement. Since China risked isolation in the socialist camp, Mao attached importance to North

Korea as part of efforts to "unite all the countries that could be united." With the U.S. threat looming within a distance from China, North Korea's position as a "buffer zone" was no less significant for Beijing. Kim Il Sung began to take a two-pronged approach: wavering between Beijing and Moscow so as to fully exploit the two communist giants' confrontation, while pursuing an independent policy under his *juche* program of national self-reliance in order to diminish the influence of the USSR and China over domestic affairs.[13]

An eccentric style of relationship formed between Beijing and Pyongyang: the DPRK sophistically manipulated China while China continually provided assistance to North Korea, refrained from intervening in North Korea's domestic and foreign affairs, and supported the DPRK's behavior and policy whatever it took. During a honeymoon period in 1957, Mao Zedong acquiesced to Kim Il Sung's purging of Kim Tu Bong, a Yanan faction leader and nominal president of North Korea, and the Chinese People's Volunteers unilaterally withdrew from North Korea in 1958. In July 1961, North Korea and China signed a Treaty of Friendly Cooperation and Mutual Assistance. In 1962, the two allies signed a Border Treaty, in which China conceded 54.5 percent of Chang-bai Mountain's Tianchi (Mount Baekdu's Heaven Lake, regarded by Koreans as a legendary place of their ancestral origin).

The ten years of 1958 to 1963 and 1971 to 1976 were generally favorable for North Korea and China. Various factors gave rise to the warming of ties. First, Mao was very generous to Kim Il Sung, while fully supporting the cause of Third World countries and standing firmly against the West. Second, Pyongyang sympathized with many of Beijing's views, such as opposing de-Stalinization, the elimination of the cult of the individual.[14] Third, Mao Zedong and Kim Il Sung shared a close cultural affinity; Mao regarded himself as a leader of the socialist camp and assumed the obligation of protecting Kim's small country. Kim in turn adopted a relatively pro-China policy and categorically supported China in the Sino-Indian border conflict of October 1962. Fourth, the withdrawal from North Korea of the Chinese People's Volunteers left North Korea with a sense of anxiety that intensified as South Korea and Japan resumed talks on the normalization of relations in October 1960.[15] Although the North Koreans had signed military pacts with the Soviet Union and China respectively in 1961, they were fully aware that in any future conflict against U.S.–South Korean forces, only China would be their reliable backer.

In the spring of 1962, *Rodong Sinmun* featured several articles criticizing Soviet revisionism. The key points of criticism were that (1) the Soviet revisionist trends, such as "peace transition and peaceful coexistence," conflicted with North Korea's assertion of imminent American aggression against the DPRK;[16] (2) the Soviet Union restrained the national economic development of soviet countries through its principle of "international division of work";

and (3) as the self-proclaimed "No.1" party, the communist party of the Soviet Union forced other communist parties to accept its position and views. At this time the Soviet Union pursued a relatively moderate policy in the international arena, even toward the United States.[17]

The period from 1960 to 1964 was one in which Moscow–Pyongyang relations steadily deteriorated.[18] Moscow considered the DPRK as a Chinese puppet and sharply cut aid to Pyongyang in 1961. Faced with economic difficulties at home, China's assistance to Pyongyang was also limited. But two years of intense Sino–North Korean military cooperation in 1963–1964 led Pyongyang to drift in China's direction.[19] Only after the leadership transition in the Kremlin did the Soviet Union resume high-level exchanges with North Korea and military aid to the North from late 1964 to early 1965.[20]

Paradoxically, the more Pyongyang reached out to Beijing, the less trust there developed between China and North Korea. Despite differences on some issues, North Korea–Soviet Union relations were neither friendly nor aloof during the period of 1960 to 1964. North Korea's open criticism of the Soviet Union did not mean that Pyongyang fully sided with the Chinese position. In private talks, Kim Il Sung expressed his disapproval of Beijing's assertiveness toward the Soviet Union, but he also did not support the Soviet Union's "vicious attack against Chinese" in August 1963.[21] At the same time, Kim viewed the Soviet leaders as the "elder brothers" of North Korea.[22] Despite amicable relations between Beijing and Pyongyang on the surface, North Korea complained about China's interference and self-conceited stance, which subtly strained their normal relations during their honeymoon period.

North Korea in principle did not get deeply involved in the disputes between Moscow and Beijing and sought to avoid criticizing Soviet behavior on the international stage. In June 1961, Kim Il Sung visited Moscow and signed the Treaty of Friendship, Cooperation and Mutual Assistance. Since North Korea's main enemy was the U.S.–South Korean alliance, it had to maintain allied relations with both China and the Soviet Union.[23] And by carefully maneuvering between the two competing giants, North Korea could gain significant amounts of needed assistance.[24]

While the new Soviet leader took active measures to improve relations with the DPRK in late 1964, China and North Korean began to differ on some issues, including assessments of Brezhnev and Soviet assistance to Vietnam.[25] Beijing doubted any substantive changes in the new Soviet leadership as well as the importance of Soviet aid to Vietnam.[26] Pyongyang meanwhile refuted Chinese premier Zhou Enlai's claim that China had become the center of world revolution.[27] Some skirmishes occurred along the Sino-DPRK border in 1965.

China–North Korea relations were suspended by the Chinese Cultural Revolution, during which Mao and his followers launched an ultraleftist campaign against revolutionary officials and the existing economic and political order. North Korea found itself among the foreign victims of the Cultural Revolution, as the Chinese Red Guards denounced Kim Il Sung as a revisionist. The North Korean media responded by accusing China of representing "Left" opportunism, dogmatism, great-nation chauvinism, and even the "Trotskyist theory of permanent revolution."[28] From 1965 to 1969, China and North Korea halted all economic and cultural agreements and top-level visits. China closed its border with North Korea in 1968, and the DPRK shifted away from China to the Soviet Union.

Pyongyang's policy during this period has been described as Moscow-inclined neutrality.[29] It can rather be seen that the DPRK abandoned a one-sided orientation toward China at the end of 1964 and in the beginning of 1965.[30] In 1965, the DPRK attended the Twenty-Third Soviet Communist Party Congress and secured a military aid agreement with the Soviet Union; in 1966–1967 the two countries reached agreements of economic and technological cooperation and military and economic aid, including Soviet provision of 150 million rubles in military equipment. Rather than demonstrating an inclination toward the Soviet Union, these acts of cooperation were consistent with North Korea's wavering policy, under which North Korea shuttled opportunistically among external powers. From time to time, the North Koreans would seek Soviet support to deal with their political struggle against Seoul and to obtain economic and military assistance.

Nevertheless, despite some difficulties in China–North Korea relations in 1965, new developments on the Korean Peninsula pushed Kim Il Sung closer to Beijing. Kim began to prepare for a unified war against South Korea amid Japanese–South Korean rapprochement and the heightening of protests in the South. In separate meetings with Yang Yong, the former commander-in-chief of the Chinese People's Volunteers, and Hao De-qing, the outgoing ambassador to the DPRK, Kim Il Sung directly asked China to support him if a new war broke out.[31]

The principal change in North Korea's China policy during the Chinese Cultural Revolution was a shift in Pyongyang's previous uncritical position toward the PRC. However, the DPRK did not seek to simply join the Soviet camp. In August 1966, Pyongyang proclaimed its independence from both Moscow and Beijing.[32] The cooling relations between China and North Korea again shifted when North Korea shot down an American spy plane in April 1969, during which the Soviet Union did not give the North its full support. Choi Yong Gon, president of the Presidium of the DPRK Supreme People's

Assembly, visited Beijing in October 1969, and Zhou Enlai reciprocated with a visit to Pyongyang in 1970 for the normalization of bilateral relations.

Friendly relations between China and North Korea began to reach a second climax in their history as Kim Il Sung resumed his regular visits to China, beginning with a secret one in October 1970 (Kim Il Sung visited China altogether forty times, mostly in secret, once or twice a year). China agreed to provide all military assistance, except for nuclear weapons, upon request when a North Korean military delegation visited Beijing in 1971.[33] Soon after Kissinger visited China and announced President Nixon's planned visit to China in 1971, Zhou Enlai made a secret trip to Pyongyang to brief and reassure Kim Il Sung on the development. From September 1982 to June 1992, China–DPRK high-level exchanges reached eighty-five, among which North Korea made seventy-one visits and China fourteen.[34]

North Korea maintained cordial relations with China after the death of Mao Zedong and other first-generation leaders and with the conclusion of the Cultural Revolution in 1976, but the colors of the Cold War alliance had faded. North Korea perceived that China's North Korea policy remained unchanged in rhetoric, but North Korean private attitudes toward Beijing revealed a degree of perplexity and suspicion about Chinese reform and their approach to Western countries. China still attached importance to North Korea, however, mainly because (1) Sino–Russian competition was still quite intense, and China needed North Korea to side with China; (2) Chinese reform master Deng Xiaoping inherited Mao and Zhou's friendly attitudes toward Kim Il Sung and held on to the perception that DPRK was a buffer zone for China.

China–DPRK exchanges continued from the late 1970s to the early 1990s. Chinese visits to North Korea included premier and CPC chairman Hua Guofeng and CPC general secretary Hu Yaobang in 1978 and 1982, respectively; Deng Xiaoping in 1978 and 1982; Premier Zhao Ziyang and Li Peng in 1981 and 1991; Hu Yaobang, Zhao Ziyang, and Jiang Zemin respectively in 1982, 1984, 1985, 1989, and 1990; President Li Xiannian and Yang Shangkun in 1986, 1988, and 1992; and Defense Minister Geng Biao in 1982. Kim Il Sung paid five official visits to China, in 1982, 1984, 1987, 1989, and 1991. DPRK premier Li Jong Ok, Kang Song San, Li Gun Mo, and Yon Hyong Muk, respectively, visited China in 1981, 1984, 1987, and 1990.

Before Deng Xiaoping's formal retirement, he invited Kim Il Sung to China in 1989 soon after the Tiananmen incident. During that visit, Deng introduced him to Jiang Zemin and other third-generation leaders, entrusting them to continue cordial relations. According to some unconfirmed reports, Deng also agreed that the PLA would offer assistance in the event of a North Korean crisis if requested by the DPRK.

A BITTER PERIOD FOR NORTH KOREA'S CHINA POLICY: ACCEPTANCE AND ADJUSTMENT

With China's marketization of its external assistance and development of good relations with Western countries from the mid-1980s, North Korea adopted a series of measures to adjust its foreign and economic policy for attracting foreign capital. In 1984, it initiated three-way talks with the United States and South Korea, and it also established a "Joint Venture Law." Facing a new situation in the early 1980s during which more than one hundred countries established diplomatic relations with the two Koreas, Deng Xiaoping acceded to the Chinese Foreign Ministry proposal of softening relations with South Korea.[35] China made subtle changes to its no-contact, no-recognition policy toward the South in the mid-1980s, allowing sports and academic exchanges, and beginning entrepôt trade with South Korea. Such moves raised worries in the DPRK about Beijing's policy toward the South.[36]

Three developments prompted Kim Il Sung to adjust his China-centered foreign policy: South Korean president Roh Tae Woo's North–South reconciliation from 1988; the disintegration of the Soviet Union; and the Tiananmen incident in 1989. Kim was clearly aware that the times of benefiting from Sino–Soviet competition were over, that North Korea's diplomatic space had narrowed, and that North Korea's heavy reliance on Chinese assistance was not sustainable. Beijing ceased to provide any advanced weapons to Pyongyang by the end of the 1980s,[37] after which North Korea had to diversify its diplomacy for new resources.

From the mid-1980s, Kim Il Sung realized that Beijing would eventually shift to a two-Koreas policy and establish formal relations with Seoul, given China's prioritization of economic considerations and interests in the "South Korean model."[38] Kim Il Sung requested that China delay its decision, pledging to solve the problems with South Korea, Japan, and the United States within a few years.

It is likely that Kim Il Sung made three strategic decisions at the time: (1) establishing an inter-Korean peace mechanism to replace the armistice regime and proposing a confederal system to realize unification in form; (2) improving relations with the United States and Japan, even refraining from making the long request that U.S. troops should withdraw from South Korea;[39] and (3) developing its nuclear deterrence capabilities against U.S.–South Korean forces to ensure its long-term security in the face of a rising South Korea.

Consul-level contacts between the United States and North Korea began in Beijing at the end of 1988. Workers' Party of Korea secretary Kim Yong Sun met the U.S. assistant secretary of state in January 1992, the first official meeting between the two countries. The United States and North Korea exchanged thirty consul-level contacts by 1992.[40] A series of inter-Korean primary-level talks resulted in the successful conclusion of a Basic Agreement on Reconciliation, Nonaggression, and Exchange and Cooperation in 1991, while North Korea's nuclear program was also rapidly proceeding.

China–DPRK bilateral relations reached a turning point in 1991 when China's foreign minister Qian Qichen visited Seoul for the annual Asia-Pacific Economic Cooperation (APEC) meeting and the two Koreas simultaneously joined the United Nations, paving the way for China to normalize relations with South Korea while justifying its actions to Pyongyang. After Beijing and Seoul established formal relations in 1992, the deterioration in Beijing–Pyongyang relations was widely evident. Beijing's pragmatic approach indeed inflicted a heavy blow on North Korea as an isolated country and a small partner of China. North Korea initially considered some retaliatory steps against China's betrayal, such as the development of relations with Taiwan,[41] but it ultimately withdrew such plans out of fear that China might sever all relations with Pyongyang. North Korea's disappointment was also partly assuaged by China's dismissal of such South Korean demands as an apology for acts in the Korean War and explanations for the clause of military intervention on the Korean Peninsula under the China–DPRK Treaty of Friendship, Cooperation and Mutual Assistance.[42]

While North Korea was receptive to the new reality of Sino–Korean relations, it began to realize one point: that only through acceleration of its nuclear weapons program and pursuit of independent diplomacy could North Korea perpetuate the viability of its regime and protect its security interests. North Korean mentality was lagging far behind during the post–Cold War transition period and continued to assume that Chinese interests and policy should unconditionally be subject to a shared socialist ideology. China's pragmatic pursuit of its own national interests and establishment of diplomatic relations with Seoul thus became a significant source of North Korean resentment.

Pyongyang maintained a cold shoulder to Beijing for twelve years after 1992. Several reasons accounted for this attitude: face-saving; unfamiliar and asymmetric relations between Kim Jong Il and Deng Xiaoping/Jiang Zemin; the three-year mourning period for the late Kim Il Sung; defection by Hwang Jang Yop, the former secretary for international affairs in the Workers' Party of Korea, to the South through China; and uncertainty about China's policy toward North Korea. However, Pyongyang did not take any hostile measures to deteriorate relations with China. Pyongyang kept silent on China's normalization of relations with South Korea compared to the media's open attacks toward Soviet–South Korean normalization. In 1993, Hu Jintao, then a member of the CPC Standing Committee, led a delegation to Pyongyang in an effort to mend fences with North Korea, and both countries maintained contacts and reciprocal visits at the middle and working levels.

North Korea resumed sub-top-level contacts with China in 1994, during which important visits included North Korean vice president Lee Jong Ok and Defense Minister Choi Kwang's respective visits in 1994; Vice Premier Hong Song Nam's visit in 1996, when the two sides signed a new economic cooperation agreement and China agreed to provide 500,000 tons of foods to Pyongyang; and the visit in 1999 by Kim Yong Nam, North Korea's ceremonial head of state and Chairman of the Supreme People's Assembly, which marked North Korea's official resumption of friendly relations with China.

For China and North Korea, this was also a period of searching for a new basis and framework of bilateral relations. The handling of the first nuclear crisis suggested to Pyongyang that Beijing still wanted to avoid conflict between North Korea and the United States. China first forced a draft of a sanctions resolution to be changed into a President's Statement at the UN Security Council, and then pressed the DPRK to accept a negotiations approach, which led to the Geneva Framework Agreement in 1994.[43] Pyongyang gradually perceived Beijing's bottom line: disapproval of North Korea's provocative behavior or other brinkmanship on the Korean Peninsula; keeping a balance between the two Koreas; preventing any new inter-Korean conflict or foreign military intervention to topple the DPRK regime; and maintaining its influence on Korean affairs, but keeping a distance with the DPRK. While trying its best to maintain normal relations with Beijing, Pyongyang decided to actively talk with the United States, but sought to exclude China from talks on a Korean Peninsula peace mechanism. North Korea's China policy can be generally summarized as keeping a distance while being sure not to openly offend Beijing.

PYONGYANG'S CHINA POLICY IN THE TWENTY-FIRST CENTURY: INTENSIFICATION OF HIGH-LEVEL CONSULTATIONS AND UPGRADING THE ALLIANCE

Kim Jong Il's visit to Beijing in 2000 suggested the beginning of recovery in China–DPRK traditionally friendly ties. Held just before Kim Jong Il received Kim Dae Jung in Pyongyang, this summit revealed North Korea's prioritization of relations with China over inter-Korean relations, and Kim Jong Il's desire to use close relations with Beijing to enhance his bargaining position with the South. More importantly, Kim's visit to Shanghai drove much speculation among outside observers that he would actively reform North Korea by learning from the Chinese experience. The 2000 summit between Kim Dae Jung and Kim Jong Il furthered the expectations about a relaxed situation on the Korean Peninsula. The failure of North Korea's 2002 pricing system reform and Kim Jong Il's lack of strategic determination for systematic reform, however, pushed North Korea's economic development into a direr situation. U.S.–North Korea relations faced severe setbacks when North Korea began to develop its highly enriched uranium program in 2002 and the United States halted its fuel supply and light-water reactor construction in North Korea.

From 2002 to 2008, North Korea adopted a two-pronged policy toward China. On the one hand, North Korea pretended to be a close and loyal partner, seeking every possible means to learn from the Chinese experience of economic reform.[44] Kim Jong Il visited China four times from 2000 to 2006, touring dozens of cities across China and examining the achievements of many sectors. On the other hand, North Korea prioritized nuclear weapons development and rendered China as an honest mediator between Pyongyang and Washington in the Six-Party Talks.

The Six-Party Talks did produce some significant progress, as reflected in the September 19 and February 13 Joint Statements, respectively, in 2005 and 2007. Although North Korea successfully disabled part of its nuclear reactors in Yongbyon, such progress did not prevent the DPRK from testing its nuclear weapons twice, respectively, in 2006 and 2009. Pyongyang knew well that Beijing's position on denuclearization was resolute, while China sought to demonstrate its diplomatic capabilities on the international stage by taking an active role to resolve some hot issues.[45] Given North Korea's reliance on China's support for its survival, Pyongyang usually adopted a seemingly docile and positive attitude toward Chinese advice to forgo nuclear weapons, but actually this response was tied with some preconditions.

Possession of nuclear weapons is North Korea's strategic goal to become a "prosperous and powerful country" in 2012. Participation in the Six-Party Talks has been a North Korean tactic to buy time and obtain economic and political rewards from the United States, Japan, and South Korea, and it has also been a symbolic approach to satisfying China's demand for denuclearization from 2003. North Korea's China policy in terms of the nuclear issue was subject to its above national goal, and Pyongyang sophisticatedly capitalized on two Chinese goals on the Korean Peninsula: denuclearization and stability. These two Chinese goals have had somewhat complementary as well as offsetting functions, giving the DPRK some leeway for playing off one against the other between China and the United States. North Korea's China policy during the Six-Party Talks has been to persuade China to understand its security dilemma and help the DPRK deal with American pressure, allowing North Korea to maximize rewards from the United States, South Korea, and Japan. Respecting China's role, but not accepting China's instruction, has characterized DPRK tactics in its China policy during the Six-Party Talks.

The DPRK has generally adopted three approaches toward China: (1) when North Korea and the United States encountered deadlock in some phrases in implementing the Six-Party Joint Statements, the DPRK urged China to exert influence on the United States and prevent a breakdown of the talks; (2) when North Korea–U.S. talks went smoothly, Pyongyang sought to marginalize China's role, even highlighting its strategic assets for U.S. hedging policy toward China;[46] and (3) when the Six-Party Talks stalled and the United States imposed sanctions against the DPRK while China just sat idle or even coordinated with American action, Pyongyang flagrantly took provocative actions, including nuclear and missile tests despite Chinese concern and appeals.

The third approach suggests that North Korea has framed China's role under North Korean national interests and *juche* ideology. The 2006 nuclear test angered China and forced Chinese diplomatic mediation into a plight.[47] Even if faced with more punishment and isolation, as well as more distancing from China, North Korea is likely to choose to go nuclear based on the assumption that the United States will not dare to strike its nuclear facility so long as the China–North Korea military pact remains valid.[48] The limited role of the Chinese in the Korean nuclear issue has not just been a result of North Korea's stubborn resistance to Chinese pressure, but is also related to China's own definition of its role as an "honest broker" and host of the Six-Party Talks. China didn't accept such a role as an enforcer. Beijing has clearly opposed "regime change" in Pyongyang or comprehensive sanctions, which has undoubtedly affected China's influence on DPRK denuclearization.

Incidents on the Korean Peninsula in 2008–2010 not only had an impact on inter-Korean relations and U.S.-DPRK relations, but also marked a turning point in China–North Korea relations. Kim Jong Il's reported stroke in 2008 drove many speculative reports about the survival of the Dear Leader as well as the DPRK regime. The *Cheonan* sinking and the shelling of Yeonpyeong Island made the DPRK a target of international condemnation and also made China "a criminal protector" in the eyes of the international community. Kim Jong Il faced three key issues during this period: resolving the issue of hereditary succession, leaving a better economic legacy to his son, and consolidating strategic relations with China.

China–DPRK relations are moving into a new direction based on these strategic decisions, as reflected in three aspects. First, North Korea feels an urgent need to strengthen relations with China in order to ensure regime survival in the post–Kim Jong Il era. Kim Jong Il at the end of his rule most probably emphasized to his subordinates relations with China as a top priority on the North Korean agenda, and the need to put aside all the differences with China. In order to gain China's trust and commitment to cooperation, the DPRK is likely to adopt a more preferential policy toward Beijing than it has ever offered before.

Second, China's active opposition to a unanimous UN Security Council resolution to condemn North Korea for the *Cheonan* sinking favorably changed Kim Jong Il's impression of China as a low-principled country.[49] Kim perceived subtle changes in China's North Korea policy as a chance to further consolidate the China–DPRK alliance.

Third, Chinese prime minister Wen Jiabao's visit to Pyongyang in October 2009 was interpreted in North Korea as a shift in China's policy of prioritizing denuclearization over stability or pursuing both goals in parallel. Beijing's new policy is regarded as centering on stability, with denuclearization as a long-term goal.

Kim Jong Il's intensified visits to China demonstrated many purposes, including learning from China's experience of reform and opening; seeking support for his power transition and DPRK regime stability; displaying the unbreakable China–DPRK friendship in the face of South Korean and American pressure; strengthening economic cooperation with China in border area development in line with Kim's combined goals of domestic economic revitalization and capitalization on Chinese economic growth; and persuading China to provide more economic assistance and even military supplies such as a JH-7 fighter, C-802 ship-to-ship missiles, PHL-03 artillery, and ZTZ-99 armored vehicles.

To win Chinese support in confronting South Korea and the United States, Kim Jong Il during his summits with Hu Jintao in 2010–2011 stressed the importance of strategic cooperation in several ways. He maintained that if North Korea collapses, China would face heavy losses as suggested by the Chinese proverb, "Once lips are gone, the teeth will be cold." According to Japanese media in April 2011, North Korea unprecedentedly proposed a joint military drill in which DPRK sailors would embark on Chinese submarines to collect American aircraft carrier data to counter U.S.–ROK exercises in the Yellow Sea, a proposal that Beijing rejected.[50] North Korea's mouthpiece in Japan, *Chosun Shinbo*, claimed that Kim Jong Il's visit to China in 2011 was a strategic move to confirm mutual interests and strategies in preparation for 2012, in which "North Korea is on the verge of becoming the strong and prosperous nation," and "China is expected to undergo major leadership shift."[51] The North Korean media have also elevated the importance of Kim Jong Il's meetings with Chinese leaders to display an image of close and highly interdependent relations to the outside world.

Based on the high-level exchanges between China and North Korea and North Korean reports on joint commemorative events since 2010, it is possible to identify some new characteristics and lines of thinking in North Korea's China policy. First, Pyongyang has actively touted the bilateral friendship with China as the best it has ever had in the last thirty years. Kim Jong Il during his 2011 visit to China stressed that the relaying friendship from one generation to the next is the "great historic task" for two countries, twice emphasizing the importance of the bilateral treaty and affirming the correctness of Chinese reform and opening. The intention behind such unprecedented statements was clear: to make China happy and willing to embrace North Korea as an ally just like in the Cold War era. Kim Jong Il's frequent visits seemed to remind both Chinese and North Korean officials of the close political-military alliance of the Cold War. For instance, the great procession upon Kim Jong Il's return from his May 2011 China tour replayed the scenes that only his father had enjoyed after he visited China.

Second, North Korea is placing greater emphasis on improving its dire economy, especially mitigating the inadequate supply of food and other daily necessities. During Kim Jong Il's visit to China in May 2010, he requested $10 billion in assistance for infrastructure, 1 million tons of food supplies, and 800,000 tons of fuel.[52] The unsuccessful results of North Korean economic development presented Kim Jong Il with an enigma: a thriving economy on the Chinese side of the border area and a stagnant North Korean side despite the same geographic conditions.[53] Determined to explore new ways to revitalize the DPRK economy, Kim Jong Il made more economic inspections, amounting to a total of sixty-three official activities in the first half of 2011, twenty-eight (or 45 percent) of which were economic related and only fourteen military related, the lowest number ever recorded.[54]

Third, the shadow of escalating tensions loomed large on the Korean Peninsula following the *Cheonan* and Yeonpyeong crises of 2010: South Korea and the United States held a series of joint military exercises, Seoul openly discussed Korean Peninsula contingency plans (the 5029 plan), and U.S.–Japan–South Korea trilateral military cooperation tightened. Such external developments raised Pyongyang's anxieties about some kind of retaliation from the South.[55] Pyongyang actively commemorated the fiftieth anniversary of its treaty with China, holding a series of joint events to mark the anniversary, including an exchange of visits by Zhang Dejiang, Chinese vice premier, and Yang Hyong Sop, North Korea's vice president of the Presidium of the Supreme People's Assembly. North Korea's official media, *Rodong Sinmun*, published an editorial that highly praised the treaty as a dynamic force for advancing bilateral relations. Through such activities, North Korea could demonstrate to the United States and South Korea, though China keeps its military intervention option in ambiguity, that its military treaty and friendship with China remains valid and the friendship with China is as powerful as it was fifty years ago, and China is always behind Pyongyang in the case of a preemptive attack on the North.[56] China and North Korea have thus reinforced the importance of their bilateral treaty as a counterbalance to the U.S.–ROK Mutual Defense Treaty.[57]

THE FOCAL POINTS IN PYONGYANG'S CHINA POLICY: JOINT ECONOMIC DEVELOPMENT AND COORDINATION

To realize its goals of improving its economy and attracting foreign investment, North Korea has to draw China deep into its economic development. Kim's delegation in May 2011 included many high-level officials in charge of economic affairs such as Jang Song Taek, vice chairman of the National Defense Commission, and Thae Jong Su, secretary of the Party Central Committee. He subsequently sent more provincial-level officials to China, including many provincial-level party secretaries, to support his efforts in drawing up a blueprint for North Korean economic development and introducing foreign investment.

As part of his new efforts to rehabilitate the DPRK economy, Kim Jong Il pursued joint development projects along the border with China, including the establishment of an industrial belt connecting Rason and Hwanggumpyong, which not only supports his basis for building Sinuiju as a center of future economic development, but also grants China access to the Sea of Japan while luring Chinese investment into North Korean border areas. Pyongyang's joint development efforts with China also demonstrated that the impact of South Korean economic sanctions could be balanced out by economic cooperation with China.[58]

However, on China's side, there was some caution toward Kim Jong Il's lines of thinking. China's main interest lies not in Hwanggumpyong Island but Rajin Port, access to which could join China's commercial shipping routes of its northeast region and east coast. Technical assessments have indicated that Hwanggumpyong is not an ideal place for development; since this island doesn't sit on the solid ground, it is not suitable for massively building infrastructures without having a mole to prevent the river from flooding. Chinese entrepreneurs hold that Hwanggumpyong Island cannot produce any significant economic benefits.[59] Yet China ultimately accepted North Korea's proposal for joint development based on the importance of Rajin Port and China's Chang-Ji-Tu Development Plan, as well as the overall effort to advance bilateral relations.

Soon after Kim's China tour in May 2011, groundbreaking ceremonies for China–North Korea Hwanggumpyong and Wihwa islands and Rason Economic and Trade Zones took place on May 28 and 29, respectively, with the attendance of more than 1,000 dignitaries, including powerful officials Jang Song Taek and Chen Deming, minister of commerce of the PRC. The Chuangli group of China has obtained the right for exclusive use of Pier No. 1 in Rajin Port, which will serve as a transportation hub for Northeast China as the maritime outlet for products from the region to the east coast of China.[60]

The details of the Hwanggumpyong and Rason projects had been discussed by the two countries for some time. North Korea initially rejected China's proposed market-driven model (governments guiding, enterprises in charge, markets driving, and reciprocity in benefits), but with Kim Jong Il's full support, Rason was elevated into a special city in 2010,[61] and the Law on the Rason Economic and Trade Zone and the Special Law on the Hwanggumpyong Zone were passed in January 2010. China and North Korea signed a memorandum of understanding (MOU) on a Joint Development Plan for the Rason and Hwanggumpyong Economic and Trade Zone in December 2010. The lease of Hwanggumpyong Island will last fifty years, with possible extension for another fifty years. North Korea's Supreme People's Assembly in June 2011 issued the Decree of Development of the Hwanggumpyong and Wihwado Economic Belt.

Although these two joint development areas are not very big, the designated goals look very ambitious, and once realized they will significantly reshape the North Korean economy. In addition to gaining the rights to develop the No. 1 dock at Rajin port in 2008, China also reached an agreement with Pyongyang at the end of 2010 to invest about $2 billion in a project to build an oil refinery plant and port facilities in the Rason Special District. Four major industrial complexes will be constructed in the Rajin area consisting of storage, logistics, and distribution centers as well as projects in clothing, food manufacturing, petrochemicals, cars, machinery, shipbuilding, and high-tech industries. The Hwanggumpyong area will be a hub of light industry, including software outsourcing, and will also have four major industrial complexes for information, tourism and culture, modern protected agriculture, and food processing. Hwanggumpyong will connect information between North Korea and the border city of Dandong in China.[62]

In general, these two zones play three roles as an experimental area for North Korean external communication, the creation of a "strong and prosperous" nation, and China–North Korea economic cooperation, respectively. Compared with the inter-Korean Kaesong Industrial Park project, North Korea's joint projects with China have received better terms. Preferential treatment will be granted to foreign investors in order to turn the area into a major entrepot, export producer, and financial and tourist hub of Northeast Asia.[63] The main special terms include the following:

1. An investment protection clause.
2. Specific provisions for large-scale development.
3. An advanced system for communications, traffic, and customs, including mobile phone connections.
4. North Korean workers and foreign companies will be permitted to sign their own labor contracts. The companies will be granted autonomy in managing hiring and firing, pricing, bankruptcy, liquidation, and other business practices based on market principles.
5. Chinese can freely travel between Dandong and Rason and Hwanggum-pyong.
6. A three-tiered cooperative system consisting of a joint steering committee, joint development management committee, and investment development corporation, which will be responsible for amending and negotiating any issues that may arise during the development process, oversee various areas of investment, enterprises, environment, land and commerce development, and basic facility operations. Jang Song Taek and Chen Deming are serving as cochairs of the Joint Management Committee on Development of the Special Economic Zone.
7. A tax refund policy will be implemented and tariffs lifted from any imported equipment and materials necessary for production. For investment in infrastructure, there are five-year tax exemptions and three-year exemptions of half tax.
8. Foreign investment companies will be allowed to choose their own banks or even establish financial institutions to assist their business management.

Despite these concrete plans, many uncertain issues remain. First, since the cost-benefit analysis is not attractive, it remains uncertain how many enterprises will invest in these projects; previous investments by many Chinese companies have failed due to the inconsistency in North Korean government attitudes and local fraud.[64] Second, it is unclear where the produced goods will go. If they go to the North Korean market, how they will be priced—fluctuating with the market or fixed by the government—remains a question; another problem is the very low demand in the DPRK. If they go to the Chinese market, they will encounter serious competition given their relatively small economic scale and low sale price, which will not make their return profits large enough for luring more investment. Third, the situation in Rason will be much better than in Hwanggumpyong given the potential role of Rajin Port in driving storage, logistics, and distribution industries, although the commercial impact of this shipping line remains to be seen.

FUTURE TRENDS IN PYONGYANG'S CHINA POLICY: CHANGES AND CONTINUITIES

North Korea's China policy had been changing from 2009 to 2011, and now the death of Kim Jong Il on December 17, 2011, will certainly accelerate the Korean Peninsula transition over the long run. But in order to know how this event will have an impact on the direction of North Korea compared with the current one in the near term, we need more time and evidence to observe the development within North Korea.

Will these previous changes continue, implying a strategic move? All remains to be seen. Will China cooperate on this policy transition? Such questions require careful consideration of what the needs are for North Korea in the diplomatic area and how North Korea can maximize its diplomatic gains; whether the new top North Korean leader, Kim Jong Un, has real power and the intention to make a strategic decision to abandon the nuclear weapons program; what Kim Jong Un's greatest concerns will be over the next one to three years; and what China's general strategy of foreign affairs and approach will be to North Korea's new government and to Northeast Asia. It is possible to highlight several points regarding the future direction of Pyongyang's China policy.

First, in the Kim Jong Il era, North Korean diplomatic priorities included establishing normal relations with Washington, Tokyo, and Seoul, which were based on the assumption that all three countries could accept a nuclearized North Korea. The establishment of formal relations with the United States would give North Korea much greater benefits than what China can offer. Most importantly, North Korea would be able to improve its international reputation and seek admission into the world's financial institutions. Another potential benefit from developing good relations with the United States is the possibility of U.S.–China–DPRK triangular diplomacy.

However, for Kim Jong Un, his priorities are to build his own power base; to search for a way of cooperating with the several powerful protectors, Jang Song Taek, Kim Kyong Hui, and CMC Vice Chairman Choe Ryong Hae; and to prove the authority and power that his title embodies as the supreme leader.[65] Since, for the time being, Kim Jong Un lacks confidence and skill to deal with the United States and its allies, he will delay the process of establishing normal relations with Washington, Tokyo, and Seoul for the next one to two years.

Even if in the future Kim Jong Un has the authority and willingness to repursue talks with the United States about normalization, the prospects for such a relationship with the United States are limited. The main obstacle is North Korea's nuclear weapons program. The United States will not recognize a nuclear North Korea in the foreseeable future. Pyongyang will not easily abandon its possession of nuclear weapons as its strategic goal and the teachings of the deceased Kim Jong Il. North Korea is likely aware of the U.S. bottom line but unrealistically expects that the United States will sooner or later accept North Korea's nuclear status just like the status of India and Pakistan. Based on this assumption, Pyongyang hopes to maintain negotiations with the United States by dividing the bargaining chips and prolonging the denuclearization process, and to also use other limited means such as joint excavation of the missing in action (MIA) from the Korean War.

Second, the late Kim Jong Il held a lot of resentment against China based on the asymmetry of relations with Beijing, and Kim Jong Un must largely inherit his father's perception. Three points of North Korean dissatisfaction with China can be identified:

1. The DPRK often could not fully satisfy its demands toward China. During Kim Jong Il's 2010 visit, Chinese leaders turned down North Korea's request for economic and military assistance. According to South Korean media, the weapons North Korea requested included items that have not appeared on its Chinese assistance list for over twenty years.[66] China only offered 200,000 to 300,000 tons of fertilizer aid and suggested that South Korea and the United States would be unable to attack North Korea if Kim Jong Il continued to insist that the North did not torpedo the *Cheonan*. Beijing's rebuff of North Korean demands is likely to drive perceptions in Pyongyang that China is not a real strategic partner and that China's position too often takes into account American and South Korean concerns when handling China–DPRK bilateral relations.

2. From the North Korean perspective, China has overemphasized its own interests in the nuclear issue. Pyongyang may be disappointed with the Chinese approach of seemingly remaining neutral but in essence siding largely with the U.S. and South Korean position on the complete, verifiable, and irreversible dimantlement (CVID)-based principle of denuclearization. Pyongyang is also disappointed with the atmosphere of some high-level meetings during which Chinese leaders made sharp and direct criticisms about the nuclear issue and other North Korean provocations, which the North Koreans perceived as an insult to Kim Jong Il.

3. North Korea certainly dislikes the ways in which China assumes the role of an instructor. Whenever North Korean leaders request assis-

tance, Chinese counterparts will teach North Korea how to adjust its economic policy based on the world trend of reform and opening. During his meeting with Kim Jong Il in May 2011, Chinese premier Wen Jiabao responded to Kim's request for massive Chinese investment in Hwanggumpyong Island and the Rajin-Sonbong special economic zone by stating, "China hopes that economic cooperation is achieved through normal business processes and we believe provinces and businesses need to become more proactive." This remark clearly suggested that China wanted the DPRK to accept the market model and not governmental guidance as the principle for joint development.[67]

Despite these resentments, North Korea must rely on this unequal relationship with China since only China will offer what North Korea needs most for regime survival: food and fuel, which accounts for some 70 percent of North Korea's oil imports, and the shared ideology of socialism and communist leadership, which, though differing in nature, supports the strategic interests of maintaining the status quo on the Korean Peninsula. Kim Jong Un is fairly young, so he will have fewer psychological impediments to humbly listening to China's advice. The continuity in North Korea's policy toward China is also in line with China's North Korea policy, which emphasizes North Korean regime stability based on the perception of North Korea as an important buffer zone inhibiting any possible hostile presence near China's borders.[68]

Third, it appears that the DPRK does not want to realize its goal of normalization with the United States at the expense of forgoing nuclear weapons and exposing its society to outside influences.[69] So far, Kim Jong Un's mind might not be fully mature on the denuclearization issue, but he is encircled by conservative generals who will force him to continue his father's policy and ensure the regime's survival by maintaining a nuclear program. The Arab Spring in the Middle East and the NATO air strike on Libya in 2011, and particularly the fact that Libyan leader Colonel Muammar Qaddafi eventually conceded to U.S. demands to destroy all of his chemical, nuclear, and biological weapons based on the principle of CVID, really served as a warning lesson for North Korea.

Fourth, if Pyongyang does not consider abandoning nuclear weapons, it will have to prepare for long-term hostility and possible conflict on the Korean Peninsula. Without a powerful dictator after Kim Jong Il's death, his son Kim Jong Un might be unable to control the power by himself; he has to rely on powerful officials in the party and military for several years. Since this core collective leadership has the function of checks and balances, which was smartly installed by Kim Jong Un in 2011, and has the common interests of maintaining regime survival and previous policy, it has to do its best to prop up Kim Jong Un's rule, the heir to the Kim dynasty. Therefore, it is less likely that a power struggle within the party-military complex will occur in the near term. However, given the priority of keeping the status quo for Kim Jong Un, the impact of sanctions and North Korea's rigid planned economic system may aggravate the grievances of ordinary people in North Korea and intensify antigovernment pressures. In order to avert or mitigate such risks within the next five to eight years, the DPRK regime must continue to turn to China for support and protection, even if this is a forced option.

Fifth, China's general strategy of foreign affairs will continue on the path of the past thirty years: developing a benign external environment and prolonging strategic opportunities for sustainable economic growth and balanced economic cooperation. Reducing tensions and instability in China's peripheral areas and balancing the offensive power of the U.S.-led alliance are part of this strategy. Securing the North Korean regime's survival partially meets China's strategy, but the precondition is that the regime should halt its nuclear weapons development and provocative behavior toward the region. China seeks to avoid being dragged into confrontations on the peninsula and becoming a hostage of North Korean brinkmanship, and even facing extended nuclear deterrence from the United States. Through more and various economic assistance and expertise support, China will lure Kim Jong Un into building a peaceful nation and a better-off economy. A stable, gradually reformed and denuclearized North Korea is in the interests of China. Based on these considerations, Beijing will take great efforts to shape North Korea's China policy.

Whether North Korea's China policy transition will succeed depends not only on the actions of the DPRK regime but also on Chinese thinking, interests, and general international strategy. Another significant factor is the development of Sino–American and U.S.–North Korean relations, which is characterized by an asymmetric triangular relationship. Chinese and North Korean commemorations of the friendship agreement reflect the gap in the bilateral relationship despite the high-profile and typical rhetorical approach. Beijing is definitely not willing to return to the era of Mao Zedong and Kim Il Sung, and will not strengthen its military cooperation with the North vis-à-vis the U.S.–South Korean alliance. At the same time, Beijing will offer Pyongyang some security confidence, which implies that it neither supports the United States in extending its nuclear deterrence to North Korea, nor accepts a contingency plan designed by Washington and Seoul to reunify the Korean Peninsula through a unilateral and coercive approach in case of instability in North Korea. Both Chinese and North Korean state security ministries will develop cooperation and share information on how to restore order in a crisis situation.

Of course, the development of North Korea's China policy may be shaped by some specific changes. First, when North Korea encounters some internal power or policy conflicts under the Kim Jong Un leadership, it is likely that the DPRK will lean more on China, and even ask Chinese leaders to mediate between divergent factions lest the United States and South Korea intervene. With Chinese support, Kim Jong Un and his supporters might accept Chinese demands to abandon nuclear weapons and open to the outside while reforming the North Korean domestic system.

Second, as U.S.–China competition intensifies in East Asia, and as Japan and South Korea actively coordinate with U.S. military maneuvers in the region, North Korea will face a new opportunity to choose sides. It is not certain that Pyongyang will side with China; a kind of weaving policy between China and the United States will be North Korea's desired option.

Many aspects of continuity can be found along the path of North Korea's China policy transition. Although Pyongyang has undertaken active efforts to develop joint projects in the China–North Korea border area, it maintains a high alert on shielding North Korean society from any kind of liberal or capitalist thought. Since the new joint projects with China provide relative freedoms for North Koreans, the more North Korean workers participate in the joint projects, the more they will learn about the outside and ways of Chinese reform. Pyongyang has thus ordered North Korean monitoring agencies to tighten security measures in the border area.[70]

At the same time, North Korea will adopt measures to avoid too much reliance on Chinese economic cooperation. Soon after Kim Jong Il's death, an order of banning the Chinese RMB was issued.[71] North Korea's recent effort to deepen economic cooperation with China has been a necessary policy alternative under unfavorable external circumstances. Just three months after Kim Jong Il visited China, he went to the Russian Far East to talk with then-Russian president Dmitry Medvedev about economic cooperation on the building of a gas pipeline from Russia to South Korea via North Korea. This move reflects the traditional balanced approach that North Korea has pursued in its very narrow diplomatic space. On January 25, 2012, Russian energy minister Sergei Shmatko told the South Korean diplomat that Russia and North Korea have reached an agreement that they would soon start the project negotiation.[72]

If North Korea can open up its economic relations with the United States, Japan, and European countries, it will certainly diversify its sources of external dependence. If Chinese economic influence in North Korea expands extensively, the DPRK will take measures to prevent Chinese business from dominating certain sectors; for example, North Korea offered the chance of establishing a cell phone system to the Egyptian company Orascom. Pyongyang will not allow China to intervene in its domestic affairs; all foreign contacts beyond the joint project areas will be monitored and controlled, and North Korea will not fully emulate the Chinese economic reform model.

Changes in North Korea's China policy have generally pushed North Korea closer to China through increased contacts and consultations at various levels and in various sectors. The most important development has been North Korea's reliance on Chinese support for the future of the DPRK regime under Kim Jong Un as well as an effort to revive strategic relations with China. In principle, North Korea will increasingly respect Chinese demands and interests in terms of restraining further military provocations.

In sum, North Korea's China policy transition faces strategic considerations in dealing with potential internal and external crises. Based on the historical development of China–DPRK bilateral relations, North Korea will not easily follow the will of its "big brother." Pyongyang certainly will not abandon its expectation of developing normal, even strategic relations with the United States, but it understands that the time is not yet mature. North Korea's future China policy is situated between its respective relations with China and the United States.

As for the Chinese side, Beijing will not unconditionally respond to Pyongyang's call for deepening strategic relations. What Beijing is willing to do is to amplify the traditional bond so as to better influence and manage North Korea's behavior, ensuring its viability and peaceful political transition. By this token, North Korea's China policy transition still bears tactical implications.

NOTES

1. Byung Chul Koh, *The Foreign Policy Systems of North and South Korea* (Berkeley: University of California Press, 1984), 204–10.

2. See Kongdan Oh and Ralph C. Hassig, *North Korea: Through the Looking Glass* (Washington, DC: Brookings Institution, 2000), 155–56.

3. Shen Zhihua, "*Zhongguo Beipo Chubing Chaoxian* [China Was Forced to Send Its Forces]," *Wangyi History*, June 29, 2009.

4. Shen Zhihua, "*Jiemi Zhiyuanjun Chejun ji Zhongchao Tongmeng Qianyue* [Decoding Chinese People's Voluntary Forces Withdrawal and China–North Korea Signing Alliance Treaty]," *Fenghuang Weekly*, no. 8 (2011).

5. At the end of 1949, with the request from Choi Yong Kun (former chief of staff of the Second Army under the Anti-Japanese United Forces in the Northeast of China, later he became North Korea vice commander of People's Army and vice president of DPRK), 28,000 Korean soldiers in China were first sent to North Korea; in 1950, North Korea Army's Chief of Operation Department came to China, asking that 14,000 Korean soldiers, who were then in the Fourth Field Army of China, be sent back to North Korea. See Shen Zhihua, "*Zhongguo Beipo Chubing Chaoxian:*

Jueceguocheng Jiqiyuanyi [China Was Forced to Send Its Forces: Decision Process and Causes]," July 23, 2004, http://www.aisixiang.com/data/3648.html.

6. See Wikipedia under the subject "Workers' Party of Korea," www.wikipedia .org, July 30, 2011.

7. Sergey S. Radchenko, "The Soviet Union and North Korean Seizure of the USS Pueblo: Evidence from Russian Archives," Cold War International History Project, Working Paper No. 47, Woodrow Wilson International Center for Scholars, USA, 41.

8. Shen Zhihua and Dong Jie, "*Zhongsu Yuanzhu Yu Chaoxian Zhanhou Jingji Chongjian* [China and the Soviet Union's Assistance and North Korea Economic Recovery]," *Yanhuang Chunqiu*, no. 6 (2011).

9. Shen Zhihua and Dong Jie, "*Zhongsu Yuanzhu Yu Chaoxian Zhanhou Jingji Chongjian.*"

10. Shen Zhihua and Dong Jie, "*Zhongsu Yuanzhu Yu Chaoxian Zhanhou Jingji Chongjian.*"

11. Shen Zhihua and Dong Jie, "*Zhongsu Yuanzhu Yu Chaoxian Zhanhou Jingji Chongjian.*"

12. For North Korea action at the Bucharest Conference in 1960, see Cheng Xiaohe, "The Evolution of Sino-North Korean Relations in 1960s," *Asian Perspective* 34, no. 2 (2010): 179.

13. See Byung Chun Koh, *The Foreign Policy Systems*, 205.

14. See Byung Chun Koh, *The Foreign Policy Systems*, 205.

15. Cheng Xiaohe, "The Evolution of Sino-North Korean Relations," 183.

16. Radchenko, "The Soviet Union and North Korean Seizure of the USS Pueblo," 6.

17. Li Chun-hu, *Zhanhou Chaoxian de Jueze: 1945–1995* [North Korea's Choice in the Post World War] (Dawang Press, 2003), 37.

18. Li Chun-hu, *Zhanhou Chaoxian de Jueze*, 37.

19. Radchenko, "The Soviet Union and North Korean Seizure," 8.

20. Radchenko, "The Soviet Union and North Korean Seizure," 205–6.

21. Radchenko, "The Soviet Union and North Korean Seizure," 6.

22. Radchenko, "The Soviet Union and North Korean Seizure," 41.

23. The original view was from Robert A. Scalapino and Jun-Yop Kim, *North Korea Today* (Berkeley: Institute of East Asian Studies, University of California Press, 1983), 40, which is cited from Cheng Xiaohe, "The Evolution of Sino-North Korean Relations," 184.

24. Byung Chun Koh, *The Foreign Policy Systems*, 205–8.

25. Cheng Xiaohe, "The Evolution of Sino-North Korean Relations," 190.

26. Cheng Xiaohe, "The Evolution of Sino-North Korean Relations," 190.

27. Cheng Xiaohe, "The Evolution of Sino-North Korean Relations," 190.

28. See Wikipedia under the subject "Workers' Party of Korea," www.wikipedia .org, July 30, 2011.

29. Kim Hak-joon, *Korea's Relations with Her Neighbors in a Changing World* (Elizabeth, NJ: Hollym, 1993), 494.

30. Radchenko, "The Soviet Union and North Korean Seizure," 45.

31. See declassified diplomatic files, Archives of China's Foreign Ministry, File Nos. 106-01479-08 and 106-01480-07, cited from Cheng Xiaohe, "The Evolution of Sino-North Korean Relations," 185–86.

32. Byung Chun Koh, *The Foreign Policy Systems*, 206.

33. See Li Zuo-peng's memoir, *Junren Yongsheng* [Soldier Is Invincible] (Hong Kong: Beijing Press, 2011).

34. Liu Jinzhi and Yang Huai-sheng, eds., *Zhong Guo Dui Chaoxian He Hanguo Zhengce Wenjian Huibian* [A Compilation of China's Policy Documents on North and South Korea] (1949–1994) (China Social Sciences Press, 1994), 2553–610.

35. Cited from Chinese former ambassador to South Korea, Zhang Ting-yan's recollection in July 2009, Beijing; see Phoenix TV column on August 8, 2009, www.ifeng.com.

36. Han Sung-joo, "The Emerging Triangle: Korea between China and the US," *East Asian Review* 12, no. 1 (Spring 2000): 7.

37. Gloria Koo, "China and North Korea: A Changing Relationship," *Stanford Journal of International Relations*, 2006.

38. Han Sung-joo, "The Emerging Triangle," 8.

39. Han Sung-joo, "The Emerging Triangle," 18.

40. Kongdan Oh and Ralph C. Hassig, *North Korea: Through the Looking Glass*, 167.

41. Hwang Jang Yop confided that there were officials suggesting to Kim Il Sung to play the Taiwan card to restrain China, cited from an excerpt from a translation of Hwang Jang Yop's memoirs; see www.chinaiiss.com.

42. See Zhang Rui-jie "Zhonghan Jianjiao Wangshihuigu [Recollection on Establishing Diplomatic Relations between China and South Korea]," *Bainianchao* magazine, November 2010.

43. Han Sung-joo, "The Emerging Triangle," 20.

44. From January 10–18, 2006, Kim Jong Il visited Hubei, Guangdong, and Beijing; in his trip, he highly valued the achievements of Chinese economic reform, which, as he put it astonishingly, proved the correctness of the reform. After his visit, Jang Song Taek, then first deputy minister for Capital Construction under the Workers' Party, led thirty economic officials for an eleven-day field inspection tour along the trail that Kim Jong Il traveled in China.

45. Zhu Feng, "Zhongguode Waijiaowoxuan Yuchaohewenti Liufanghuitan [China's Diplomatic Mediation and Six Party Talks on North Korea Nuclear Issue]," *Diplomatic Comments*, no. 4 (2006).

46. Zhang Zuqian, "Hebaozhihou, Meichaohudong Nairenxunwei [The U.S.–North Korea Interaction Carries Deep Implications in the Wake of Nuclear Test]," *International Outlook* (Chinese), no.11 (2006).

47. Li Hua and Feng Xiu-yu, "Waijiao yu Weishe: Lun Zhongmeizai Chaohe-weijizhongdezhengce quxiangjiqixiandu [Diplomacy and Deterrence: On China and the US Policy Options and Limits in the North Korea Nuclear Crisis]," *Guojiwenti Luntan* [International Studies Forum], Spring 2007, 73.

48. Li Hua and Feng Xiu-yu, "Waijiao yu Weishe," 74.

49. This saying is just the author's guess from some conversations with North Korean people; maybe there are two typical examples to prove this: Beijing abandoned its loyalty to its traditional ally of North Korea in 1992 and established diplomatic relations with Seoul, which made two Koreas a fait accompli; on April 14, 2009, after a series of intensified consultations, China together with Russia supported a UN Security Council President's Statement condemning a North Korean rocket launch, which violated UN Resolution 1718, whereas, before the launch, Chinese Foreign Ministry spokeswoman Jiangyu said in a press conference on April 7 quite the opposite: "Launch satellite, testing missile and nuclear test are all different in nature, and it involves each country's peaceful use of outer-space exploration rights, so Security Council needs to respond to it cautiously."

50. See BBC: "North Korea Invited China to Conduct A Joint-Drill, but Succeeded," August, 8, 2011.

51. "The DPRK-China Summit: A Strategic Meeting in Preparation for 2012," NK Briefs, No. 110529, Institute for Far Eastern Studies, Kyungnam University, May 30, 2011.

52. *Tokyo News*, August 13, 2010.

53. Kim Jong Il asked that question to the officials who escorted him to visit China. This remark is based on a well-informed briefing.

54. "Official Activities of Kim Jong Il Centered on Economy," NK Briefs, No. 110718, Institute for Far Eastern Studies, Kyungnam University, July 19, 2011.

55. The treaty was extended twice, in 1981 and 2001, and it will run through 2021.

56. Editorial, "China-DPRK Friendly Cooperation and Mutual Assistance Treaty," *Chosun Ilbo*, July 11, 2011.

57. "It Is Not a Time to Commemorate the 50-Year Anniversary of Signing TFMC," *Joongang Daily*, July 11, 2011. According to the U.S.–ROK Mutual Defense Treaty, the United States agrees to help the Republic of Korea defend itself against external aggression.

58. "North Korea, China to Launch Joint Construction Projects in Border Area," BBC, May 20, 2011.

59. "Huanggeumpyong Economic Zone Breaks Ground," *Chosun Ilbo*, June 9, 2011.

60. Editorial, "Across the Tumen River," *Korea Herald*, June 15, 2011. In July 2012 an investment team from Hong Kong's China Merchants Group (CMG) reached an agreement with North Korea about the Rason Economic and Trade Zones future development. The CMG will lead an enterprise union to take over the development projects of Piers No. 1, No. 2, and No. 3 in Rajan, which are currently run respectively by Chuangli Group, North Korean, and Russian enterprises.

61. Rason became a special economic zone in 1991, but never fulfilled its proposed role as a transportation hub.

62. "The Blueprint for the Development of the Rajin-Sonbong (Rason) Economic and Trade Zone Is Released," *North Korean Economy Watch*, Institute for Far Eastern Studies, May 26, 2011.

63. "North Korea Pushes Forward with the Modernization of Rajin Port," NK Briefs, No. 110620, Institute for Far Eastern Studies, Kyungnam University, June 21, 2011.

64. See *North Korea Today*, August 3, 2011.

65. Ken Gause, "Leadership Transition in North Korea," Council on Foreign Relations Press, released in January 2012.

66. "China Rejected North Korea's Request for JH-7, C-801, C-802," April 2010, see http://joongangdaily.joins.com/article/view.asp?aid=2935931.

67. "Cracks Open in North Korea-China Ties," *Chosun Ilbo*, June 7, 2011.

68. Jonathan Pollack, a famous North Korea expert, held that there were three schools of thinking on North Korea in China, but the current prevalent policy is stability-first. See Bona Kim, "China's Policy toward North Korea Redefined," *Daily NK*, October 20, 2009.

69. Han Sung-joo, "The Emerging Triangle," 27.

70. See Yonhap News Agency, August 16, 2011.

71. *North Korea Today*, www.goodfriends.or.kr, January 11, 2012.

72. Associated Press, January 26, 2012.

Chapter Eleven

Changes and Continuities in Inter-Korean Relations

Haksoon Paik

This chapter will deal with changes and continuities in inter-Korean relations during the transition era (1991–2011), with a prediction of where North Korea (the DPRK) is headed. The transition era was the period in which North Korea first explored an "exit" strategy out of the difficulties it faced since the collapse of the Soviet Union in 1991, then concretized a strategy of survival and development for the twenty-first century, and finally sought to accomplish the key goals of the strategy by making critical choices.

The transition era came to an end for North Korea at the end of 2011 with the death of Kim Jong Il on December 17, 2011, and with Kim Jong Un assuming full power as the new "supreme leader." The transition in North Korea's external environment will end in 2012 due to the expected power change by presidential elections in the key countries surrounding North Korea: in March in Russia, October in China, November in the United States, and December in South Korea. The coming of new governments in all these countries at the time of an emerging new international order signifies the coming of a new era for the twenty-first century in East Asia, which will have a serious impact on the course of North Korean politics and inter-Korean relations.

What are the changes and continuities in inter-Korean relations during the transition period of the past two decades, and what does the future hold for North Korea? In an effort to answer these questions, we will begin with an analysis of the key agential variables (the leadership's ideas, identities, and interests[1]) and structural variables (domestic and external) that interplayed to produce the strategies and policies of both Koreas, and the political opportunity structures for them to make critical choices. Then we will examine North Korea's strategy of survival and development for the twenty-first century and the critical choices North Korea made to implement its strategy under changing political opportunity structures—all to see how strategy and policy

239

choices influenced inter-Korean relations. Afterward, we will briefly review inter-Korean relations for the past two decades to identify changes and continuities. Finally, we will deal with prospects for both Koreas' strategies and policies toward each other, inter-Korean relations, and North Korea's future based on all of the above.

It should be pointed out that the weight of focus in analysis will be on North Korea, not South Korea, in view of the prediction of this study, that is, where North Korea is headed. So the scope of analysis of South Korea will be limited only to South Korea's strategy and policy toward the North and inter-Korean relations.

THE LEADERSHIP'S IDEAS, IDENTITIES, AND INTERESTS

Multiple variables at the agential level in both Koreas interplayed to produce the two Korean states' strategies and policies and ultimately the changes and continuities in inter-Korean relations. Specifically, what were the ideas, identities, and interests of the North and South Korean leadership, respectively?

North Korea

The North Korean leadership explored several key ideas on how to survive and develop when the Soviet Union and other East European socialist states collapsed and underwent a systemic transformation. The key ideas included "Korean-style socialism" based on "people-centered socialism," the "military-first" idea, a "do-or-die spirit" and "all-bomb spirit" to protect the supreme leader, a peace settlement in the Korean Peninsula, and détente and cooperation with the capitalist world.

The most basic idea was to differentiate its "Korean-style socialism" from all other socialisms. The North Korean leadership criticized the Gorbachev reform as a reform done by "contemporary revisionists"[2] and emphasized the distinctive character of North Korea's "people-centered socialism."

Another key idea searched for ways to protect the leadership and system at the time of increasing security threats coming from the outside world. The idea that surfaced was "military-first" politics. Military-first politics was first introduced on New Year's Day of 1995 after North Korea experienced serious security threats coming from a U.S. plan to strike the Yongbyon nuclear facilities in 1994.[3]

Still another idea was to achieve a peace settlement in the Korean Peninsula and promote détente and cooperation with the capitalist world. It was to end the Korean War, sign a peace treaty, normalize relations with the United

States, and reconcile with South Korea and Japan to improve the external political opportunity structure for survival and development. As for inter-Korean relations, it sought peaceful coexistence and peaceful co-prosperity.

The aforementioned ideas served as the basis for establishing the identity of the North Korean leadership as the introducer and manager of the "Korean-style socialist state," equipped with military-first politics, and as the seeker of a peace settlement and détente, and economic cooperation with the capitalist world. This identity was independence seeking and defensive, but simultaneously sensitive to new opportunities and adaptive to changing environments.

Based on the aforementioned ideas and identities, the basic interest the North Korean leadership wanted to promote and secure was "survival and development" for the twenty-first century. Concretely, it was to protect and preserve the North Korean regime and system including the "supreme leader system," to achieve peace settlement in Korea, and to revive the economy.

It should be noted that the aforementioned ideas, identities, and interests contain noticeable tensions or contradictions in them. The military-first politics helped strengthen North Korea's military capabilities through developing nuclear and ballistic missiles, but it has not been in harmony with efforts to promote a peace settlement and peaceful coexistence, normalization of relations, and economic cooperation with the capitalist world. This contradiction has brought about rounds of tension in inter-Korean relations as well as in DPRK–U.S. and DPRK–Japan relations.

South Korea

The ideas the South Korean leadership had in dealing with the North basically had to do with the type of unification it preferred to achieve. One group of South Korean leadership—Presidents Kim Young Sam and Lee Myung Bak—encouraged by what happened in the Soviet world and Germany, sought "unification by absorption." The other group—Presidents Roh Tae Woo, Kim Dae Jung, and Roh Moo Hyun—recognized the tenacity of the North Korean regime and the need for cooperation with it in pursuit of the common good in inter-Korean and international arenas, and pursued peaceful coexistence and a gradual unification. This difference in ideas on unification produced crucial differences in their strategies and policies toward the North.

Another key idea was the leaderships' focus on inter-Korean relations versus South Korea–U.S. relations. Those leaders who were more focused on inter-Korean relations often faced attacks from the conservative circles as not valuing the South Korea–U.S. alliance enough. On the other hand, those who appreciated the U.S.–South Korea alliance cooperation more tended to criticize those who sought reconciliation and cooperation with the North as "nationalist" or even "pro-North Korean," while they themselves were often criticized as "internationalist" or "pro-American."

Still another idea had to do with the extent to which the South Korean leadership was aware of the change of the times. The so-called nationalist group of leaders tended to be keenly aware of a power shift between the United States and China and the restructuring of a new international order in East Asia. By contrast, the so-called pro-American leadership by and large tended to believe in the relative supremacy of U.S. power over China despite the dramatic rise of China and unambiguous signs of U.S. decline.

What was then the identity of the South Korean leadership based on the aforementioned three key ideas? As already alluded to, it was a divided identity: "absorptionist" versus "engager." The former took on the identity of "unification by absorption" of the North with U.S. support; the latter was the identity of "believer of engagement and a gradual process of unification."

What were the interests of the South Korean leadership? In principle, there was no difference between the absorptionist and engager leaderships in that they all tried to promote the cause of unifying the nation and to strengthen their grip on power by doing so. However, the key interests of the leaderships were not identical when they said they wanted to promote the cause of unification of the Korean nation: the absorptionist group sought rather immediate and direct political benefits such as the collapse of North Korea, while the engager group envisioned peaceful, gradual unification, albeit time consuming, by lengthening the shadow of the future in its favor.

STRUCTURES: DOMESTIC AND EXTERNAL, AND POLITICAL OPPORTUNITY

What were the key variables at the structural level, domestic and external, that helped open or close political opportunity structures for making critical choices for the leaderships in both Koreas? And how favorable were their political opportunity structures in that regard?

North Korea

First, the key domestic structural variables of North Korea included the domestic power structure called the *Suryong* (supreme leader) system, the three-generation power succession, military-first politics, an efficiency-lacking socialist economic system, a shortage of food and daily necessities, and the introduction of economic reform (market elements) and opening up in 2002.

The prominent external structural variables were the collapse of the Soviet Union and the East European socialist states; Russia's and China's diplomatic normalization with South Korea; the signing of the Agreement on Reconciliation, Nonaggression, and Exchanges and Cooperation with South Korea (hereafter referred to as the "inter-Korean basic agreement"); the September 11 terrorist attack on the United States and the global War on Terror; deterioration in DPRK–U.S., DPRK–Japan, and North–South Korean relations, and the UN sanctions because of the nuclear and missile problems; and the military conflict with the South due to the *Cheonan* incident and the Yeonpyeongdo shelling incident in the West Sea (Yellow Sea) of Korea. And a power transition characterized by the rise of China and the decline of the United States has been an overarching external structural environment for the countries in the region including both Koreas.

More importantly, inconsistencies in policy toward North Korea, resulting from the change of governments in the United States, South Korea, and Japan brought about by democratic elections, were most treacherous and damaging for North Korea.[4] North Korea policy underwent a complete reversal from one government to the next: from the Clinton administration to the George W. Bush administration in the United States, from the Kim Dae Jung government and the Roh Moo Hyun government to the Lee Myung Bak government in South Korea, and from the Junichiro Koizumi government to the Shinzō Abe government in Japan. These inconsistencies and reversals have seriously limited North Korea's strategic capabilities to implement its long-term strategy toward those countries and to consolidate its gains and minimize its losses in dealing with the respective governments.

Finally, how favorable was North Korea's political opportunity structure? As shown above, both domestic and external structural variables were for the most part "not" favorable for North Korea in making strategic choices to implement its strategy for survival and development for the twenty-first century. In fact, some of the domestic variables, agential and structural, could be held under control by the leadership, but it would not be possible for external variables, which is a common reality for a small country like North Korea.

South Korea

The most salient domestic structural variables for South Korea with regard to inter-Korean relations included the division of South Korean society along ideational, identity-, and interest-based lines; structured preferences and choices of the people based on their own socioeconomic status; the influence of regionalism; and the generational gap.

South Korea is a highly divided society along political lines based on their ideological orientations and identity- and interest-based preferences about what desirable inter-Korean relations should be. Public opinion about North Korea has been under the heavy influence of major conservative newspapers and government-controlled broadcasting companies. Socioeconomic status or the bipolarization of wealth has also had significant influence on the making and implementation of North Korea policy. By and large, the well-to-do strata of the society tended to support the conservative governments' confrontational policy with the North, while other strata have tended to support the policy of reconciliation and cooperation with the North. In addition, regionalism along the division of Gyeongsang versus Jeolla Province was also correlated with North Korea policy. The Gyeongsang people, who were major beneficiaries of the wealth accumulated during the period from the 1960s to the 1990s under the rule of Gyeongsang Province–born leaders, tended to oppose the engagement policy toward the North, and vice versa for the relatively poor Jeolla people. And young generations tended to be more supportive of engagement with the North, while old generations tended to be opposed.

What were the key external structural variables for South Korea? Basically, the aforementioned North Korean domestic and external structural factors were South Korea's external structural variables for their North Korea policy. They were full of "conflicting" elements, still "amorphous," albeit "post–Cold War" and "order forming" in character.

Then how favorable was the political opportunity structure for South Korea's North Korea policy? On the whole, they were "not" favorable, as was the case with North Korea. This had much to do with the fluctuations in South Korea's policy toward the North from one government to the next during the past two decades, as we will see later in detail.

As examined above, there were elements of cooperation and conflict between the two Korean states at the agential and structural levels. All those elements interplayed to help produce political opportunity structures, favorable or unfavorable, for both Koreas to make and implement their strategies and policies toward each other.

NORTH KOREA'S STRATEGY OF
SURVIVAL AND DEVELOPMENT

With agential and structural variables interacting between them, what was North Korea's strategy of survival and development for the twenty-first century? It was basically for achieving national and regime security on the one hand, and economic development on the other. The immediate goal was to open a "strong and prosperous state" in 2012.

North Korea's strategy of survival and development for the twenty-first century could be expounded in three different domains: domestic, inter-Korean, and external. In order to establish a framework for survival and development in the domestic realm, the North Korean leadership focused on two key tasks: achieving political stability and regime security through power succession from father to son, and opening up a "strong and prosperous state" through domestic mobilization and economic cooperation with the outside world.

With regard to inter-Korean relations, North Korea pursued peaceful coexistence and co-prosperity with the South. It may have been sure of success in achieving that goal by having two rounds of inter-Korean summits and joint declarations. To its disappointment, however, the Lee Myung Bak government upset North Korea's aim by pursuing a policy of "denuclearization, opening, and 3,000," which North Korea perceived as tantamount to an outrageous insult and confrontation aimed at collapsing North Korea.

In the external realm, North Korea wanted to settle peace with the United States by ending the Korean War, signing a peace treaty, and normalizing relations, among other things. In order to make the reluctant United States come to the negotiation table, North Korea used the nuclear and missile cards. It is noteworthy that North Korea has been rather consistent in proposing the exchange between the denuclearization of the Korean Peninsula and a peace regime. Such resolution was to lead to peaceful coexistence between the two countries, not to be disturbed much by the change of governments in Washington, D.C.

NORTH KOREA'S CRITICAL CHOICES

What were the critical choices North Korea made to carry out the strategy of survival and development for the twenty-first century? Since the early 1990s, North Korea has made a series of critical choices, which were results of the interplay between agential and structural variables in the form of conflict and cooperation between politics and economics.[5] The first choice was made in 1991–1994, the second in 2000, the third in 2002, the fourth in 2005, the fifth in 2006–2007, the sixth also in 2007, the seventh in 2009, and the eighth and ninth in 2010.

Concretely, the first critical choice North Korea made in 1991–1994 just after the demise of the Soviet Union and East European socialist states included the following: the inter-Korean basic agreement, the Rajin-Sonbong free economic and trade zone, the first-ever high-level dialogue with the United States since the Korean War (the Kim Yong Soon–Arnold Kanter meeting), three preliminary meetings and eight rounds of normalization talks with Japan, UN membership obtained simultaneously with South Korea, the unrealized 1994 inter-Korean summit, and the Agreed Framework between the United States and North Korea for the resolution of the North Korean nuclear issue.

The second critical choice made in 2000 was the first-ever inter-Korean summit and the June 15 North–South Joint Declaration, and the DPRK–U.S. Joint Communiqué in October 2000. The third choice was the introduction of market elements and economic opening in Sinuiju, Mt. Kumgang, and Kaesong in 2002. The fourth was the September 19 Joint Statement in 2005 for nuclear resolution. The fifth choice was the nuclear test in October 2006, the February 13 Initial Actions Agreement in 2007, and the October 3 Second-Phase Actions Agreement in 2007. The sixth was the second inter-Korean summit in October 2007. The seventh was the rocket launch in April 2009 and the second nuclear test in May 2009. The eighth included the *Cheonan* incident,[6] Yeonpyeongdo shelling incident, and the revelation of the uranium enrichment facilities in Yongbyon. Finally, the ninth choice was the official promotion of Kim Jong Un as the heir to his father Kim Jong Il at the Third Party Conference in September 2010.

All in all, the nine critical choices above show that North Korea's decisions were accommodating in meeting the demands from within and without at certain times, but confrontational with such demands at other times. The choices covered a wide spectrum of political, military-security, and economic areas, as well as domestic, inter-Korean, and international issues.

North Korea's Critical Choices for Inter-Korean Relations

Of the nine strategic choices above, at least six were related to inter-Korean relations. During the period 1991–1994, there were groundbreaking developments in inter-Korean relations: the inter-Korean basic agreement, simultaneous entry into the UN as a member with South Korea, and Kim Il Sung's decision to have an inter-Korean summit through the good offices of former U.S. president Jimmy Carter, which was aborted due to Kim Il Sung's sudden death in July 1994.

The most critical choices both Koreas ever made in inter-Korean relations were the first-ever inter-Korean summit in June 2000 and the June 15 North–South Joint Declaration. These provided a new momentum not only for the improvement of inter-Korean relations but also for the United States and the international community to review and revise their policies toward the Korean Peninsula.[7]

In the second half of 2002, North Korea also made another choice: the designation of Sinuiju as a special administration district, the Mt. Kumgang area as a special tourist zone, and Kaesong as a special industrial zone. It is to be noted that this opening up was preceded by North Korea's introduction of market elements in its economic system in July of that year. The Mt. Kumgang Tourism Project and the Kaesong Industrial Park were to be the most visible and tangible symbols of inter-Korean economic cooperation.

Still another critical choice was the second inter-Korean summit that was held in October 2007 and the October 4 Summit Declaration. This summit declaration helped to concretize and enrich the June 15 North–South Joint Declaration. One of the key achievements of the second inter-Korean summit was the agreement on the "special peace and cooperation zone" in the West Sea. The idea was to combine security and economy in such a way that security concerns in the West Sea, where naval clashes recurred along the Northern Limit Line (NLL), could be offset by economic cooperation there. But it failed to materialize because of the reversal of the policy by the Lee Myung Bak government.

On the contrary, the *Cheonan* incident of March 2010 and the Yeonpyeongdo shelling incident in November of that year were the most serious disasters in inter-Korean relations since the Korean War.[8] These incidents caused unprecedented mutual distrust, throwing cold water on all preceding positive developments in inter-Korean relations. On May 24, 2010, just two months after the *Cheonan* incident, the South Korean government put a comprehensive ban on inter-Korean trade, personnel exchanges, and even humanitarian aid to North Korea (the "May 24 measure").

Finally, there were other critical choices that indirectly influenced inter-Korean relations. Some of the choices targeting the domestic realm had an indirect influence on inter-Korean relations: the July 2002 "market" economic reform and Kim Jong Un's coming to power as the heir to his father in September 2010. As for the choices targeting the external arena, there were some that had positive, favorable bearings on inter-Korean relations: the 1994 U.S.–DPRK Agreed Framework, the October 2000 U.S.–DPRK Joint Communiqué, the September 2001 DPRK–Japan Joint Declaration in Pyongyang (dubbed the "Pyongyang Declaration"), and the September 19 Joint Statement of 2005 and the agreements that followed to implement it—the February 13 and October 3 agreements of 2007. Other choices that had a negative, unfavorable impact on inter-Korean relations included the two nuclear tests in 2006 and 2009, multiple test firing of ballistic missiles, two satellite launches with long-range missile technology in 1998 and 2009, and the revelation of uranium enrichment facilities to U.S. experts in November 2010.

INTER-KOREAN RELATIONS SINCE 1991:
CHANGES AND CONTINUITIES

A review of inter-Korean relations for the past two decades from 1991 to January 2012 is in order. What were the continuities and changes in inter-Korean relations? What distinctive features were present?

A Roller-Coaster Trajectory

Inter-Korean relations are the result of both Koreas' strategies and policies toward each other. First of all, what were North Korea's strategy and policy toward the South?

It is worth recognizing that there has not been much change in North Korea's strategy and policy toward the South for the past two decades. North Korea consistently desired peaceful coexistence and co-prosperity with the South as an integral part of its larger strategy of survival and development for the twenty-first century.

But this does not mean that there was no change in tactics and policy instruments. North Korea employed carrots or sticks depending on the situation. There were times when it cooperated with the South, reciprocating the South's policies toward the North: during the Roh Tae Woo, Kim Dae Jung, and Roh Moo Hyun governments, North Korea chose carrots such as government-to-government dialogues, economic cooperation, social and cultural exchanges, humanitarian cooperation, and the like. There were other times when it confronted the South, again reciprocating the South's North Korea policy: during the Kim Young Sam and Lee Myung Bak governments, North Korea employed sticks such as harsh verbal attacks, the termination of Mt. Kumgang tourism, the suspension of reunion of separated families, the use of force, and so forth.

It could be argued, then, that inter-Korean relations for the past two decades have followed a roller-coaster trajectory due mainly to changes in South Korea's strategy and policy toward the North. Those changes were more than changes in tactics and policy instruments, as will be seen below. Such changes reflected the change of governments in the South through presidential elections.

At the beginning of the 1990s, there was rapprochement between the two Korean states under the Roh Tae Woo government (February 1988–February 1993): it pursued Nordpolitik, exploiting the opportunity provided by Mikhail Gorbachev's reform and opening. The thrust of national reconciliation between both Koreas was fully expressed in the 1991 inter-Korean basic agreement, ushering in a post–Cold War transition era in inter-Korean relations.

But this initial rapprochement was followed by the confrontational years during the Kim Young Sam government (February 1993–February 1998). There was a time when an inter-Korean summit was agreed on, but the inter-Korean relationship turned dramatically sour when President Kim put the South Korean army on maximum emergency alert instead of expressing his condolences for the death of Kim Il Sung. Inter-Korean relations were aggravated further due to President Kim's pursuit of unification through absorption of the North following the German example, and the worsening of the North Korean nuclear issue.

But there came a dramatic turnabout in inter-Korean relations during the Kim Dae Jung government (February 1998–February 2003). The success of President Kim's policy of engaging the North (dubbed the "Sunshine Policy") was highlighted by the first-ever inter-Korean summit held in June 2000 and the historic June 15 North–South Joint Declaration. This monumental accomplishment ushered in a paradigm shift from distrust and confrontation to trust, reconciliation, and cooperation between the two Korean states.

The Roh Moo Hyun government (February 2003–February 2008) pursued the Policy of Peace and Prosperity, which basically succeeded the Sunshine Policy, even though there were differences in priorities and policy instruments. Both Koreas held a second inter-Korean summit in October 2007. The October 4 Summit Declaration, another landmark document in inter-Korean relations, symbolized the continuing efforts of both Koreas to promote peaceful coexistence and co-prosperity in the peninsula.

However, the efforts were soon followed by another reversal in inter-Korean relations. The Lee Myung Bak government (February 2008–) disparaged the two previous governments' engagement policies with the North as the "lost ten years." President Lee adopted a policy of applying pressure and sanctions on North Korea with the ulterior motive of collapsing it. But it is worth noting that a certain degree of fluctuation existed even within the Lee government's policy toward the North.

Fluctuation within the Lee Government's North Korea Policy

In March 2008, just less than one month after the inauguration of the Lee government, South Korea put forth a new policy that would make the expansion of the Kaesong Industrial Park conditional on the progress of the North Korean nuclear issue. North Korea was grossly upset.

In an effort to ameliorate the situation, President Lee prepared a goodwill message to the North, but on July 11, 2008, a South Korean woman tourist trespassed on the forbidden North Korean military control zone outside the Mt. Kumgang tourism zone and was shot to death by the North Korean soldier on sentry duty. The Lee government immediately shut down all Mt. Kumgang tourism.

On December 1, 2008, North Korea announced a strict control and ban on traffic by land across the Military Demarcation Line (the "December 1 measure"), and on January 17, 2009, North Korean military authorities announced North Korea's "entry into a full-scale confrontational posture toward the South" (the "January 17 measure"). This was followed by North Korea's announcement that it was nullifying all agreements on settling inter-Korean political and military conflicts.

North Korea's launch of a satellite rocket and second nuclear test followed consecutively in April and May 2009. Tension on the Korean Peninsula rose dramatically. In early August 2009, former U.S. president Bill Clinton visited North Korea. In mid-August, Chairman Hyun Jeong Eun of Hyundai Group visited Pyongyang and agreed with Kim Jong Il to an early resumption of Mt. Kumgang tourism. But the Lee government did not accommodate the agreement.

On August 18, 2009, former South Korean president Kim Dae Jung died, and North Korea sent a condolences delegation to his funeral in Seoul. The condolences delegation met with President Lee Myung Bak at the Blue House and delivered Kim Jong Il's message to the effect that he wanted to improve inter-Korean relations and have a summit with President Lee. But President Lee explained his government's "consistent, firm principle" in its North Korea policy that there should be progress in the denuclearization of North Korea first.

In late August 2009, both Koreas held an inter-Korean Red Cross meeting, and about nine hundred separated family members from both sides were reunited at Mt. Kumgang in late September on the occasion of Chuseok, Korean Thanksgiving. Also in mid-October, inter-Korean working group meetings were held in Kaesong for the prevention of flooding at Imjin River and for the discussion of humanitarian issues including family reunions.

Against this backdrop, officials from both Seoul and Pyongyang secretly met in Singapore in mid-October 2009 to explore an opportunity for an inter-Korean summit. They were reported to have discussed agendas for the summit, but this secret channel of negotiation was exposed to the press. The Ministry of Unification officially took over and held two rounds of meetings in Kaesong in November 2009. Soon after the first round of negotiations, however, another naval clash broke out in the West Sea.

Inter-Korean cooperation continued in December 2009 when both Koreas had a joint North–South observation tour for overseas industrial areas in China and Vietnam and when South Korea provided H1N1 flu vaccines to the

North. And in his New Year's Address for 2010, President Lee emphasized the need to make a turning point in inter-Korean relations.

But all these developments in inter-Korean relations came to an abrupt stop due to the *Cheonan* incident that took place in the West Sea of Korea on March 26, 2010. On May 24, 2010, the South Korean government announced the "May 24 measure," a comprehensive sanction on the North. The next day, North Korea responded by announcing its decision to renounce government-to-government contact and dialogue with the South during the remaining tenure of the Lee government. Tension mounted during the summer and autumn of 2010 to the point that anything could happen in inter-Korean relations. The Yeonpyeongdo shelling incident took place in November 2010 under exactly such circumstances.

As the need to stabilize the Korean situation grew and the intervention of the United States and China in Korea intensified, the two Koreas resumed secret contacts in April 2011 to explore an inter-Korean summit. The representatives of both Koreas met in Beijing and elsewhere in May 2011. But North Korea was discontented with South Korea's behavior and revealed publicly the contents of the clandestine negotiations.[9] The prospects for inter-Korean dialogue became all the more gloomy due to the fiasco in Beijing.

Still willing to explore opportunities to improve inter-Korean relations, as well as with the pressure coming from the United States and China to restart inter-Korean dialogue, both Koreas held their Six-Party Talks chief negotiators' meeting at the ASEAN Regional Forum in Bali, Indonesia, in July 2011. As inter-Korean dialogue was taking place, the United States did not lose time to resume dialogue with North Korea by inviting Kim Kye Gwan, North Korea's first vice minister of foreign affairs, to the United States. And both Koreas held a second round of meetings between their Six-Party Talks chief negotiators in Beijing in September 2011.

Kim Jong Il died on December 17, 2011, and the Lee government expressed comfort to the North Korean people, but not to Kim Jong Un. North Korea regarded the Lee government's distinction between the leader and the people as an "unbearable insult and ridicule to our [North Korea's] dignity."[10] The Lee government did not permit any condolences delegations to go to Pyongyang. Only the bereaved families of former president Kim Dae Jung and former Hyundai Group chairman Chung Mong Hun were allowed to visit Pyongyang to reciprocate Kim Jong Il's expression of condolences for their respective family members' deaths through past dispatches of condolences delegations to Seoul. And North Korea expressed its anger, announcing that it would "not deal with the Lee Myung Bak government, the immoral traitor, forever as had been announced before."[11]

On January 5, 2012, the Ministry of Unification briefed President Lee Myung Bak on its "2012 Work Plan," where it revealed its intention to open a "high-level dialogue channel" with the North to deal with the key pending issues: the *Cheonan* incident, the Yeonpyeongdo shelling incident, reunion of separated families, expansion of the Kaesong Industrial Park, resumption of Mt. Kumgang tourism, and implementation of the June 15 North–South Joint Declaration and October 4 Summit Declaration.[12] Note that the *Cheonan* incident and the Yeonpyeongdo shelling incident were mentioned as the items for negotiation, which is a clear departure from the previous position that North Korea's admission of and apology for the two incidents were the precondition for any dialogue and negotiation with the North. North Korea responded to South Korea's offer to open a high-level dialogue channel in the negative.[13]

As shown above, we found fluctuation even within the Lee government's North Korea policy. President Lee's policy toward North Korea was characterized from the very beginning by the incongruence between its official policy of "mutual benefits and common prosperity" with the North and its hidden agenda of seeking its collapse. This discrepancy brought about a trust issue. Tension between the official and hidden agendas, combined with the conflict of interests between the need to stabilize and improve inter-Korean relations and the need to deal with North Korea's provocation in a resolute manner, contributed to fluctuations within its policy toward the North.

Changes and Continuities in Inter-Korean Relations

What were the changes and continuities in inter-Korean relations for the past two decades? What were its distinctive features?

Fundamentally, there has not been much change in North Korea's strategy and policy toward the South, as pointed out already. For the most part, the changes in South Korea's strategy and policy—which were expressed often in the reversal of the previous government's strategies and policies—were more responsible for the changes in inter-Korean relations, good or bad. The alternating governments with contrastive ideas, identities, and interests in the South—that is, the "engager" versus "absorptionist" governments—brought about inconsistency in policy toward the North. But this inconsistency in strategy and policy should be understood as an innate character of a democratic political system, resulting from the changes of governments through democratic elections.

Surely there were times when the absorptionist leaderships in the South, with overconfidence in South Korea's power over the North and an underestimation of the North's power and geopolitical locations, awaited and pursued the collapse of North Korea. Needless to say, this caused serious confrontations with the North. But it should be pointed out that there were more powerful elements of reconciliation and cooperation in line with the spirit of the post–Cold War era, and such elements persistently came back to the fore with the engagement policies toward the North. Even under the Lee Myung Bak government, such need and impetus of seeking reconciliation and cooperation with the North surfaced repeatedly as shown above.

PROSPECTS FOR INTER-KOREAN RELATIONS AND NORTH KOREA'S FUTURE

Finally, what are the prospects for the two Korean states' strategies and policies toward each other and inter-Korean relations in terms of changes and continuities? And in what direction is North Korea headed?

Prospects for Both Koreas' Strategies and Policies toward Each Other

Considering North Korea's track record, North Korea is almost sure to continue, without any serious change, its pursuit of peaceful coexistence and co-prosperity with the South to stabilize the Korean Peninsula as an integral part of its strategy of survival and development for the twenty-first century. In addition, North Korea is in desperate need of food and energy assistance, among other needs, from the outside world including South Korea. Wary of overgrown Chinese economic influence, North Korea will have to promote economic cooperation with South Korea, the United States, Japan, and Russia to countervail against China. Furthermore, an improved relationship with the South has always been an asset for North Korea in its negotiations for improved relations with the United States.

Under the circumstances, North Korea appears to have decided to wait for South Korea's presidential election to be held in December 2012. This does not mean, however, that it will never resume talks with the Lee government even when the South offers food aid or lifts its May 24 measure. North Korea appears to be well aware that whoever comes to power in the South in 2013, conservative or liberal, will have to change North Korea policy in one way or another. In fact, let alone the Democratic United Party's presidential hopefuls who have consistently opposed President Lee Myung Bak's North Korea policy as an anachronism and a historical anomaly, even Park Geun Hye, the most powerful presidential hopeful in the conservative circle, has differentiated her North Korea policy from President Lee's in her contribution to the September/October 2011 issue of *Foreign Affairs*.[14]

With regard to South Korea's future policy toward the North, two features are likely to continue to play: overall confidence in an ultimate unification of the country largely on South Korea's terms, and the fluctuation of its North Korea policy resulting from government changes through presidential elections.

On the whole, it appears that President Lee will continue his "principled approach" to the North, unless North Korea makes face-saving concessions for the resumption of talks with the South. It is a pity, however, that President Lee has not made the best of the window of opportunity opened by the death of Kim Jong Il. President Lee should have valued more the political implications of expressing condolences for future developments in inter-Korean relations with the new leader in the North than the past enmity associated with Kim Jong Il. It is noteworthy that despite the unification minister's idea of opening a high-level dialogue channel with the North and negotiating a resolution of the *Cheonan* and Yeonpyeongdo incidents, President Lee advised the Ministry of Unification that "being impatient or upsetting principles in inter-Korean relations will not be of help for real cooperation with the North,"[15] meaning that he did not want to have any abrupt change in his "principled" policy toward the North.

Prospects for Inter-Korean Relations

Then what are the prospects for inter-Korean relations in terms of changes and continuities? Again, changes and continuities in inter-Korean relations had much to do with the democratic election system that produces changes in government and power in Seoul and Washington: North Korea policy has alternated from one government to the next depending on the result of presidential elections in both countries.

There are many reasons to expect inter-Korean relations to be more reconciliatory and cooperative in the future than it is under the Lee government. Again, on the North Korean side, there will not be much change in its pursuit of peaceful coexistence and co-prosperity with the South and also in its demand for the faithful implementation of the two inter-Korean summit declarations.

On the South Korean side, despite the fluctuations in its policy toward the North, the political thrust among people to peacefully coexist and co-prosper through reconciliation and cooperation with the North in a win-win fashion has always existed. This political impetus is more likely to express itself in the future with a new government in power in 2013, liberal or conservative. After years of unswerving mutual hard-line policies, what is left for both Koreas is a more volatile, treacherous situation with the specter of a war hovering nearby, an alarm bell for an unrealistic and excessive policy toward the North for South Korean voters before the critical presidential election in December 2012.

Results of opinion polls about the Lee government's policy toward North Korea in chronological order confirm the above argument: in August 2008, 55.6 percent of the respondents supported implementing the June 15 North–South Joint Declaration and October 4 Summit Declaration, while only 21.4 percent felt no need to do so;[16] in August 2010, 60.5 percent of the respondents were dissatisfied with the Lee government's North Korea policy, while only 39.5 percent said they were satisfied;[17] in February 2011, 43.6 percent were of the opinion that the Lee government's North Korea policy was not as good as the Roh Moo Hyun government's, while 23.0 percent answered in the positive;[18] and on December 31, 2011, about two weeks after the death of Kim Jong Il, 53.3 percent supported a forward-looking policy toward the North for improved inter-Korean relations even without the North's apology for the *Cheonan* and Yeonpyeongdo incidents, while 37.3 percent were opposed.[19]

However, it is fair to point out that there is no guarantee that inter-Korean relations will be consistently stable and peaceful in the future, considering the stumbling blocks still in the way: change of governments and policies through elections in South Korea and the United States, failure to find solutions to the *Cheonan* incident and the Yeonpyeong island shelling incident, and the North Korean nuclear and missile issue. Eventually, however, it is expected that both Koreas will find "political solutions" to the two incidents in the West Sea, once a new government is inaugurated in the South. As for the North Korean nuclear issue, the United States and North Korea have already begun bilateral talks to seek solutions, holding a third round of which is under discussion.

North Korea's Future: Where Is It Going?

Kim Jong Il's era is gone, and Kim Jong Un is now the new supreme leader in North Korea. How solid is Kim Jong Un's grip on power at the moment? Can Kim Jong Un continue to consolidate his power into the future? What kinds of policies will the new leader pursue toward the United States and South Korea? And where is North Korea headed?

First of all, by all indications, Kim Jong Un appears to have consolidated his power successfully. Nothing out of the ordinary has been detected so far in the power succession from father to son. What we see today is basically the reflection and extension of hitherto progress in power succession in North Korea. A few facts lend weight to this argument.[20]

First, even before officially becoming heir apparent at the Third Party Conference of the Korean Workers' Party (KWP) in September 2010, Kim Jong Un is known to have focused on taking control of the military and the intelligence apparatuses with the full support of the two key power holders, Jang Song Taek and Ri Yong Ho, under the tight supervision of Kim Jong Il. It is also noteworthy that Kim Jong Il had placed a double layer of safeguards for his son when he named him the heir at the party conference. One protective layer was that Kim Jong Il reorganized the lineup of the KWP and restored its authority fully so that it could keep the military in check. The military's power had grown disproportionately strong under the strategy of military-first politics. The other safeguard was that Kim Jong Il placed some key military and party figures in positions overseeing the military and party, respectively, to counterbalance any potential threat to his son from Jang Song Taek (Kim Jong Un's uncle-in-law), the most powerful figure in North Korea after Kim Jong Un.

Specifically, the key military figures included Vice Marshal Ri Yong Ho (vice chairman of the Central Military Committee [CMC] of the KWP, chief of the General Staff of the Korean People's Army [KPA]); General Kim Jeong Gak (member of the CMC of the KWP, first vice director of the General Political Department of the KPA);[21] General Kim Won Hong (member of the CMC of the KWP, vice director of the General Political Department of the KPA in charge of organization, former chief of the Military Security Command of the KPA);[22] General U Dong Cheuk (candidate member of the Politburo of the Central Committee [CC] of the KWP, member of the CMC of the KWP, first vice director of the National Security Department of the National Defense Commission [NDC] of the DPRK); and Vice Marshal Kim Young Chun (member of the CMC of the KWP, minister of the People's Armed Forces of the National Defense Commission [NDC], full member of the Politburo of the CC of the KWP).[23]

The key party figures included Kim Gi Nam (full member of the Politburo of the CC of the KWP, secretary of the Secretariat of the CC of the KWP, chief of the Propaganda and Agitation Department of the Secretariat of the CC of the KWP); Choi Tae Bok (full member of the Politburo of the CC of the KWP, secretary of the Secretariat of the KWP, chairman of the Supreme People's Assembly of the DPRK); Choi Ryong Hae (candidate member of the Politburo of the CC of the KWP, secretary of the Secretariat of the KWP, member of the CMC of the KWP);[24] and Ju Gyu Chang (candidate member of the Politburo of the CC of the KWP, chief of the Machine Industry Department of the Secretariat of the CC of the KWP, member of the CMC of the KWP, member of the NDC, lieutenant general of the KPA), among others.

It is to be noted that key figures who hold at least three positions of the following power institutions—the Politburo of the CC of the KWP, the Secretariat of the CC of the KWP, the CMC of the KWP, the NDC, and the KPA—included Ri Yong Ho, Kim Young Chun, Kim Jeong Gak, U Dong Cheuk, Jang Song Taek,[25] Kim Kyong Hui (Jang Song Taek's wife and Kim Jong Un's aunt),[26] Choe Ryong Hae, and Ju Gyu Chang.

Second, the December 19, 2011, obituary report of Kim Jong Il's death accorded Kim Jong Un the title "the leader" of North Korea. In it he was called the "outstanding Leader of the party, the military, and the people."[27] This hints that during the two days that followed the death of Kim Jong Il, the key power holders in the North had discussed and agreed to continue to support the son as they had been preparing to do. Had Kim Jong Un's power not been that solid, the obituary would have evidenced his weaker status with more equivocal phrasings than "the leader" with superlative modifiers such as "outstanding," "great," and "respected." As early as December 24, the North Korean media had described Kim Jong Un as the "supreme leader of revolutionary armed forces."[28] On December 25, North Korean media accorded him the titles "Dear Leader," "supreme leader of the armed forces," "supreme commander-in-chief," "sun of the twenty-first century," and "people's leader and father."[29] On December 26, Kim Jong Un was called "the head of the central committee of the party" and "the pre-eminent Leader of the party, the state, and the military."[30] On December 30, 2011, the Politburo of the CC of the KWP held a meeting and decided to have Kim Jung Un as the supreme commander-in-chief of the KPA in accordance with the "October 8, 2011, will" of Kim Jong Il.[31] All this points to the fact that Kim Jong Un, as the new "supreme leader" of North Korea, has control over and will officially assume the top positions in the party, the military, and the government before long.

Can Kim Jong Un continue to consolidate his power into the future? At the time of this writing in early January 2012, his path to power appears free of outstanding obstacles. Any internal power strife will only be possible in a future scenario where Kim Jong Un proves inept in the eyes of the ruling elite by failing in the areas of economy, security, foreign policy, and so forth. By and large, the key power holders are more likely to work in concert than not, for their own interests, as they are stakeholders and key beneficiaries of the Kim Jong Un regime.

What will Kim Jong Un's policies be toward the United States and South Korea? Since stabilization of the domestic situation and improvement of the living standards of the people are at the top of Kim Jong Un's agenda, it is less likely that North Korea will provoke first, unless South Korea and the United States pose a threat to or provoke North Korea, except for the possibility of having a satellite rocket launch in April 2012 for the commemoration of the centenary birthday of Kim Il Sung, the founder of North Korea.

Finally, what does the future hold for North Korea? The problems Kim Jong Un will struggle with are exactly the same problems his father faced: provision of food and energy, economic recovery and development, resolution of the nuclear issue, a peace settlement on the Korean Peninsula, and improvement of inter-Korean relations, among others. These problems are real tough challenges for the new leader in the North, the solutions to which require cooperation from the outside world.

In the domestic realm, whatever critical choices the new leader makes will inevitably have much to do with further economic reform and opening. There will come a time when Kim Jong Un's capabilities as a leader will be seriously tested in terms of maintaining the regime and system and simultaneously accommodating more liberalized political and socioeconomic demands from below. North Korea will have to be more responsive to and accountable for the needs of its people.

In the external realm, North Korea will continue to seek help from and make efforts to improve its relations with the United States, South Korea, and Japan. There are many reasons to predict that inter-Korean relations will be more reconciliatory and cooperative in the future than they have been under the Lee Myung Bak government. Ultimately, North Korea has no other choice but to be more cooperative toward the United States and South Korea. North Korea will have to continue its effort to end the Korean War, sign a peace treaty, and normalize its relations with the United States as a quid pro quo for resolving the nuclear issue. Finally, it is also worth noting that North Korea may want to engage the United States as a countervailing force to dilute Chinese influence over the state as a way of promoting its diplomatic independence, just as it did when it played the Soviet Union and China off against each other in the past.[32]

NOTES

1. This study will adopt a constructivist perspective in explaining changes and continuities in inter-Korean relations. It will pay special attention to the ideas, identities, and interests of both North and South Korean leaderships. Their ideas served as the basis for their identities and interests in making strategies and policy choices toward each other and in structuring inter-Korean relations. See Alexander Wendt, "Anarchy Is What States Make of It: The Social Construction of Power Politics," *International Organization* 46, no. 2 (Spring 1992): 397–98; Alexander Wendt, *Social Theory of International Politics* (Cambridge: Cambridge University Press, 1999), 1; and Robert Jackson and Georg Sorensen, "Social Constructivism" (chapter 6), in Robert Jackson and Georg Sorensen, *Introduction to International Relations: Theories and Approaches* (New York: Oxford University Press, 2007), 163.

2. Kim Il Sung, "The Historic Experience of the Construction of the Korean Workers' Party," *Kim Il Sung Works, Vol. 40* [*Kim Il Sung Jeojakjip 40*] (Pyongyang, DPRK: Joseonrodongdangchulpansa, 1994), 244.

3. *The History of the Korean Workers' Party* [*Joseonrodongdang Ryeoksa*] (Pyongyang, DPRK: Joseonrodongdangchulpansa, 2004), 531–33.

4. This was expressed as "the lesson learned from North Korea's twenty years' relationship with the U.S." by one of the North Korean participants in the "Triad Track-II Seminar on Peace-Building and Reintegration of the Korean Peninsula," sponsored by the Center for the Study of Global Issues (GLOBIS), University of Georgia, Athens, GA, USA, October 16–18, 2011.

5. Haksoon Paik, "North Korea's Choices for Survival and Prosperity since 1990s: Interplay between Politics and Economics," *Sejong Policy Studies* 3, no. 2 (2007): 250–64.

6. The *Cheonan* incident has been controversial in terms of whether North Korea sank the South Korean corvette *Cheonan* or the *Cheonan* sank due to an accident North Korea was not involved in.

7. Secretary of State Madeleine K. Albright, "Address at National Press Club," Washington, DC, November 2, 2000.

8. Senator John Kerry, "Opening Statement for 'Breaking the Cycle of North Korea Provocations,'" March 1, 2011, for U.S. Senate Committee on Foreign Relations, "Breaking the Cycle of North Korea Provocations," 419 Dirksen Senate Office Building, Washington, DC, Tuesday, March 1, 2011, http://www.foreign.senate.gov/hearings/breaking-the-cycle-of-north-korea-provocations; "Richardson Presents Proposals to North Korea Aimed at Easing Crisis," CNN, December 18, 2010.

9. "National Defense Commission Spokesman's Reply to Korean Central News Agency (KCNA) Reporter's Question," KCNA, June 1, 2011.

10. "We Are Watching South Korean Authorities' Attitude," *Uriminjogkkiri* [Between Our Nation], December 23, 2011.

11. Statement of the National Defense Commission of the DPRK, December 30, 2011.

12. "2012 Work Plan," Ministry of Unification of the Republic of Korea, January 5, 2012.

13. "(South Korea's So-Called) Active Unification Policy—a Pet Saying That Tries to Disguise Crimes," *Uriminjogkkiri* [Between Our Nation], January 9, 2012.

14. Park Geun-hye, "A New Kind of Korea," *Foreign Affairs*, September/October 2011, 13–18.

15. *Yonhap News*, January 5, 2012.

16. *Minjungeui Sori* [Voice of People], August 10, 2008, http://www.vop.co.kr/A00000218380.html.

17. Myoung-Kyu Park et al., "2010 Unification Attitude Survey [2010 Tongil Euisik Josa]," Institute for Peace and Unification Studies (IPUS), Seoul National University, August 17, 2010.

18. *Kukminilbo*, February 21, 2011, http://news.kukinews.com/article/view.asp?page=1&gCode=kmi&arcid=0004664677&code=11121100.

19. *Dong-a Ilbo*, December 31, 2011, http://news.donga.com/Politics/NK/3/000301/20111231/42988078/1.

20. Haksoon Paik, "Kim Jong Un's Power and Policy: Current State and Future Prospects," December 27, 2011, *38 North*, http://38north.org/2011/12/hskim122711.

21. Author's Note: The manuscript of this chapter was completed in early January 2012, but two months before this book went to press, North Korea held the Fourth Party Conference of the KWP on April 11, 2012, and the Supreme People's Assembly on April 13, 2012, respectively, and had a reshuffle of the power elite lineup. General Kim Jeong Gak was promoted to full member of the Politburo of the Central Committee of the KWP in April 2012 and minister of the People's Armed Forces of the National Defense Commission of the DPRK in April 2012. Note that he had been promoted to vice marshal of the KPA in February 2012.

22. General Kim Won Hong was promoted to full member of the Politburo of the Central Committee of the KWP and director of the National Security Department of the NDC of the DPRK in April 2012.

23. Vice Marshal Kim Young-chun was demoted from minister of the People's Armed Forces of the NDC of the DPRK in April 2012.

24. Choe Ryong Hae was promoted to member of the Presidium of the Politburo of the CC of the KWP, vice chairman of the CMC of the KWP, director of the General Political Department of the KPA, vice marshal of the KPA, and member of the NDC of the DPRK in April 2012. Note that Choi became one of the most powerful figures in North Korea by April 2012, and the appointment of Choi, who did not have any military career background, to director of the General Political Department of the KPA was understood as a reflection of Kim Jong Un's strong will to have full control of the military by the party.

25. Note that Jang Song Taek possesses positions in all of the five power institutions in North Korea: candidate member of the Politburo of the CC of the KWP, chief of the Administration Department of the Secretariat of the CC of the KWP, member of the CMC of the KWP, vice chairman of the NDC, and general of the KPA. And note that Jang was promoted to full member of the Politburo of the CC of the KWP in April 2012.

26. Note that Kim Kyong Hui was promoted to full member of the Politburo of the CC of the KWP and secretary of the Secretariat of the CC of the KWP in April 2012. Also note that Kim Kyong Hui was the first among the sixteen full members of the Politburo and the first among nine secretaries of the Secretariat, which means that Kim Kyong Hui, along with Jang Song Taek and Choe Ryong Hae, became one of the most powerful figures in North Korea by April 2012.

27. "Announcement to All Party Members, People's Army Soldiers, and People," KCNA, December 19, 2011.

28. KCNA, December 24, 2011. Also see *Rodong Sinmun*, December 26, 2011.

29. *Rodong Sinmun*, December 25, 2011; KCNA, December 25, 2011.

30. KCNA, December 26, 2011.

31. KCNA, December 31, 2011. The official text of the so-called "Kim Jong Il's October 8, 2011, Will" has not been published, but parts of it were circulated informally in an unofficial form, whose authenticity cannot be judged.

32. Haksoon Paik, "Why Not Opt for a 'Win-Win' Strategy for the Korean Peninsula?" Nautilus Institute Policy Forum, July 26, 2011, http://www.nautilus.org/publications/essays/napsnet/forum/Paik_Win-Win/?searchterm=Haksoon Paik.

Chapter Twelve

North Korea's Relations with the United States and the Rest of the World

David Kang

North Korea remains both a practical problem and an intellectual puzzle, with actions that sometimes appear self-defeating, aggressive, and unpredictable. North Korea's sinking of the South Korean naval vessel *Cheonan* in March 2010 was described as "South Korea's 9/11 moment," only to have the incident superseded eight months later when North Korean artillery fire killed two South Korean marines and two civilians and wounded eighteen others in November 2010, characterized as "the most serious incident since the Korean War."[1] Both incidents followed a November 2009 skirmish in which South Korean naval vessels opened fire on a North Korean patrol ship that had crossed the disputed Northern Limit Line, "damaging it badly," with suspected heavy casualties on the North Korean side.[2] Combined with revelations in November 2010 of a uranium nuclear program, nuclear tests of a plutonium-based weapon in 2006 and 2009, and continuing fears of missile and nuclear proliferation, the peninsula is in a new cold war.[3] Even with the death of Kim Jong Il in December 2011 and the putative rise of the third generation of Kims to leadership in the form of Kim Jong Un, deterrence, isolation, and symbolic shows of force and determination are the current strategies in place, and the "North Korea problem" remains as intractable as ever.

The scholarly literature about North Korea tends to cohere around three enduring and interrelated questions: First, to what extent is North Korea's foreign and domestic policy behavior motivated primarily by internal versus external factors?[4] That is, do its leaders and people behave the way they do more as a result of circumstances inside the country such as a particular ideology, economic situation, or political mind-set, or more as a result of situational and external pressures such as its geographic or strategic position relative to other countries? Second, is North Korea strong or weak? Put differently, does the regime pursue militant and destabilizing foreign policies and repression at home because of fear, aggression, or greed?[5] Third, to what extent is North Korea predictable or unpredictable?[6] On the one hand, North Korea continues to defy outsiders' expectations about both its own endurance as well as the patterns of conflict and cooperation it pursues, while on the other, its behavior is seen by many to follow a pattern or cycle. In short, the regime survived long beyond most expectations, despite obvious internal weaknesses and external pressure, and it continues to pursue policies that often appear to be puzzling or at least contradictory to outside observers.[7]

Depending on how one answers these questions, the policy implications that follow are fairly straightforward. For policy makers, the questions have always been whether to engage and interact with North Korea, or whether to contain it and attempt to isolate the people and leadership. If one sees North Korea as fundamentally insecure, predictable, and concerned about its external relations, then engagement and carrots are the best way to lure the leadership into accommodating outside powers. However, if one sees the regime as fundamentally aggressive, unpredictable, and motivated by internal or self-regarding factors, then pursuing deterrence and isolation is the best way to deal with the regime.[8]

Yet North Korea is both an intellectual puzzle and a practical problem beyond the issues of nuclear proliferation and international security, and these same fundamental questions motivate debate about the North Korean economy and its deplorable record of human rights abuses. Why and how can the country survive with an economy that is so poor, backward, and isolated compared to its rapidly developing neighbors? Why has North Korea not pursued economic reforms and opening? Should foreign countries promote marketization, economic reforms, and capitalism in North Korea, or should they prohibit and limit foreign economic interactions with North Korea? Regarding human rights, profound ethical questions face both scholars and practitioners of international relations: How do we effect human rights in North Korea and improve the lives of the people? Should external actors—governments, NGOs, and other groups—work with a regime that is so obviously repugnant in many ways if doing so can improve the lives of innocent citizens? Or do we isolate the North Korean regime and subject it to external pressure and embarrassment over its human rights record, and not deal with it until it changes? Does engaging with the regime support it and allow it to continue its reprehensible ways, or does engagement induce internal improvement?

This chapter will examine North Korea's relations with the United States and the rest of the world and make two overarching arguments. First, North Korea's continuing nuclear and military challenge is only one aspect of its overall relations with the world, and policies designed to affect its security policy may work at cross-purposes with policies designed to affect its economy and the lives of its people. That is, North Korea is both strong and weak and reacts to both external and internal pressures. Outside governments, NGOs, activists, and policy makers face a series of difficult trade-offs in crafting policies toward both the North Korean regime and its people. The complexities that arise in dealing with North Korea lead to a number of contradictory policy choices, and making progress in one issue area has often meant overlooking a different issue area or even allowing it to worsen. Second, North Korea's search for status is as important as its search for military power or economic wealth. While there is intense speculation about the North Korean regime's motivations for its behavior, one aspect that generally is not as central to analyses is status seeking. Most analyses see North Korea as motivated by greed or ambition, as noted above. But it is possible that status—that is, social recognition—is as important a goal to the leadership. After all, this is a regime that pays particular attention to its position in the world. While this approach is speculative, it may perhaps provide some new insights into North Korea's relations with the United States and the rest of the world.

RELATIONS WITH THE UNITED STATES

This chapter focuses more on the DPRK's perspective on the United States than on a U.S. perspective on North Korea. North Korea's second nuclear test, its long-range missile tests, and its two attacks on South Korea in 2010 once again threatened stability in Northeast Asia. Once again, North Korea has engaged in bluster designed to project strength and resolve in the face of international disapproval. The North Korean nuclear issue has been the most important security issue in the region for almost two decades, and despite newer developments, such as the death of North Korean leader Kim Jong Il and new leaders in both South Korea and the United States, the underlying issues remain depressingly the same: how to rein in North Korea's nuclear programs and entice North Korea to open its markets and borders to greater foreign interactions.[9] North Korea itself has been one of the most enduring foreign policy challenges facing the United States over the past half century. From a bitter and divisive war in 1950–1953, through the Cold War, and now to the successive nuclear crises, the United States has made little progress over the years.

North Korea itself may be at a major turning point: Kim Jong Il's death and the naming of his son, Kim Jong Un, as the "great successor" marks only the third leader in North Korean history. Whether Kim the third can hold power, and what his policies may be, is the subject of enormous speculation.[10] North Korea also faces recurrent food and energy shortages, and its economic system is barely functioning. The opportunities and dangers of rapid regime change or collapse in North Korea are immense. Yet North Korea may yet again find a way to muddle through, with its basic ruling regime and leadership intact. If there is continuity in the North for the time being, the underlying task will remain the same: how to draw North Korea into the world and away from its dangerous, confrontational stance.

In the United States, most observers from across the political spectrum agree on the goal: a denuclearized North Korea that opens to the world, pursues economic and social reforms, and increasingly respects human rights. Disagreement only occurs over the tactics—what policies will best prod North Korea on the path toward these outcomes? These debates over which strategy will best resolve the North Korean problem remain essentially the same as they were decades ago: is it best to engage North Korea and lure it into changing its actions and its relations with the outside world, or is it better to contain the problem and coerce North Korea into either changing or stopping its bad behavior?[11]

Furthermore, the questions and debates surrounding North Korea tend to center on discrete and identifiable challenges: Can the United States contain the North Korean nuclear problem? Can the United States change Pyongyang's behavior on human rights and encourage economic reform in North Korea? Can the United States coordinate the diverse interests and priorities of its allies and counterparts in Northeast Asia and still retain a focus on solving the numerous challenges with North Korea? These are all difficult issues in and of themselves; jointly they make the North Korean challenge exceedingly difficult to manage.

Yet underlying all these questions is an even more fundamental question to which there is no clear answer: Is the United States willing to coexist in a long-term relationship with North Korea and grant it equal status? This question is actually much more difficult to answer than any of the preceding questions, and indeed how one answers this question may condition the responses to the other questions. That is, the United States is certainly willing to normalize diplomatic relations with North Korea if it changes completely by abandoning its nuclear weapons programs, opening up its economy, and respecting human rights. But this is also essentially pointing out that the United States is willing to live with regime change in North Korea. The real question is whether the United States can live with North Korea if it changes just enough to pose little threat to U.S. interests, but remains essentially the same in character, outlook, and other policies. As Robert Litwak has pointed out, historically the United States cared about other states' behavior. Recently, however, the United States has been concerned with their character.[12]

These discrete policy challenges facing the United States—nuclear, economic, humanitarian, and coordination—are difficult enough to solve. But behind each one of them lies a much more fundamental challenge for the United States: whether it should grant North Korea equal status as a normal nation-state. Can the United States live indefinitely with North Korea, grant it diplomatic normalization, and treat is as an equal like all other recognized states in the world?

Social status is one of the most important motivators of human behavior, yet for over a generation international relations scholars largely ignored it. As Richard Ned Lebow has noted, scholarly research in international relations has been framed by overarching grand theories that foreground other motivations, primarily fear (security) and appetite (wealth).[13] Yet as Nicholas Onuf noted two decades ago, "standing, security, and wealth are the controlling interests of humanity. We recognize them everywhere."[14] Status is "an individual's standing in the hierarchy of a group based on criteria such as prestige, honor, and deference," where status is an inherently relational concept and manifests itself hierarchically.[15] While it may be intuitively plausible that states value material gains such as economic wealth or military power, it is just as plausible that states and individuals value their social standing and desire social recognition and prestige.[16] As Max Weber wrote, "A nation will forgive damage to its interests, but not injury to its honor, and certainly not when this is done in a spirit of priggish self-righteousness," while John Harsanyi has written that, "apart from economic payoffs, social status seems to be the most important incentive and motivating force of social behavior."[17]

I have spent so much time on the scholarly discussion about status in international relations because it appears that both the United States and North Korea recognize that the status of North Korea is a central—but implicit—element of their relationship. The U.S. reluctance to grant North Korea status similar to other states is evident across administrations and the political spectrum. More recent informal examples include Hillary Clinton's verbal sparring with North Korea, complaining that North Korea acts "like small children and unruly teenagers and people who are demanding attention."[18] Previously, former U.S. defense secretary Donald Rumsfeld called DPRK leaders "idiotic," while then-president George W. Bush was quoted as saying, "I loathe Kim Jong-Il—I've got a visceral reaction to this guy."[19] Put that way, it is not at all clear that the United States really does want to live with North Korea. Our hesitance and skepticism about North Korea is evident across administrations and thus renders any more specific policy agenda quite difficult. As Victor Cha has written, "North Korea doesn't just want the bomb. It wants to be accorded the status and prestige of a nuclear power."[20]

More concretely, the United States implicitly and explicitly realizes that formal recognition and diplomatic status for North Korea as a sovereign nation-state deserving to be treated equally in the international community is a tremendous honor for North Korea, and withholding it is also a strategic U.S. tool. While normal relations hardly stop nations from going to war if they choose, it does confer legitimacy, prestige, and status. The United States is clearly reluctant to confer such status on North Korea as long as it so willingly violates international norms in so many different areas. As President Obama said in August 2009, "We just want to make sure the government of North Korea is operating within the basic rules of the international community."[21]

The North Korean desire for this status as a nation-state equal to all others runs deep. There is an (in)famous museum in Pyongyang that houses only gifts from foreign dignitaries attesting to North Korean "greatness." Although this normally provokes snickers outside of North Korea, it reveals a deep-seated insecurity and desire on the part of the North Korean leadership for recognition. Similarly, Barbara Demick of the *L.A. Times* reported, "North Koreans are obsessed with the United States. They hold the U.S. responsible for the division of the Korean peninsula and seem to believe that U.S. foreign policy since the mid-twentieth century has revolved around the single-minded goal of screwing them over. *The cruelest thing you can do is tell a North Korean that many Americans couldn't locate North Korea on a map.*"[22]

A recent example of North Korea's intense desire for "normal" status came from the arrest of two U.S. journalists who had crossed the border from China into North Korea. It appears that North Korea's main purpose in arresting, sentencing, and now releasing the journalists to a major U.S. political figure has been to be treated as a sovereign nation with its own laws and territory. North Korea's actions from the beginning of this incident have displayed a heightened desire for recognition of its status as a nation-state like any other. Thus arresting the two journalists for "illegal entry" was a statement that its borders are sovereign and must be respected; putting them through the judicial process (however maligned) was a performance that emphasized that North Korea also has laws and processes.

Both the United States and North Korea kept the issue of the two journalists quite separate from their other diplomatic and political problems, and Bill Clinton's visit was aimed solely at getting the two journalists released. North Korea charged the journalists with "illegal entry" and did not charge them with espionage or politicize their arrests in a way that linked them to the nuclear crisis. The United States as well did not attempt to link the two issues. Perhaps most importantly, releasing the two journalists to a major political figure after the process had run its course was a way of gaining the status the North Korean leadership so clearly craves.

Indeed, much of the criticism that came from the U.S. side focused on the dubious wisdom of sending a former president to North Korea. Despite the fact that the trip was explicitly a private, nongovernmental affair, many U.S. observers were skeptical about sending a former U.S. president to North Korea. The implication is clear: North Korea does not deserve a visit from a man of such stature. As former vice president Dick Cheney commented, "I think when a former president of the United States goes and meets with the leader and so forth, that we're rewarding their bad behavior, and I think it's a mistake."[23]

Status as I use it here does not mean diplomatic niceties of being polite and providing "face" for the North. That is an element of status, to be sure. But my point is more fundamental—much North Korean behavior exhibits a clear recognition that the DPRK does not have the formal status of a sovereign nation-state equal to other nation-states in the modern world. Furthermore, the behavior of the United States and other regional states reveals that they, too, implicitly recognize that granting North Korea status as a sovereign nation-state is a tremendous honor, one that can be awarded to the North only after it modifies its ways. There appears to be little room for compromise on this issue, on either side. Would it be possible for the United States and other countries to live with a North Korea that somehow abandons its nuclear programs but remains a totalitarian, closed, militaristic, and repressive regime? Although there is no obvious answer to that question, such a question surely does pose a challenge for other states as they decide how to deal with the reclusive leadership in Pyongyang.

RELATIONS WITH THE REST OF THE WORLD

DPRK relations with the rest of the world understandably receive less attention than do its relations with those countries most involved in its foreign relations, such as the United States, South Korea, China, and Japan. What is less commonly known is that the DPRK has normalized relations with most of the rest of the world. The countries that matter most to it—the United States, the ROK, and Japan—still do not have diplomatic relations with the DPRK. However, most ASEAN member states, the European Union, and other countries around the world do have normal diplomatic relations with North Korea. This is perhaps more telling with regard to how North Korea sees itself—as just another country in the world, like any other.

Yet these relations remain superficial at best. In terms of economic relations, the DPRK does have a penchant for trading its missile and weapons technology with other countries considered to be "rogues," such as Syria, Iran, and Iraq. However, Joshua Pollack shows that DPRK weapons sales have fallen dramatically since 1994. Between 1987 and 1993, North Korea sold 420 missile systems to international buyers; from 1994 to 2009, North Korea sold a total of 100 missile systems. As Pollack notes, "The subsequent fall-off took place a decade too early to be explained by the Proliferation Security Initiative of 2003."[24]

"Regular" economic relations between the DPRK and the rest of the world are also falling. At present, China and South Korea account for almost 60 percent of total North Korean trade, and trade with the rest of the world accounts for less than one-third of total trade. In short, North Korea interacts with much of the world through normal diplomatic channels. However, because of its intensely complex foreign relations with key countries such as the United States, the ROK, China, and Japan, those relations remain minimal and superficial.

CONCLUSION

As Bruce Cumings wrote about North Korea, "We look at it and see ourselves."[25] That is, outsiders more easily project their own fears and hopes onto North Korea rather than viewing North Korea on its own terms. North Korea presents no easy conclusions, and thus, what does a careful exploration of the available research about North Korea itself tell us? Most clearly, international relations, and the North Korea problem, comprise more than simply the security issues involving nuclear and missile programs. Dealing with the economy, human rights, and humanitarian concerns is just as important.

North Korea in 2012 is not the same as North Korea in 2000—the political institutions, economy, and society have all experienced major and possibly enduring changes since then. North Korea contains more diversity of opinion and people than is commonly thought. Although a totalitarian regime, within the regime there are identifiable institutional differences, and undoubtedly personal differences. Largely as a result of weakened state control, the economy has experienced a growth of commercialization and marketization. North Korea's economy is both stronger than we might believe, in that it has proven remarkably enduring and adaptable, and many people are now working in the black, or private, markets (a probable target of the 2009 currency devaluation). The regime itself is clearly weaker than it was a decade ago: the unplanned marketization has shriveled the central government's control over the periphery, despite episodes of retrenchment. The people themselves are not simply brainwashed robots, nor are they all proto-democrats; they are real people with many different opinions. As North Korea becomes increasingly penetrated by informal and sporadic information that trickles back through traders or family members in South Korea or China, the question is how this will affect them.

But these changes do not necessarily mean that North Korea is headed toward collapse or that the state institutions are close to failing. Outsiders have been predicting North Korean collapse for twenty years, if not longer.[26] Yet North Korea has managed to survive. State officials benefit from marketization because it provides a measure of human security that lessens domestic resistance even while it weakens officials' control. Corrupt officials benefit personally from marketization even as it undermines their position. Civil society is almost entirely absent in North Korea, and while there are occasional reports of spontaneous "rice riots," there is very little evidence that the North Korean people themselves could engage in a Libya-style uprising of any sort. Society is too divided, there are almost no "bottom-up" institutions around which political protests could cohere, and there are no social or civic leaders that could become political leaders in protests against the government.[27]

What does this mean for policies of countries concerned about the North Korea problem? Does engagement or isolation work more readily toward change in North Korea? On the security issue, as with the economic and social issues, North Korea today is not in the same place it was ten years ago. Regarding the nuclear and missile programs, those ten years have led both sides to conclude that there is little likelihood for a negotiated solution. The U.S., South Korean, and Japanese governments have chosen a policy of containment and isolation, of pressuring the North Korean regime to make concessions before making any moves of their own. This has been fairly successful in the domestic politics of both the United States and South Korea, and there is little indication that either government plans to change its strategy.

Yet the larger North Korean problem involves more than simply the security issue, and a strategy of isolation and minimal interaction with North Korea means that the weakest and most vulnerable North Korean people will continue to lead a hazardous existence, with near-famine conditions possible each year. The only way to truly solve the hunger issue is to bring North Korea into the world market and help it earn enough abroad through trade so that adequate food can be imported. The North Korean government also continues to engage in horrific and systematic human rights abuses, and international isolation has done little to curb those abuses, and may in fact encourage them. Thus, dealing with the immediate and present economic and social issues in North Korea and interacting with the government and people of North Korea may work at cross-purposes to policies designed to pressure North Korea into making concessions on its nuclear and missile programs. Even sanctions that are targeted only at the North Korean elite appear to have little impact. The youngest and oldest, the weakest and most vulnerable, will be most directly affected by most sanctions, not the elites at the top of the hierarchy. As Haggard and Noland conclude, "A coordinated strategy of cutting North Korea off from international assistance would increase the probability of regime change . . . [but] that rests on a highly dubious utilitarian logic: that it is morally acceptable to sacrifice the innocent today in the uncertain probability that lives will be saved or improved at some future point."[28]

The changes that are taking place in North Korea will continue whether or not the international community engages North Korea. Most assuredly the regime will continue to look after its own survival first without any consideration for the people. And thus North Korea presents no easy solutions for policy makers in Seoul, Washington, and other capitals, but rather a series of difficult trade-offs: engagement of some type may have an impact on the current economic and humanitarian issues, but some fear this will reward the regime for its international behavior. Containment is an obvious response to belligerent North Korean foreign policy behavior, but it is not clear that North Korea will bow to such pressure, while such actions would probably exacerbate difficulties for the North Korean people themselves. For outside powers, there is the difficult task of crafting policies toward North Korea that recognize the inner workings of North Korea itself and that manage the trade-offs across issue spaces of engagement and pressure.

NOTES

1. Donald Kirk, "Holed *Cheonan* Stern Ups the Ante," *Asia Times*, April 17, 2010, http://www.atimes.com/atimes/Korea/LD17Dg01.html; Tom A. Peter, "North and South Korea Clash across Tense Border," *Christian Science Monitor*, November 23, 2010, http://www.csmonitor.com/World/terrorism-security/2010/1123/North-and -South-Korea-clash-across-tense-border.

2. Choe Sang-hun, "North Korea Warns South after Naval Clash," *New York Times*, November 11, 2009, http://www.nytimes.com/2009/11/12/world/asia/12korea.html.

3. This uranium facility opens up the possibility of a second pathway to nuclear weapons development. However, its revelation in and of itself is not immediately indicative of a weapons program. Many in the United States and the ROK believe that this facility raises the probability of many hidden uranium facilities, however.

4. Victor D. Cha, "Korea's Place in the Axis," *Foreign Affairs* 81, no. 3 (May/June 2002): 79–92; David C. Kang, "International Relations Theory and the Second Korean War," *International Studies Quarterly* 47, no. 3 (September 2003): 301–24.

5. Michael O'Hanlon, "Stopping a North Korean Invasion: Why Defending South Korea is Easier than the Pentagon Thinks," *International Security* 22, no. 4 (Spring 1998): 135–70; David C. Kang, "Preventive War and North Korea," *Security Studies* 4, no. 2 (Winter 1995): 330–63; Stuart Masaki, "The Korean Question: Assessing the Military Balance," *Security Studies* 4, no. 2 (Winter 1995): 365–425.

6. Denny Roy, "North Korea as an Alienated State," *Survival* 38, no. 4 (Winter 1996–1997): 22–36; Hazel Smith, "Bad, Mad, Sad, or Rational Actor? Why the Securitization Paradigm Makes for Poor Policy Analysis of North Korea," *International Affairs* 76, no. 3 (2000): 593–617; David C. Kang, "Rethinking North Korea," *Asian Survey* 35, no. 3 (March 1995): 253–67.

7. David C. Kang, "Rolling with the Punches: North Korea and Cuba during the 1980s," *Journal of East Asian Affairs* 8, no. 1 (Winter 1994); Marcus Noland, "Why North Korea Will Muddle Through," *Foreign Affairs* 76, no. 4 (July/August 1997): 105–18; Andrei Lankov, "Staying Alive: Why North Korea Will Not Change," *Foreign Affairs* 87 (2008): 9–16.

8. Victor D. Cha and David C. Kang, *Nuclear North Korea: A Debate on Engagement Strategies* (New York: Columbia University Press, 2003); Michael O'Hanlon and Mike Mochizuki, *Crisis on the Korean Peninsula: How to Deal with a Nuclear North Korea* (New York: McGraw-Hill, 2003); John Delury and Chung-in Moon, "Analytic Failure and the North Korean Quagmire," *38North*, April 7, 2011, http://38north.org/2011/04/quagmire; B. B. Bell, "What Must Be Done about North Korea," CSIS Korea Chair Platform, December 14, 2010, http://csis.org/publication/what-must-be-done-about-north-korea.

9. Cha and Kang, *Nuclear North Korea*; David C. Kang, *China Rising: Peace, Power, and Order in East Asia* (New York, NY: Columbia University Press, 2007).

10. Victor Cha, "China's Newest Province?" *New York Times*, December 19, 2011, http://www.nytimes.com/2011/12/20/opinion/will-north-korea-become-chinas-newest-province.html; Scott Snyder, "Who Are the Generals Surrounding Kim Jong-un?" *Asia Unbound*, Council on Foreign Relations, January 13, 2012, http://blogs.cfr.org/asia/2012/01/13/who-are-the-generals-surrounding-kim-jong-un.

11. For example, Moon Young Park, "Lure North Korea," *Foreign Policy* 97 (Winter 1994–1995): 97–105.

12. Robert Litwak, "Living with Ambiguity: Nuclear Deals with Iran and North Korea," *Survival* 50, no. 1 (2008): 91–118.

13. Richard Ned Lebow, *A Cultural Theory of International Relations* (Cambridge: Cambridge University Press, 2008).

14. Nicholas Onuf, *World of Our Making: Rules and Rule in Social Theory and International Relations* (Columbia: University of South Carolina Press, 1989).

15. Alastair Iain Johnston, *Social States: China in International Relations, 1980–2000* (Princeton, NJ: Princeton University Press, 2007), 82. Gould defines status as "the honor or prestige attached to one's position in society." Roger V. Gould, *Collision of Wills: How Ambiguity about Social Rank Breeds Conflict* (Chicago: University of Chicago Press, 2003).

16. James Fearon notes that it is also reasonable to assume that states pursue and satisfy a number of other goals in addition to material power as measured relative to

other states. James D. Fearon, "Domestic Politics, Foreign Policy, and Theories of International Relations," *American Review of Political Science* 1 (1998): 294.

17. Max Weber, "The Profession and Vocation of Politics," p. 356, quoted in Lebow, *A Cultural Theory*, 20; Harsanyi, *Essays on Ethics, Social Behavior, and Scientific Explanation* (Dordrecht, Holland: D. Reidel, 1976), 204, quoted in William Wohlforth, "Unipolarity, Status Competition, and Great Power War," *World Politics* 61, no. 1 (January 2009): 28–57.

18. Quoted in Ryan Witt, "Secretary of State Hillary Clinton and North Korea Have a Verbal Brawl," Examiner.com, July 24, 2009, http://www.examiner.com/ x-5738-St-Louis-Political-Buzz-Examiner~y2009m7d24-Secretary-of-State-Hillary -Clinton-and-North-Korea-have-a-verbal-brawl.

19. U.S. Department of Defense, "DoD News Briefing—Secretary Rumsfeld and Gen. Myers," December 23, 2002, http://www.defenselink.mil/transcripts/transcript .aspx?transcriptid=2960; Bill Powell, "Nuclear Blackmail: North Korea Is No Iraq. There's No Military Option. So How Do You Get a Defiant Kim Jong Il to Give up His Nukes?" *Fortune*, January 20, 2003, http://money.cnn.com/magazines/fortune/ fortune_archive/2003/01/20/335652/index.htm.

20. Victor Cha, "Up Close and Personal, Here's What I Really Learned," *Washington Post*, June 14, 2009, http://www.washingtonpost.com/wp-dyn/content/ article/2009/06/12/AR2009061202685.html.

21. David Sanger, "Coming to Terms with Containing North Korea," *New York Times*, August 8, 2009, http://www.nytimes.com/2009/08/09/weekinreview/09sanger .html.

22. Barbara Demick, "Barbara Demick on Life in North Korea," *New Yorker*, October 26, 2009, http://www.newyorker.com/online/blogs/newsdesk/2009/10/barbara -demick-conversation-north-korea.html; italics added.

23. Hwang Doo-hyong, "Cheney Depicts Clinton's North Korea Trip as Mistake," *Yonhap*, August 3, 2009, http://english.yonhapnews.co.kr/national/2009/08/31/26/03 01000000AEN20090831000200315F.HTML.

24. Joshua Pollack, "Ballistic Trajectory: The Evolution of North Korea's Ballistic Missile Market," *Nonproliferation Review* 18, no. 2 (July 2011): 411–29.

25. Bruce Cumings, "We Look at It and See Ourselves," *London Review of Books* 27, no. 24 (December 15, 2005).

26. Nicholas Eberstadt, "The Coming Collapse of North Korea," *Wall Street Journal*, June 26, 1990; Fareed Zakaria, "When North Korea Falls," *Washington Post*, October 18, 2010; Robert Kaplan, "When North Korea Falls," *Atlantic Monthly*, October 2006, http://www.theatlantic.com/magazine/archive/2006/10/when-north -korea-falls/5228.

27. David C. Kang, "They Think They're Normal: Enduring Questions and New Research on North Korea," *International Security* 36, no. 3 (Winter 2011/2012): 142–71.

28. Stephen Haggard and Marcus Noland, *Famine in North Korea: Markets, Aid, and Reform* (New York: Columbia University Press, 2007), 230.

Part V

CONCLUSION

Chapter Thirteen

North Korea in Transition

Evolution or Revolution?

Scott Snyder and Kyung-Ae Park

North Korea's system does not fit easily into modern theories of international relations, nor does its dynastic, family-centered, military-first system fit well into the modern world. Despite the systemic failures revealed by the famine of the mid-1990s, followed by over a decade of information penetration and marketization, the North Korean system persists as an anachronism in twenty-first-century politics. Founded by Kim Il Sung as part of the socialist bloc with major support from the Soviet Union, North Korea survived the collapse of communism and the loss of significant political and financial support from the Soviet Union. Three generations of family succession have made it the world's only remaining dynasty. North Korea has survived by its relative isolation and has perpetuated a totalitarian system based on a cult of personality that is out of place in the twenty-first century. The state's thoroughgoing exploitation of its citizenry has consistently placed it among the worst systems of government in the world. But neither the failure of North Korea's leaders to deliver to the public on their own promises, the challenges posed by inward flows of information from the outside, nor North Korea's extensive economic dependency on external sources of trade and financial support have resulted thus far in its demise. However, each of these factors is arguably a catalyst for transition that will require the system to either adapt or fail.

None of these challenges are new to North Korea's leaders, and most of them have been front and center for decades. The North Korean system has already been forced to adapt to momentous challenges resulting from a transformation of North Korea's international environment following the end of the Cold War and the catastrophic implications of that transformation for North Korea's internal circumstances. Yet North Korea's leadership and its system have endured despite those challenges, and it has adapted to new circumstances more successfully than most observers expected. At the same

275

time, international pressure on the system continues to build as North Korea grows increasingly out of place with its surroundings. The seeming contradictions between the internal requirements for North Korea's continued survival and the international environment increasingly impinge on the capacity of the North Korean system to endure in its current form.

NORTH KOREA'S TRANSITION FROM KIM IL SUNG TO KIM JONG IL

Given these pressures, it is clear that North Korea is in transition, but it is unclear what the end result of North Korea's transition is likely to be or how quickly the transition is likely to unfold. Moreover, the character, direction, and momentum of transition in North Korea are both hard to measure and potentially reversible, given the crosscurrents and contradictory forces at work in North Korea. The foregoing chapters explore the extent to which transition in North Korea is occurring in three main areas: (1) the instruments and capacities of state control, both through examination of institutions such as the party, the military, and the influence of state ideology as a mechanism for demanding public loyalty to the North Korean leadership; (2) the declining ability of the state to control the economy, and the extent to which marketization has led to a sphere of activity outside the control of the state that might be an instrument for introducing reforms and driving political changes inside North Korea that directly or indirectly challenge the state's capacity to impose its will on the people; and (3) changes in the international environment, including cross-cutting positions and actions by China, South Korea, and the United States to influence the international context to which the North Korean system must accommodate itself.

The overall picture for North Korea is one in which there are several clear trends. First, ideology is on the wane inside North Korea and has been replaced by patronage as the primary means by which the leader exerts influence on his people. As the founder of the North Korean state, Kim Il Sung commanded ideological loyalty and exercised complete control over functional institutions within North Korea, including the party, the military, and the state bureaucracy. His exposition of *juche* ideology and his assertion of North Korea as an independent actor in international affairs reinforced his preeminent position on the national and international stage. However, Kim Jong Il's power came more from patronage than from ideology, although he still provided an ideological justification for his rule that relied firmly on military power and control. Under Kim Jong Il's rule, money became the means for advancement within the North Korean system, and patronage combined with punishment for disloyalty became the primary means by which Kim Jong Il was able to maintain discipline and ensure the centrality of his role within the North Korean system. An ideology of military-first recalls Mao Zedong's statement that power flows from the barrel of a gun. No longer was power in North Korea cloaked in an ideology; rather it depended entirely on Kim Jong Il's singular ability to exert power over the North Korean system. As chairman of the National Defense Commission, Kim Jong Il's position gave him control over the gun, while expressions of allegiance and rewards for loyalty were expressed through exchange of tangible resources. The exchange of material gifts is the primary means by which to demonstrate the loyalty necessary to move up within the system and the means by which the leader shows appreciation for that loyalty. Terence Roehrig illustrates in his chapter on the Korean People's Army that the shift from ideology to patronage has also brought the military into civil and economic affairs as a powerful actor, both as an instrument through which patronage is exerted and as an institution that needs to be placated first among all, given its material power within the North Korean system.

A result of Kim Jong Il's emphasis on the military at the expense of the party and government was the relative weakening of nonmilitary institutions within North Korea. The atrophying of institutions may have also been a means by which Kim Jong Il could assure his control since institutions were otherwise relatively powerless to act beyond their own narrow prerogatives. This weakening of institutions lessened the likelihood of challenge, but it also served in the long term to weaken the sustainability of the state. As Ken Gause details, it appears that Kim Jong Il only sought to rectify this imbalance in 2010 when he realized that a successful generational succession to Kim Jong Un would require more balance among North Korean institutions. Kim Jong Un appears to have few resources to work with as he attempts to reassert his own control over the institutional mechanisms of power while facing unprecedented challenges from the influx of information and goods that are no longer under the direct control of the state.

Second, North Korea has moved in the past two decades from relative isolation to partial integration with its neighbors as a result of its dependency on external sources to meet its economic needs. North Korea's increased economic integration with its neighbors has had mixed effects. Marketization has lessened the public's dependence on the state and has allowed for inward flows of information about the outside world that may further challenge North Korea's capacity to impose political control, and the leadership's dependence on patronage networks has reinforced the overall dependency of North Korea on economic exchange. This transition has created constituencies within North Korea that are no longer directly dependent on the state for their survival, even if there is not yet space for civil society–based resistance to the state. But this situation also appears to have created a backlash in which the state has struggled for means by which to reassert its control over the markets, and by extension to ensure that its political control remains unchallenged, even as the state's reliance on economic flows from abroad has also increased.

Bradley Babson's analysis of North Korea's economic situation argues that North Korea's sheltering of its people from external influences will no longer be possible—and the scope of its need for external economic interaction will continue to grow—as the aims of North Korea's external economic interactions broaden from efforts to extract subsidies and foreign exchange to a need for economic development as a foundation by which to maintain political power. Following an initial experiment with reforms in 2001 and 2002, North Korea's leadership has moved toward economic retrenchment, highlighted by a history of failed efforts to reassert control over the markets (for instance, through revaluation of North Korea's currency in November of 2009) or to reassert political controls as a means by which to limit the potentially politically challenging effects of marketization within North Korea. (Kim Jong Il ordered two successive 150-day and 100-day speed battles in 2009 with the apparent objective of heightening productivity, but this mobilization also had the effect of restricting the amount of time and effort within the society available to pursue market-oriented activities.) Following this retrenchment, Babson describes the latest North Korean efforts to create institutions such as the newly established State Development Bank and Joint Venture and Investment Commission, and to establish various investment groups and special economic zones on the border with China as a means by which to attract capital without opening, under the guise of "controlled capitalism."

These steps illustrate how the leadership's granting of permissions to be involved with trading activities can be used to reinforce loyalty to the state by providing concessions primarily to politically powerful individuals or institutions, so as to reaffirm elite control rather than allowing upward mobility within the North Korean system by potential enemies of the system who might challenge it. The state's ability to award concessions and to restrict market access and activity to unauthorized entities is a powerful instrument by which to reinforce loyalties among market participants, but also a means by which to discourage upward mobility by individuals who are not politically "approved" in the North Korean system. Widespread reliance on the markets has become a fact of life, but the state has retained the right to punish market activities carried out by those who are not formally qualified to engage in trade, whether it be at the local level through the inspection and bribe taking of local security forces or at the central level by restricting only authorized companies related to various branches of the North Korean bureaucracy to do business in China and to move goods internally throughout North Korea.

Third, North Korea still has political space to play off the United States and China against each other as a tactical means by which to perpetuate its survival. China continues to view U.S. motives on the Korean Peninsula with deep distrust, while the United States follows a multitrack policy that involves both cooperation with China and hedging against the effects of China's growing power and influence in the region. The apparent gap in perspectives and interests of the United States and China works to North Korea's advantage, enabling it to occupy the gap between the two countries caused by China's distrust of U.S. motives on the Korean Peninsula and U.S. uncertainty regarding China's broader strategic design. China made its bet on North Korea's strategic value in the months following the North's second nuclear test in 2009, despite the considerable reputational and material costs to China of continuing to support the North. China is concerned that the United States might take advantage of Korean reunification to create a presence close to China's borders that could threaten Chinese strategic interests. This perspective inhibits cooperation with the United States and South Korea to manage the shared risks that might result from North Korean instability. On the other hand, Sino-U.S. strategic coordination to determine the future of the Korean Peninsula would be the North Korean nightmare most likely to constrain North Korean choices (although such a development would also likely be strongly opposed by South Korea).

FIVE DIMENSIONS OF NORTH KOREA IN TRANSITION

Beyond these major trends, analysis of North Korea too often becomes a Rorschach test that reveals more about the observer than about North Korea.[1] This is because there are other dimensions of North Korea's transition on which it is harder to make definitive judgments based on available data and the current low level of understanding of system dynamics within North Korea. The ability to clearly understand these dimensions of North Korea's transition are absolutely critical for making a definitive judgment regarding the likely direction and impact of change within North Korea. Yet the available information leads scholars to contradictory judgments, or their assessments of these issues lead to opposing expectations for how the situation might unfold.

Is the North Korean System Rigid or Flexible?

The first dimension of North Korea's transition about which there are clear disagreements among analysts is the question of how adaptable the North

Korean system is to new circumstances; that is, should we see North Korean institutions as characterized by flexibility or rigidity? If North Korea's institutions are rigid and brittle, should one expect that growing external pressures may eventually result in a breakdown of the current political system? If they are supple, is there likely to be sufficient space for North Korea's leaders to continue to adjust tactically to external challenges by muddling through? Charles Armstrong's analysis of the regime's manipulation of ideology in support of Kim Il Sung and Kim Jong Il suggests an approach in which ideological concepts have proven to be quite malleable, and he argues that the system has in fact shown "remarkable resilience." Bruce Cumings comes to similar conclusions. He notes that based on North Korea's history and culture, its monarchical governing structure, its postcolonial nationalism, and its neo-Confucian philosophy, we are likely to see Kim Jong Un at the helm for a "long, long time." Widespread perspectives to the contrary, he points out, reveal a fundamental misunderstanding of North Korea and an inability to objectively see our own biases.

Juche ideology appears to be less an ideological system of thought than a statement of Korean nationalism; that is, that North Korea will stand up for itself and must not be ignored. But the concept is supple enough to be used to justify any number of specific policy directions that Kim Il Sung might have wanted to pursue, and to cloak whatever actions he took as actions that ultimately were implemented as being in the highest interest of the nation. Kim Jong Il's military-first ideology brought with it greater institutional constraints, namely by placing the military exclusively on the institutional front lines within the society, but a "military-first" ideology ultimately doesn't predetermine the directions that the military might take, even if it does suggest that whatever the military does will be for the purpose of preserving the state. It remains to be seen how ideology will be defined under Kim Jong Un, but his use of ideology will reveal much about the sustainability of his rule even while his ideological choices are likely to be flexible enough to justify whatever course of action he decides to take—and to affirm that his actions are being undertaken out of motives that are in the highest interest of the North Korean nation.

The transition to a third-generation leadership, and presumably the formation of a new ideology under Kim Jong Un, will carry with it both the burdens of the past and the opportunity to establish a new baseline and vision for North Korea going forward. If past practice proves to be a guide to understanding how ideology might be shaped under Kim Jong Un, he most likely faces some institutional constraints from existing vested interests within North Korean society, but he may also have the flexibility to make choices and to reorder the existing institutional hierarchies and priorities within North

Korean society according to his own needs. The establishment of an ideology under Kim Jong Un may be a powerful tool for reordering North Korea's internal priorities in potentially unexpected ways.

Those who see North Korean institutions as flexible are more likely to emphasize the overlap in personnel and functions between party and military institutions in the current North Korean leadership, and even to discount the role of the party as an "artifice of the *Suryong*'s ('Great Leader's') leadership style," as Ken Gause has argued. In a system led by the *Suryong*, the significance of bureaucratic politics should be virtually eliminated. This idea is reinforced by overlapping personnel roles in North Korea's system; many of the same individuals that are in the KWP's Central Military Commission are part of the National Defense Commission, which also has overlapping membership with the Politburo. Although oversight for various functions and appointments may be held under differing institutional frameworks, those frameworks are ultimately both stovepiped in such a way that they can only serve the top leader, and layered or overlapped in ways that diminish the significance of any potential division among institutions. In this view, the potential for open bureaucratic rivalry or factionalism within North Korea is greatly reduced by the predominance of the central leader, although it remains a subject of great debate and uncertainty with the succession to Kim Jong Un how this system has evolved and whether there is greater room for collective support within a *Suryong*-centered system.

The idea that there is flexibility in North Korean institutions might also reinforce the view that North Koreans have always been exceedingly pragmatic in their adherence to institutional constraints, effectively finding work-around approaches to solve problems despite the apparent rigidity of institutions. Ultimately, that pragmatism creates flexibility and toleration for any necessary deviations from institutional requirements within the system. A pragmatic approach to institutions provides the flexibility and suppleness to respond to emergencies or unexpected situations, even despite institutional constraints.

On the other hand, Victor Cha and Nicholas Anderson's analysis of North Korea and the Arab Spring argues that North Korea's "political institutions cannot adjust to the changing realities in North Korean society." They argue that North Korea's ideology and fundamentally rigid system will ultimately meet its downfall as a result of its inability to adjust to new realities and new demands, either from the North Korean people or from the outside world. In this view, ideology, tradition, and the immobility of personnel and institutions serve as a constraint and obstacle to the regime's ability to adapt flexibly to new circumstances. Cha and Anderson's analysis finds five active ingredients in the political protests in the Middle East—wealth accumulation, rates of growth, demography, contagion effects, and regime type—that seem unripe in the North Korean case, a circumstance that might be ascribed to North Korea's relative isolation, if not its system's rigidity. However, North Korea is clearly less isolated than it was before, raising the prospect that external changes could overwhelm the North Korean system. The assumption of regime rigidity suggests that there is no way to release pressures that are building on the regime other than to break the old system and replace it with something new.

The assumption of rigidity within the North Korean system results in greater expectations of political friction among various parts of the North Korean bureaucracy, including the view that North Korean institutions may conflict or work at cross-purposes with each other. From this perspective, the likelihood of conflict between the party and the military rises, long-standing conflicts between the state security bureau and other power holders might come to the surface, and the reality that everyone in North Korea is watching each other and being watched for signs of political incorrectness creates a system in which rising internal conflicts heighten implosion, and difference or deviance must be eliminated. Equilibrium only exists with a single dominant ruler and within a system that requires conformity as a condition for survival.

The assumption of rigidity may also inform analysts' understanding of the goals of the regime, as is the case in Nicholas Eberstadt's description of North Korea's unwavering commitment to a system that purposefully and systematically impedes economic performance, seeks to extract economic assistance for its own political ends, and remains committed to an absolutist political vision of unification on its own terms.

Is Transition in North Korea More Likely to Be Bottom-Up or Top-Down?

A second dimension of change is whether the motive forces likely to drive a transition within North Korea are likely to come from the bottom up or whether they will be driven by top-down changes in the North Korean system. This analysis also tends to borrow from a wide range of recent experiences with political transition, including those that Cha and Anderson treat in their analysis of the Arab Spring and its implications for North Korea. In addition, China offers a model of top-down political transition accompanied by economic reform that has proven to be peaceful, gradual, and successful. But Kim Jong Il never moved North Korea meaningfully onto China's reformist path, perhaps for fear of becoming a shadow of South Korea and perhaps because the political dangers of navigating the road to reform in a modern political environment so clearly threaten North Korea's ability to put forward a distinctive raison d'être. Kim Jong Il's reliance on "close aide politics" described in Ken Gause's chapter, suggests that the only meaningful opportunities for policy input are likely to come at or near the top, since the level of influence on leadership from the bottom-up through institutions is likely to be constrained.

The most recent and nascent potential model for the economic and political reform of North Korea has been forged by military leaders in Burma who have exposed themselves sufficiently to the outside world to recognize that their path was unsustainable and that Burma continued to fall behind its neighbors. This military leadership, led by Prime Minister Thein Sein, appears to recognize that failure to integrate Burma politically and economically is a cul-de-sac, and that long-standing civil wars must be set aside if Burma is to pursue peace and prosperity.[2] The South Korean historical precedent for this approach is represented by Park Chung Hee, a military man who grasped political power and brought South Korea onto a path that placed export-led economic development as its top priority. But even if North Korea were to take this course, another concern is that there is little evidence that North Korea has the human resources available to effectively guide its adjustment to an economic system that is highly integrated with the outside world.

The challenge for external actors who might want to facilitate North Korean reforms is that top-down reforms will only be pursued if a reformist leader is able to consolidate power, and the ability of external parties to influence North Korea's leadership has remained exceedingly limited. Moreover, there are few leading indicators for determining which leaders within closed societies such as North Korea might be potential advocates for reform, as is evidenced by current unfounded speculation over whether Kim Jong Un might have determined based on his years abroad at a Swiss secondary school that North Korea must pursue the path of reform or whether his uncle Jang Song Taek might be a closet reformer. Although the inclination to pursue reforms presumably requires a certain level of exposure to and understanding of the outside world, it also will likely entail risks and engender internal political opposition among vested interests in North Korea's current system.

Since there is so little knowledge or ability for external actors to overtly and directly influence thinking among North Korea's top leadership, considerable attention has been given to the prospect for bottom-up reform, including the promotion of markets and the expansion of opportunities for international exposure, especially to technocrats. Cha and Anderson's chapter in this volume provides a partial set of criteria by which to make judgments on the probability of a top-down versus a bottom-up transition in North Korea. The bottom line from their analysis is that the conditions in North Korea do not yet exist for an effective option for bottom-up transformation of the North

Korean system, in large part because there is no space for a public voice of opposition inside the North. While there may be a growing exile community of over 20,000 North Korean refugees in the South, there is not an organized political movement among North Korea's diaspora (which consists primarily of poor agrarian females) that has meaningfully been able to project political views back into North Korea.

Even if the conditions for an Arab Spring seem unlikely to obtain, there is widespread evidence of grassroots changes that could lead to bottom-up reforms. Certainly, those changes appear to provide empowerment, if not true self-reliance, at the individual level, where the average North Korean has no reason to expect that the state will provide for his or her critical needs. Instead, the market has now been the primary medium of exchange for over a decade.[3] This market activity frees individuals from dependence on the state, but it does not free individuals from interference by state agents in the ability of individuals to earn a livelihood. The form of capitalism practiced in North Korea at the grassroots level is a ruthless form of jungle capitalism in which individual traders who are trying to survive might face any number of predators and parasites, including demands for bribes and possible expropriation of goods by local authorities, potential competition for business from more politically powerful market competitors, and all manner of schemes to swindle the hard-earned value of goods in the marketplace. As Andrei Lankov points out in his chapter, a hierarchy of levels and types of capitalist exchange has emerged in North Korea, with those who are closest to the state most able to extract profits and exploit the markets to their own benefit. This structure suggests that while marketization may result in considerably less direct control by the state over people's lives and livelihoods, the lessening of state control may not be a near-term threat to the political survival of North Korea's current leadership.

Marketization also catalyzes the exchange of information, especially from the outside world, that might prove deleterious to the control of information, which is one of the fundamental conditions that has helped perpetuate state authority and control. However, in the absence of a politically viable organized opposition within North Korea that is able to utilize that information to mobilize a political threat to the existing regime, it appears that while increased information flows into North Korea may erode the political control of central authorities over time, there is no immediate threat from a grassroots-based opposition movement in North Korea.

Will Transition in North Korea Be Gradual or Sudden?

A third dimension of change that derives from the first two is whether the pace of change in North Korea will be gradual or sudden. The quickening pace of change in North Korea is a development that would potentially pose a serious challenge to the capacity of the state to maintain centralized control and could lead to institutional failures or a systemic failure of political leadership. In this circumstance, either a vacuum in leadership or a factional split within the existing power structure, which could result in a competition for political control, might result in sudden changes in North Korea. This scenario for transition in North Korea would clearly involve a transition to a new leadership structure inside North Korea, or the possibility that neighboring powers might assist in stabilizing a security vacuum in North Korea while assisting a new leadership structure to restore order and institutional capacities inside the country. The sudden transition to a new leadership structure in North Korea presumably would also open up new possibilities for external involvement in North Korea's stabilization, either led by the United Nations representing the international community or led by South Korea or China, as immediate neighbors of North Korea with the capacity to assist in North Korea's stabilization under new leadership. The scenario of a sudden transition in North Korea is the one that is most associated with the possibility of Korean reunification, if for instance South Korea were able, with the support of the international community, to extend its political authority over North Korea as part of a process that also achieves North Korea's stabilization and a plan for political integration with the South.

If the pace of change in North Korea takes a more gradual form, it most likely will involve the continued assertion of political authority by the existing leadership, which could either take a form that continues to assert political control while resisting forces for economic change and regional integration or which might in fact choose to pursue economic reforms and regional integration. This path is most often described as a path that would follow a Chinese model for reform, at least in the sense that the existing leadership would maintain political control while opening up new possibilities for economic reforms that would enhance North Korea's prosperity. A January 2012 Bank of America–Merrill Lynch study projects that under such circumstances, an economically reforming North Korea might achieve 10 to 12 percent growth over a period of years.[4] Although there is strong conventional wisdom that an economically reforming North Korea might not be able to exert legitimacy in the face of the success of a wealthier, industrialized South Korean political system, it is also possible to argue that sustained growth under an economically reformist North Korean leadership might be the best way to ease the potential burdens to South Korea likely to accompany rapid unification given the wide economic gap between the two. In any event, there is no question that the pace of change in North Korea will have direct ramifications for the cost of reunification as well as for the main potential sources of financing for North Korea's stabilization and economic revitalization.

Will North Korea Be the Agent or Object of Transition?

A fourth and related dimension of change in North Korea surrounds the question of agency. Will change be controlled by forces and institutions within North Korea, or will the North Korean system ultimately be the object of externally initiated changes in the international environment or of actions by other states in the international system? Are the penetration of outside information and the growth of markets inside North Korea eroding the power of North Korea's core political institutions in ways that pose a direct challenge to the viability of North Korea's elite, or are the elites managing the introduction of these new forces in ways that will perpetuate their political power?

Haksoon Paik's analysis of North Korean ideas, identities, and interests presents the leadership's strategy of "survival and development" for the twenty-first century as an unchanging objective that is likely to endure. Nonetheless, in a world characterized by contagion, North Korea appears to have been remarkably immune to external developments, but it is sufficiently connected that North Korea is increasingly sensitive to external influences. Reports of North Korean efforts to close its borders in 2003 at the height of the SARS epidemic show an awareness of North Korea's vulnerability to outside forces over which it is unable to exert control.[5] Likewise, North Korean grain prices have not been immune to fluctuations in the international price of grain, demonstrating North Korea's relatively newfound vulnerability to external forces over which it has little control. Evidence provided by Seo and Lee in their examination of the impact of South Korean "cultural pollution" on North Korea suggests a widespread impact on North Korean culture that has severely eroded official controls and has created space for an unofficial culture that is highly resistant to North Korean political control. However, it is hard to say how far such trends have advanced, especially given the absence of observable institutionalized private or civic networks beyond the control of the state.

North Korean leaders must be acutely aware of their vulnerability to both marketization and dissemination of information from the outside world (especially from South Korea), and have taken steps to limit the potentially corrosive impact of both of these forces on their capacity to exert political control. The efforts of the North Korean leadership to discipline the market, both by providing opportunities to control external sources of trade and investment to politically trusted elites and by limiting opportunities by nonelite groups within North Korea to profit from market activity to those same elites, serve to minimize the prospect that new actors might develop sufficient social mobility to emerge as threats to the existing power holders in North Korea. Nicholas Eberstadt's description of North Korea's political economy and the aims of its leadership suggests that the leadership has an absolute commitment to sustaining political control in the face of these challenges, despite the transformative impact of cultural pollution from the South and the emergence of various forms of capitalist entrepreneurship in North Korea's markets.

North Korean authorities clearly recognize the vulnerability of the regime to externally controlled sources of information and their inability to control it, as illustrated by the regime's attempts to crack down on the spread of information or cultural programs from South Korea that might challenge North Korean authority. But North Korean authorities have also recognized that they cannot completely stop the flow of information from the outside world and have taken limited steps to use international media as a venue for disseminating messages that can serve to reinforce the position of the leadership in Pyongyang. This logic may be behind the decision by North Korean authorities to allow a wider range of foreign news agencies, including the Kyodo and AP wire services, to have reporting privileges in Pyongyang, as well as to allow external access to the events surrounding the September 2010 Korean Worker's Party Conference in Pyongyang. These reports in the international media may reinforce the credibility of messages being delivered by domestic media, over which North Korea retains absolute control. To the extent that North Koreans are hearing external reports about political issues in North Korea that coincide with official propaganda, the external messages serve to reinforce the credibility of official information sources, and by extension reinforce perceptions that the North Korean leadership's political control capabilities remain intact.

How Will the International Environment Affect North Korea in Transition?

A fifth and final dimension of change is related to the international environment for sustaining North Korea. Do external actors such as China, South Korea, and the United States have leverage to influence the course of the North Korean leadership, and if so, which parties will be able to use their leverage so as to effectively manage the course and outcome of North Korea in transition in accordance with their respective interests? North Korea has always benefited from its ability to manipulate gaps in the perceptions and interests of major power supporters. This is evident from the ways in which Kim Il Sung played Soviet and Chinese interests and support off of each other to maximize his independence during the 1960s and 1970s. But in the absence of the Soviet Union, North Korea has long suffered from the lack of an effective foil against which to play off Chinese interests. One result has been North Korea's unprecedented economic dependency on China, which presumably should also result in greater Chinese political influence and control over

North Korea's capacity to pursue provocative actions that result in damage to Chinese interests. Yet in practice, China has not yet been able to effectively control North Korea, but instead must always worry that North Korea is likely to tack toward South Korea and the United States, not only to expand economic resources available to perpetuate North Korea's survival, but also as a means by which to enhance North Korea's independence from larger powers. In fact, Nicholas Eberstadt's analysis of the influence of external assistance on North Korea argues that any assistance will only be used by the current regime in pursuit of the self-interest and aggrandizement of its top leaders.

The worst case scenario for North Korea is a situation in which China, South Korea, and the United States are all on the same page in their policies toward Pyongyang. But lingering strategic distrust and differing visions regarding the most desirable end state on the Korean Peninsula provide ample opportunities for North Korea to manipulate the situation so as to reduce the possibility of a coordinated stance among China, South Korea, and the United States. From 2003 to 2007, North Korea appeared to have been quite successful in inducing a competition for market share in North Korea between China and South Korea, as reflected in the fact that both trade relationships gradually increased in line with each other during that period. But the Lee Myung Bak administration abandoned such an approach, with the result that inter-Korean trade leveled off in 2009 and remained stagnant in the aftermath of the *Cheonan* and Yeonpyeong incidents in 2010, while Sino-DPRK trade continued to grow rapidly in consonance with Chinese efforts to increase top-level consultations between the two countries. Under these circumstances, North Korea may quietly be looking for opportunities to reduce its economic dependency on China by improving its relationships with South Korea and the United States. China's support allows North Korea to minimize the political risks that might result from efforts to reach out to these two countries and to wait out approaches by the United States and South Korea to the extent that they are perceived as dangerous to North Korea's interests in survival as a nuclear weapons state.

However, China's dominant economic influence in North Korea has rekindled a debate in South Korea that highlights the downside of Lee Myung Bak's approach, which placed the objective of denuclearization as a priority over efforts to increase influence and leverage by growing inter-Korean relations. In his chapter, Bruce Cumings notes how a great deal of Pyongyang's overwhelming dependence on China really kicked into high gear with the advent of the Lee government in 2008. The South's curtailing of inter-Korean economic exchange, with the exception of activity at Kaesong, following the 2010 Cheonan and Yeonpyeong incidents may have been a necessary short-term vehicle for expressing outrage, but perhaps at the relative cost of the loss of South Korean economic influence in the North. Haksoon Paik delves into the inter-Korean dynamic at the ideational, identity, and interest levels to illustrate the depth of complexity of inter-Korean interaction. He effectively illustrates that when it comes to inter-Korean relations, the tactical motive of playing off one against the other tells only a small part of the story, given the perceived strategic and existential ramifications associated with the management of the inter-Korean relationship. Paik's analysis suggests that South Korean or U.S. failure to adapt to and accept that this constitutes a primary source of tension will continue to consume the attention of the leaderships concerned.

With regard to the U.S.-DPRK relationship, David Kang asks a fundamental question: "Is the United States willing to co-exist with North Korea and give it equal status?" This has been a perennial question at the heart of the U.S.-DPRK relationship, but it appears that both sides provided a clear negative answer in 2009. Just days prior to Barack Obama's inauguration as president of the United States, the DPRK foreign ministry spokesman effectively delinked U.S.-DPRK normalization and denuclearization, which had been the long-standing U.S. precondition for improvement of diplomatic relations between the United States and North Korea. Months later, in June 2009, the United States signed on to a U.S.-ROK Joint Vision Statement, which appears to reject coexistence with North Korea, stating clearly that the United States seeks a unified Korean Peninsula that is a market economy. This may explain why North Korea has been such a low diplomatic priority under the Obama administration. Likewise, Bob Carlin and John Lewis have argued clearly that North Korea's attention is no longer fixed on the long-standing objective of normalization with the United States, in which case the question of whether the United States and DPRK can coexist has already been decided by Pyongyang's preference for a nonrelationship with the United States.[6] But can both sides afford to walk away from or repudiate some form of relationship? In late 2011, both the United States and North Korea resumed bilateral dialogue, despite the reluctance on the part of either side to provide status to the other. Neither side can live with the other; and neither side can live without the other.

This circumstance has been particularly perplexing and complicated for China in its management of both its relationship with North Korea and its management of the North Korea issue as a component of China-U.S. relations. North Korea's economic dependency has also complicated Pyongyang's strategy in dealing with China and has made North Korea an issue of tension in U.S.-China relations, even as China pursues a strategy designed to promote stability and reduce tensions that might lead to military conflict. Liu Ming's analysis that North Korea has been relatively passive in its relationship with

China while insisting on its independence from China reflects the complexity of a Sino-DPRK relationship in which North Korea assiduously avoids providing any concession of strategic value to China at the same time that China is perceived internationally to have decisive influence over North Korea. The paradox of Chinese influence as both overwhelming and limited is the critical contradiction China must address as it weighs North Korea's survival against its own broader interests and international pressures. Barack Obama and Hu Jintao were able to identify a clear but limited set of common interests regarding North Korea in their January 2011 Joint Statement, including the need for stable inter-Korean relations and a common interest in the peninsula's denuclearization;[7] however, the relative priority that Beijing and Washington accord to these respective interests, and the actions they are willing to take in order to achieve those interests, remain in conflict with each other given the apparent difference in American and Chinese visions of a preferred end-state on the Korean Peninsula.

One clear illustration of how Chinese and U.S./South Korean policy preferences contradict each other is the contrast between international efforts to implement UN-mandated sanctions as a means of punishing and denying North Korea access to dual-use technology that could be used to advance its nuclear program versus China's use of increasing engagement with the North as an economic tool for stabilizing the DPRK. Bradley Babson's exploration of commercial motives for expanding China-DPRK interaction, quite apart from political factors, illustrates how the promotion of market-based interactions designed to integrate North Korea economically with its neighbors works at cross-purposes to North Korea's political isolation in ways that may equally frustrate political leaders for very different reasons in Beijing, Washington, and Seoul. Until North Korea's neighbors can come to terms with these deep contradictions in their approach to North Korea, it is unlikely that international pressures will converge in a direction that will decisively influence North Korea's prospects for survival, much less shape North Korea's future prospects.

CONCLUSION: ASSESSING THE VULNERABILITY AND LEGITIMACY OF NORTH KOREA'S TRANSITION

As North Korea attempts to consolidate its third-generation leadership under Kim Jong Un, it must address two primary issues that are likely to determine the outcome of its effort to persist in justifying its quest for "survival and development": how to overcome its vulnerability and how to establish its legitimacy. In both cases, there are internal and external dimensions to the challenge.

The early days of transition to a third-generation succession mark a period of acute vulnerability for North Korea, both internally and externally. Although leadership succession plans had been put into place in 2009 and were announced in 2010, no one could know with certainty whether such arrangements would remain in place in the absence of Kim Jong Il. Although the succession plans seemed designed to carefully take into account institutional and personal stakes so as to perpetuate a leadership structure in which a new *Suryong* would be placed in control of the party and the military, the relative power of personalities and institutions in the post–Kim Jong Il era could inevitably be determined only following Kim Jong Il's death, enhancing sensitivity and vulnerability internally during this sensitive time of transition. In this context, the decision to publicly unveil a succession plan in September of 2010 with Kim Jong Un clearly announced as Kim Jong Il's successor has provided a first-mover advantage that may force potential challengers for power to accept the formal structure, even while competing to enhance their influence within the post–Kim Jong Il system.

Now that Kim Jong Un has taken over formal titles and is being treated as North Korea's supreme leader, he must learn how to exercise power. But it remains to be seen whether he has the personal skills to turn the post–Kim Jong Il system he has inherited into a Kim Jong Un leadership system. The relative weakening of institutions and ideology within North Korea are two factors that will make it more difficult for Kim Jong Un to assert the levels of political control that his father and grandfather enjoyed, especially, as Cha and Anderson point out, in the face of transformational changes in the markets and minds of the North Korean people that have resulted from North Korea's partial exposure to the outside world. All these factors are corrosive to the system of political control that Kim Jong Un has inherited, and it is not clear that he has either the skills and relationships to authoritatively assert sufficient political control to stanch those external influences or the acumen to transform the North's political and economic system so as to maintain political control and assure the regime's survival.

The early days following Kim Jong Il's funeral have featured significant efforts by North Korea's top propagandists to place Kim Jong Un firmly in the footsteps of his father and grandfather by having Kim Jong Un "turn sorrow into strength" through on-the-spot guidance and other images designed to perpetuate Kim Jong Un's image as a leader, rather than observing a lengthy mourning period as was the case with Kim Jong Il following the death of Kim Il Sung. The emphasis has clearly been on stability, continuity, and control in North Korea's domestic and foreign policies. But one can't help but feel that these propagandistic messages are also attempting to obscure vulnerability and potential disorder under the surface that inevitably must accompany the dramatic shift in power from Kim Jong Il to his son. The pointed comments of Kim Jong Nam that a third-generation succession is unsustainable and that his half-brother is only a puppet of other forces provide a strong counterpoint to North Korean propaganda from someone with sufficient inside knowledge to discern the real situation.

Even as Kim Jong Un grapples with both his own vulnerability and that of the North Korean system, the other factor likely to weigh heavily on North Korea's external relations in its post–Kim Jong Il era is the widespread dismissal of the system under Kim Jong Un as a serious system. Given its accumulated failures, it seems implausible, in comparison with the governance structures of other nations in the twenty-first century, that a not-yet-thirty-year-old successor can be accepted as an international leader. This means that North Korea's legitimacy as a governing system is being questioned by outsiders as never before, while external acceptance has always been a source of prestige and affirmation of legitimacy within North Korea. One need only visit the large museums at Myohyang-san that have been built to catalog the gifts that outsiders have given to Kim Il Sung and Kim Jong Il to understand that external legitimation is a powerful tool for enhancing legitimacy inside North Korea. But that source of legitimation is likely to be harder for North Korea to earn under Kim Jong Un at the same time that it may be needed more than ever to assure the perpetuation of the regime. Oddly, China's early validation of North Korea's generational succession, including the display of condolences to Kim Jong Il by the entire Chinese Politburo, serves as an early indicator of just how important external legitimation may ultimately be to North Korea under Kim Jong Un, both as a reinforcement of his own claims to legitimacy internally and as a means by which to perpetuate North Korea's survival both politically and economically.

As North Korea's succession process unfolds under Kim Jong Un, therefore, there are two factors that will bear careful scrutiny. First, how will Kim Jong Un formulate an ideology that can both consolidate his rule and open the way for greater integration between North Korea and the outside world? Second, in what ways will North Korea under Kim Jong Un seek international affirmation for his system, despite its obvious economic failures, its provocative actions contributing to inter-Korean tensions, and its challenge to the international community's nonproliferation norms, and what might the international community require in exchange for symbols of North Korea's validation and legitimation under Kim Jong Un? The answers to these two questions are likely to influence the prospects for and pace of North Korea's further transition and transformation going forward.

NOTES

We would like to acknowledge the Academy of Korean Studies for its financial support on this book project.

1. Mark E. Manyin, "Kim Jong-il's Death: Implications for North Korea's Stability and U.S. Policy," Congressional Research Service, Washington, DC, December 22, 2011, 4.

2. "Thein Sein: No Turning Back on Burma Reforms," AP News, January 20, 2012, http://asiancorrespondent.com/74259/thein-sein-no-turning-back-on-burma-reforms.

3. Yoshihiro Makino, "Side Jobs, Black Markets Flourish in North Korea," *Asahi Shimbun*, December 26, 2011, http://ajw.asahi.com/article/asia/korean_peninsula/AJ201112260001.

4. Kim Yoon-mi, "North Korea Could Grow up to 12% under Open Economy, Says Report," *Korea Herald*, March 2, 2012, http://www.asianewsnet.net/home/news.php?id=27282.

5. "North Korea Acts against Sars," BBC News, April 26, 2003, http://news.bbc.co.uk/2/hi/asia-pacific/2978173.stm.

6. Robert Carlin and John W. Lewis, "North Korea's New Course," *Los Angeles Times*, December 8, 2011, http://articles.latimes.com/2011/dec/08/opinion/la-oe-carlin-nkorea-20111208.

7. Office of the Press Secretary, "U.S.-China Joint Statement," January 19, 2011, http://www.whitehouse.gov/the-press-office/2011/01/19/us-china-joint-statement.

Index

About the Contributors

Nicholas Anderson is a graduate of the Security Studies Program at Georgetown University's Edmund A. Walsh School of Foreign Service in Washington, D.C. His research interests include political theory, international relations theory, and the international relations of East Asia. His work has been published in *The Washington Quarterly* and the *Cornell International Affairs Review*, among other publications. He previously worked for the Office of the Korea Chair at the Center for Strategic and International Studies (CSIS) and has lived and worked in both Seoul, South Korea, and Tokyo, Japan. He received his BA from the University of British Columbia.

Charles Armstrong is the Korea Foundation Professor of Korean Studies in the Social Sciences in the Department of History and the director of the Center for Korean Research at Columbia University. His books include *The North Korean Revolution, 1945–1950* (2003); *Tyranny of the Weak: North Korea and the World, 1950–1992* (forthcoming in 2013); and *A History of Modern East Asia, 1800–Present* (forthcoming in 2014). Professor Armstrong holds a BA in Chinese studies from Yale University, an MA in international relations from the London School of Economics, and a PhD in history from the University of Chicago. He has taught at Princeton, Seoul National University, and the University of Washington in Seattle, and has been a member of the Columbia faculty since 1996.

Bradley Babson is a specialist on Asian affairs with a concentration on North Korea and Myanmar. He worked for the World Bank for twenty-six years before retiring in 2000. Since then he has consulted for the World Bank and United Nations and been involved in projects sponsored by various institutes, foundations, and universities. He presently is chair of the DPRK Economic

Forum at the U.S.-Korea Institute, Johns Hopkins School of Advanced International Studies and serves on the executive committee of the National Committee for North Korea. Mr. Babson received his BA degree from Williams College in 1972 and his MPA degree from the Woodrow Wilson School of International and Public Affairs at Princeton University in 1974. He lives in Brunswick, Maine.

Victor Cha (PhD Columbia, MA Oxford, BA Columbia) is director of Asian studies and holds the D. S. Song Chair in the Department of Government and School of Foreign Service at Georgetown University. In 2009, he was named as senior adviser and the inaugural holder of the new Korea chair at the Center for Strategic and International Studies in Washington, D.C. He left the White House in May 2007 after serving since 2004 as director for Asian affairs at the National Security Council. He is the award-winning author of *Alignment Despite Antagonism: The United States-Korea-Japan Security Triangle* (1999), coauthor of *Nuclear North Korea: A Debate on Engagement Strategies* (2004) with David Kang, author of *Beyond the Final Score: The Politics of Sport in Asia* (2009), and author of *The Impossible State: North Korea, Past and Future* (forthcoming in 2012).

Bruce Cumings is chairperson of the History Department at the University of Chicago and Gustavus F. and Ann M. Swift Distinguished Service Professor in History and the College there. His first book, *The Origins of the Korean War*, won the John King Fairbank Book Award of the American Historical Association, and the second volume of this study won the Quincy Wright Book Award of the International Studies Association. Professor Cumings recently published *Dominion from Sea to Sea: Pacific Ascendancy and American Power* (2009). He is the editor of the modern volume of the *Cambridge History of Korea* (forthcoming) and is a frequent contributor to the *London Review of Books*, *The Nation*, *Current History*, the *Bulletin of the Atomic Scientists*, and *Le Monde Diplomatique*. He is working on a synoptic single-volume study of the origins of the Korean War, and a book on the Northeast Asian political economy. He received his PhD from Columbia University.

Nicholas Eberstadt holds the Henry Wendt Chair in Political Economy at the American Enterprise Institute in Washington, D.C. He is also a senior advisor to the National Board of Asian Research, a member of the visiting committee at the Harvard School of Public Health, and a member of the Global Agenda Council at the World Economic Forum. He researches and writes extensively on demographics, economic development, and international security. His books include *Policy and Economic Performance in Divided Korea during the Cold War Era: 1945–91* (2010); *The Poverty of the Poverty Rate* (2008); *The North Korean Economy: Between Crisis and Catastrophe* (2007); and *The End of North Korea* (1999). Mr. Eberstadt received his BA, MPA, and PhD from Harvard University as well as an MSc from the London School of Economics.

Ken Gause is the director of the Foreign Leadership Studies Program at CNA, a research organization located in Alexandria, Virginia. Gause began his career as a Kremlinologist with the U.S. government. Since the mid-1980s, he has worked for a number of defense-related think tanks, where he has strived to push the boundaries of leadership analysis. He is the author of the book *North Korea under Kim Chong-il: Power, Politics, and Prospects for Change* (2011). He also authored a recent paper entitled "North Korea after Kim Chong-il: Leadership Dynamics and Potential Crisis Scenarios," which can be obtained on CNA's website. Gause holds a BA in political science and Russian from Vanderbilt University and earned an MA in Soviet and East European affairs from George Washington University.

David Kang is professor of international relations and business at the University of Southern California, with appointments in both the School of International Relations and the Marshall School of Business. At USC he is also director of the Korean Studies Institute. Kang's latest book is *East Asia before the West: Five Centuries of Trade and Tribute* (2010). He is also author of *China Rising: Peace, Power, and Order in East Asia* (2007); *Crony Capitalism: Corruption and Development in South Korea and the Philippines* (2002); and *Nuclear North Korea: A Debate on Engagement Strategies*, co-authored with Victor Cha (2003). Kang has published numerous scholarly articles in journals such as *International Organization* and *International Security*, and his coauthored article was awarded "Best Article, 2007–2009" by the *European Journal of International Relations*. He received an AB with honors from Stanford University and his PhD from Berkeley.

Andrei Lankov is professor in the Social Science Department at Kookmin University in Seoul, South Korea. Prior to his position at Kookmin University, he worked at Leningrad State University and Australian National University. His major research interest is the social and political history of North Korea. Lankov has had his work published in journals such as *Foreign Affairs* and *Foreign Policy*, and in newspapers including the *New York Times*, *Wall Street Journal*, and *Financial Times*. His books include *Crisis in North Korea: The Failure of De-Stalinization, 1956* (2007); *North of the DMZ: Essays on Daily*

Life in North Korea (2007); *The Dawn of Modern Korea: The Transformation in Life and Cityscape*, with Sarah L. Kang as editor (2007); and *From Stalin to Kim Il Sung: The Formation of North Korea, 1945–1960* (2002). He completed his undergraduate and graduate studies at Leningrad State University and also attended Kim Il-sung University in 1985.

Woo Young Lee is an associate professor of sociology at the University of North Korean Studies in Korea who specializes in sociology of knowledge, social thought, and North Korean culture and society. He has published numerous works in Korean on North Korean culture, symbolic system, and literary politics including *Consistency and Change in the Literary Politics of Kim Jong-il, A Study of North Korean Social Control System*, and *Private Sphere and People of Cities in North Korea*.

Liu Ming currently is professor, director of the Institute of Asia-Pacific Studies, and director of the Center for Korea Studies at the Shanghai Academy of Social Sciences (SASS). Liu holds a PhD from the World Economy Institute, Fudan University, 1998. He has also been a visiting scholar at Columbia University, Seoul National University, and Stanford University. Over his twenty-two-year career, Liu has contributed extensively to several leading Canadian and South Korean journals, including the papers "Opportunities and Challenges for Sino-American Cooperation on the Korean Peninsula" (*Korean Journal of Defense Analysis*) and "China and the North Korean Crisis: Facing Test and Transition" (*Pacific Affairs*).

Haksoon Paik is a senior fellow and the director of the Center for North Korean Studies at the Sejong Institute in South Korea. He received his PhD in political science from the University of Pennsylvania and was a postdoctoral fellow at Harvard University. He is currently a member of the South Korean government's Committee for the Development of Inter-Korean Relations, and an advisor to the Kim Dae-jung Peace Center. Among his books and monographs are *The Military in North Korean Politics: Its Character, Status, and Role* (in Korean) (2011); *The History of Power in North Korea: Ideas, Identities, and Structures* (in Korean) (2010); and *North Korea in Distress: Confronting Domestic and External Challenges* (coauthor, coeditor) (2008).

Kyung-Ae Park holds the Korea Foundation Chair at the Institute of Asian Research of the University of British Columbia (UBC). She is a former president of the Association of Korean Political Studies in North America. Professor Park is the author, coauthor, and editor of many scholarly publications on issues ranging from North and South Korean politics and foreign relations to gender and development, such as *Non-Traditional Security Issues in North Korea* (forthcoming), *New Challenges of North Korean Foreign Policy, Korean Security Dynamics in Transition,* and *China and North Korea: Politics of Integration and Modernization.* She has also written articles in a number of journals, including *Comparative Politics, Journal of Asian Studies, Pacific Affairs, Asian Survey,* and *Pacific Review.* Since the mid-1990s, she has made several trips to Pyongyang and has hosted North Korean delegation visits to Canada, playing a key role in promoting Track II exchanges and diplomacy between Canada and North Korea. Most recently, she established the Canada-DPRK Knowledge Partnership Program at UBC, which hosts North Korean professors for long-term academic exchanges at the university. The program is unprecedented and groundbreaking, being the first of its kind in North America where North Korean nationals are being educated for a long-term period.

Terence Roehrig is a professor in national security affairs and the director of the Asia-Pacific Studies Group at the U.S. Naval War College. He is the author of the forthcoming book *Japan, South Korea, and the U.S. Nuclear Umbrella: Extended Deterrence and Nuclear Weapons in the Post-Cold War World* and has published articles and book chapters on Korean and East Asian security issues, North Korea's nuclear weapons program, and the U.S.–South Korea alliance. He received his PhD in political science from the University of Wisconsin–Madison and is a past president of the Association of Korean Political Studies.

Jungmin Seo is an associate professor in the Department of Political Science and International Studies at Yonsei University, Korea, where he teaches Chinese politics and nationalism. His main research interests are the various forms of nationalism in contemporary East Asia. Currently, he is conducting a number of research projects on inter-Asian migration and the politics of memory in Northeast Asia.

Scott Snyder is senior fellow for Korea studies and director of the program on U.S.-Korea policy at the Council on Foreign Relations (CFR), where he had served as an adjunct fellow from 2008 to 2011. Prior to joining CFR, Snyder was a senior associate in the international relations program of the Asia Foundation, where he founded and directed the Center for U.S.-Korea Policy and served as the Asia Foundation's representative in Korea (2000–2004). Snyder has written numerous books and book chapters on aspects of Korean politics and foreign policy and Asian regionalism. He is editor of *The U.S.-South Korea Alliance: Meeting New Security Challenges*

(2012) and coeditor of *Paved with Good Intentions: The NGO Experience in North Korea* (2003). Snyder is also the author of *China's Rise and the Two Koreas: Politics, Economics, Security* (2009) and *Negotiating on the Edge: North Korean Negotiating Behavior* (1999). Snyder received a BA from Rice University and an MA from the Regional Studies East Asia Program at Harvard University and was a Thomas G. Watson Fellow at Yonsei University in South Korea.